For those who don't want to purchase the book, it is available online for a free download at, www.RestoreTitle.com

CONTENTS

PREFACE

I grew up with a very logical and pragmatic mind. I grew up with a strong drive for two things, to become a top professional freestyle BMX athlete and to learn everything until I came to fully understand this thing we call life.

I eventually reached utter fulfillment in my career winning ESPN's X Games multiple times in grand fashion. Among my world travels I sought all manner of wisdom. After reaching that utter fulfillment in my career my entire focus again was turned to seeking wisdom.

Eventually I went beyond quantum physics and consciousness until I 'understood,' rather deeply, the deep spiritual 'wisdom' of the world that relatively few hold. My deep search and study had finally led me to 'perfect understanding,' or so I thought. I became one of those few in the world who 'know;' I continued to gain more deeply.

As I continued yet deeper in this I eventually watched it entirely collapse and confound in a significantly profound fashion that surprisingly confirmed religious truth to me. I came to surprisingly see just as the Bible promises that the "wisdom of their wise men shall perish, and the understanding of the prudent men shall be hid."

I came to understand fully that true truth was that Jesus Christ is real, alive and utterly necessary.

I came to see deeply and clearly how certain 'wisdom' can be used by real powers of deception and darkness to steer us away from real singular truth that is in Jesus Christ; He truly is the way, the truth and the life.

Since this 'confounding' I left a large corporate sponsor and have sought entirely the will of my Father in Heaven for I've seen the reality and perfection of Him.

I have had a constant realization of the many in the world still 'robbed and spoiled' in such 'wisdom' who cannot clearly extrapolate to truth that is truly in Jesus Christ.

I see many in the world who pride themselves thinking they 'know' of themselves. I couldn't stand by, saved out of a vast stumbling block and do nothing for the many still therein.

I write this to them to help extrapolate to true truth in our necessary Savior. I judge none; I simply know the depth of the stumbling block and seek to show clearly for the pragmatic mind like mine. I write this also to all to stay steadfast on the rock of Christ amidst the deep deceptions in the world.

My story is similar in many instances to that of the Apostle Paul or Alma the Younger, for in my own wisdom I greatly hardened my heart

3

in what the Lord would later prove to be incredible truth in significant fashion. I am forever grateful.

My story has many incredible miracles. All of these miracles came by recognizing the vastness and closeness of our loving Father in Heaven, Almighty God. My story has become that of my utter weakness and the utter strength, power and true wisdom in our perfect, saving, and loving Father in Heaven.

I seek to show three things. To show the many miracles of my life; to help those ensnared in 'wisdom,' those twisted away from our Savior, extrapolate to true wisdom in Him; and to help all better stand on the rock of our Savior Jesus Christ, giving some simple guidance to help us exercise true wisdom. True wisdom is humility before our Father in Heaven.

Truly the singular focus of this book is to glorify my Father in Heaven. All is His. He is so good and His love and glory is beyond all things. Upon realizing this incredible love I seek to help all to come to Him and know His love as I know it.

He lives; take it from one who had to go entirely full circle and to understand such all the way around. I am forever grateful.

Isaiah 42:18 "Hear, ye deaf; and look, ye blind, that ye may see.

19 Who is blind, but my servant? Or deaf, as my messenger that I sent? Who is blind as he that is perfect, and blind as the Lord's servant?"

1 Nephi 14:1

"And it shall come to pass, that if the Gentiles shall hearken unto the Lamb of God in that day that he shall manifest himself unto them in word, and also in power, in very deed, unto the taking away of their stumbling blocks-"

RESTORE
C. Satterfield

In gratitude to my ever praying Mother.

     1 Peter 1:7 That the trial of your faith, being much more precious than of gold that perisheth, though it be tried with fire, might be found unto praise and honour and glory at the appearing of Jesus Christ:

Chapter 1

I WILL NOT FAIL THEE, NOR FORSAKE THEE

A young boy sat on the back of large brown horse in the hills of Idaho. Behind the saddle and directly on the horse he sat with his sure-handed young aunt guiding it. This boy wasn't entirely fond of horses, but when one grows up in Idaho and your grandparents own a farm, horses seem to be the norm. A mild fear was always had in this young boys mind, he trusted his teenage aunt knew what to do and what she was doing, but still knew all too well that no matter what anyone thought they knew, that horse was, in the end, in charge of itself and no manner of trust in another could help him gain the fullness of trust required to be entirely at ease; especially after this day. Or maybe it was a shadow of a beginning of learning just that trust.

Regardless of the uneasiness of being on the back of this powerful animal, this had been a normal and occasional occurrence, a common activity on the farm, and the boy had essentially gotten used to it with growing confidence each successful outing.

Generally these adventures didn't venture too far from the barn or house of the farm. Today however, the boy and his aunt felt confident to venture a bit further this time, beyond the property of the family farm. The farm was vast, even at the ends of the property they were a fair ride away from the house, but it had already been explored over and over. Adventure, always seeming to be the root of excitement and name of the game. What is on the other side? Adventure, at the very least, something new, something different.

The horse was always the most trusted of the boy's Aunt, after all she had handled 2 on her back all the while and many farm rides and adventures had been enjoyed with her. Coming to the end of the farm the horse walked slowly through a narrow opening in the barbed wire fence, beyond the property of the family farm.

Through the fence the majesty of a new adventure set in, this was no longer another simple boring ride around the farm, this was new territory, this was adventure. The other side of the fence was not well taken care of ground, as the farm was. The ground was weed covered, all kinds of tall brown weeds; even the worst kind, the kind that get into your socks and stay there until they are plucked out. The other side did not have paths as the farm did, but this was the point, adventure.

The horse started up a hill not far from the fence line of the farm boundaries, being sure to at least keep it in eyesight and not to stray too far. The young boy held on the back, a little apprehensive of the new adventure. Horses really never were his thing, but when your other

6

option is sit back at Grandma's house and miss out on an adventure you go. Especially when being asked to go over and over, the norm of the farm often prevailed.

The boy had found himself yet again going up another hill, clinging to his Aunt's back, sitting on the rear of the horse, off the saddle. As they started up the hill the days when he was small enough to share the saddle and how much more comfortable it had been, came to his mind. Especially with the extra bumpiness of this new untamed 'trail'.

Hills never seemed too bad, they had hills on the farm and the horse could go up and down easily, but this hill had no path. It was covered in tall weeds and gopher holes were round about; the boy quickly noted how much more uncomfortable and bumpy this adventure was going to be. Shortly into the adventure on the other side of the fence the hill got to a point of steepness much steeper than the rest of the hill, the horse came to a stop.

The boy's aunt had been on horses her whole life and didn't think twice trying to kick the horse into gear to hop itself up this bit of steepness so they could get to the top. The horse didn't move. Again she kicked the horse and gave it a few audible encouragements, the horse made a small attempt and reared back.

This was enough to send the boy into thoughts of fear, he had never been on such a place on a horse, and if the horse was saying no, well then he wanted off. But getting off was not a decision he could make alone and by himself, and he wasn't going to walk the whole way back.

His aunt told him to hold on tighter, he did, and she kicked the horse with a "Yah!"

The horse jumped into gear to give all it had up the steep part of the hill. The horse immediately struggled and started slowing and began falling back.

In what seemed like an instant of shock the horse came backward down the steepness, lost it's footing, tripped, and began to fall. The boy and his aunt both instinctively jumped off in the best way they could in the shocking situation only to find the horse falling down following right after them.

The boy and his aunt were suddenly, and in what seemed like in an instant, in a position they had never before experienced. In an instant they went from the comfortable position from atop the horse to being slammed hard into the dirt, in shock.

The horse had fallen directly on top of both of their legs, trapping them both beneath its immense weight. Their faces and bodies, covered in dirt, the entirety of their legs slammed hard, stuck, under the large horse.

Shock began to set in as they began to come to realize their situation. The boy could barely tell what was happening before he found himself in their dire situation. The aunt looked to the boy and the boy back but they were both wide eyed and no words could at first suppress the shock.

They both instantly tried to pull themselves out from under the horse. It was of no use; the entirety of its weight was holding them down completely. They began to hit the horse and trying to get it to get up, only to realize the horse wasn't responsive at all, whether knocked out or dead, hitting it and yelling didn't prevail. Thoughts began to fill the boys mind of his legs, they were really pinned down and wouldn't budge, were they ok? Was he ok?

After making every effort to get out from under the horse and to get the horse to get up they began to fully realize the predicament they were in.

Shortly after talking over and exhausting every simple idea they had, they began to start to yell as loud as they could, hoping someone might hear them. As soon as this final idea began it ended, realizing just how far they were from the farm, even past the farm.

When anyone finally came looking how would they even know where to look? They were past the farm and against the ground. The thought of not being found came and was unbearable, leading to the same desperate attempts at trying to get the horse up and to get out from under it, to no avail.

The horse showed no signs of life or movement. As hope was dwindling the thought entered to pray. After all, what else could be done?

"Let's say a prayer," they decided. "You say it." His aunt agreed to. They folded their arms as they had been accustomed and raised to and opened their humble prayer.

"Heavenly Father, please bless us, help us that we can get out, bless us that we are ok, bless the horse that she is ok and will get up. In the name of Jesus Christ, Amen."

Immediately following the 'Amen', the horse got up and stood up strait and steady.

Realizing they were free they slowly got up. They both realized they were both ok, the boy was in shorts and had a few scrapes on his legs, but otherwise was ok. He left the horse to his aunt and began running back to the farm, in amazement his legs were ok and not broken; cutting over the fences the entire way back. Making it back to tell his family the story of the horse tripping and falling on them and getting up;

and for some reason of perceived shame, leaving out the seeming coincidence of the story of the prayer. This interesting moment was reflected back on from time to time throughout his life.

I am this boy.

Chapter 2

MINDSET

I grew up in the Church of Jesus Christ of Latter-day Saints. When I was about 16, I was done with it. Whether it was the things of the world that I was focused on or simply lost interest I'm not sure, probably both. But what I do remember is seeing simple people that 'knew' the gospel was true. And in young ignorance I would wrongly judge it as people deceiving themselves in one way or another. I perceived only the carnal things and the worldly wisdom of these.

This type of mindset led me on a very logical and pragmatic search for real truth as best as I could find it. I always loved reading and learning more and hearing other perspectives. I had a strong feeling that perhaps I would be the one to finally figure it all out for good.

All the while in this search, the focus of my life was Freestyle BMX, the bikes you see guys flipping and spinning on. I loved it and it was the passion at the center of my life.

I remember trips to California with friends to go ride. I would tell one of my friends on our trips, I didn't know what it was, but I really felt that I could, and perhaps it was my calling, to figure this life thing out, to figure everything out. I always was driven to figure it out.

The difference between me and seemingly everyone else is that I believed it could be done and that I could do it, just as I believed I could become a professional BMX athlete and win the largest contests in the world.

Life went on, I started doing incredibly well in BMX, I became pro, qualifying in the top tours of the world such as Dew Tour and then X Games, appearing live on large TV networks, doing well and achieving my dreams.

Obviously that sentence includes a lot, hard work and studying that is impossible to convey to anyone, and impossible to achieve without having an incredible passion. To achieve in action sports also means to be able to be mentally un-effected by injuries, which came more often than I liked. But I had done it.

I had become pro and started doing very well. Winning my first major professional contest being one of the top twelve invited to the middle of Times Square, NY where they shut the road down just for our contest, 'Air in the Square,' it was called. An epic setting to get my first major win in 2011.

I went from traveling the country a lot to traveling the world, and my perspectives on life really started to grow.

10

I am far different than most people, and I think in action sports, because it is such a mental game, weighing risk and technique and so many things mentally, that most of us spend a lot of time in our heads. Because of that many of us are far different from the next with only action sports in common.

In action sports, you have to be meticulous. With how to move your body and what techniques to use and when to be able to progress and learn new tricks. Perhaps the greatest gift of action sports is the confidence and faith required. Often you didn't win unless it was with brand new, never before done tricks. And often the year prior they were tricks people didn't even think were possible. Confidence and faith in ourselves is something that each of us became very good at.

On top of that, being humble is something we all get very good at, especially to be on a professional level. We had all been sent to the emergency room many times, we had all become used to our lifestyle and people constantly asking us, "Woa, what did you do?" Often we reply confused because we forget that its not normal for everyone to have scabs up and down their arms. Humility and respect for new things was something we all learned to gain; often through wrecking and injury, yet it is a part of what we do.

The amount of mental focus that goes into certain tricks only becomes more impressive when anyone weighs the fact that if we don't perform it perfectly that we likely could be hurt. Especially after seeing a few great friends have career ending injuries and their whole lives changed. We could spend years and injuries on one new trick, but the day you finally landed it was an experience that had such a high cost that the payoff is more than what I can possibly convey to people.

The time we didn't spend on action sports, in other hobbies, we attacked with the same confidence and work ethic. Whatever else we were into we're really into, whether it be cars or whatever. For me it was different than most, it was learning all manner of things.

I would get on the plane reading books on quantum physics and other things, I spent a lot of time riding and progressing as well as learning the things that I wanted to understand. For me it was going from one place to the next trying to figure everything out.

I had no idea then just how important BMX and the habits and confidences I had gained would play a part in learning. When I would go riding with friends, even small shows, and friends and other pros would say, "Dude, you don't have to go so hard all the time, you can chill out. You don't have to do such hard tricks and you don't have to ride so hard."

11

I enjoyed progressing. To the point I tore my ACL at a random school assembly doing a trick far beyond what was needed to impress.

Thankfully, I was blessed with same passion for another thing, learning. So many things struck my interest. I wanted to understand how the mind worked, why society was how it was, how history shaped it, why people were the way they were, how and why we are here, why do certain things happen, why hardships happen, what is truth?

I was always happily engaged in a full time course of history, the world, culture, the powers that be, psychology, philosophy, consciousness, physics, quantum physics, world economy, the mind and the human condition as a whole.

Pragmatically as I could I went from one to the next, learning what was before me.

Divine direction I couldn't then perceive was taking place. I was then spiritually 'blind,' but I was not forsaken. I was being brought in "ways I knew not" as it is so greatly put in the book of Isaiah. And eventually the "crooked paths" would be made strait. The promise of "seek and ye shall find" was unfolding, even for one seeking in all the wrong places.

"These things will I do unto them, and not forsake them." I am forever grateful.

Chapter 3

GUIDED BY LOVE

I love love. I had always been drawn to love and kindness and appreciated any religious or personal approach that was centered thereon.

I perceived relatively early in life the importance of love. The lack of love was the only thing ruining the world. Pride and insecurity were great destroyers. In my eyes pride was the lack of giving love, and insecurity was the lack of receiving it. All the problems of the world stemmed from a lack of love and love was the 'not just cliché' answer. Love is a big thing for me.

The first X Games I won I was wearing a shirt with the word 'love' on it. And the next year I won again with a picture of Martin Luther King Jr., a great person and symbol of love.

The picture was a mug shot of him. I removed the numbers and put the word 'love' in red on the shirt. It was such a big message to me, someone who suffered much for love and the care of many. Although I was nowhere near perfect, love and kindness is something I did my best at and really appreciated in the world and in people.

This was surely instilled in me at a young age, just as many other important lessons that surely led to the determination that I have been blessed with in life. And it all was a blessing through the example of my amazing mother.

My parents were divorced when I was still quite young. My amazing Mother was certainly called to do much in this life, and she has handled every step of it incredibly. It is apparent to me now how much the Lord has trusted her with.

Going from a seeming perfect member of The Church of Jesus Christ of Latter-day Saints, with her focus on a temple marriage in the church and raising an eternal family, her life changed quite quickly a few years into her marriage. My Dad struggled with his testimony and it led him away from the church. I have a lot of compassion for him and all who have struggled with faith, as I too did and left church at a young age. My Mother always ensured I saw the situation clearly, with a kind and understanding heart. My Dad is a great person who learned life through different avenues. I was blessed to see that at a young age. What an incredible blessing.

When I was 3 my brother was born and shortly after that it was just the three of us, my brother, my mom and I. We had moved from UT, away from my Mother's family to Idaho and began a new life together. Luckily my Dad's family lived there and since then essentially adopted my Mother as their daughter ever since that day, some incredible people that I'm very proud to share a last name with.

My Mother, my baby brother and myself were all living in a small apartment in a new place, and we were poor. It was something I didn't realize much at all growing up. I always felt very spoiled on birthdays and always had too many things to open up on Christmas. We always had plenty of food in the house; we were very well taken care of. I have been incredibly blessed with a very loving mother.

The financial struggles of our family led to so many incredible lessons by example from my Mother. Incredible lessons that we got first hand growing up. I wouldn't trade any of them. Many things I wouldn't even come to realize until we were much older.

For us to have juice, our Mother would water it down more and more and make it last as long as possible, we never knew. For us to stay fed, there were times she didn't eat, we never knew. We were always very well taken care of, and as I became older I could really gain a larger sense of how dire at times our situation was. Most months the entire bit of the money we had would be eaten up in bills, and food, and then there was very, very little to nothing left. Some months it was harder than that.

For us to get out of the poverty we were in, she put herself through college while raising 2 boys. Every night, she would put us to bed, then begin hours of homework in the living room, going to bed late. I remember the light being on in the living room all the time through the night. Eventually she graduated and became a teacher, an incredibly low paying job; but truly her calling in life.

18k for the first year as a teacher seems like incomprehensible poverty, yet she felt rich for the first time ever; going from nothing, to suddenly making some money was a huge change. This would go up a little over time but still remained very little. Teachers certainly make far less than they should and to me is a symbol of how skewed our cultural priorities are. It certainly takes some incredible selfless people to be teachers.

After a few years, we found a really run down house that my Mother could just barely afford to get into, as long as the basement was rented out. Our family helped greatly to renovate it to a livable condition and we found ourselves in a good neighborhood. Down the street older neighbor kids built BMX jumps, foreshadowing my future.

All the while I was instilled with one of the many great examples of my Mother, work hard, at all costs, to get where you want to go. This lesson was not lost on me and I simply saw it as a norm. This translated well to me in school and later would do the same in BMX and learning and pursuing all that I had interest in.

14

My mother often used the phrase with her lucky classroom kids, as well as my brother and I, "Whether you think you can or think you can't, you're right." A huge and deep phrase attributed to many famous people of the past. A true phrase. She was always a great motivator and supporter.

Beyond the lesson of working hard we were taught grander things in ways that really stuck.

One Christmas, shortly after we had moved to the new neighborhood, I had an interesting lesson that was taught a lot, but this time in a way I could never forget.

We were still poor, although better off and well taken care of, we were told all the time not to expect much for Christmas or birthdays. We always had great gifts, no money spent on wrapping paper. Our gifts were always wrapped in newspaper, borrowed newspaper from my grandparents who could afford to get it; it was a great tradition. We always felt very, very spoiled. My Mother must have saved and saved all year for Christmas.

One Christmas, at church there was a Christmas tree. On the tree were age numbers with a gender attached. Those with plenty were to pick ornaments of genders and ages and buy and wrap gifts for those kids. This was done so that kids of poor families that probably wouldn't receive Christmas gifts would have something to open on Christmas. Our Mother talked to us about this and asked us if we would want to trade some of what would be affordable for us for Christmas, and instead get some gifts for some of these kids. We decided it was a great idea.

Each of us grabbed a couple paper ornaments off of the tree and later that week went to the mall and stores to find what those kids might like. We chose ages near ours so that we could pick something accurate that we knew those kids may like. We bought real wrapping paper, wrapped them up, and brought them back to set them under the tree.

As Christmas neared, one day a man of the leadership of the church came over with a bag full of gifts for us for Christmas. I was confused at first and later found out that there were gifts for my brother and I as well. We quickly realized we were thought of as one of those families whose kids might not get much for Christmas. I remember being somewhat embarrassed at first but then noticing the reaction of my mother swept that away. She was so grateful and thankful. And genuinely appreciative, even though she really didn't expect or need it.

We opened the gifts and found some of the very gifts we purchased; in the same wrapping we wrapped them, among a few others. We all laughed together about how funny this was. We were opening gifts that not long ago we had picked out and wrapped. This was a powerful lesson then and has been again at times throughout my life.

15

I think now of the second of the two great commandments, after the first of 'Love God with all your might, mind and strength.' It is, 'Love your neighbor as yourself.' And what we sow, that we also will reap.

There is a grand temporal lesson here in always being grateful, so much so that you don't even see yourself in a hard situation, perceiving only the good; something that is truly a great and necessary life 'skill'. Furthermore, choosing to give to others and love others.

Beyond the temporal lesson here is the grander spiritual lesson. And to those seeking spiritual discernment of this cool lesson can see much there. We are all brothers and sisters and of the same eternal and grand family, this is true. We are all beloved Sons and Daughters of God. What we give to others we give to ourselves in the end. We are all a part of something grand, of God our Father, divine and precious.

"Verily I say unto you, Inasmuch as ye have done it unto one of the least of these my brethren, ye have done it unto me."

With this scripture we can keep it to just one great commandment, the first.

"Thou shalt love the Lord thy God with all thy heart, and with all thy soul, and with all thy mind."

When we understand that He loves all of His children so much that He places even Himself upon each of us. When we understand this, we can see the importance of the second great commandment. We can begin to understand just how much we all mean to Him. If you had a child who was hurt or offended by someone, would we not feel hurt or offended? He loves us this much and more.

The grandest lessons in life were taught to me by example. Not just example but genuine example. I still learn from these today. I am forever grateful for the incredible loving examples of my Mother that shaped all the good things in my life.

Although I was nowhere near perfect, I was blessed to have an understanding of what hard work can achieve and how important love is to the world.

Furthermore, I am exceedingly grateful for the constant prayers of a faithful mother.

Chapter 4

LEARNING AND SEEKING

It was at the new house that I found guys that rode BMX; it was a great blessing. Down the road there was a spot to build small dirt jumps and a bunch of kids who liked to ride them. My pure focus on BMX and the world began to make my focus on church diminish.

Shortly after I turned 16 I stopped going to church and it became a thing of the past. I didn't have the testimony I had had before. Looking back I can surely see how things of God are living, including the faith we have. And like muscles, must be worked out to grow. Muscles are only as strong as the tests they can pass, how much weight they can lift. If we neglect working out entirely for a long period of time, our muscles no longer can lift the weight we used to.

Likewise, faith is only as strong as the test it can survive. Shortly after 16 I hadn't worked out the things that matter, so much that I didn't perceive it to be there and it couldn't pass the small test of the world. I stopped going to church, thinking that there must be more to know. Pride and hardheartedness were guised as normality. I didn't know then the vast knowledge that could be found there in the gospel and with God as our guide, and eventually began to perceive "wisdom" in other areas more interesting.

I began focusing so much on BMX that almost everything took a back seat. It was a great passion that I am grateful for as it had many good elements to it, even elements that taught divine lessons. I can look back now and see the great wisdom in God in teaching me the way He did.

As I grew older and traveled the world and became very successful in BMX I began searching and learning about everything. For some reason, I loved BMX and I love learning more and more, about many things.

The first thing that I really took an interest in learning was the current world and how it came to be, what drove it and how certain things happened and operated.

It is hard to describe to people how I liked to learn. I spent a lot of time in very deep things. I just loved to learn and really understand what I thought other people couldn't see fully or didn't care to look at or understand.

I had always grown up getting good grades, and finding myself spending more and more time thinking about life, existence and why things were the way they were. This led to very deep study of many things.

17

As I traveled the world more, I spent more time learning and digging for learning as well. I learned a lot of history, the powers that helped create the world as it is, the inaccuracies of many things, the false perceptions that changed societies. I began to see things differently and more clearly.

Before I seem to aggrandize this search for wisdom, know this, Jesus said, the greatest in the Kingdom of Heaven is he who humbles himself before God as a little child. The humble and faithful gain the truest wisdom.

If anyone reading seeks true wisdom, seek a closer relationship with God, in humility, and meekness. One cannot dispel ignorance while retaining arrogance; especially when it comes to finding truth. I simply have to tell my story; and I had to go full circle.

That said, I'll continue.

The multi year and very deep search of the world as the world was and is and has become, regarding society, can be summed up in this. I became exceedingly more astonished, to the point of sadness, as I learned more and more of how things worked; essentially the sad state and darkness of the true situation. And how far removed the people were from it. Furthermore, how little people cared about it and were significantly deterred from ever seeing many things. It was more deception than I could imagine. Significant.

The extent of the explanation I will give is one given in Ether 8:24, "Wherefore, the Lord commandeth you, when ye shall see these things come among you that ye shall awake to a sense of your awful situation, because of this secret combination which shall be among you;"

I have no intention to delve into this. I will simply say that it is just as in the days of the 'Gadianton robbers' the people and even the people of God were incredibly deceived in nearly all areas of society for deeper agendas not of God.

Alas all is God's and we need not fear. Love is the way.

I wont get into it, I simply want to show where my search started, and it was rather deep before my interests in learning evolved and progressed.

It was significant and of later great value that I delved into this area first. It directed the rest of the search and where to and how to and what to learn about.

This was mainly driven by understanding where and why many things had come to be and the sources of much of those things. They either could not be trusted or were under guidance of things in the world that couldn't be trusted. Or rather were driven for specific purposes with beginnings that began where certain few felt they should and ended where certain few felt they should, regardless of actual progress.

18

Essentially I had seen each average avenue for learning, college, university, etc., although great for a specific field, was directed for specific purposes to fulfill specific needs for a society that was intended with very deterministic ends and purposes. People were taught for specific overall reasons, things and how things would actually be learned. Society was very well ran and orchestrated deeply by few. Anything of true value seemed incredibly controlled. Alas, I judge none and love all, as imperfect as I am; I want love and good for all.

I recognized that understanding and learning all I sought to learn could not be provided in common ways, to say the least.

I continued my search on my own in many areas. A vast search, constant reading about everything was something I really enjoyed, and BMX. Among the search I would even delve into learning of other religions, what they believed, motivations etc.

There is one very interesting story that comes from this. Sadly, at this point I had all but been very over the religion I had grown up in. I vaguely remember even a time of sadness, feeling I had been lied to all growing up. For those just this far into reading, I was mistaken; the church is indeed incredibly true. Yet then that was how I felt.

At one time someone from the church came over because my records had been moved to my address I moved to. I was so annoyed and upset and even thought that perhaps I would remove my records. I am very grateful I didn't do this. But feeling I had been lied to and learning what I thought was correct things really bummed me out and I felt bad for everyone I thought was wrong or misled. This is hard stuff to write now, knowing of the truthfulness of the gospel; but it is important to illustrate the process and this story.

I had been reading all sorts of everything. One day it felt somewhat comical to pull out the Book of Mormon and read it. I opened to a random page, I don't remember what. And began reading the random verses. I felt the Spirit incredibly strong. I was very surprised. I kept reading. It was significantly strong. I still had believed in God and occasionally prayed at this time, as I felt it silly to discontinue such as signs still pointed to the existence of Him. I obviously know now the immense truth and exceptional goodness of God, which is really what this whole grander story is about.

I felt the Spirit very strong. Amazingly strong. I was amazed. I wasn't sure what to do, but I felt it was true. The feeling was powerful and of the greatest peace I had felt and it was shouting one thing at me that I felt but had no real spiritual discernment then; it was shouting, "This is true."

I was amazed, and being a pragmatic and logical truth seeker I could not deny how strong and powerful this was. I decided I would drive back to my Mother's house that weekend and go to church with her. Something that I'm sure was hard for her to believe at the time.

I hadn't been to church for years. It was odd at first, remembering singing hymns and talks and everything. While I was there it happened to be a missionary homecoming for one of my childhood friends. We were best friends kindergarten to third grade. In fourth grade his parents sent him to a religious school for the year. I had no friends that whole year and had to try to fit in with different kids not of my faith. Kids that later became my friends, into skateboarding and other things. I look back at that and wonder how my life would have been different if I would have been able to keep a good friend with the same standards, beliefs and values that I had then. Instead I was a bit of a loner for a while, trying to figure things out. It certainly changed much.

He spoke about his mission, and I talked to a couple people. I didn't feel the Spirit how I felt it the night I read a few verses. The reason is probably that the entire time I was there I was silently judging. I judged that 'these people don't actually seek to understand like I do, they just believe it because they are raised in it.' These thoughts were false and wrong and generated the next great big lie in my head. I thought at times "oh call it the devil, what a great cop out to get me to do whatever you want." It was these types of thoughts that made feeling the Spirit impossible. Oh how I wish I knew what I know now. How grateful I am to my Father in Heaven.

I basically looked around, wrongly judged what I saw; I saw the people as simple minded and misled and on the drive back home decided that a feeling, even a strong feeling, couldn't mean all of this was immediately true. I was spiritually blind because I really prided what could be learned in a pragmatic fashion logically.

Oh how I wish I knew then what I know now. One of the great things about the Spirit is that it is a revealer of truth. How spiritually blind I was and how blessed I was to have a love that never would give up on me.

I would have loved for it to be true for me then. The day I found it was all true I was very, very, very happy. A perfect loving Father in Heaven? And I'm one of His children?! And He loves me that much? And wants me to be with Him forever? One can see the state I was in then, yet I still always held out a possibility for God and occasionally prayed; too many things were unexplainable.

I can only imagine that my Father in Heaven just sighed and kept helping me along, knowing full well I would be a harder case. I am eternally grateful for His great love and long suffering. All wisdom in Him for what I needed to learn.

As I continued seeking my paths certainly got crooked. I began to get deep in understanding how the brain perceived things and how many things were snuck by it.

I learned the principles of hypnotism and how the brain functioned. I was further shocked to see how many of the principles are absolutely everywhere in our world, even in deep ways, and I became even more saddened at it's state.

From very sad and deep things to even things as seemingly simple as Neuro Linguistics, a form of communication that seems innocent yet mildly coerces a subconscious and distracted mind to certain action, even these things were all over advertisements and in news and things to get people to act certain ways or feel a certain way toward things. The subversive power was all over and extremely prevalent.

A simple principle that messed with me was that of pre supposition. For a time it scared me off of anything to seek after with a pre supposition of something happening given, even if they were true things. I took so many psychological things and twisted them in the wrong way. Like many who err in this area, we were spiritually blind, seeing such things as foolishness, seeing only in the temporal. Yet I was learning much more about the world around me and getting the greater picture physically.

1 Corinthians 2:14 "But the natural man receiveth not the things of the Spirit of God: for they are foolishness unto him: neither can he know them, because they are spiritually discerned."

And so they are.

I used to think the feeling of the Spirit must have been able to be felt by all religions that believe what they learn, a mental trick alone. This is untrue and the Holy Spirit truly can testify in incredible ways of real truth.

People that used to be in other religions when they experience it, experience it in truth for the first time. It is nothing like they have experienced before and many are converted. Furthermore, the Spirit of the Lord can attest deeply and through many incredible avenues that completely and utterly shatter anything wordly and anything not of truth; light can prove light vastly.

I will get into some of my experiences later on. But utterly, light can prove light. The Spirit can incredibly, far beyond this world, prove truth.

"Cognitive Dissonance," as the term is, is something that I saw throughout thinking myself wise in. It essentially is that if someone is so entrenched in their beliefs they will not even allow themselves to look at the physical evidence, or evidence contrary to their belief.

This was another huge deception for me as I saw things pragmatic, logical and physical. Not understanding the possibility that the Spirit of God could make anything in the physical world utterly laughable to say the least. Yet another physical perception that I thought myself wise in.

Truly the foolish things by the worlds standard are chosen by God; for even His foolishness confounds the wise and mighty. If I could have known then.

Learning how powerful the mind was and how easily it could be manipulated really scared me off of so many things. This opened my eyes to essentially a whole new even deeper world, and I was mostly disgusted in sadness at the greedy world as I saw it applied in many aspects of business and coercion in many areas throughout the world.

I must add again here, the Spirit of God can absolutely shatter all this, and this was truly me seeking and being deceived at every turn. Yet in the wisdom of God, my crooked path was very slowly being made strait, leading me right where He wanted me to be led.

The way of the worldly average physical perception, including much taught in schools, is such a stumbling block.

I began to think myself wise in a few things, even setting aside very deep truths; that I now, very thankfully, KNOW to be true. I then set them aside because I thought the things I had learned in the physical carnal world meant anything. I began to 'understand' many things and wisdom was deceiving me.

1 Corinthians 2:18 "Let no man deceive himself. If any man among you seemeth to be wise in the world, let him become a fool, that he may be wise."

One of the greatest deceptions is the lie that 'there is no deception.' Any who are prideful in "wisdom" are certainly not led in true wisdom.

"Oh be wise; what can I say more?"

Over time, although I kept learning about many things, I began to focus more and more on quantum physics. This was a great curiosity to me as it had so much that is incredibly unexplainable. Basically, the things that make up the physical reality on the subatomic level, behave in no way that is predictable or even definitively measurable. This began to open my mind up exceedingly.

'You mean to tell me the things that make up our physical world don't behave on the properties of the laws of physics? At all? Like not even close?'

Not only that but no one understands it? To the point where famous physicists that dabbled with it and tried to learn much now look back and say, "I don't like it, and I'm sorry I ever had anything to do with it." – Schrodinger

The more people thought they came to know about it, the more things totally changed; at least that is what is reported and given to the public.

For instance, quantum entanglement is a thing, where two subatomic particles can become entangled and one will affect the other regardless of space and regardless of distance. It gets even more wild when some properties of particles become paradoxical; impossible seeming.

Needless to say all of this kept me praying and knowing that we knew nothing.

If you ever want to blow your mind go look up 'The Measurement Problem" or the "Double Slit Experiment." In a quick attempt to explain it simply and without detail it is this in a nutshell. An electron is a 'particle' or a 'wave'. Well, it's both. Well, depending on if you're looking at it. Well, actually, if there is any conscious observation whatsoever.

Really, a quick youtube search of the "double slit experiment" may help get the general laymen explanation out of the way.

Think of the electron as a small marble. When shot through one slit, with a measurement device on the back, we can see the slit expressed. As it is the only placed the 'marbles' can be shot through. Now when there are two slits, and we shoot an electron or a marble through suddenly the electron does something very weird. It reacts with itself and instead of being a particle becomes a wave and an interference pattern is shown (the pattern a wave makes through 2 slits).

Now here is the wild part. When a measuring device is set up to catch how and what slit the electron is passing through, suddenly the electron that had been a wave, is no longer a wave and is acting as a particle, going through a specific slit as a particle. The act of measuring the particles that make up everything, changes their very nature ENTIRELY. Things took shape as it was consciously observed. This is a far bigger deal than it sounds.

Furthermore, as more measurement experiments took place another wild thing appeared. They would switch on the measurement with different and more measurements after it was 'shot' either a particle or a wave ('it hadn't decided yet,' or so was perceived). As the

23

measuring device was switched on or not, each time it was as if the particle looked forward in time and knew before hand exactly what would happen, acting before exactly as we expected it to; or rather, from 'it's' perspective, as 'it' expected us to.

All particles that make up all things behave incredibly bizarre. All particles are the same particle, yet different in any fathomable way. Man's popularly pushed philosophies of how things are and came to be are based off of physical laws that are undermined by what matter is made up of. Which is a set of laws known to God and are God's, though some understand in part.

Consciousness and perception surely played a great part in reality I learned and began the depth of understanding in. As we faithful know, it is God who is the creator of all things. These findings make us smile. Because we know who's all things are and are by.

Doctrine and Covenants 88:41 "He comprehendeth all things, and all things are before him, and all things are round about him; and he is above all things, and in all things, and is through all things, and is round about all things; and all things are by him, and of him, even God, forever and ever."

Learning this bit of quantum physics took me directly to choosing to seek understanding of consciousness, something I had dabbled in seeking. I decided to dedicate the majority of searching here.

Soon I realized, logically and pragmatically, it would be most beneficial to not any longer seek the things that other people had researched and reported. I read books even research on how many different compounds affected people's minds and thoughts and consciousness, countless theories and ideas.

I read doctors studies of many theories from dimethyltryptamine, the pineal gland, psilocybin, other glands and areas of the mind; all interesting subjects to research, all based physically. All largely touted and talked about, I saw symbolism and realized the answers couldn't be without.

I began to realize if perception could affect subatomic things so greatly that perceptions of others could affect mine, and clearly they were getting to no final ends of understanding.

Everyone thought the same in a general sense and most had come through the same filter of schooling, which seemed detrimental to trying to discern things of an entirely different nature. One book a guy did a study and recorded body temperature and other things that physical science cares about during peoples serious spiritual experiences.

24

Einstein had said, "We cannot solve our problems with the same thinking we used when we created them."

I slowly began to realize that looking at the physical world or the brain for consciousness and understanding was as silly as breaking open a radio and trying to find the announcer. Boy how that understanding grew over time.

I eventually made the choice, logically and pragmatically, to cut off entirely outward sources of learning, and focus on consciousness by pragmatically assessing my own thoughts and consciousness. I still dabbled in reading things but the "research" turned into meditation and self-focus. This didn't become as profound until after BMX passed as the main and more sole focus by way of total fulfillment in my career.

The next bit I would learn however would make all I have learned up to this point seem laughable in hindsight. Further along, and more crooked paths the Lord would make strait.

Reader's Note: Again, I only relay this information to show the full circle way I had to go. Do not seek wisdom the ways I sought it, for all wisdom falls before the truth of God and Christ. I am simply telling the wild path that I had to take to get there. The greatest wisdom is humility and meekness before God.

You can spend forever to find all wisdom of the world and see your ignorance in attaining it as it shatters before the truth. Real wisdom is in our Father in Heaven.

James 1:5 "If any of you lack wisdom, let him ask of God, that giveth to all men liberally, and upbraideth not; and it shall be given him."

Oh if I had had the true wisdom to humbly ask and trust God to show me truth in a way that I would know it forever. I had to go full circle. All wisdom is in Him."

Chapter 5

BMX, FULFILLMENT, LEARNING

BMX was the main focus still. X Games is like our Super Bowl. In 2014 I had finally won my first X Games Gold Medal in Big Air. The top 8 in the world are invited. BMX Big Air is the flag ship event for BMX at X Games, (skateboarding also has a big air event). I had done quite well in Dirt for a while and set my sights on what seemed to be a wild level in 2011, the highest and almost ridiculous level of competition, Big Air.

Big Air was something I wasn't sure I would ever even do. Few guys did it and you had to be really proficient on big jumps, which I was from Dirt (big dirt jumps in a row), and you had to be proficient in vert. Vert is a half pipe, with higher risk and takes a long time to become good at. Fewer guys do it on BMX because it is so much harder and more dangerous. I had qualified into Dew Tour for vert as well; I was probably the only guy in dirt and vert at the same time. I began to make televised finals in that discipline as well and did well. Big Air was next on the list.

The Big Air ramp is nearly 9 stories tall. You have to take an industrial elevator to the top. You drop in a very steep and tall roll in, hit a 70 foot gap jump, land on a big landing that is also another roll-in to gain speed to hit the 27.5 foot tall quarter pipe.

The quarter pipe sends you strait up into the air; this is why you want to be proficient on vert type ramps. It's very important to find your way back to the ramp in the right spot. If you are in or out of the ramp by 3 or 4 inches it the difference between falling much further and either hitting the deck or landing far lower and wrecking. Wrecks on the Mega Ramp, another name for the Big Air ramp, are really gnarly. Knockouts happen often, and everyone has been slammed on it a time or two.

I like to describe it as the Formula 1 of Action Sports. It is significantly faster, significantly higher, significantly more dangerous. You pull more G's and slam much harder. Sometimes I laugh about it and ask myself, "What the heck are we even doing." It's that gnarly, and it gets wild when you get used to the speed and height and distance; it becomes the most fun thing to ride once you get dialed in on it. Basically it is gnarlier in every way, by far, than anything comparable.

Danny Way, a legendary skateboarder pioneered with BMX legend Mat Hoffman the ramp type. He is one of 3 people with his name in gold on the Great Wall of China for building a Big Air ramp to jump over it. It looks big on TV and it looks ridiculous in person.

I had been riding X Games Big Air since 2011 and finally won in 2014, which is no small task. It was a bizarre feeling. I felt then that I

26

could die happy. I had worked my entire life for this. Something many thought was totally a crazy dream at times, even through rough injuries and hardships.

I had won X Games, and the biggest event of the X Games, live internationally on TV. My family was watching live on ESPN and I had experienced something so grand that I wish everyone could experience it, utter life fulfillment. What else was there to do? It is a very weird bizarre feeling.

I completed the biggest goal I could imagine for myself from a kid; so I made a couple more big goals. I wanted to win again the next year in absolutely serious fashion. I also wanted to bring some top X Games dudes in BMX and Freestyle Moto Cross to the town I grew up in. The town, I felt, was cut off from many inspirational influences. I wanted to bring something that I would have loved as a kid and would have motivated me to. On top of making that happen, I would work the whole year on a trick so big that I didn't even know if I could make it happen on a ramp that size.

I spent a huge chunk of the year dedicated to learning a very big trick called the 'double flair.' This is a trick for the quarter pipe, the strait up into the air and back down ramp. This ramp is the most dangerous to do tricks on and I was stepping it up into a level significantly beyond where it had been at.

A double flair is a double backflip with a 180, so you can land back in the direction you came up. You have to come down in the pocket perfectly, where even inches matter greatly. Too close to the deck you can hit it, falling a couple stories, to a deck, then bouncing down almost 3 more. Too far from the deck you just fall all 5 of the stories to however you happen to land. It's a serious ramp and I had to make sure the trick was perfect.

I spent a bunch of time working on the trick making it perfect as well as making the event happen that we called 'Ramp Riot'.

Ramp Riot happened for us that next year in 2015 right before X Games. It was a ton of preparation and we had the top dudes in BMX and Moto X in the entire world, in a small town, in a stadium of 12k that we ended up getting just over 7k. I think the town had absolutely no idea the immensity they were getting.

I had traveled all over the world and the same names would sell out large arenas, but in towns in Idaho it seems things with hay bales and horses is cooler. Regardless, the people who did support it were die hard in their support and we gave something really big to an area that get's nothing like it. We gave something many of the kids who came would never otherwise have been able to experience. Most importantly they

27

knew they could come from anywhere and do anything. I would have loved it as a kid and that's what mattered for them.

A very cool experience happened at that event. We heard through the grape vine that some kid from Utah who had cancer had made a wish, through a similar organization, to become a professional BMX rider of all things. We brought him out to the event, made him a pro and had him ride with us. The whole crowd was on their feet and it was an epic moment. This is something I will never forget, for a few reasons.

My good buddy Ben Voyles who was an incredible rider and Pro who was there riding with us, he had previously gone through cancer and been able to put it far behind him and continue riding on a ridiculous level. It was the perfect two people to be at the same event together. The kid with the dream and things to overcome and the kid who is standing right there showing him he can do exactly that. It can be done.

That had a big impact on me, being able to inspire any and all, even those with low hopes or extra difficulties. It really made the event special, it seemed the whole event was about inspiring people who maybe hadn't even seen their potential, in that area there was little inspiration toward youth; at least that I saw.

My mother being a school teacher would always give me sad stories of these poor kids with really very hard lives and hard things to overcome. This was a driving force behind making the event happen, as well as making ticket prices cheap, 15$, so that anyone could afford them as well as gave a lot away. We covered all the ramps in banners of big words like, Humble, Inspire, Dream, Grateful, and Believe. The point of the event was to get across to kids, that no matter what you want to do, you can do it.

After the event we had all the athletes stay as long as they had to in order to do every single autograph desired. Everyone got a free program and there were posters and shirts and we spent so much time, hours, talking to kids, giving autographs etc. The line was massive.

This type of thing doesn't happen often. The top dudes in Freestyle Moto Cross, and I mean the top dudes, the most winningest X Games dudes were there in BMX and FMX. Really big name dudes, some of which, like Nate Adams, that I had grown up watching on TV, only to later become friends with them and drag them to Idaho.

The big impact was this, seeing how excited and truly inspired these kids were, and not just the kids, the adults alike. The vibe at the event was moving; everyone standing up for the one kid and his dream of overcoming a disease to keep following his dream alone was absolutely epic. The newspaper and news did stuff about the event all weekend. The vibe was strong and inspirational. The biggest impact was on me.

28

I saw these kids, the way they acted and looked at us, and suddenly the accolades that don't matter, mattered, because it showed them what they could do. If I could come from this place that seemed broken to so many, and there are so many broken kids with broken homes, I really feel for them. But if I could come from there and make something happen they could too. I really began to see in a big way that I owed it to these kids to keep going and to keep doing my best to do big things. That was my perspective.

I had been working that whole year on the goal of the double flair; it wasn't working. It was on such a level that I wasn't even close to making it happen on a ramp. X Games was a few months away and I wasn't anywhere near making it happen for real yet, although I had put a ton of work in. And I had to make it happen on the gnarliest ramp in existence.

After the event was over I made a big decision. I would forgo the next event the next month in China and choose to spend all the time leading up to X Games to work even harder than I had all the year thus far to make the dream of that trick happen. And I was going to do it to really show these kids, it can all be done.

Inspiration was a huge driving factor for me. I suddenly saw myself as the guy in the seat that the guys I looked up to on TV growing up were in. I remembered how much I was inspired. I wanted to live up the inspiration I had received growing up from my heroes. From my perspective then, it was of the most worth to work towards, to inspire others to pursue their dreams.

I started training hard. A bunch of friends were at Travis Pastranas house for an event and he had a perfect setup to practice the trick; a ramp not as big as Big Air but bigger than anything else around. I decided to make it happen. I booked a flight, got a car and hotel nearby and decided to make learning them happen no matter what.

I happen to show up the day that Josh Sheehan did the first and only triple backflip on a motorcycle on a wild and highly specialized setup. So seeing that basically made me feel like a wus if I didn't get done what I set out to do. One of my buddy's that was there also kept asking me, "Are you really gonna send it and try em?" Over and over. I was determined.

I came to the setup to try them on one day, and realized everyone around was already doing other things way back in the back of the property, basically I was alone, trying gnarly stuff. I would wait for one of the camera guy's kids to come skate the ramp nearby, then I would climb up the roll-in and start sending the trick. If I got knocked out or hurt at least he could run and tell someone, hopefully. It was the most interesting way to learn a trick ever. I spent the whole first day working it out and eventually, after many wrecks, got them dialed in. I ended the day doing 4 in a row.

This was a big deal. Only one double flair had ever been done before on a vert ramp type. It was by my friend and legend Kevin Robinson who had become known for it. One ever had worked. This ramp was bigger. And the Big Air ramp was far, far bigger still. I had finally figured it out. If I went as absolutely fast as I could, rotated as fast as I could, really paid attention to where I was in the blur, I could just barely make it happen.

I woke up the next day, no warm up, and did 4 in a row cold turkey to make sure I really had them dialed. The trip was worth it.

I went home and a month before X Games made my way to Woodward West. Basically paradise, Woodward is a summer camp for kids into BMX, Skateboarding, and really all action sports. They have the best facilities and it is also a training camp. Professionals frequent it often as we go there to train and ride and hang out and teach the new generation of kids. It's a win win-win for everyone and they are always so good to us. Paradise on earth for us.

The major win is that Woodward West has the only permanent full size Big Air Ramp outside on a mountainside, other than legend Bob Burnquist's private backyard one, but I think he was using it for his helicopter landing pad. How would it be?

My buddy Ben and I went out to ride the Big Air ramp. Generally when I ride it, it's me riding it, and a friend watching to make sure I survive. It's rare to get another person, even a pro, to want to ride it with you. It's just a gnarly thing.

After getting a few warm ups and some warm up single flairs on the ramp I felt good to give it a go. I decided to not go full height and keep it safer, at a still decent height.

I went for it, it felt good, and then all of the sudden I hit my hip on the deck and the coping, the metal pipe at the top, hard. I bounced to the flat and some all to familiar pain set in. I had slammed, and hard. To put this in perspective, jump out of 4 stories, do a double backflip, hit your hip on the balcony of the 2nd or 3rd story then fall to the ground. It was awesome.

Slowly the pain went away enough to know I could walk. I got up; realized nothing serious had been broken. We packed up and left. I spent the rest of the time up to X Games recuperating.

The point of all these details is to illustrate the dedication and intensity of the search for the goal. This intensity became the normality in all areas; from BMX, to seeking 'wisdom' to being guided in truth. It becomes important.

X Games time came. I felt great on my bike, knew I knew how to do the trick and tried to put the wreck out of my mind. Barreling at the quarter pipe in practice and trying to imagine myself, going that fast, into a wall that was going to toss me so high into the air, it was hard for me to imagine pulling back as hard as I could and actually sending the trick. It was so gnarly. All I could do was laugh at the utter seriousness of it. I'm still not sure if it's a strength or a weakness to be able to 'control alt delete' serious fear and just focus and do it full bore. Regardless it is a necessary skill for that ramp.

The night came around for the event. We were a big one; prime time on ESPN and tens of thousands of people lined the hillside watching the highly anticipated event. I was going last of the 8 of us as I was the defending gold medalist. We had 3 runs each.

I decided I was going to go for the double flair each run. The first run in, I did the gap trick, and went for it. I nearly hit the deck and coping and sliding out of it ok. I had kept the trick quiet and a secret and only a small select few knew about it. It was a big surprise to many.

The contest continued. I took the elevator back to the top, brandishing my 'love' MLK shirt. My second run came around. I dropped in, went higher on the quarter pipe to get around the last little bit of the rotation that lacked on the first run as well as pushed away from the deck a little more. I went low and slightly over rotated hitting my head. It was a decent knock but no big deal. I got up, knowing I needed to do a mid range between my first and second run to make it happen.

It's a weird thing when you're the last guy to go. I was the defending champion and last to go. By the final run, everyone has done their total runs and down on the ground looking up. I found myself atop the roll in by myself with a camera guy and a contest official.

I looked out from atop the big roll-in. I had been blessed to see many different views from that giant roll in across the globe. In Brazil alone, I had been able to look 360 degrees around and see an ocean of only city skyscrapers in Sao Paulo, look around and see an ocean of only rain forest in Foz Do Iguacu, and look around and see the favelas of Rio de Janiero under the statue of the Christus. I had been greatly blessed.

This was the second occasion I had been able to look out and see the hillside in Austin Texas full of people. This time was different than them all. I was up there alone, trying something big, something I had just got out of twice on the previous two runs. I looked out; then looked at the ramp, incredibly focused on the minor variances I had to make to make this happen.

At this time in my life I prayed every so often still. What better time than now? I knew this wasn't a joke. I said a quick one, remained focused, I was called to drop and I rolled in.

31

I did a 360 backflip no hander over the jump again, and barreled at this huge wall and yanked for all I could, making the tiny changes. The moment I could spot the landing I realized I was coming in low, very low, how could I ride out of this? I braced to take a landing like I never had before and before I knew it my body had held and I was riding away.

There is nothing to describe tons of people going from quiet anticipation to an explosion of elation cheering and applause. I know all to well how it can go from the same anticipation to sounds of, "Ohhhh," when someone slams hard. But when they explode with that energy, there is nothing like it; especially when something big new and thought impossible just happened.

I basically could barely wrap my head around it. It had happened. Tons of work the whole year panned out, barely. I was certainly blessed to be able to have landed it and I'm forever thankful for it. My family was there to watch and see it. A great blessing.

According to my mother, my step dad had told her right before I was about to drop in that he had a strong feeling I would land this one, he felt that Heavenly Father told him that this was the one. Interesting to think of. It wasn't something I heard about till long after.

In the post contest TV interview I remembered why I worked so hard. 'It wasn't long ago I was at home watching some of these legends, and I wanted kids to see this and think they should be able to do something awesome with their lives.'

Legends like Kevin Robinson who I thanked, who was a good friend I had grown up watching with posters on my wall, who helped me sort out the double flair here and there as well and one of the first I told after I got the practice ones at Travis's. He was the only one to ever do it on any vert ramp, and he announced the contest for television as I landed it, jumping out of his seat. I was quick to remember all he had done for me to get there physically as well as inspiring me and hoped kids would see that message again related.

I was inspired through injury and hardship to keep going all the way. ACL reconstructions and rough things from the very beginning; and this was an even bigger payoff than the first win.

It was done in a big fashion with next level progression that I worked very hard for, in Cinderella story fashion, on the last run. It even made the #1 Moment on ESPN Sport Center that night amidst the NBA Finals.

If I ever could have maxed out 'utter life fulfillment' of my childhood goals even more than the year before, I sure did it. It is an incredible blessing to look back on.

Chapter 6

COMING TO 'KNOW' 'WISDOM'
Clarity for those within the stumbling block

Right after that X Games I instantly began working hard for the next year, wanting to do my best to relive that incredible night. I learned a lot of new great things, none to get anywhere near simply again landing the double flair; it is a weird thing when you jump the progression up 10 steps instead of 1; it starts to become expected every time.

The next year went around, training; we did Ramp Riot again once more for the second and last time and X Games came around again.

The weather was bad the whole time. Crazy storms ended up cancelling Big Air for BMX and Skateboarding, a seriously wild thing to happen. No one had ever 3-peated Big Air wins and I had been really looking into giving it my best effort. There is nothing like working hard all year again to have nothing to work hard for.

I ended up going home, moved, and had a bunch of down time. The major tours I was on were done before X Games and the contest was cancelled. After one other smaller event I had a lot of down.

I found myself back in 'loving to learn' mode.

I had given everything to BMX hard for the last many years and on a ridiculous training level the last 3 years. And although I wasn't going to stop, I was finding increased focus in learning; something I also hadn't stopped but began to dedicate more time to.

Readers Note: I am going to be incredibly vague and non-detailed in this next part; for good reason. Remember, ALL man's 'wisdom' falls before God, for all is of Him. If you seek wisdom, seek revelation from Him. I will later get into how all wisdom is confounded and the deepest true wisdom is humility before God.

Having learned a lot since leaving quantum physics behind for personal consciousness, I began to gain a lot of headway in meditation and self-learning; consciousness was all I sought to understand. Understanding that others perspectives were in a certain way of thinking, and understanding the irrelevancies of time and locality at the subatomic level was plenty to get me thinking deep all the time.

I spent a lot of alone time, a lot of deep reasoning with myself. Personal honesty and openness in thought and reasoning began to lead to deep understandings. I began to discern and control my thoughts and escorted myself through the maze, finding keys, opening locks, as some philosophers and others have called it.

33

I had come to learn much that many in the world would call 'secret knowledge' or something; but I was finally understanding it all very deeply.

I began to understand everything, so I thought. The 'spiritual laws,' though taught in the very wrong context in the world (in deception), were being understood deeply.

I began to see philosopher's deepness and the things they alluded to and the esoteric things in the world that many don't think about or perceive. Furthermore, I understood the root. The 'oneness' and 'enlightenment' eastern religions talked about made sense and I began to respect their points of view; although the very 'knowledge' itself negated any point for religion; as it was, in my perspective.

And perspective was everything. It opened my heart up more to love, I saw everyone closer than they seemed, by a lot, it was harder to judge; and the rabbit hole went deeper. After getting past the many pitfalls and wrong and incorrect assumptions many have come to in this search in the past, like some thinking they are all that exists, and other deceptions, I came to "know." A term used often to separate those who 'understand how things are' and those who don't. Those who 'know' the 'wisdom' of the wise of world.

Looking back, how foolish the 'wisdom of the wise' as it is taught in the world. Yet I felt I finally understood everything, perfectly. So perfectly, I thought. Boy is existence far bigger than we can imagine, and to limit it to our own imagination and mind is a pitfall.

I began to understand and see people all over the world in high places with this knowledge. I finally figured out, for myself, what secret societies all over the world teach. Those with this 'deep wisdom' are all types of people, referring to others as simply people who 'know'; people who understand how things are or people who 'get it.' After all it was a finite and understandable end that seemed to perfectly explain everything; though it was understood and pushed in a false fashion.

Let me interject. First of all I will not explain this 'wisdom,' but speak in ways that those stuck in them can understand and see their way out. It is unfruitful and true wisdom comes from God and the milk of the word is perfect. God will teach the greater things that make even the deepest 'wisdom' in the world seem utterly foolish. All is His.

In part the 'wisdom' of the wise is not all bad if understood right in utter humility before God, though it still becomes quite small and to be left behind in a sense as even His foolishness confounds the mighty and wise of the world. Humility before Him and faith on our Savior Jesus Christ is the true wisdom. The law of Christ supersedes.

As the world gives 'wisdom' it can do so much more harm then good, and does. The way it is given in the world is such a stumbling

34

block and becomes a tool of the adversary to ever distract us from the truth of God, keeping in pride. The very 'wisdom' or 'law' becomes fulfilled only in Christ and becomes confounded entirely by simple childlike faith in our Savior Jesus Christ.

Seek wisdom from God; for the wisdom of the wise and understanding of the prudent truly collapses just as the Bible says. Humility before God is all wisdom.

For the compassion of those in this deception and stumbling block I write this; as well as for those who will come to see it; that they will not be persuaded from the rock that is Jesus Christ.

It became interesting to see people throughout history who would imbed this understanding into their art, or books or poetry or music or symbolism anywhere in an esoteric manner to somewhat tout their personal wisdom to others who 'knew' and to lightly tease the 'average populace.' Art often uses all manner of things; sacred geometry, and patterns of creation in art like Fibonacci and tons of general natural things that are of a deeper nature.

This existence is essentially seen as rather light hearted and pointless; none had the ability to be correct in their beliefs for anyone but themselves. The perspective was that perspective alone is what matters. Understandable as one can come to understand the vast agency and freedom God has given us, but the stumbling block can be so vast that one cannot perceive a specific truth because of the belief there is none. It is highly skewed to keep us in an endless deception.

It is thought that there could be no specific perfect avenue of truth but that any path was a personal truth. Infinite possibilities. People stuck in this cannot discern that for their 'truth' of 'no specific truth' to exist, the opposite of a 'specific truth' would exist; then making their perspective of 'truth' better described as one grand deception keeping them from the singular specific truth, Jesus Christ. The way, the truth and the life.

They really had come to discern the depth of agency and freedom God gives His children, in a very wrong and diluted way, away from God. Alas at the end, there is truth alone, in Jesus Christ; I'll get to it in good time.

Per Capita this is a very rare 'wisdom,' few have it and most I have seen in it are so deceived as it is steered deep and wrong. I can judge none. Many in high places have it, it is being pushed more and more and is a grand deception in the way it is given. Many can go very far in all the wrong direction. For this reason I say, "Restore." I will get deep into explaining the truth and necessity of Christ clearly for those who are in it and so much more as we go along.

I will say, even this 'knowledge', that the world has prided itself on for a long time, confounds the physical understanding of time and matter in the grandest general sense immensely. So for any to assume things that co exist with those being fact (big bang, evolution, etc.) they do themselves such a disservice; all utterly and absolute fall before necessity of a conscious being. God lives.

Many have come before and debunked silly things, and even base deep understandings or 'wisdom' few in the world hold, even though exercised in the wrong way, utterly destroy any idea of the physical being wholly relevant including the thought of evolution or others that are centralized on time or physical. It becomes irrelevant with even the wrong understanding of deep 'wisdom' of the world.

"The flesh profiteth nothing." It is a Spiritual battle. Christ is necessary. Deception and the powers thereof take a bit of truth and twist it vastly and bring others to pride in it and guide them all the wrong ways in endless deception. This will become evident as we go along and I cannot judge any as you will see as my story goes along.

Time itself is relative and even satellites experience time differently than we do on earth. There are many ways, even by 'physical laws' and understandings, to experience it differently. It is pointless to get into this other than to say it is irrelevant to a point that the snare of deception that I am trying to get people out of, is still beyond that.

This book is simply going to be cram packed with information and different perspectives to show that all confound and show the truth in and utter necessity of Jesus Christ and His atoning act.

From the humblest of learning to the deepest as far as 'wisdom' attained by man, all will be shown the truth of Jesus Christ.

Those in the stumbling blocks of 'wisdom' will by the end of this come to see their way out of it to true wisdom, that is humility before our good Father in Heaven. There will be much information given on how to do all such things with so much of my personal experiences peppered in.

X Games freestyle moto cross champ and legend Travis Pastrana explained action sports tricks in an interview once regarding how a 2 second jump can feel like 20 seconds, "There are a lot of people who experience this in sports . . . if you can block out every feeling, emotion and thought, you can actually slow down time." He acknowledges how people can wrongly assume this sounds like witchcraft or something, as it is new to them. He explains it is, "simply when your adrenaline takes over and everything else doesn't matter, it really feels in your mind, I don't know if it's something speeding up, but it really feels like time slows down."

This is similar to someone who might be in a car accident and feels like time slows down. As Travis says, "I don't know whether something speeds up or time slows down."

It is as though your thoughts can speed up, and in your perspective time can slow down based on focus. Neither side is correct. It doesn't speed up or slow down it is simply whatever perspective you choose to see from. Many experience this daily, in sports and otherwise.

I wont get into this deeply, and it is a bit of an odd divergent to the topic, I simply wish to show a grander point. There IS a deep 'understanding', 'wisdom' that is beyond all these other theories. And I am mainly addressing those ensnared in that. They perceive it the wrong way and the adversary pushes 'wisdom' as something to pride oneself in and a part of truth is greatly distorted to become a cage that keeps us from God our Heavenly Father.

I feel 'wisdom' in deception will be pushed more into the future; ignorantly guiding away from truth of our Savior. For anyone ensnared in the growing deceptions that are prophesied to have the ability to deceive even the elect in the future and now, I want to greatly lessen this impact and restore those ensnared. I intend to paint this clearly and set a highway out of the pit back to truth that is Jesus Christ our absolutely necessary Savior. Praise God.

This 'wisdom' should not be sought as something to gain. What should be sought is TRUE WISDOM, which is Jesus Christ. The 'wisdom' is taught and given in such a twisted and wrong way that it can make one into their own prison keeper, thinking themselves wise in it.

Again, before we continue and as we continue, if you want true wisdom, seek God. Walk uprightly, become humble before Him, seek and ye shall find. In due time, in wisdom of Him He will teach you grander in truth; the way the world is currently getting such things is generally very twisted as it very often guides in deception; regardless such becomes very deeply confounded and faith in God is the greatest wisdom. I will explain this far more.

"But to be learned is good if they hearken unto the counsels of God."

1 Peter 5:5-6 "...and be clothed with humility: for God resisteth the proud, and giveth grace to the humble. Humble yourselves therefore under the mighty hand of God, that he may exalt you in due time."

For those who struggle to part with their physical understanding and silly theories of evolution and things I give a few quotes about our solar system. Keep in mind here I am taking a huge backward step to illustrate these points. I hope some may find it fruitful.

37

The physical world is confounded in spiritual laws that are confounded in God, who has created all things. The law of Jesus Christ supersedes. Seek and follow God in faith. Stay on the rock of Christ. Regardless I will, for the sake of some, digress and show in a physical way a few simple quotes.

These quotes are about the computer models and ideas to create the solar system, many say they have it figured out, it is lies and they cannot get anywhere near with their physical understanding and infinite time, to make the solar system. This is shocking to come to find when we realize it is these 'wise men' who often refuse to ever entertain a creator, it is their theories that are relied on to teach kids in school.

Here is one from a Nobel Prize winner, "To place the Uranian satellites in their present (almost coplanar circular) orbits would require all the trajectory control sophistication of the modern space technology. It is unlikely that any natural phenomenon, involving bodies emitted from Uranus, could have achieved this result." H. Alfven and G. Arrhenius, Structrue and Evolutionary History of the Solar System, 1975, D. Reidel Publishing Co.

The further scientists get into it, the more they learn, the more problems they find. Each planet to exist as it does generally needs a large asteroid impact and many other anomalies that have no proof of existence. Each planet gets more complex and needs more very rare additions to make it happen.

Eventually for galaxies and things to work scientist must invoke the 'tooth fairy,' their words not mine, of 'dark matter' and 'dark energy,' which there is no evidence of. Anything to keep the theory of evolution over time from the big bang alive.

Interesting to note how when we don't see in light and truth of God that quickly the deception is darkness is responsible for what is. How deception controls.

Continual things are added with zero evidence to hope to get to the result of what we have today, and yet they cannot. Isn't that interesting, they seem so confident when they give it to us and teach children. There are real powers that push us from God. God lives, He created all things.

"To sum up, I think that all suggested accounts of the origin of the Solar System are subject to serious objections. The conclusion in the present state of the subject would be that the system cannot exist." Sir Harold Jeffreys, The Earth: Its Origin, History, and Physical Constitution. P 359

In the end, and as we experience things here, all things require an opposite. There is everything and nothing. ALL IS GOD'S! I will extrapolate further on in future chapters. 0 is 0, nothing. -1 +1 is also 0. And -10000 +10000 is zero. Within 0 is everything. $0/0=E$.

Physical is nothing, God reigns. And we want to be on the side of life and light. We need Christ, He is the way, the truth, the life; we will get to it.

Scientists are 'baffled,' according to Michio Kaku, because those at the Large Hadron Collider cannot understand why they get the same levels of matter and that of antimatter. They see in terms of the "Big Bang" and creation and that with this understanding, "we shouldn't be here!"

"We have more matter than antimatter in our galaxy," he says. He also states that at the instance of the "big bang," (that wording shows some real faith in that 'big bang,') there was a slight overabundance of matter over anti matter; which consequentially means, us. He even says comically there should be 'anti love.' I would say it's called hate and is how we can know and understand love. (I will get more into this in future chapters.)

Michio continues by saying that there is a Nobel Prize waiting for someone to figure it out. Glory to God, all is His.

He explains they want the theory to "naturally come out, with this over abundance of matter, over anti matter." Again they are set on a big bang with time and other irrelevancies that I assume God chuckles at, or is sad about. He ends with the question, "why should we be here?"

More and more scientists are coming to faith and more are coming to understand deeper things, leaving behind the old ways.

The truth again is that, as we experience it here, there must be opposition of everything to exist. One can extrapolate this to understanding certain things; I will get into it further on.

Be absolutely sure to keep God and Christ at the center. All true wisdom begins with humble faith in Him. In the end we get to a VERY REAL need of Jesus Christ and His atonement. Why would He have to pay for the opposite of our sins? There are things that must be. When we see clearly, we owe all to Him. All is God's.

I cannot blame or judge this scientist. We are constantly pushed this type of stuff to keep us thinking in a certain aspect or way. Truly pride in any wisdom not taught by God will keep us all in deception, whether in physical or spiritual.

Scientists want anything to match up with a big bang and evolution etc. etc. etc. It is all nonsense even to the people that I am trying to help now. They are beyond the physical though they see in much deception. God lives. All is His.

When they start seeing that there is a creator, they can become humble before Him, resonate in truth with Him, utilize the Saviors

Atonement through faith, resonate with our Father in Heaven and finally be taught some real truth by way of revelation through His Holy Spirit. Then such will begin to have spiritual vision. Then the doors are blown off and we can laugh and rejoiced like a child at the goodness and glory of God our Father in Heaven.

Man is nothing, yet we are everything to God. How grateful I am.

1 Corinthians 1:28-29 "And base things of the world and things which are despised, hath God chosen, yea, and things which are not, to bring to nought things that are: That no flesh should glory in His presence."

For people in the proverbial stone age of 'understanding', (not to sound unkind or judgmental, I have been there myself and full circle,) trying to figure things out physically, their answer is to come up with newer and newer ideas that will get closer to what is created based on their base and corrupted and fallen theory of evolution. It is almost taboo for them to ever think in terms of a creator. They are creating their own prison just as those on a higher level of understanding by not even seeking God.

All must leave 'logic' and try faith; things of the spirit are simply significantly above physical understanding. Alas, God lives. We must seek Him for ourselves.

Romans 8:5-6 "For they that are after the flesh do mind the things of the flesh; but they that are after the Spirit the things of the Spirit.

6 For to be carnally minded is death; but to be spiritually minded is life and peace."

1 Corinthians 2:14 "But the natural man receiveth not the things of the Spirit of God: for they are foolishness unto him: neither can he know them, because they are spiritually discerned."

People in the 'know' of this 'wisdom,' (remember true wisdom is of and from God,) scoff at those researching such areas and simply say that one day they will get to the 'knowledge,' even though they understand it partially and in the very, very wrong context. Though they can see through many lies of the physical understanding, still they are yet deceived, deeper in pride of 'wisdom', and miss God who is and who created all things. They are able to see more and understand more, yet they are in a worse place than they know; and it is because they don't know it. I will show this more clearly as we go on.

They are worse still if they are persuaded to believe themselves that they alone are Christ, one grand deception of many that those in 'wisdom' must get past. All manner of stumbling blocks to get past throughout it, all orchestrated by deception. It is one of the many twists and turns and deceptions people must get past in this 'wisdom.'

Some get far and deeper and clearer, some get stuck. Some think it's a mirror(s) and only them, or just them, some get further, some get stuck in other parts. Some get past deep parts, some get to places not understanding the 'wisdom' and are even more stuck by lies. Some come to think there is just a negative power and lose hope for anything more. Yet all who are in it, even with a 'fuller' understanding are ensnared in deception and kept from God.

Jacob 4:14 "…Wherefore, because of their blindness, which blindness came by looking beyond the mark, they must needs fall; for God hath taken away his plainness from them, and delivered unto them many things which they cannot understand, because they desired it. And because they desired it God hath done it, that they may stumble."

Many have the 'wisdom' only in portion and people have called it a maze, it is deeper and deeper deception. The more 'understanding' one gets, the further away from the rock of faith in Christ. At least until the hopeful case it falls away and one can see through deception or extrapolate to truth.

Such can become entrenching and prison of our own creating. Those who walk in pride of wisdom cannot accurately see the vastly larger things behind it guiding all the wrong ways. Though on one side it can be perceived as 'great knowledge,' it becomes utterly confounded by the weak things of the world. The foolish things, in the eyes of the world, truly confound the things which are mighty.

1 Corinthians 1:27 "But God hath chosen the foolish things of the world to confound the wise; and God hath chosen the weak things of the world to confound the things which are mighty;

28 And base things of the world, and things which are despised, hath God chosen, yea, and things which are not, to bring to nought the things that are:

29 That no flesh should glory in his presence."

We will get into it further on. This may seem confusing to many reading. If so, good. Hold on to God and never be persuaded from the rock of Christ. Some of this will be given in a way for specific few stuck in stumbling blocks. All of this will be helpful for both parties. Humility before and faith in God is true wisdom. His ways are above and more perfect. We will get into it.

A simple analogy that comes to mind is this: A drop in the ocean can be falsely coaxed in specific 'wisdom' to see themselves as the entire ocean and not a drop; an incorrect extrapolation in deception, for they are but a child of the ocean. The drop cannot imagine yet the powers that are about. The Spirit of the ocean, who allows his drop to believe as he wishes, looks at his little drop and little child in concerning love. What is really happening is the drop is being coaxed away from the ocean, to a hot fire on the shore, it will be evaporated and lost and lose its belief that the ocean is the omniscient Father of the drop and all things.

When truth is not paid attention to, so much so that the drop believes a lie in opposite of the truth, not seeing what created him, the only thing the drop becomes influenced by is the opposite of truth, deception and lies. The drop thinks itself wise. Because it sees itself as wise, it can only see what is below it, and cannot perceive that it, by its understanding and knowledge, is actually quite small and deceived. For compared to the drops around it is very wise.

The drop may seemingly cause the ocean to roll its waves toward the shore in joy, realizing too late that it was only that little drop on the end that was burned and evaporated by a fire waiting on the shore. The ocean is the necessary and only source of love and all good things for that drop. The drop cannot be the ocean of itself, it needs the source, the ocean.

Because the drop believes so opposite of the truth, deep in 'wisdom' deep in deception, the drop is led high and mighty to then come to realize it is just a drop in a fire and was deceived. The drop is that oceans beloved child, a child who is learning for itself. Greater truths only seen when it is humbled to look above itself.

The truth of this is on a grander scale and will be extrapolated further on. In faith we can come to realize our Father was always far, far bigger than just the ocean, and there were things far bigger deceiving us.

Our Father can catch us by the wind back into the ocean of His arms, heal us, and restore us as His beloved drop in His arms of the ocean when we see truth. Then through faith He can teach us the right way, humbly, in truth. And oh how His wisdom is significantly beyond what the drop before thought was wisdom.

Simple extrapolation of 'wisdom' even can show true truth, and we will get there. There is deception. Oh be wise, what can I say more.

If God lives and is true, and He is, all that pushes away from Him is deception. I will extrapolate to truth in more pragmatic ways in future chapters.

Isaiah 47 10-11 "Thy wisdom and thy knowledge, it hath perverted thee; and thou hast said in thine heart, I am, and none else beside me. Therefore shall evil come upon thee; thou shalt not know from whence it riseth:"

I do not judge any; I have been there and I will tell you a little about it. But it is for this cause that I choose to write this. For those ensnared thinking themselves wise. Many in high places of the world hold themselves wise in this, I hope to restore all to truth. He loves us dearly.

This wisdom, as spoken of a bit in Isaiah and many places throughout the Bible, is the knowledge of the wisdom of Egypt. Remember even Pharaoh's men could do some of the miracles that Moses could do. They were perverting the very laws that are God's; priding themselves in their own wisdom. Alas it all confounds.

Isaiah 44:25 "That frustrateth the tokens of the liars, and maketh diviners mad; that turneth wise men backward, and maketh their knowledge foolish;"

1 Corinthians 1:21 For after that in the wisdom of God the world by wisdom knew not God, it pleased God by the foolishness of preaching to save them that believe.

I will not detail it nor get into it much and certainly won't describe it. True wisdom is from God; revelation is real. There are truths of deeper things pushed and taught in the very wrong way, by deception that can become great stumbling blocks to truth. There are many walking around thinking they are one who 'knows' how things are, and they need help.

The truth is, even the foolishness of God truly confounds all of this on a hilariously vast scale. Everything is His and of Him. Faith in and humility before God is true wisdom. He can then teach us true wisdom. He can wash us clean to resonate with His perfection, in faith, through the very real Atonement of Jesus Christ. He has done all for us.

Why do I write all of this? I have been through this. In the last days it is said that knowledge will increase and also that deceptions would grow strong; and that even many of the elect will be deceived. I have seen many who think themselves wise in this stuff as it is very

43

convincing. It takes truths and distorts them, pulling us away from God. So in a sense, I simply write this to say, "Restore."

Isaiah 42:18 "Hear, ye deaf; and look , ye blind, that ye may see.
19 Who is blind, but my servant? Or deaf, as my messenger that I sent? Who is blind as he that is perfect, and blind as the Lord's servant?"

Remember it is prophesied that knowledge will increase; if the knowledge is from God and centers Him and testifies of the necessity and truth of Jesus Christ it is true. However, it is easy to see and understand some laws in a VERY skewed way. God respects our freedom and His arm is outstretched to help. As we realize our weakness we can rely on His strength.

His Spirit can influence and help us if we desire it and if we are worthy of it through the merits of our Savior. On the opposite, there is an opposite force that leads always and pecks and pecks at us, not caring about our freedom. Commandments are a guardrail to protect His beloved children from a very real influence that pulls away in deception.

Many embark on learning and seek deep things, very few get to the ends and 'understand,' yet still in their 'wisdom' they are led by the wrong powers. I will extrapolate this in further chapters. Oh be wise. What can I say more?

Remember that Christ said about the last days,

Matthew 24:24-25 "For there shall arise false Christs, and false prophets, and shall shew great signs and wonders; insomuch that, if it were possible, they shall deceive the very elect. Behold, I have told you before. "

We will know them by their fruits.

Isaiah 42:22 "But this is a people robbed and spoiled; they are all of them snared in holes, and they are hid in prison houses: they are for a prey, and none delivereth; for a spoil, and none saith, Restore."

23 "Who among you will give ear to this? Who will hearken and hear for the time to come?"

I simply must give ear. I simply must do all I can for Him who has done all for me; and so I will forever.

Isaiah 43:8 "Bring forth the blind people that have eyes, and the deaf that have ears.

44

9 Let all the nations be gathered together, and let the people be assembled: who among them can declare this, and shew us the former things? Let them bring forth their witnesses, that they may be justified: or let them hear, and say, It is truth."

This is the modern day spiritual equivalent of Moses leading the children of Israel out of slavery in Egypt. The Lord is gathering Israel as promised and is guiding us out of and saving us from spiritual Egypt. It is a spiritual slavery of the worst kind. The 'wisdom' and 'knowledge' of Egypt, spiritual slavery of the deepest kind as many are in the wrong ways. It is many thinking themselves wise, not understanding what they are doing to themselves; not seeing how greatly deceived they are; simply having pride in all that they 'know.'

I judge none, I was right there, believing and perceiving incorrectly, priding myself on deep understanding. Unwitting to what was greatly behind much. Bait on hooks. Trust God and have faith in Him, His simplicity confounds all. I am consistently overwhelmed by His goodness and perfection.

A good analogy is this. It is as though understanding of metal making is given to an ant, and they boast themselves of the sword and spear and the understanding of making metal; not knowing or understanding they are an ant, in a bigger imaginable 'world' than they can ever understand, they are less than children. And on the other side of the veils that large creatures set up, they await with apache helicopters and armies to destroy the anthill, or better yet, lead the ant by deception to destroy it themselves.

Many still priding themselves in these "wisdoms" may claim they understand a certain base law well enough that it doesn't matter what comes upon them. Have you analyzed the source of all your thoughts? You have no idea what you're messing with and how small you are. We need to be on the side of our Father in Heaven and in His protection.

There is a source of light and life, and we should seek that truth and want to be there. Our Father in Heaven becomes vastly necessary. We NEED the Lord; we NEED God. The atonement truly fulfills and confounds and makes perfect the law. I'll get into it all, but our Savior is so necessary.

These are things withheld and are Biblically called a stumbling block as it would take an average person maybe even 1000 years of stumbling before they realized that the necessary perfect key to their problems is Jesus Christ and His perfect atonement and attributes; then come to see how they were deceived.

45

There is a reason that in scripture we are called children, and cannot bear meat, but must be fed on milk. At the very bit of it many pride themselves and are totally ignorant and arrogant. I have seen instances of those walking away from the gospel after receiving it in part, deceived.

I am grateful in the wisdom of the Lord in taking me the way I went that I could see it in the correct order. Faith becomes the grand key and confounds. The milk is perfect and the faith in Christ and His atonement truly confounds the 'wisdom.' The way the 'wisdom' taught in the world is a vast stumbling block. Any who think of themselves as wise and seek not the council of God also will find deception. Pride must be left behind, humility before Him must be embraced, for humility before Him is all wisdom. His wisdom is so vastly beyond all.

1 Corinthians 1:27 "But God hath chosen the foolish things of the world to confound the wise; and God hath chosen the weak things of the world to confound the things which are mighty;"

Humility is the polar opposite of pride. Many of us walk thinking we are wise in some way or another, but when it comes to things of eternity, we truly must rely on He who created ALL things, even our Father in Heaven. Walking in pride is walking in deception.

I will get into this more of why soon, but I often think someone should make a painting with someone sitting on a throne with a crown that says wisdom, and dark things speaking words that turn to perceived light, "you are so wise," "you have so much understanding," etc. and the crown has an invisible shackle to the neck and every word is a chain. And Christ in the clouds of actual white whose light breaks the bands and the lies.

He loves us dearly and will leave the 99 safe ones to seek out the 1.

Many look at Christ as simply someone who had this knowledge and 'wisdom', which I'm sure He far and significantly surpassed such, being taught by God through faith. But He and His teachings are looked at wrongly as simply one who has attained this level, of many. The rest of what is taught is not weighed, and context even is set aside. The greater things discerned by the humble, and things taught through humility and faith in God are not seen and are protected. The false philosophies of man, even 'wise' men, mingled with twisted scripture.

The pride of wisdom entraps and many are guided so wrong by what they cannot perceive. I've seen it even called, 'Christ consciousness'. Interesting that the plan of the adversary of this world is to set at naught Christ and God.

46

I say much of this to foreshadow what I will say, to give you an idea, and to tell you at the same time, wisdom is through God alone. Christ has told us we will not see the Kingdom of God unless we are humble even as a child. I will get into why this necessary soon. The first drops of humble wisdom from our Father in Heaven are so far beyond such.

As for philosophy, it is rather lighthearted and becomes quite pointless, to the full-lived point. Useful perhaps as preference for personal ease in life, or logic productivity sake leaning toward stoicism (in which the base of 'knowledge' isn't in pure truth,) and better yet described as calm optimism. For truth and perfect living choose the 'philosophy' of living as Christ lives. Faith in Him will get you furthest. He is necessary.

In the end we are to be like Him. This should be our goal. He is the grand key and grand exemplar, we must seek His attributes. Seeking perfection in living in Christ in His attributes, and upon the rock of Jesus Christ, leading to salvation. Live in truth.

It is either that, or one confounds philosophy to get to the underlying understanding or 'wisdom' and quickly confounds all philosophy and confounds many things; and even incorrectly seem to put at naught the truth of God who has created all things. And be led in deception until the day you discern by what you have been led. All is God's. Do not be deceived.

I stress here, this is all in the way people perceive. The only true understanding is the one God alone can give. For the way many learn and is pushed by deception and in deception is this in plain; it is the depth of understanding that comes from, "I think therefore I am." And the very deep ends thereof taught in all the wrong ways, leading in deception. We are children of God, and oh are we children. Humble yourself.

Because our agency allows us to tune to whatever we desire many go exploring and see no specific truth simply because the path to destruction is wide and the path to everlasting life is strait and narrow and requires humility to tune to.

Because of 'wisdom' and the necessities of gaining it in the way the world does, people are caused to put themselves at the pinnacle or center; rightly allowing themselves to be guided in deception and not understanding it clearly, taking themselves away from their true home and loving Father in Heaven. Because of the perceived freedom, they become more entrenched and essentially build their own cage of lies, as they don't perceive there is singular truth.

Again I judge none, been there, deceived; thinking myself wise. I simply wish to warn anyone now, seeing that it must come more and more upon the world, this grand deception, and to restore those ensnared

47

as I have been saved and redeemed from such; which story I will get into.

The story becomes one of amazing grace and goodness of our Father in Heaven. He is pouring out His Spirit and breaking chains from off of His beloved children. I am forever grateful.

Stay in truth, which is in Jesus Christ. Faith in Him greatly confounds such things and is wisdom in God. He has protected truth perfectly and you wont find it unless you become humble before Him.

There was an incredibly famous philosopher, Friedrich Wilhelm Nietzsche; he has a famous quote.

"You have your way. I have my way. As for the right way, the correct way, and the only way, it does not exist."

Anyone who lives in his understanding, thinking themselves wise, will applaud this simple quote and see he 'clearly understands.'

When Friedrich was 44 he suddenly collapsed and lost all mental faculties. His mother took care of him.

Granted I don't know, but I submit, and I think you may agree as you continue to read, that he, very sadly, had no idea what he was getting into or dealing with; and when he got deep enough he realized what was in the pit he was being lulled into. He probably didn't have the religious understanding to piece together what was happening to extrapolate to truth and became that state.

I want to add one thought. If one thinks they can outwit dark things that have been for eternity how deep is their deception? Something I have sort of seen in others. How deep is the deception when one is led in deception, thinking they are above it all and nothing can touch them? We are less than children.

Christ is more necessary than we can all imagine. If you seek wisdom it is given to us very, very, clearly in the scriptures and they are true. I praise God for His infinite goodness, longsuffering and saving grace.

I will go onto explain this in further depth as we continue. There is much wisdom, and as we walk in the Spirit of God, in humility before Him and relying on our Savior we are led in truth and can eventually see all things clearly. As we truly walk humbly we can be taught by Him, and in no other way can we see clearly in truth the greater things.

"But to be learned is good if they hearken unto the counsel of God." "Blessed are the meek: for they shall inherit the earth."

Again, true wisdom in perfect context in truth comes from God alone. We must be humble, we must be meek, we must learn much, be cleansed through faith on our Savior and seek His teaching by the Spirit.

His simplicity confounds the wise. All things are His, and He will give all things to His children who love Him and love to serve Him.

48

Oh be wise, what can I say more.

Isaiah 47:10 For thou hast trusted in thy wickedness: thou hast said, None seeth me. Thy wisdom and thy knowledge, it hath perverted thee; and thou hast said in thine heart, I am, and none else beside me.

11 Therefore shall evil come upon thee; thou shalt not know from whence it riseth.

The scripture goes on to explain how sorceries, enchantments and things trusted in, astrologers even wont save from the fire. Eventually the chapters go onto how the Lord will save many. God is incredibly good. Perceive His outstretched arm, call out, grab hold. He is mighty to save.

Though many feel they can understand deep things, I still add this scripture, because they don't understand though they think they can.

Jacob 4:14 "But behold, the Jews were a stiffnecked people; and they despised the words of plainness, and killed the prophets, and sought for things that they could not understand. Wherefore, because of their blindness, which blindness came by looking beyond the mark, they must needs fall; for God hath taken away his plainness from them, and delivered unto them many things which they cannot understand, because they desired it. And because they desired it God hath done it, that they may stumble."

I find it interesting this scripture mentions the Jews, who of course are a strong people with incredibly rich history and by what we have much of the Bible. They are an important people and our Savior Jesus Christ is of descent.

I find this interesting as they have an aspect of mysticism about them and even their "Kabbalah" has a set of 'esoteric teachings' that lead one up to the final height of the very same 'understanding' that is expressed in, "I am." The Jewish star is a clear esoteric symbol of sacred geometry. We have gone over this and it is the same type of 'wisdom,' a bit of truth but without the things that are seriously necessary, understood incorrectly and not fully. Things come to 'naught' without our Savior.

Similarly the 'wisdom' is all over the world and is ancient 'understanding' in many societies; commonly referred to as from Egypt and the center of eastern 'enlightenment.' It is held as the height of all such 'wisdom' by many and the base of much culture around the world. Many 'secret societies' around the world hold such and the point here is that many here think that it is the grandest wisdom. It shatters and the law of Jesus Christ, in and through Him, is true wisdom. That comes

49

through faith on Him. The 'foolish' things of God our Father in Heaven vastly, VASTLY, outweigh the mighty and wise of man.

Unless wisdom is rooted on and in the Savior Jesus Christ one does not see entirely clearly. The law of Jesus Christ supersedes all. He is entirely and utterly necessary. Truly the weak and foolish things by the world's standards confound the 'mighty' and 'wise' of the world.

Truly our Savior fulfilled so much when He came, He has truly saved us. Another of the many things He did is expressed in scripture and it applies here.

John 9:39 "And Jesus said, For judgment I am come into this world, that they which see not might see; and that they which see might be made blind."

Matthew 11:25 "At that time Jesus answered and said, I thank thee, O Father, Lord of heaven and earth, because thou hast hid these things from the wise and prudent, and hast revealed them unto babes."

He has truly hidden the greater things and shown them to the humble. He has allowed 'deep wisdom' to ensnare and become a 'stumbling block' to the proud and wise in their own eyes who have looked beyond the mark, until they humble themselves and see with their eyes and hear with their ears. We must become humble before Him. We must not seek wisdom from the arm of flesh or trust our own but seek it from Him. Just as Christ teaches in Matthew 16. I certainly can judge none and have but His grace and goodness to be thankful for. We will later get into it.

Upon further understanding of the 'law' one can discern the brokenness thereof. Namely our inadequacy before God and our impossibility at resonating truly with His perfection as we are imperfect; as well as coming to discern the power that is and quietly controls without the protection and kingdom of God.

He is above all; all is His. The greater things must be given by Him. Humility, humility, humility.

Matthew 13:14 "And in them is fulfilled the prophecy of Esaias, which saith, By hearing ye shall hear, and shall not understand; and seeing ye shall see, and shall not perceive.

15 For this people's heart is waxed gross, and their ears are dull of hearing, and their eyes they have closed; lest at any time they should see with their eyes, and hear with their ears, and should understand with their heart, and should be converted, and I should heal them."

Hear now and see now! Let Him heal us all; we utterly need Him. How thankful I am for my perfect loving Savior.

We must choose to be humble now, that later and for our own good we are not compelled to be humble. I certainly was a bit of both. Realizing our own weakness is important.

"That no flesh should glory in his presence."

Isaiah 52:15 "So shall he sprinkle many nations; the kings shall shut their mouths at him: for that which had not been told them shall they see; and that which they had not heard shall they consider."

We are truly in the last days, deception in rampant. And many are deceived, sadly, when some particles of truth are highly distorted.

I will get much more into it, but the gospel of Jesus Christ is amazingly true and necessary. And just as promised Biblically the fullness of the everlasting gospel is again on the earth. True wisdom is humble faith in truth, exercising our vast agency as children of God in truth. Being aligned in truth. Light can surely prove light. We must seek it humbly.

The Lord has prepared the perfect way for the meek and the humble. The meek will inherit. We are children.

The Savior says in Matthew 16 that He will build His Church on the rock of revelation. Not trusting in arm or flesh but the revelation of God. Just as He told Peter, he was blessed because he knew He was the Son of God. Flesh and blood didn't reveal it to him, but our Father in Heaven did.

Seek true wisdom through humility and meekness before God our Father, in which we resonate in truth. His Spirit can and does teach incredibly. His children and His Church truly are led by revelation.

Never forget who is in control, God Almighty, our Father. All is His vast symphony; oh how he loves us!

Those who may be reading this in the 'stumbling block' of specific understanding, thinking themselves wise, I will come to extrapolate and explain this much further. As I get further into my story and path you will begin to see even more clearly. The humble and meek receive and inherit.

Christ IS necessary, and HE LIVES.

1 Corinthians 3:18 "Let no man deceive himself. If any man among you seemeth to be wise in this world, let him become a fool, that he may be wise.

19 For the wisdom of this world is foolishness with God. For it is written, He taketh the wise in their own craftiness."

51

Isaiah 29:14 "Therefore, behold, I will proceed to do a marvelous work among this people, even a marvelous work, and a wonder: for the wisdom of their wise men shall perish and the understanding of their prudent men shall be hid.

16 Surely your turning of things upside down shall be esteemed as the potter's clay: for shall the work say of him that made it, He made me not? Or shall the thing framed say of him that framed it, He had no understanding?

18 And in that day shall the deaf hear the words of the book, and the eyes of the blind shall see out of obscurity, and out of darkness.

19 The meek also shall increase their joy in the Lord, and the poor among men shall rejoice in the Holy One of Israel.

23 But when he seeth his children, the work of mine hands, in the midst of him, they shall sanctify my name, and sanctify the Holy One of Jacob, and shall fear the God of Israel.

24 They also that erred in spirit shall come to understanding, and they that murmured shall learn doctrine."

"Oh be wise, what can I say more?"
He lives. Restore.

Chapter 7

CROOKED PATHS

The year went by and I had gotten far deeper, incredibly deep, thinking myself very wise and thinking myself even deeper and wiser than even those who understood this. I did my best to be a good person and to love everyone and be kind, and in a sense some of this felt to promote love, yet I was in deep deception thinking myself wise. Partially having a depth of understanding, yet all the while that understanding was steered wrong and leading away from truth into deeper deception.

I saw many in the paths of consciousness, learning tiny bit by tiny bit; and in my perception, probably not going to ever get 'it.' Few, generally, I perceived, that understood it.

Some in the world looked at as the most bizarre people, yet the world having no idea the 'understanding' they were on. Many high up in areas of the world carried such and I would come to learn how deep many went and were guided deep in deception, things became sad. Stay on God's side.

I began to see people who delved or dabbled in things perceived in religion as 'dark' were simply very misunderstood most times by people who simply didn't fully 'understand.' I also thought fear of things was funny, anything like dark stuff just seemed funny and no big deal, because anyone who "knew" would be able to discern it as no big deal. "Nothing to fear but fear itself." In essence, manifesting what we felt appropriate, leaving fear behind, being a part and all of all things; perceiving 'wisdom' of ourselves regardless of the fullest extension of truth that are seldom fully perceived.

Many saw it as a slow conscious awakening that eventually everyone would get to. And until that point the few would know it. This is nonsense from a truth perspective, but able to be perceived through that perception and unblamable to anyone thinking themselves wise in it; for how deep of a stumbling block it is. It is truly a deep deception thinking there is no singular truth, and neither can be singular truth. Oh how it is one of the many buildings of a reality of lies.

The two perceptions; of everything matters and has infinite purpose, or that nothing matters and has no purpose, but perhaps inevitability of consciousness growth, the latter seemed to be the only "truth". They symphony of God was hid from my eyes for I was blind to it, not seeking or even perceiving the possibility. How 'wisdom' can surely ensnare.

The year went on, eventually the season came back around again. The first one I needed to do well at. I had spent all the money I had saved on a denim specific to BMX company that had cost a bunch. A deal had fallen through with a store that left me unpaid on a lot of ventures to make their situation work. I needed to do well, and I knew I could.

It was Nitro World Games at Rice Eccles. I had qualified into the finals and had worked on a run and pulled it before the final that could win; I knew I could do it. We had 2 runs. I really needed to do well.

The first run I somehow messed up the hardest trick in the middle set; it was 3 jumps. The second run I did it perfect, and came to the last trick on the last set. I did the trick. The bike came right back to my feet and I was landing perfect.

As I began rolling away I thought to myself, "Thank goodness, I really needed that." The thought hadn't completely finished before I realized that for no reason my feet had slid from the pedals and I was falling over. I had pulled it, began rolling away, and then fell. I finished 8/8.

I was absolutely broken. I needed it more than I've ever needed a win or at least a podium. I had been working hard for it. I got really mad, left my bike, and went out in the parking lot where my car was and basically broke down. I was devastated. I absolutely had to do well. What happened?

At this point, I was so deep in this "wisdom" that I had gone from praying occasionally at least, to no longer being able to understand that God is. This is the worst part of all of this. It is a wisdom that when pushed in the worldly way, darkness behind a veil we cannot perceive slowly pushes us to think of ourself high and mighty. The 'understandings' within the 'wisdom' can truly skew the views of what is, simply because we can perceive we are a part of something yet bigger. It seems to all makes sense in the understanding thereof. What rough endless deception keeping from the strait and narrow path of singular truth.

I vaguely remember a day I was younger and felt that I had learned the church was false; I was so devastated I felt I had been lied to. I was wrong. My heart was hardened with deception and as the promises of God are, even what we have received will be taken from us; the opposite of keeping a hope where eventually the greater things are manifest and we can know all things.

Regardless, you can imagine the pain of the situation that day. It is similar sadness that came when 'understanding' 'wisdom;' so partially in such a skewed manner of deception. I was suddenly feeling alone, that God isn't how you thought in a sense, yet a somewhat 'freeing' understanding. Oh how I want to pluck anyone stuck in these deceptions out of them. Oh how I'm grateful that God Almighty our Father in Heaven lives and reigns forever. I am so thankful for our Savior.

As I sat in the car outside of the arena, absolutely devastated, I looked and half laughed at the bumper sticker on the car in front of me. It was an Angels and Airwaves band logo that said 'Love'. It was the shirt logo I wore to win my first X Games. I loved their music and loved anything that promoted love. The main guy of the band I believe is a Free Mason and puts a lot of esoteric symbolism in things; I laughed inside. But the overall message was, 'if we are so wise sharing a base understanding, what is wrong? Why is all this going wrong?' The pant company, this contest, yet I'm confident.

The next month was X Games again. ESPN flew out and filmed a couple spots for TV. The year before had been cancelled and this year I had the opportunity to be the first to win 3 in a row.

Driving up one mountain I made a remark how the 'Mormon Church' owned so much here. This part of things is hard for me to talk about, as I am truly a new man and saved by grace, changed and healed, but for the glory of God and to show His great love and longsuffering I will tell many of the things I thought.

I had a friend who told me a hard story of her past about the Church; she had had a rough experience. My brother as well had had an experience where someone was unkind in a way that made an impression. Hearing and thinking of these earlier life experiences added to the pre conceived notion that I understood truth and that there shouldn't be things that hurt people.

I did not like that people were to feel guilt and sadness either. In the understanding I had then, I looked at it as simply one person's construct to get to a 'heaven' they personally constructed by belief. Be clear to know I was wrong and this is past.

I felt, incorrectly, that in one sense they were helping people by giving them a good direction and helping them with a few diluted points of truth, but profiting off of it, and that people should simply come to know the "truth," that would "set them free;" so many things got twisted from their true meaning, even scripture. Freedom is in Christ alone, not wisdom, but in what He has done for us. I'll get to that. It is sad how perception can be so skewed; the Church is utterly true.

It got to a sad point that I thought that there must be some in the top of the Church that "know" the "truth." Yet having no idea the deep level they are on having the keys of the Priesthood of God Almighty. And how significantly vast such is and how small even the deepest 'wisdom' of man.

I thought they must have been taking advantage or just leading along to help. At the time I couldn't see the truth of God and Christ and that He Himself was and is truly leading His Church.

This is hard for me now, as I know the Church is true, and I will get into it. But try to understand my feeling. I had come to learn how much the world took advantage, in essentially every single way; and the people at the top generally had the knowledge of such understandings, at least many people in high places seemed to. It was easy for me to see it totally incorrectly; I was clearly led wrong. Deception fights hard against pure truth. I'm so grateful for my Savior.

The hard thing about this deception is many, as I did, just want to help everyone, and just want them to have a good abundant life of happiness. Either that or they even more deceptively, not getting past one part of the 'maze', see themselves as the only thing and become twisted to see things darker. "Casting out" themselves, as they become perpetually alone in increased deception. Restore.

I wanted everyone to be happy. I saw my mother, who is a pure Saint of whom I'm so incredibly lucky to have as my Mother and whom the Lord surely placed in infinite wisdom, knowing I would need many, many prayers.

To that same incredible mother, I told her over and over she was being deceived and she needed to apply understanding to other areas. I felt bad for her; I love her. I felt bad for young kids that were brought up to learn things that I felt were not truth but simply one persons perspective of it.

It didn't seem to me that I was bashing everyone, but I have since heard a few accounts from people how I told them they were wrong or something along the lines; a friend saying I kinda gave him crap for going on a mission, or another saying I told them they were wrong, I do remember a few accounts and I pray for all of those people who I ever may have spoke wrong to every night. It breaks my heart, and I say it solely to glorify my Father in Heaven and show His truly incredible love and long suffering, His grace and infinite goodness towards me and all of His beloved children.

Oh, how new and perfect He can make us.

How grateful I am for my Savior. He has made me far more than the sum of my past mistakes and wrong choices, truly new in Him. I am forever truly grateful and will serve Him forever.

I look back and all was truly wisdom in Him in bringing me the way He did. He truly broke the bars of brass and cut in sunder the bars of iron; I am forever grateful.

Isaiah 42:16 "And I will bring the blind by a way that they knew not; I will lead them in paths that they have not known: I will make darkness light before them, and crooked things straight. These things will I do unto them, and not forsake them."

Readers Note: Some of this vague description of 'wisdom' is specifically for one reason, in hopes that those ensnared in pride in these 'wisdoms' will easily and simply recognize it and actually listen. There will be much depth for them as we go along. I believe it profitable in measure still for all to hear and much is written for all.

Truly what the gospel confounds 'wisdom' and teaches perfectly in truth. All is God's. Do not forget all confounds before the truth of God and Christ and the Holy Spirit bears witness that Jesus Christ is the truth.

I have gone full circle, so you don't have to. And if the growing deception comes your way, you will not move from the rock that is our Savior Jesus Christ.

God is sovereign over all things. Humble yourself and exercise your agency in faith to truth, to resonate in truth, which can only be properly exercised if you place yourself in truth. This means recognizing what you must be before God Almighty, be humble, be meek, remember Christ really is the perfect key, in so many ways, seek to become as He is; then we can come to see our perfect Father and be taught by Him what is true wisdom. We will forever be profoundly amazed and praise Him forever.

I went to X Games, going last again as I was the defending winner. I was confident and needed to do well; if I was prepared for anything it was certainly this.

My first run, I did the trick over the gap perfectly, coming at the quarter pipe it was time to do the double flair again, this time even higher.

I went for it. Everything went well and was coming in slightly deep which caused me to be over rotated slightly. I hit hard. I would find out after the event that I cracked a bone in my arm on this hit. I was bruised up from this hit and later would discover my black and blue hip and side.

I got up, one of the hardest things to do after big hits, but one of the best lessons BMX can teach you. I made my way to the elevator to make it happen on my next runs. By the time the last run came around I had gotten close to the trick and wrecked again. I was incredibly beat up. At this point it was solely adrenaline and the strong will to finish that kept me going.

As I was making my way again to the top for what would be the last run I found myself in familiar territory. I was in a huge stadium full of people, I was the last guy to go, and I had the ability to win in epic fashion.

I climbed my bruised and beat up self to the top of the roll-in and had a strong thought that I've had before, "Pray." This time however was far different. I immediately followed up the thought with a half depressed thought of "You're so dumb dude."

The 'wisdom' that I had gained and seen many high up people of the world carrying seemingly took out the need and understanding of God, as I had previously known it. I felt I was just deceiving myself if I prayed. I think now in obviousness knowing what spirit it is that teaches a man not to pray.

I focused up, rolled in, did the trick over the gap jump, and went for it again on the quarter pipe.

This one was different. I was coming in perfectly. My tires touched down right in the perfect spot. The feeling of elation was beginning as my tires touched down, after all those runs I had finally got it right it seemed.

As I landed and began to roll down the landing in confidence, I noticed my back wheel unexpectedly begin to wash out. My elation quickly jumped to despair and then pain as the cheering of the crowd again turned to the dreaded "Ohhhhh," that one hears when they slam. I hit hard again on that same side.

I pulled myself off, waved to the crowd, held up my arm and went with the medics strait to the doctors and X Ray room. I did however win the biggest "swell-bow" they had ever seen. I would have been surprised if anyone had ever had a larger one. I went back to the hotel and dealt with the most swelling I have ever had, stressing how I was going to handle the future with the year's opportunities now over.

Chapter 8

CONFOUNDING EXPERIENCE, REALIZATION OF TRUTH

This chapter will talk about my experience, my first experience that confounded this great 'wisdom' and brought me back to seeing truth. Understand much of this is going to be incredibly vague as getting into the depth of details of it will do no good.

I came home and was really at a loss of what to do. I had been prepared and I had thought I was more mentally prepared than I have ever been. After all I had felt I understood how all things worked for quite a while now. But why was nothing panning out? Everything seemed to be crashing, obviously including myself. I didn't know what to do.

I decided to really dedicate myself to meditation and sort this whole thing out. I spent some serious time in some incredibly deep thought, weighing the understanding that I had come to understand deeply and figure out what was going on; or at least to figure out more.

I relaxed at home and meditated. Again, understand I am choosing to be quite vague about all of this.

I eventually came to what I would consider the grandest understanding. Something I felt that even the few who understood this 'wisdom' would never be able to get to or understand on their own. It was significantly deeper, and it was already so deep.

It was getting to the very center of everything. Although the base 'wisdom' could be claimed to be such, understandings could be extrapolated to find more. What I had come to find what felt like the greatest end of all one could ever possibly wish to accomplish. It was deeper than deep and I felt very few could ever get to it, even with the 'knowledge' well understood.

I remember telling my friend even, 'everything is going to be different from today; everything is going to be amazing.' I wanted to help everyone in this world. I had always felt deeply, and seeing many in many situations really troubled me. I was nowhere near perfect but I felt things were about to change and all would be well. In a sense they would be for He was, thankfully, making my crooked paths strait.

I relaxed the rest of the day. Pleased with ends of what I had 'found'. There was incredibly much found before, incredible amounts, wholly not worth for the sake of this book to get into; and probably ever. God is good all is His. The greater things that make these vast 'wisdoms' of man come to nothing are given as we humbly have faith in Him and seek His guidance.

Keeping it vague; the next day I began meditating again. I got right into the depth of where I had been. Deep levels of understanding, extrapolated to specific means of understanding; such deep things I thought; a humble pride was present. Perhaps the worst kind of pride is when you genuinely just think you know best or better than absolutely anyone. After all, this approach, ditching ideas that Universities and scholars really could get anywhere near true truth, was in a sense a right move, though Christ is the source of true truth. Without going the singular direction I did I would never had found all that I had come to understand in the right way.

I kept meditating and a few things happened quickly.

I discerned something that I had previously discerned yet really had no depth of definitive answer for, just conjecture. This was that some of my thoughts that lightly jumped into my mind were not original thoughts. They were not of me; I would NEVER have thought such things. Whether pure randomness, or of a nudge in certain direction, they weren't of me, and I discerned it again among a few other things.

Among other things I had a clearer understanding of what I had just found, or gotten myself into. Thinking myself wise. I will not get into this.

What also happened was a discernment of a presence, spirit or other. This influence grew. I began to rout out exactly where these non-original thoughts came from.

Seeming suddenly all things exploded.

A dark presence was around. The sense of routing out the origin of these non-original thoughts turned to somewhat of the thought of, "Oh you are so smart and so wise, I guess you found me." A darkness overtook everything in power I never imagined.

I tried to calm myself, knowing within myself apparently all things of 'wisdom', not allowing fear to dictate my reality. I would try to calm myself and focus elsewhere, which one can understand is simple in the 'wisdom' I was in. At first things felt very simple, just a state of fear that I felt I would quickly would overcome in wisdom.

As I would turn my thoughts to other things, leaving behind whatever was being pushed at me, and suddenly whatever I turned my thoughts to or distracted myself with was used to further put me in fear. It was as though this thing was outside of time, and knew before hand right where my attempt in joyful focus would bring me, and there already had placed something to bring me back. The "wisdom" was entirely pointless.

Things got wilder and wilder and scarier and scarier. I would actively distract myself and focus away from things, entirely discounting whatever was happening and leave it behind and not believe it but believe good things, and wherever I would look would be changed to the exact response that would again ensnare me. It was so significantly beyond me. I was helpless though I wouldn't and I couldn't give up. In not giving up, being still and giving up wasn't either a remedy.

This influence got larger and larger, the harder I seemed to focus away I would get ensnared more. Even in attempting relaxing and focusing away entirely, it didn't change the constant barrage. It got darker and darker and bigger and bigger. Things would change instantly. The movie on the TV would jump to scenes that had never been seen by me that the character would say something or be spoken through in this darkness. Instagram wherever I looked would change and captions would be spoken through; all these people entirely clueless to what must have been effecting them then or at least knew what was going to be and yet beyond that as well, changing things entirely. A power quietly and subtly always effecting those not within the protection of light.

I however knew many things, the irrelevancy of time, and I had seen things in reality similarly before based on focus. I began to work overtime, after trying everything.

After thoroughly proving that no matter what course of action, even entire non-action, whatever this was, was real. Overwhelming, horrible. So I needed to set up walls and barriers in my mind.

I began setting up mental barriers and my mind suddenly went from thinking I had been wise, to thinking, "Ok well if you ever needed to be smart it's now."

I set up all the mental barriers I could think up, deep ones. The importance of anyone's belief in any god or god's became apparent in 'wisdom.' I quickly realized that although there was everything, nothing could stand unless it was actually truth. The power there was large. Everything I set up; would fall. I began to go into absolute overdrive as this presence got larger and larger.

This thing was showing me it's vast power, and essentially pushing me to submit to it. I think of Moses when he experienced the adversary, a real power pushing me to recognize that it was powerful, and to submit to it. Of course I would not, but I see how many would be utterly deceived.

I could see then how even as I was led in this 'wisdom' that it was behind curtain after curtain, leading me along in pride. I was pushed to see that I finally had seen it all, that this was the end of all things. This pushed to see more and more deception. It was infinite seeming beings that were significantly, so significantly, to say the very least, beyond

61

even the wisest person of the world. And of all that darkness there was even still a singular 'power' showing itself.

Much of the things I tried were in deception. I saw ways to make one think they had 'won' and I could see how some could go quietly back to letting this control quietly. I didn't know and couldn't discern then that the whole thing and 'wisdom' as I knew it was being used in deception, because it was never exercised in truth through faith in Christ.

In trying to figure such out with the 'wisdom,' I was pushed a deception that there are simply many gods that one should seek to serve and be empowered by. I began to see much in popular culture that seemed to allude to such. Many 'ways out' of the situation using aspects of 'wisdom' were recognized as deceptions; I now clearly know are simply powers of deception. Deceptions fell and the dark power that seemed then to control it all kept overpowering.

This was taking over everything and seemingly making it apparent that it alone had power to give and do anything. I did my best to focus on myself entirely and ignore. I really feel for people who may get to this point not fully understanding 'wisdom,' for they probably stare right into deception not knowing what to do. Not that I was much better off but it bought time for me to realize.

The more I tried the more humble I became. To the dust, recognizing I could do nothing of myself. I kept trying. Darkness was creeping in so exceedingly and I began to understand why certain analogies are used for such darkness. For those who uncover this, truly are tormented. It became rough.

Even in all of this, I didn't yet think, "oh this is the adversary like the Bible teaches," I was so far removed from religious thinking. I had put it so far in the past. I was explaining this by many other ways. Other conscious beings significantly beyond was enough to explain it then. I couldn't then discern exactly how long I had been deeply effected and guided in wrong paths, thinking myself wise. It is no different then darkness whispering in your ear all the time, and the world walks in ignorance on the outside of the commandments of God, on the outside of protection. I can judge none.

The things I tried were in the wisdom I learned, in the way I learned it (which I think I had much more understanding having essentially coming to it on my own, I feel for people of secret societies or otherwise who are told all of this and have none of the learned tools to help them out in any way, if it does much anyway. The greatest tool would become my previous knowledge of God and Christ.)

Darkness began to get ridiculous; everything was taken over. If I tried anything it was instantly twisted to something that would bring fear. This thing was exploiting all the things I had come to learn, in all the wrong ways, caring nothing of me, to say the very least. I was pushed to accept this thing, or be destroyed essentially. I did my best to focus on my own self and ignore entirely at this point.

At one point in my mind, after things got crazy, I said to myself something like, "It's all good, everything is good." And at that moment a friend of mine would walk into the house, mid conversation with someone else saying, "Nope, your (effed) your (effed)." Nothing around, no one, had any idea of what was happening, of what was actively within them; whether within them or whether aware of what would be said it didn't really matter.

There is the Spirit of God of all good working, and the opposite that is deceiving and guiding away through hate and animosity and anything not of God, acting on many. Not respecting freedom as God, but the opposite, pecking always.

The ability to quietly guide them obliviously wherever and however is startling. It makes sense how sins can become so normalized.

This all happened in a way that I couldn't explain to anyone. If I said something so someone else, it wouldn't be them.

Those who hold themselves wise in this wisdom prior to this confounding may say, "Oh you were fearful and manifested this in specific thoughts already. Etc. etc." I will immediately say how wrong they are. I did everything possible to pass this by. And even if it exists in any capacity, it does. The power was sad to come to know. And there have been many 'wise' people who have experienced this, some changed, some further deceived, and some come to see the truth and necessity of our Savior.

Darkness was taking over everything. In a horrific way, a being that cared about nothing at all, entirely self focused and if any seeming freedom was offered, it was, "Look at all that I could do for you." I did my best to keep my focus on anything but that thing. I focused on me independently the best I could.

I must add, anyone who has ever been here and thinks they have beaten it. How seriously enslaved that thought process is. The term "outwit the devil" has been used, even as book titles in a different way. However even the word use is ridiculous. It makes one believe that they have any control whatsoever; as they walk in their pride they are quietly motivated behind veils, something that is again quiet behind you.

It is no different that a billionaire not recognizing at any moment, a decision by one person could change currency value, and even more, that you are led by societal norms to become a certain predictable way, you can want only what you know about, your whole life is predictable, and you are guided to predetermined choices. This is perhaps a bad example but you get the idea in the main sense.

Many also will seek wisdom and take any spiritual influence in their 'progress' (deception) as they have never experienced anything like it before. They will have "cool" new experiences, so they blindly trust whatever leads them; after all many are led to new wisdoms all the time. Deception. Restore.

I was doing everything I could to stay afloat, to overcome this. To bypass this; to live. Quickly the fear turned real, I simply couldn't ignore it no matter what I did it forced itself. It was becoming horrible, I kept trying everything, some incredibly deep things.

I really put in some effort. I came to things that must be true and based off those irrefutable things, built something that absolutely must be. All in the hopes to help me figure this out.

I set up a grand necessity in my mind. Things of great intention that I would exercise great belief in and build up in a perfect order. Things that utterly must be based on what is. Then the next, then the next. And I would stand wholly in that.

Eventually I began to see things much clearer. I began to set up some things that I could see really working. And each time, no matter how perfect it would shatter. Even with attempted belief higher powers, it would all shatter and I would be in an even darker situation, being laughed at and ensnared more. This darkness is something that I hope no one will ever know. Praise be to God for healing.

Finally, in utter despair, wide eyed, humbled to the dirt realizing the horrible situation I was in and my utter inadequacy, in absolute desperation, I understood something.

No matter what I do, my attempts in things that must be are still not based off what is actually real. The power is not there, though I believe it there, it must be real. I am led where this thing wants anyway, and even if I believe there is something above it, unless there is real power in all of this perfect setup it falls. This thing has real power. Maybe this really is the end all, everything just is horrible in the end, and if its not, it's because I recognize this thing; something I would never do.

Those who continue to think themselves wise in this 'wisdom' will eventually become miserable forever without Jesus Christ and God. He has done all for us. How blessed we are. He is the only way. He is the way, the truth and the life.

Was my best bet only to live and not be affected by it and to be rid of perceiving its influence only? I realized unless there is real power all is horrible. And it must simply be significantly beyond me. I was humbled to the dirt. What more could I do. I couldn't do anything.

And obviously. . . . wait, I saw it; the thought came to me and I'm forever grateful for a Father watching me learn my lesson and never forsaking me, helping me, and always with an arm outstretched.

64

"You are kidding me." I thought. My wide eyes became wider. A bunch of things came to me quickly.

Every single thing and more that I just set up in necessity is exactly like The Church of Jesus Christ of Latter-day Saints. The next thought, "And this is exactly like the experience Joseph Smith explained he had before seeing God and Christ." An actual being from an unseen realm of powerful darkness overtook him and was then dispelled as he called out to God by the light of our Father in Heaven. (Any Christian or other who scoff at the pure truth in The Church of Jesus Christ of Latter-day Saints, rest assured we will get into it. I direct you to the History discourse chapter near the end of the book. All will be clear for those who seek.)

I had put things of religion, after all I had learned on such levels, in such a way that I couldn't even have them come to mind before that point, and this thing was leading me away from such things seemingly.

I could finally see what should have been so easily discerned; it took humility to even see. I had to fully recognize I could absolutely do nothing of myself. I could then see. For this to have being there must be an exact opposite in every bit for it to be, of good and light, to have created such darkness and bring such into being. There must be an infinite and perfect pinnacle of light and good that has created all things. God is. We simply are in a fallen realm currently. How necessary our Savior is.

At this point I was in utter despair, I was essentially drowning in this experience, in such indescribable fear and despair. The presence of this horrible darkness was beyond an unbearable point.

I saw what must be. It was either totally all true or all was lost. I saw it clearly and all around, it has to and must exist, or this thing cannot. I was in almost disbelief that all of this 'religious stuff' (truth) was so necessary and actual pure truth. I called out to God for the first time in a long time. Either He really lives and cares or all was lost. The moment I realized it all in humility I called out.

"Father in Heaven, help me, please! In the name of Jesus Christ, Amen."

In that moment, everything, all the darkness, was gone entirely. The overly loud influence, gone. In a moment everything that had been warring with me was gone. All that had beset me and exercised such incredible power to seeming destruction was gone. Peace.

Psalms 107:11 "Because they rebelled against the words of God, and contemned the counsel of the most High:

12 Therefore he brought down their heart with labour; they fell down, and there was none to help.

13 Then they cried unto the Lord in their trouble, and he saved them out of their distresses.

14 He brought them out of darkness and the shadow of death, and brake their bands in sunder.

15 Oh that men would praise the Lord for his goodness, and for his wonderful works to the children of men!

16 For he hath broken the gates of brass, and cut the bars of iron in sunder.

How incredibly thankful I am. How great is our Father in Heaven, God Almighty.

I realized in an instant how real all this was. He lives. How ignorant I had been and how led astray I was.

I remember saying, "I'm so sorry, but can you really blame me?" Knowing He knew clearly my path and my thoughts the whole way and how hard the road and how hard the world fought against truth; I had simply always sought truth. I had a serious recognition of how ever present and how infinitely big He is.

In my head the words, "Now you know." are spoken calmly and simply.

I cry writing this, as no one can know the true, very serious and utterly vast need I had of my true Savior; and He was there. He saved me, and much more.

My Father in Heaven truly had always been RIGHT THERE. The veil had always been SO THIN. He was really always right there with His hand always outstretched, just begging and waiting for me to come back to Him. What incredible perfect loving kindness.

He totally honors freedom and is there when we are humbled and need him. He guided me and He is so beyond even that power, He is total authority. Everything is His.

John 1:5 "And the light shineth in darkness; and the darkness comprehended it not."

I had been blind to it all entirely. In saying, "I'm so sorry, but can you really blame me?" It was the wrong question to ask.

I didn't yet know, that my Father is a saving Father, a teaching Father, a healing Father, a loving Father, not a blaming Father. He sent His Son to die for me so and that I would be blameless. He heals and makes perfect forever so that we can be with Him in loving glory forever. I had been stolen away, and He wouldn't let me be lost. From the moment I left in paths of 'wisdom' He plotted a course to save me, even before that; that I would learn perfectly.

Even still my pragmatic mind had to search everything. Was this another deception? Was God really entirely good?

I knew what must be, and began to see it all clearly. 'Now I knew.' And I understood the necessity and picture of it all. Though I didn't understand yet everything perfectly I could now see so much more.

All was God's. All was of Him. And we utterly need our Savior Jesus Christ. His atonement was purely vital. The law is broken for those who have sinned. And we all have. How perfect the plan of our Father in Heaven.

All these things and every detail would be incredibly proved as true as my search continued. One side was for me, the other clearly against. Light can truly prove light. The 'wisdom' itself was extrapolated that certain things had to be. It wasn't darkness tricking me. I am grateful I fully understood even the deep 'wisdom' that gets confounded, for those without that find such as I, I fear, may not last long at all. Alas it all comes to humble reliance on our powerful and perfect Father in Heaven.

I was overwhelmingly shown truth. And I was significantly so very grateful for the grace of God my Father. I had been saved in my need. He was always there.

I was finally back on the shore. My mighty Father who swam out to save me, metaphorically, hugging me with tears in His eyes and a big smile on His face, His son was saved. And me in His arms on the sand, trying to further understand everything, entirely and incredibly grateful.

He had brought me to understand entirely logically, through the meat, through the things hard to bear, the hard full circle logical way; I couldn't be confounded anymore. He knew how my mind worked, that I needed to understand. He brought me in His perfect wisdom that I would see clearly. He answered the prayers of so many that love me, because He loves me more than I can imagine.

I have since found this scripture, one of very many that I marvel at;

Doctrine and Covenants 35:25 "And Israel shall be save in mine own due time; and by the keys which I have given shall they be led, and no more be confounded at all."

This day, the day I was brought back to truth from my full circle journey through 'wisdom' was the 24th of July. I was in Utah, and it is a

67

holiday, Pioneer Day. The day the Saints of God finally made it to Zion. He made it clear that it was His plan. I am forever grateful.

The religion I left, and told my own mother she should probably leave is right. I saw it. God lives. All is His. Jesus Christ is necessary. (We will get more into it pragmatically.) The wisdom of the wise was entirely confounded. I was back in truth. Something I before entirely discounted.

I could see all the other religions of the world and how far they had come in truth and where they had stopped along the way and where non Christian religions were ran off in deception. I could see clearly. I was restored to truth, and it was absolutely amazing that it happened to be where I began. I was surprised at first; I had to eat some humble pie, but knew and was grateful for the truth. I knew it, and I knew God knew I knew it. And He was just beginning to guide me to deeper understanding.

Some will say, I'm more prone to this because of how I grew up; they lack understanding of fact. I had to eat serious humble pie to accept this, but I was pragmatic and did my best to walk in what I knew to be the right path. I was proved it. It is true.

That night I couldn't sleep at all. I was terrified. In riding I had never been scared, even of death I was never scared, this was beyond that fear. PTSD is something I can understand by that experience alone.

I didn't sleep at all; I was terrified. I slept for the next months with my old scriptures that I dug out of storage right by me. "What they don't know cant hurt em," how true in this sense. The adversary that I thought was a perfect excuse I came to find is real. And the power of my Father exceeds that, beyond significantly.

I lay on the couch with the scriptures next to me. One thing is for sure after that. I needed healing; I needed to be fixed. That would come over time and with great teaching, and it started the next day being led in the scriptures.

Regardless, I had this overwhelming thought. After that experience, if I had realized that I was the poorest kid in a third world country with no food, I would have been the happiest person in the world in comparison to what I have been saved from. I was and forever am so very thankful for the amazing saving grace, mercy and love our Father in Heaven has for us.

I was so thankful and grateful that God not only exists but also He cared and cares a great deal for me. He had not only never left my side, but had stayed with me and planned all along how to save me. He sent His only begotten Son, our perfect and entirely innocent Savior, for us. He loves us all dearly. I am forever grateful.

Isaiah 42:16 "And I will bring the blind by a way that they knew not; I will lead them in paths that they have not known: I will make darkness light before them, and crooked things straight. These things will I do unto them, and not forsake them.

17 They shall be turned back, they shall be greatly ashamed, ... "

1 Corinthians 3: 18 "Let no man deceive himself. If any man among you seemeth to be wise in this world, let him become a fool, that he may be wise.

19 For the wisdom of this world is foolishness with God. For it is written, He taketh the wise in their own craftiness.

20 And again, The Lord knoweth the thoughts of the wise, that they are vain."

1 Corinthians 1: 18 "For the preaching of the cross is to them that perish foolishness; but unto us which are saved it is the power of God.

19 For it is written, I will destroy the wisdom of the wise, and will bring to nothing the understanding of the prudent.

20 Where is the wise? where is the scribe? where is the disputer of this world? hath not God made foolish the wisdom of this world?

21 For after that in the wisdom of God the world by wisdom knew not God, it pleased God by the foolishness of preaching to save them that believe."

Readers Note: Those who are in the stumbling block of specific 'wisdom,' I will explain later ways to extrapolate to necessary truth that are understandable from where you are. Jesus Christ is the way, the truth and the life. Faith in Him is necessary.

See the necessity of God and Christ. Those who walk in pride or 'wisdom' of the world may mess with this 'wisdom' in part. Many mess with portions in part not getting to the 'end of understanding' and few do see the whole bit. Regardless the law of Jesus Christ supersedes all.

Portions of such 'wisdom' up to the full depth 'final' bit of the twisted 'wisdom,' that guides away from truth, can come in many names. Many have partial or fuller understanding of such names and see such as 'wisdom.' I relate a few so all can see a bit clearer. All are based off the same 'wisdom' often twisted in the wrong ways away from truth in our living Savior. 'New age,' the 'matrix,' reality being a 'dream,' or a 'simulation,' 'I am,' or our growing our 'consciousness,' opening 'third eye' and things with pineal gland, 'waking up,' all is man and mind,

69

'wisdom of Egypt,' nothingness, enlightenment, energy playing with itself having no real point, mysticism, etc. All are forms of deeper understanding (many not getting to base 'wisdom' still) yet all often steer away from singular truth that is in our actual real, living, and necessary Savior Jesus Christ alone.

Whatever way, name, or level of 'wisdom,' if it steers away from God Almighty at the center, or steers to personal pride in 'wisdom,' it is in deception. Furthermore, powers of deception aim to make Christ a small thing, simply a level of knowledge or understanding that we all can 'awaken' to. Be not deceived with a portion of wisdom twisted in vast deception. Jesus Christ lives and He is the only way. He is the way, the truth and the life. We will later extrapolate to such. Seek His guidance above all.

I could go on with the different terms and things that are twisted of relative levels of the same deeper understanding; the point is, even the deepest confounds and comes to naught before the necessary truth of God and Jesus Christ, who live. He has created all things perfectly and the meek will inherit.

One can walk and explore in endless deception as they will, agency and freedom is given them, but until they humble themselves to seek light and truth they will not see it.

In such 'wisdom' at least some things are better understood; but at the cost of walking in deception and not finding real truth. Real peace, real wisdom, real knowledge that greatly, GREATLY outweighs such 'wisdom' of the world is given by the Holy Spirit of our Father in Heaven through our Savior Jesus Christ to our Father in Heaven's humble and faithful children. Wisdom exercised in truth.

The 'foolishness' of faith in our Savior perfectly fulfills and confounds. The law of Christ vastly supersedes all things. Humble yourself and let our Father in Heaven show you. We will get much deeper and clearer into understanding such in truth as we go along.

"But to be learned is good if they hearken unto the counsels of God."

Most all in 'wisdom' are truly deeply led and deceived by darkness. For the law of Christ through faith confounds and fulfills it and gives truth far beyond. If there is ANY understanding that leads from God Almighty and our humility before Him then we are being led in deception. This is why it is dangerous.

Understanding certain base laws or coming closer to them is no more than coming to realize the agency and freedom God Almighty has given His children. Be not deceived. Alas, all is done in wisdom of Him who has created all things and knoweth all things. Even so here you are, reading this.

True wisdom comes through faith in God. All is His. He must be at the center for us to be led in truth; and as we seek of Him, we sure do find.

Later in chapter 12 we will show how often this same experience has happened and the extent it has, in entertainment and other. We will further extrapolate to truth in Jesus Christ as well.

"The law discovers the disease. The gospel gives the remedy." - Martin Luther

Do not be deceived. Wide is deception, strait and narrow is the gate to truth and to true freedom. Oh be wise!

Matthew 7:13-14 "Enter ye in the strait gate: for wide is the gate, and broad is the way, that leadeth to destruction, and many there be which go in thereat: Because strait is the gate, and narrow is the way, which leadeth unto life, and few there be that find it."

Chapter 9

GUIDANCE
Personal Story Continued: Revelation

The immediate and drastic change must have startled everyone. I went from being increasingly critical of the Church to my own mother and had discounted religion basically entirely, thinking myself wise; to suddenly humbly reading the scriptures and praying all the time, telling everyone it's true and seeking wisdom humbly from the Lord.

All things had been allegories that alluded to a certain understanding of a 'truth' before; then I was shown the absolute real truth; truth which confounded even the deepest 'wisdoms' of men, Jesus Christ.

Things quickly went from, "Oh this is just another bit pointing to 'wisdom.'" To, "Wow all things in heaven and earth point to Jesus Christ our living Savior, by whom all things even are." Even the deepest 'wisdom' of the world was fulfilled in and by, as well as confounded perfectly in Jesus Christ the Savior of us all. This understanding became even clearer and deeper all the while.

I was finally tuned to truth. Jesus Christ truly is the way, the truth and the life.

Many must have been so confused at first, but I had been shown clearly and I truly didn't care what anyone thought. I simply needed to figure the rest of all of this out, given the new and incredible information by way of love in the saving grace of God my Father in Heaven.

The day after the experience I texted so many friends and told them basically, "Hey, this is really true, just so you know."

I began reading scriptures and studying. I had some serious questions I needed answers to. And I knew God was right there to answer them. I had understood by weighing the past 'wisdom' in the new light and how it was confounded, that He is what is claimed. But I still needed to know, and I needed to know so many things. However, I now knew that God is, and I had the faith necessary for revelation. He was right there. How incredible the 'wisdom' of God to bring me in the perfect way to finally see clearly.

I have since seen stories of people who became converts, their lives were brightened and then they come to understand this 'wisdom' and they leave the church thinking that they 'finally get it all now, they finally understand.' What a stumbling block it can be.

I will touch briefly on this for the benefit of some and then I will get back into my story.

72

Every time I see someone like that in any way, I get shown the importance of writing this. Jesus Himself said that in the end times deceptions would be everywhere and that even some of the elect would be deceived. And in this understanding people are pushed to look at themselves simply on the same 'level of understanding' as Christ, things are twisted in a horrible and deceiving way. Obviously one on the rock of truth can see the deceptive plan of the adversary.

Matthew 24:24 "For there shall arise false Christs, and false prophets, and shall shew great signs and wonders; insomuch that, if it were possible, they shall deceive the very elect.
25 Behold, I have told you before."

As Christ has told us before, we know it will come. And it has and will more so. The basic understanding is so 'clear' and seems to confound and explain all things; though in 1000 years that it may take someone to see clearly on their own, they will finally see how Christ is necessary and God is Almighty and the perfection of the plan and what is really deception. I will get into explaining this more later.

I simply want to stress beforehand, over and over, the only way to gain PURE truth and TRUE knowledge is by revelation from God. And light can prove light, in ways that are significantly beyond our potential to understand.

Understand that this will be increasingly pushed in the future; in one smaller sense (though world changing) doing some good by showing the true nature of many things; time, space or locality, the nature of many things that are far from current perception. In a sense some things can be understood more clearly. Technology may be given far grander and more revealed as these things are understood and pushed, but I perceive they may be presented in a way that will destroy truth. And this will be because they do not understand truly where they are and the utter vastness of things; that or they seek to deceive.

What a deception to say, "Look, here are all the understandings of our reality, and look at all this technology to 'free' you greatly, and oh ya here is all this blasphemy and lies because we will only give you a portion of the truth to walk prideful in it and steer you away from truth in God." Beware of such.

I perceive many technologies may not be given easily as they will lose the control grip that is had on the masses. I perceive deception will be so rampant that these technologies and things will be given in further deception. I wouldn't even be surprised if the rapture of the Saints or other tech is brought out and is masqueraded as aliens for further subjugation and control. It may sound silly now, but deception

73

will be rampant and I feel to write such. Many agendas may be pushed and 'wisdom' taught incorrectly away from the truth of God. I can perceive 'wisdom' twisted and pushed as a world religion. Oh how deep the deception. I don't know for sure in what way, but I know in many ways there will be vast deception. Keep Christ at the center; stay on the rock.

He has told us before. Signs and wonders are possible in deception. Pharaoh's people did such and God obviously did the more and is the creator of all things. Jesus Christ is the way, the truth and the life. He is utterly necessary. Be not deceived.

Alas, God is at the helm.

Be ready for this; and for what way and in what adverse power they are pushed. Do not look beyond the mark of Christ; stay built thereon and there is safety. Remember that Christ says in Matthew 16 that He will build His church on the rock of revelation. Revelation from Him and His Spirit, which always testifies of Christ, and not wisdom from the arm of flesh. He later tells us of the last days and the deception that would surely come, even 'signs and wonders' to deceive.

Again, there is a chance this 'wisdom' will be introduced to many at first through newly revealed technology, (in partial or twisted truth, or deception), that may drastically help many. There are good things that may be accomplished, though the understanding is exercised, and 'wisdom' pushed, in deception and in incorrect fashion in vast deception; remember there is true truth.

Be careful that you do not accept any 'wisdom' in any way that takes God and Christ from the very center of your life. Though there is potential for grand tech to be revealed, it will likely come in more deception and the base of it likely will be pushed in the wrong way. The ways it is pushed and taught is totally in deception and many are stuck in the stumbling block.

* (Note: There are many things that I will repeat and reiterate throughout this book. Furthermore, I will get far more into and deeper into such things in a clearer manner to show the law fulfilled in Jesus Christ alone. I do not care to make this perfectly polished but write in a way that I have faith is wisdom to convey importance.)

There are some in the world who even see the adversary of truth as a 'light bringer,' they see this opposite of truth and are deceived. We are scripturally warned to not see light for darkness and darkness for light.

Isaiah 5:20 "Woe unto them that call evil good, and good evil; that put darkness for light, and light for darkness; that put bitter for sweet, and sweet for bitter."

I judge none but I find it seemingly common to see in many 'secret societies' that seemingly teach 'wisdom' that some seem to later get to seeing the adversary of truth as the 'light bringer.' This is wholly a wrong assessment and a detrimental deception. They become led by a spirit of deception to deeper deception. Sadly those that become so deceived cannot perceive the 'wisdom' has become twisted vastly to steer them away from all truth, they become so steered that eventually can see things so wrong and inversed. Restore.

I was amazed and saddened to learn that some were this far deceived to see things fully backward. It becomes those lulled away with a piece of desirable candy, guiding the opposite way from their home and Father who has created and is the source of all good things. I think of the movie 'Hook' where the kid was deceived to believe the villain was his father and was giving him more, when in reality he was deceived and later saved by his loving dad. It is this on a vast scale. These are they who truly are snared in holes. Restore. See clearly.

Jesus Christ is the way, the truth and the life! He is breaking chains.

Isaiah 42:22 "But this is a people robbed and spoiled; they are all of them snared in holes, and they are hid in prison houses: they are for a prey and none delivereth; for a spoil, and none saith, Restore.

23 Who among you will give ear to this? Who will hearken and hear for the time to come?"

If we are not led by God, in light and truth, and seeking His guidance we will be guided by those things of darkness on the other side, which don't care about freedom and will guide to all deception.

Again, I perceive many societies of such teach things increasingly from the understanding of the 'wisdom' and teach the deeper and deeper perceptions and further utilization, if you will. They seemingly teach this in all pride in 'wisdom,' after all they are seeking wisdom of themselves. Pride ensnares so deeply. Some eventually get to the mother of all ensnaring lies, seeing the things of darkness for light and light for darkness. That or they finally come to realize their awful situation.

They compare their extended 'wisdom' in spiritual law, though twisted, with that of average man and see themselves superior in understanding. They cannot yet see that their vast seeming 'wisdom' is utter foolishness in the grand scale of things and are confounded by things so far beyond them. They cannot yet see by what they are guided and the 'wisdom' is the cheese in the mouse trap in many cases. They lead themselves there, in a sense, rather, allow themselves unknowingly to be led, and keep themselves there and dig deeper until some eventually realize what is going on or become further ensnared.

Many, when they do realize it all simply believe it in opposite and become servants, in a sense, of things very not good.

How sad that one can be convinced that terribly harsh things are not. How sad it can be that harsh things done in the world are seen as no big deal because they are convinced by darkness it simply doesn't matter; that all is only a cosmic giggle, an infinity of pointlessness. Many things are simply not original thoughts but given by darkness. Oh be wise.

2 Nephi 9:28 "O that cunning plan of the evil one! O the vainness, and the frailties, and the foolishness of men! When they are learned they think they are wise, and they hearken not unto the counsel of God, for they set it aside, supposing they know of themselves, wherefore, their wisdom is foolishness and it profiteth them not. And they shall perish.

29 But to be learned is good if they hearken unto the counsels of God."

2 Nephi 2:5 "And men are instructed sufficiently that they know good from evil. And the law is given unto men. And by the law no flesh is justified; or, by the law men are cut off. Yea, by the temporal law they were cut off; and also, by the spiritual law they perish from that which is good, and become miserable forever.

6 Wherefore, redemption cometh in and through the Holy Messiah; for he is full of grace and truth.

7 Behold, he offereth himself a sacrifice for sin, to answer the ends of the law, unto all those who have a broken heart and a contrite spirit; and unto none else can the ends of the law be answered.

8 Wherefore, how great the importance to make these things known unto the inhabitants of the earth, that they may know that there is no flesh that can dwell in the presence of God, save it be through the merits, and mercy, and grace of the Holy Messiah, who layeth down his life according to the flesh, and taketh it again by the power of the Spirit, that he may bring to pass the resurrection of the dead, being the first that should rise."

Be bound no longer. The Lord God Almighty, our loving Father, is breaking chains. How blessed we are.

76

All is infinitely more than pointless, in fact the opposite. There is infinite vast and perfect purpose. The grand symphony of God is imperceptible for those walking outside of the strait and narrow path and the protection it provides.

Humble yourselves. Those who see wrong as though nothing matters, oh what a deception. See that the opposite must also be true. Restore now. As we go along this will be made deeply more apparent and you will be able to see your way out of the deception. (Speaking to those that walk in such 'wisdom.' All words will still be profitable for all to stay on the rock of our Savior.)

"The only true wisdom is in knowing you know nothing." – Socrates

Even the man that said "Know thyself," has some deeper and true wisdom in the above; even the deepest 'wisdom' of man gets swallowed up in the truest wisdom, humility before God. We must be humble before He who has created all things. We are children. We can be shown all things by Him.

We must be humble.

I judge none; I seek simply to help.

Going back to the Isaiah scripture of putting light for darkness and darkness for light, the very next scripture in Isaiah 5 is,

21 "Woe unto them that are wise in their own eyes, and prudent in their own sight!"

(Isaiah does a good job at directly depicting much true wisdom in the area. Deep stuff made clear.)

Do not take the 'wisdom' as it is pushed if ever away from God. True wisdom is faith in God and Jesus Christ. Those who hold 'wisdom' see it wrong, incorrectly, in all the ways of continuing deception. The humble realize they know nothing and seek Him to guide. Some things learned can be a relative help to discern how perfect Christ is and how He fulfills, though faith in Christ becomes the grandest and only way to go and all grander understanding and truth comes from faith in Him. The weak things confound the mighty. Most that come to learn such 'wisdom' are led in pride and by things they don't perceive, ever away from the strait and narrow path of truth in Jesus Christ. Restore.

I surely can judge none and how great our Father in Heaven is in His grace and mercy. His words are being fulfilled, His goodness and mercy is vast. He is bringing His children home; we but have to hear His voice and seek Him.

It is certainly wild to spend so much time deeply seeking and learning all wisdom to then see it all collapse, in a sense. I judge none, but feel something needs to be said for those 'learning' in these specific areas of the world. Become humble before God that you may resonate with truth through faith in Him and, "Restore." Hear.

Continuing on, all of this will be made very clear in many ways. Those in 'wisdom' will be able to clearly see their way out to be guided in pure truth. The way is being opened if you will but seek humbly.

It will soon become a great blessing that this has collapsed and soon you will see the amazing goodness of God. We must be meek; we must be humble. How great is our Father in Heaven who has saved us continually, even out of spiritual Egypt.

True wisdom is humility before God. Just as Jesus taught, the one humbled as a little child before God is the greatest in the kingdom of heaven.

Matthew 18:4 "Whosoever therefore shall humble himself as this little child, the same is greatest in the kingdom of heaven."

We will get much more into this as we go along, pragmatically, logically and spiritually.

Jesus Christ will show us all wisdom and true wisdom will be taught from and begin from Him at the center of our lives and relying on Him. Many simply understand things in the very wrong context, and an adverse power pushes it wrongly. Though there may be new things that seem to bring 'light,' the true light is Jesus Christ. Oh be wise! Though I reiterate it over and over, remember it.

Be careful of deception. Christ has told us before. I tell you again. Do not be coaxed off of the rock of Christ. If you think you 'know' and 'understand' how things are and it doesn't involve the absolute necessity of our resurrected Lord and Savior, the actual Jesus Christ, then you are in paths of deception. Jesus Christ is the way, the truth and the life. Be prepared; stay on the rock.

Doctrine and Covenants 38:30 "I tell you these things because of your prayers; wherefore, treasure up wisdom in your bosoms, lest the wickedness of men reveal these things unto you by their wickedness, in a manner which shall speak in your ears with a voice louder than that which shall shake the earth; but if you are prepared ye shall not fear.

31 And that ye might escape the power of the enemy, and be gathered unto me a righteous people, without spot and blameless-"

Again, "lest the wickedness of men reveal these things unto you by their wickedness, in a manner which shall speak in your ears with a voice louder than that which shall shake the earth; but if you are prepared ye shall not fear."

I feel for everyone; there is simply an adversary and we need our Savior! I have seen full circle. I see those beloved sons and daughters of God 'robbed and spoiled, snared in holes, hid in prison houses, for a pray, for a spoil;' as it says in Isaiah 42.

Over and over it has been laid on my heart, it is as if the Spirit of the Lord is saying, "Look how much I love you, I have saved you, and now you see clearly and I will show you yet clearer. You see them there ensnared, can you turn your back on them knowing how much I love them too? Who else can understand as you do? Have I not chosen you? Can you see yet your calling?"

For a while it was myself recognizing my pure weakness, each time He made that weakness perfect in His strength. I of myself can do nothing; I seek no glory or praise of myself but that all will recognize the hand of our Father in Heaven in His mighty works to save and strengthen His beloved children. Though there is great weakness of myself I know that such will be made perfect in His strength for His purposes and may it abound to His glory forever. If one soul is strengthened, if one soul is saved, how great was the worth of the effort.

I am forever grateful He loves us all that much. For I am one, and you are one; how He loves us.

I will forever do all I can for my perfect Father in Heaven and He will give me strength in my weakness to do all He would have me do. I pray that He give everyone humility necessary to receive truth by His Spirit, that the blind eyes will be made open and the deaf ears be unstopped.

Rely on the Lord; Israel will be saved by His mighty hand.

Doctrine and Covenants 136:22 "I am He who led the children of Israel out of the land of Egypt; and my arm is stretched out in the last days, to save my people Israel."

Today we are having the need to be saved from modern day spiritual Egypt. His arm is outstretched and is mighty to save.

Understanding that we are children of God, and truly children before Him. Trusting Him and in His wisdom is important. We must seek to be led and live to be led by the Holy Spirit. We have vast agency the

Lord has blessed us with, be wise and exercise yourself in truth. Jesus Christ the living Son of Almighty God and His atonement is the only way. Humbly rely on Him.

REVELATION BEGINS

As I begin to get more into my story, which will be peppered in again and again, even to the end of the book, consider the following.

"Could we read and comprehend all that has been written from the days of Adam, on the relation of man to God and angels in a future state, we should know very little about it. Reading the experience of others, or the revelation given to *them,* can never give *us* a comprehensive view of our condition and true relation to God. Knowledge of these things can only be obtained by experience through the ordinances of God set forth for that purpose. Could you gaze into heaven five minutes, you would know more than you would by reading all that ever was written on the subject. ... I assure the Saints that truth ... can and may be known through the revelations of God in the way of His ordinances, and in answer to prayer." – Teachings of the Prophet Joseph Smith

Personal revelation is very important; there is a discourse on it later on. The point I was at the day after this was utter reliance on revelation, reliance on God. I will detail some of it. I had come to know in my own path why Christ would build His Church on the rock of revelation. Although I had learned much, and was beginning to learn much more, this was only the very beginning of so many amazing things learned.

I had questions I needed answers to right away. I needed to understand why certain things were acceptable and others weren't, and many other things.

I pulled out my phone. I had downloaded the LDS library that held the KJV Bible and Book of Mormon and other scriptures.

Understanding that God was right there, and being able to finally know this, it made being directed and exercising faith in revelation easily possible now. I knew He was above all things. Furthermore, I understood much how certain things worked now and how our gift of agency worked, as well as the power and tuning of faith, and in what ways, and how even that seemingly 'deep' understanding was confounded by He who created all things, by whom all things are.

Doctrine and Covenants 35:25 "And Israel shall be saved in mine own due time; and by the keys which I have given shall they be led, and no more be confounded at all. "

I prayed to understand, not thinking at first to take out my scriptures. I need to know, I had many things on my mind I needed to understand.

Immediately the thought in my head was a scripture I had sadly often recited to people about the church. I didn't know where it was but I knew it went something like this. "God is not the author of confusion but of peace and sound mind."

I would tell this to people occasionally that I genuinely wanted to help and 'enlighten' and say, "Well do you understand God fully? Well then this must not be the right path, because He is not the author of confusion."

This thought was interesting as it not only led me to where I was going to seek answers but it entirely confounded the way I had used it before.

"For God is not the author of confusion, but of peace, as in all the churches of the saints." 1 Corinthians 14:33.

He proved the scripture by giving me the scripture to show me the answer to even where I was going, proving He will lead and guide and showing my past understanding of the scripture obviously as wrong. Something I discern even more now. He solved many things in an instant with one thought. Fulfilling His word perfectly and confounding past 'wisdom.'

The scripture had come to mind so I searched where it was at. 1 Corinthians 14. "Cool, I'll check it out." I knew the Lord was leading me in truth, understanding the importance of faith and how to exercise it and why to exercise it in truth and what truth is; how greatly I had been blessed, how merciful the Lord is. I'm forever grateful. It was amazing to finally see clearly and I was and forever am so grateful.

I open up to the chapter and read through it all. At the time I knew next to nothing about where I was reading and who was talking but it was deep. The chapter has much about deep things of the gospel, prophesy, tongues, etc. I saw how those who sought certain gifts and had been blessed with any manner of things should be used for the help and guidance of others, to edify, for the glory of God.

I understood a lot, learned a lot, and my mind quickly realized the unreal depth of understanding these guys had. In one chapter I saw, in a sense, how much could be learned and shown in truth by the Spirit in just one chapter of scripture. The Spirit conveyed incredible depth of how true wisdom is truly humility before God. The Spirit was conveying things of importance to me at the time regarding being quickened in the Spirit. Furthermore I was being humbled with an overload of information that I was a child to try to grasp.

This vast and incredible guidance has always been at our fingertips? If we would but humble ourselves and trust our Father in Heaven and exercise faith? I wanted to know and learn more and more.

After this chapter I had another question. "All this is great, but I feel like it just has to be about love. Like it has to be all about love. It is the only thing that makes sense to me."

Some things of the Church just weren't fully understood yet to me, (though over time serious amazing understanding of all has come,) I simply felt love is really what has to matter. It was what made sense to me then and I just wanted to know the truth on such matters.

My next thought is something like this. "God you are fully capable to say the least, I know you'll keep showing me."

I will break off for a moment from the story to convey a few points of clarity.

This was understood especially as I had previously discerned how much of these types of things work based on base understanding, furthermore how all things were swallowed up in His utter vastness and perfection.

I was finally seeing furthermore how real and ever present He is and how well we can be taught if we but exercise our vast agency in faith to tune to truth in Him, that we may be shown truth.

Doctrine and Covenants 50:11 "Let us reason even as a man reasoneth one with another face to face.

12 Now, when a man reasoneth he is understood of man, because he reasoneth as a man; even so will I, the Lord, reason with you that you may understand.

19 And again, he that receiveth the word of truth, doth he receive it by the Spirit of truth or some other way?

20 If it be some other way it is not of God.

21 Therefore, why is it that ye cannot understand and know, that he that receiveth the word by the Spirit of truth receiveth it as it is preached by the Spirit of truth?

22 Wherefore, he that preacheth and he that receiveth, understand one another, and both are edified and rejoice together."

I had seen things similarly extrapolate this way prior. Some in 'wisdom,' (of the world that should be left behind, in a sense, for faith in God,) may see what I mean in the extrapolation of expectation.

I intend to show that true wisdom is in God and is shown by His Spirit, who gives freedom for us to go as we will and seek as we will and asks us to have faith in Him. Once we do, oh how light proves light and how small and miniscule everything else becomes in comparison to His immensity and perfection and truth and light.

How the grand things of men quickly come to nothing in comparison to even the "foolish" things of Him. All things are His! And when the dews of wisdom of Him come down, how great it is! May we be humble that we in faith can tune to truth and see the immensity of Him. Our Father in Heaven is so good! Truly our Savior has built His Church on the rock of revelation.

Now I understood it in the right way, in faith in truth. Truly the way we are taught in the gospel is true. Faith is such a big deal, and the deeper things are stumbling blocks when seen the way most do. Faith becomes the grandest wisdom and in this the Lord can explain all things deep and proper.

We must tune to the correct station of truth to hear truth, and the truth is all-powerful God Almighty, our loving Father in Heaven. The greatest wisdom is faith in Him and humility before Him. All things are His; He confounds and magnifies all things for His purposes in love.

Back to my story, I know that I will be shown. I feel strongly and pray, 'it must all be about love, and I just need to understand that.' I realize God is significantly above all and no matter what I do I will find what I need, rather, He will show me. So, knowing the Lord can do all things well I chose entirely randomly to simply go back one chapter to 1 Corinthians 13.

The entire chapter is about love and charity being the greatest of all things. And describes it in a way that is deep and beautiful. In it one can see why our Father in Heaven has such incredible long-suffering for us. He loves us so dearly. The grandest thing, was that although 14 was about all this deep learning of the gospel to help and edify myself and others, even above that, love confounds and is more important than it all.

In 14 I saw such importance on 'prophecy' and spiritual relatively deeper things and 13 made clear how much charity, the pure love of Christ, matters to our Father in Heaven.

1 Corinthians 13:2 "And though I have the gift of prophecy, and understand all mysteries, and all knowledge; and though I have all faith, so that I could remove mountains, and have not charity, I am nothing.

13 And now abideth faith, hope, charity, these three; but the greatest of these is charity."

I had always loved love. I will in further chapters talk a little bit more about love and the science behind it. It is deep. And the Lord was showing me how love is the grand point. I had known the scripture, 'God is love,' but I was just only beginning to glimpse His vast perfection and pure love.

Having my faith strengthened yet again, I exercised another question. "If love is the grand end all, and all that matters, why all the stuff that I have now come to understand as real of The Church of Jesus Christ of Latter-day Saints?"

I could answer my first question partly immediately in my mind, rather my thoughts were guided there, by what had happened the day before. I could see clearly the power of the ordinances in the power of God and the wisdom therein of the path in His power; they must have even more significant meaning as I would later come to learn.

I could see also, powerfully and clearly the importance of the Priesthood and being given authority directly by God to act in His name. But I still wanted to be sure. Why are these other things important? Some things taught in the gospel I wasn't yet entirely sure about in that I didn't yet fully understand all the way around. I wanted to be sure I was led in truth.

"If it's all only about love why these other things?" Again, even though there were vast difference of the topics I asked about, I knew God is above all and couldn't fail me as I walked in faith.

I went back a chapter from 14, why not go forward a chapter to 15? Totally a random choice. In it I realized for the first time, that it is not the Book of Mormon or Church of Jesus Christ of Latter-day Saints only that teaches of the degrees of glory or baptism for the dead, but Paul in Corinthians. Things the Church gets bashed about, things I couldn't earlier in life understand were right there.

Let me just say this, Paul knew things very, very, very, deeply, a very wise man. I came to re-learn that Paul had been against the Church of Christ in the early days and God saw fit to save him. Christ came to him and taught him deeply. Paul became a strong and incredibly wise Apostle of Christ. Paul went from watching prophets being stoned to bringing about the salvation of millions through Christ by now.

Then and since, I have further seen how incredible and merciful the Lord is. Teaching me deeply things that I needed to know, by an apostle that needed saving just as I did. He showed me how deeply wise this man was, how blessed of God he was, and how much good he could do for God; all the while teaching me through him.

I understood some deep things in that chapter of 1 Corinthians 15 and simply began to see that the Lord has and will always pour out more and more blessings to His faithful children. The fullness of His everlasting gospel was promised by Him, and He loves His children so much that He wants to bless us all the more.

If you have children and love them, you cannot yet comprehend the love He has for us as His children.

My questions I had at that time were answered. Remember my question being about the specific gospel as it was shown to me and inquiring to be shown clearly. (A full clarity of everything came over time and required much to be accepted simply on good faith first, then the grandest revelations later came of how perfectly things fit together and how grand the blessings are. The greater things and blessings of our Father in Heaven are protected by a meek and humble faith.)

Consider the first scriptures in the chapter reading of 1 Corinthians 15, remembering the question I asked about the specific gospel.

1 "Moreover, brethren, I declare unto you the gospel which I preached unto you, which also ye have received, and wherein ye stand;
2 By which also ye are saved, if ye keep in memory what I preached unto you, unless ye have believed in vain.
3 For I delivered unto you first of all that which I also received, how that Christ died for our sins according to the scriptures;
4 And that he was buried, and that he rose again the third day according to the scriptures:"

I was essentially wowed with the first verse. The chapter goes on and speaks of baptism for the dead and degrees of glory and much deep.

I could understand the need for such baptisms, even in bits of 'wisdom,' as we are still connected to those and how they all still exist and still need to come in by the strait and narrow path that is our Savior Jesus Christ.

It became more normal to see how direct and perfect of answers the Lord could always give and in the plain answers of God through His word and by His Spirit. His Spirit will give the understanding and help us see things deeper and clearer.

I was further wowed by the depth I learned. Truly He has chosen the foolish things to confound the wise and the weak things to confound the mighty. One tiny ray of His revelation or goodness, (that can be overlooked or seen as weak by those not seeing,) can shatter any thought of mans 'wisdom,' thoroughly explaining the weakness of it while thoroughly explaining whatever we seek and so much more. Truly we can gain all true wisdom as we are humble and faithful before Him, 'as fast as we are able to bear.' And all things are His.

The next bit goes on to testify of the resurrection of Christ; even over 500 men saw Him and many remained that day Paul wrote it. And the depth of these scriptures in 9 and 10.

9 "For I am the least of the apostles, that am not meet to be called an apostle, because I persecuted the church of God.
10 But by the grace of God I am what I am: and his grace which was bestowed upon me was not in vain; but I laboured more abundantly than they all: yet not I, but the grace of God which was with me."

This bit mingled with what I was shown in 14 gave me a good direction of the Lord's good intentions for me. It was amazing to see that I would be given answers and taught all the more seemingly at the same time. I could see how the Lord used Paul so well in His amazing grace.
I have since heard a great quote. "Often the Lord recruits from the pit and not the palace." How good our Father in Heaven is. I truly will labor the best I can; I know that with His help my weakness will be made strong.
The next scriptures explained through my experience, and that of others, how Christ must be risen and resurrected. The 'wisdom' was confounded yet again. I discern and learn much clearer and continue more so as I go along.

* (Note: When being taught in and by the Spirit of the Lord He can bring things to our understanding and help us see and understand deeper things than meet the eye. He can enlighten our minds greatly and we can truly be 'taught from on High.'
Doctrine and Covenants 76:12 "By the power of the Spirit our eyes were opened and our understandings were enlightened, so as to see and understand the things of God-"
I personally have seen that in a single moment vast concepts can be understood all the way around. Though the immediate vast concept form does happen it is seemingly more rare than the "line upon line, precept upon precept" form given Biblically in scripture; bit by bit, eventually coming to understand a greater whole, then another and

another. Sometimes the line upon line is all vast concepts. I find faith as well as the level one is "quickened in the Spirit" to be a factor in depth of revelation received. And all is wisdom in the Lord. Sometimes we need to seek diligently for ourselves; sometimes we can be very close to the Lord, which is what we should seek. There is a whole discourse on revelation later on.)

(Further note: I am going through reading through this book for errors and adding things and I check these scriptures again in 1 Corinthians 15. I take a break, have a Spiritual conversation with my Mom on the phone and am edified by the Spirit of things that I have been seeking and gaining deeper further understanding on and can better discern such by re-reading about the Spirit edifying. I come back to read the scriptures and learn again the same lesson even deeper that I am trying to convey; and am taught very large things scripturally by the Spirit that I have been learning lately of the Spirit. Truly our Father in Heaven is so amazing. Constant learning, all for His glory!

John 6:63 "It is the spirit that quickeneth; the flesh profiteth nothing: the words that I speak unto you, they are spirit, and they are life."

We are called to live 'above,' in the Spirit, not in the physical. In the Spirit where He is ever present; we simply must recognize He is always right there.)

Seek the scriptures. Read them and pray for guidance in faith.

I had received my answers and I came to discern, learn and understand other deep things. There are many things I have learned that I will keep incredibly vague or simply not talk about. God is there to teach you all things.

Even if I were to try to teach some things that are deeper you must walk the steps yourself to them first to understand clearly. We all have our time and season, take it from someone who had to go full circle. If we seek diligently we will learn quickly. Christ taught often and constantly said things over and over and finally more began to hear or discern better.

Often times, like most scriptures, I read over His words and am astounded by the new level of wisdom I discern that He was getting across for those that the Spirit was teaching and showing clearly. Then I can read them another time and gain an even deeper understanding by the Spirit again. It is the Spirit that quickeneth. We simply must have faith that He is there. I will get more into it in later discourse chapters.

I was blessed with answers as well as the strong understanding of essentially this thought, "Yes, there is incredibly many more significant things to learn. Things of truth that are far beyond all you can know now. Humble yourself, and learn them the only way you can, from Me." Not that that was said, but those were the understandings of my thoughts in the Spirit.

I have since learned very much, and still do so. The words of God are living, and have deeper and deeper meaning and more always to teach through the Holy Spirit.

I will say, there is so much given to know. I will get more into revelation later. There are promises that we can know all things. There is endless knowledge to those led by the Lord to receive it and especially those who seek whole-heartedly His will in all things. We will get into this more as we go along.

I was shown a lot out of 1 Corinthians chapter 15, I still am if I seek for different things now. The things of God are alive.

My faith was again strengthened. The Lord's perfect answer, as my faith was exercised. (Later I will help you, in a discourse on faith, discern how to approach and look at faith in ways that will help.)

I knew I was being led to the scriptures but I wanted to know of absolute understanding, that absolutely the Lord was leading me in wisdom beyond my own and that I wasn't leading myself. I knew I was receiving vast information in deep and new and vast ways but it was as though I wanted to be so sure.

I knew the way certain laws worked and wanted to be sure that this was Him and that He was the one taking me there. As I knew it I wanted to be sure that I was resonating with Almighty God and truth and not leading myself or other things, as I understood these laws. I was being overly careful and knew He could and would show me.

I opened the app, and this time entirely clicked on random books, random chapters and scrolled to entirely random verses. I was led to Galatians 3. Now, wow. I scrolled down and hit on some scriptures that are as follows.

23 "But before faith came, we were kept under the law, shut up unto the faith which should afterwards be revealed.
24 Wherefore the law was our schoolmaster to bring us unto Christ, that we might be justified by faith.
25 But after that faith is come, we are no longer under a schoolmaster.
26 For ye are all the children of God by faith in Christ Jesus.
27 For as many of you as have been baptized into Christ have put on Christ.

28 There is neither Jew nor Greek, there is neither bond nor free, there is neither male nor female: for ye are all one in Christ Jesus.
29 And if ye be Christ's, then ye are Abraham's seed, and heirs according to the promise."

Now this is just SOME of the chapter. I STONGLY URGE you all to just go read Galatians 3. It is the Lord explaining the law and how humble faith is above. It gave me a far, far deeper understanding of Moses and the Law of Moses and why he did certain things and all I can say is wow. I strongly urge you to read it. It gave me a very deep understanding. In all things, pray for understanding and discernment for the things that you are ready for.

My question was perfectly answered in a depth of understanding that I had no idea scriptures touched. It validated everything I had been taught and came to know by the Spirit and reminded me again how perfectly Jesus Christ confounds and fulfills the law and how necessary He is for us all.

Furthermore the first verses of the chapter I was led to were seemingly a quick rebuke to see clearly in a sense. When reading I thought something to the extent of, "Yea, I know, I've seen more than enough, I know more than enough. I see it clearly and you've shown it clearly." Consider the question I asked, then the answers.

1 "O foolish Galatians, who hath bewitched you, that ye should not obey the truth, before whose eyes Jesus Christ hath been evidently set forth, crucified among you?
2 This only would I learn of you, Received ye the Spirit by the works of the law, or by the hearing of faith?
3 Are ye so foolish? having begun in the Spirit, are ye now made perfect by the flesh?
4 Have ye suffered so many things in vain? If it yet be in vain.
5 He therefore that ministereth to you the Spirit, and worketh miracles among you, doeth he it by the works of the law, or by the hearing of faith?"

The first bit of the chapter truly was a bit of like a, "Dude, wake up, see all these things, and you know how clearly I have shown you grand things in grand ways by you finally seeing in faith, how can you be deceived any more? See clearly. I am with you. I have saved you. And here is more to help you understand."

And the rest of the chapter continued to make it clear just as I stated above. The law was our schoolmaster to bring us unto Christ.

Humble faith in Him and seeking the guidance of the Holy Spirit is true wisdom. How the 'foolish' things confound the 'wise.'

I was reminded of the depth of things I have been shown and realized my ignorance in asking the question. I knew He could answer and still felt to ask. More was taught even in this alone, the answers aplenty aside.

Understand at times the same words like 'law' can mean different things and most scriptures have deeper and deeper meanings, spiritual, physical, historical, and they all seem to have so many levels, the Lord can speak to each of us perfectly if we exercise faith and have eyes to see and ears to hear; recognizing the Spirit.

Certain scriptures that seem physical can have deep spiritual meanings that seem deep today, then tomorrow are yet significantly deeper, then the next a deeper physical meaning then next an even deeper never before discerned spiritual meaning, then yet deeper physical. The works of God are endless. He is endless. That which is of Him is endless.

I was really beginning to see the depth of true wisdom these ancient apostles had and gave in scripture. I had a vastly renewed zeal to learn for I now knew what truth was and that scriptures are the very word of God and He longs to teach us.

If it is His will we can be given immense spiritual wisdom out of a random seemingly pointless word on a rock. As Christ has told us in John 6:63 It is the Spirit that quickeneth.

Christ truly came to do it all and make it all easy for us and save us all; we need Him and owe Him so much. Oh how He loves us and how thankful and grateful I am.

I can see some of the many ways of how many of the wise of the Jews were confused at first; but Jesus Christ is necessary and the law and all things are confounded and fulfilled by faith in Jesus Christ. He supersedes all things. We must become humble. He has built all things perfectly. God is so good.

Here are some scriptures that are worth adding. My answer was given incredibly deep. The Spirit makes perfect, God makes perfect, Jesus Christ makes perfect, not the work of the flesh but of God. Not the law, not wisdom, but the things above, faith and the Spirit of God.

The whole chapter is worth reading but here are a few more verses. Again, understand there is MUCH more deep wisdom about all of this, and we will get into more in a logical sense in future chapters, but it is so far beyond when it is spiritually discerned in truth by the Spirit of truth which is the Spirit of God. How blessed we are by our Father in Heaven.

11 But that no man is justified by the law in the sight of God, it is evident: for, The just shall live by faith.
13 Christ hath redeemed us from the curse of the law, being made a curse for us: for it is written, Cursed is every one that hangeth on a tree:
19 Wherefore then serveth the law? It was added because of transgressions, till the seed should come to whom the promise was made; and it was ordained by angels in the hand of a mediator.

I think of a fitting quote I once saw, "Praise the Lord, He is the only reality, everything else is only our means to reach him. Don't let our time be wasted, it's so little time, lets make the most of it, before it's too late."

Consider the last scripture there, 19. The seed to whom the promise was made. See that if you are coming into faith now that you have been called. If you have a humble heart, you have been called.

John 6:44 "No man can come to me, except the Father which hath sent me draw him: and I will raise him up at the last day."

Recognize the immense blessing we are all given, all of us who know of the truthfulness of our Savior. We have been drawn and called and chosen of our Father. Yes you. May we recognize this and do His work in the little time we have. May we seek His perfect glory, His perfection that has saved us in his amazing grace and perfect mercy.
Oh the immensity and perfect symphony of our loving literal Father in Heaven.
I will further get into the importance of faith and why later on, but let me say now, even though I was blessed with much I surely still had to go through a great trial of faith. I learned and have been strengthened thereby. I had to rely entirely on faith in God to get through much of it, and how blessed am I for it.
This story is a perfect example of relying on Him in faith to overcome things not yet wholly sure about and be shown by Him perfect truth in a way we can perfectly understand. We simply must walk meekly and humbly, for guidance is ever present for those who can be meek and humble. We must not harden our hearts or think we or men know, we must listen and seek His guidance.
We can continue to learn, continue revelation and eventually we are molded and have strong desires to become even as our Savior is; loving and seeking our perfect Father in Heaven's glory above all things. Then we are open to even grander things. How perfect our Father is!

91

Doctrine and Covenants 50:24 "That which is of God is light; and he that receiveth light, and continueth in God, receiveth more light; and that light growth brighter and brighter until the perfect day.

25 And again, verily I say unto you, and I say it that you may know the truth, that you may chase darkness from among you;

Faith is incredibly important to God and is different than the understanding of law. It is choosing to exercise our hope in good, in a sense choosing it for ourselves and voting and hoping for good for all. Our earnest choice until we come to learn and are able to wholly and entirely rely upon Him. It is our guidance to perfect joy. We are exercising purely our agency humbly toward what we need. We rely wholly upon God and Jesus Christ. Faith becomes and guides to knowledge of truth and is incredibly precious.

Just as we learn and appreciate joy by knowing sorrow we can grow faith as we choose to overcome doubt with faith. Faith is grown as we overcome. Israel in specific translation means, "overcomer." We are the children of Israel; the Lord is gathering Israel now.

Let us be strong in faith. It wont be easy every day to be strong and be edified of the Spirit, and because of such days we will learn to let go of the world, let go of our fears and stresses more and trust in Him more, we become strengthened as we recognize our weakness and trust in His strength. And as we do, we recognize His strength is beyond ample.

Let us wholly rely upon our Father in Heaven and recognize He is right there. Let us not doubt it in thought in any degree but be strong mentally earnestly seeking Him, for we will find Him!

For a while I thought, 'I am going to learn all of this logically and teach everyone,' to later find out, 'Oh the Lord's way is perfect, faith is that important. And I again am praising Him for His perfection. I have learned over and over that He lacks nothing His ways are abundantly perfect. I am weak, in Him alone I am strong. Oh His strength.

We are given the perfect duty in the perfect way in the perfect time. He is significantly beyond us and all things. I had the Moses realization that 'man is nothing' before God. How grateful I am that He is such a loving and good Father. His work and His glory is to bring to pass the immortality and eternal life of man, to perfectly love His children. We are His. It is true!

I will get more into this as we go on, but know that all you need is humble faith, and everything is opened to you. Simply exercise it, little by little. All confounds and it is the perfect way; our Father in Heaven is truly perfect. I forever praise Him and glorify His name and serve Him forever!

Galatians 3:5 "He therefore that ministereth to you the Spirit, and worketh miracles among you, doeth he it by the works of the law, or by the hearing of faith?

6 Even as Abraham believed God, and it was accounted to him for righteousness.

7 Know ye therefore that they which are of faith, the same are the children of Abraham."

Pertaining to 'wisdom' I think of these scriptures of Moses performing miracles. The Pharaoh's people being able to do many as well, but it was Moses' humble faith in God and God and His Almighty Power that parted the Red Sea and saved His people. Even the weak things of our Father in Heaven are so vastly above all things of man.

Again remember the importance of faith and the trial of it. The Lord truly brought me back in His wisdom. I see the path how perfect it was for me and how it even fulfilled many of His words.

Though, in a sense, 'wisdom of the world' can make trying faith somewhat harder, I was blessed greatly. I was still taught all that I needed to know, yet was put in the place to then try faith and then learn through faith; which are far, far grander things.

Truly the things of God are protected by faith. The greater things a more humble faith, the greatest things, an eye single to His glory with a full desire to serve Him.

1 Peter 1: 7 That the trial of your faith, being much more precious than of gold that perisheth, though it be tried with fire, might be found unto praise and honour and glory at the appearing of Jesus Christ:

Readers Note: I must absolutely stress this. All of these blessings were absolutely NOTHING of myself, but the grace and mercy of God. He truly does all good, and all good truly originates from Him. I am forever grateful. Only when we are humble before Him, recognizing all is His and all good is of Him, is when we can properly be prepared to be humble enough to receive His goodness.

Should the pot counsel the potter by which it was made?

All I write is not to show anything of myself other than my fallacy, incorrect paths, previously fallen ways in deception in 'wisdom,' essentially my utter weakness. I was truly lost. I write to show His perfect glory, love, kindness and perfection. I desire simply to bring those ensnared to Him that they may know His love as I know it. Our utter weakness is made perfect in His perfect strength.

93

In this the glory of God is manifested through my experience. This is all written to show the glory of our loving Father in Heaven. To show His love, mercy, long suffering, kindness, true wisdom, perfect guidance and perfect glory. I cannot even begin to glorify Him or praise Him or thank Him enough for all that has been done for me. I will serve Him forever in His wisdom. I am so thankful that He is the perfection that He is and that we are His children.

I write that we can all more clearly see His perfect goodness and great love and become closer to Him.

Chapter 10

EXPERIENCES CONTINUE

Alma 5:7-9 "Behold, he changed their hearts; yea, he awakened them out of a deep sleep, and they awoke unto God. Behold, they were in the midst of darkness; nevertheless, their souls were illuminated by the light of the everlasting word; yea, they were encircled about by the bands of death, and the chains of hell, and an everlasting destruction did await them. And now I ask of you, my brethren, were they destroyed? Behold, I say unto you, Nay, they were not, And again I ask, were the bands of death broken, and the chains of hell which encircled them about, were they loosed? I say unto you, Yea, they were loosed and their souls did expand, and they did sing redeeming love. And I say unto you that they are saved."

More experiences happened a few days after. I really wanted everyone to know what the truth was. I had truly come to know it, vastly. I understood it so much that the 'wisdom' of the world many prided themselves in were perfectly confounded. I could see clearly how Christ is necessary to fulfill the law and how grateful I am that He did; without Him we were all truly lost.

I texted everyone, friends and family and didn't care about reactions. I was humbled to the absolute dirt and above all wanted to stand for the Lord.

I had to overcome much and relied on the grace of God and His healing power. I wanted everyone to know. As far as I was concerned now, there was a new world, one in which God is intimately real and constantly acting. It was as it always had been, now I could see clearly.

I was hoping people would see how I was before, them knowing that I knew some deep things, and that they would be compelled to seek for themselves and find. Regardless of hopes, I wanted them to know the truth of our Savior. I wanted them to seek that they may find. I'm sure it was a huge surprise to many. Yet it is true, and I stood for it.

I had one newer friend I felt to reach out to. I felt incredibly bad as I kind of taught her a little bit of the things I understood. She had grown up in The Church of Jesus Christ of Latter-day Saints and had had a bad experience that took her completely away from it. It really hurt me that I had ever spoken in any way ignorantly against what now I knew to be so perfect and true.

I still to this day pray every night for every person that I ever spoke in error to. I truly always had the best intentions. Which is worth note for all of us to see how we can be acted upon in deception even in good intentions.

Many in the past who thought they have served God have done things God would not want. How we must love above all!

I really felt for her specifically because she knew about the Church, and I wanted her to know it was actually true.

I felt increasingly prompted to tell her as well. She had a hard story. I've learned the strongest people get the hardest challenges to grow and are of great use in love to our Father in Heaven to uplift His children. Humility before God and trust in Him is incredible strength.

Those with the most they have gone through generally have Christ-like love. They don't judge, they have been judged harshly and know how it feels. They aren't unkind; they have felt what it feels like to be treated harsh. They are more compassionate; they know what real hardships are like. In general hardships can help us become truly humble. The world is somewhat of be humble or be humbled situation; humility and meekness before God is a grand key.

Parts of her story were very sad. Her and her boyfriend moved away together. And unexpectedly he committed suicide. She was then forced to move back home. This was obviously devastating and I had never known much detail about it.

What little I did know is that he was a smart guy. They both grew up in the Church and both left. She would tell me occasionally that I reminded her of him because we would talk about similar things, referring to wisdom and the nature of things. He had a goal essentially to build a utopian society where everyone relied on everyone and helped everyone. I didn't know much about him but I always felt sad for her, she cared a lot for him.

It had been only a few days after the experience I had that brought me to the truth of Christ and the gospel. I had told many friends but I was being constantly prompted to contact and say the same to her.

I was driving to my mothers; I was heading to church that weekend. I could discern a strong difference as well between my house and the comforting Spirit in her home. I needed to be close to the Lord and His peace. All who seek healing as I needed in fear, seek the constant Spirit of the Lord. Stand in Holy places. Be prayerful, His Spirit will heal you.

I sent her a text that night as I was pulling into my mom's house. I told her God was real. That she knew I was well thought out. That I believe the LDS faith to be true; and although man sometimes makes mistakes and we aren't perfect (in thought of her past experience,) I wanted her to know, the gospel is profoundly true.

I wanted her to know especially that she can pray and He will be there to protect and has immense love. I quickly explained that at the end of all understanding is the truth of the Church and that I knew and understood what Joseph Smith was talking about.

I really felt to say something to her. I felt pressed in the Spirit, "You know the logical mind too perfectly, who can help her like you can?" I needed to say something and I finally had. I got a text back. But it was weird.

My phone said I had a message, so I opened up my messages. On the screen where it shows all the different peoples messages come up on an I-phone is where I saw the message first. I won't divulge her name so I will simply put underlines where her name is.

On the page with all the messages, I could see the blue dot on the left and top indicating an unread message, with words of the message next to it.

'___(her name)____ is thinking, "What came first the concept or the idea."' Or something along those lines, I would say that's 98-100 percent accurate. But that gives you the perfect idea.

I thought to myself. What an interesting thing to write back to that. Speak in third person? I had known her to often say things like, "What came first the chicken or the egg." I wasn't particularly surprised.

I clicked on the message to open up the conversation. The new message was not there at all. I went back to the screen before. There it still was. And it was the perfect length to fit in the small area of the text preview. I clicked again to get into the specific message thread. It was again not there. It only existed in the screen before in the messages preview.

It said "_____ is thinking, ...," and then gave what she was thinking. It had only been a few days since the experience I had and everything was changing. I was becoming nervous though I knew it must be the Lord.

Before she actually wrote me back, I wrote her again saying basically, "Hey, did you write this? Cuz my phone said this, and it didn't make sense. And if not, were you thinking it?"

It turns out, she had not written me that, and informed me she hadn't responded and wasn't sure what to think or say. But in fact yes, she had been thinking along the lines of exactly what was told me she was thinking.

I was fearful and quickly prayed. After what I had seen just a few days ago of a power taking over all these things, I didn't want to see such fearful things again.

Yet this time I had the feeling that this was an important prompting. The Lord had protected me from such before and this

97

occurrence was showing me that, 'Yes, this is important; she needs to know.'

I was still very fearful, this is hard to explain, but given what I had experienced I didn't want to see such things again. I prayed quickly something like, "Lord, I'm still scared of this; I know you'll protect me. Please, if you have something to show me, please do it in a way that I will not be scared." I didn't see anymore of anyone's thoughts broadcast to me illustrating the importance of helping them in such a physical manner after that. But it was truly wisdom in the Lord and I had again my faith yet the more strengthened.

The moment I messaged her after seeing the message the new message took its rightful place on the screen with all the messages on the preview screen, and the message that was there was gone. I thought how I should have screenshot it, but was entirely too scared and texted her again quickly trying to figure out what was going on then.

Regardless I had my answer; and more importantly I realized again how close the Lord was to His own work and children. And if I was prompted to speak to someone it was for a very wise purpose in Him. He knew everyone's thoughts and wanted to help all of His children.

(If anyone struggles with the same type of question such as what came first the chicken or the egg, allow me to quell such with this. Time is hilariously irrelevant before God. All things are His, that includes the understanding of time, and as we understand it here is sensed for us to learn. He is eternal. All is eternal; time is not. Don't hold yourself up on such things, I wont get too much into it, but move on, we are less than babies in comparison to what He's got going on for us.

We are children learning on the other side of 2-way glass; trust God, our loving Father in Heaven.)

The next thing she said was profound and began to illustrate some of what the Lord already knew and wanted to help with. Oh the goodness of our Father in Heaven!

She told me that the last time someone told her exactly what I was saying to her now, "literally word for word," she said, was her ex that she had sadly found dead the very next day after he had said them to her. Among all of it she re iterated how he said that Joseph Smith was right and the church is true. She explained the fear he was in the night before and a story of sadness.

She further explained that it was very weird for her to hear that from him as they had both had been on the same page about the church and God. And she let me know it was hard to hear these things from me as well. And that it was perhaps God reminding her through me. She told me she had been having an incredibly difficult time feeling anything but

98

hopelessness; and after all she had been through how could anyone blame her. It clearly was our loving Father in Heaven reminding her. He cares so much for all of His children.

As she explained the situation I could tell her ex had probably got to similar places that I was in. Something truly beyond fearful to discover and I wish none to ever know it. I had been explained this person in some manner many times by her and it seemed he was on similar deceptive paths, always seeking good, but being pulled in wrong directions unwittingly. Deep worldy 'wisdom' is a snare and great stumbling block. If God is, and He is, truth can only be resonated in as one is humble before Almighty God; all else that pulls away from truth is then deception.

Alma the Younger, in the Book of Mormon, similar to Paul, after his experience, spent the rest of his life doing his best to bring everyone he could to the truth of the gospel. He had finally truly seen truth and seen how important it is. Furthermore, he said that he couldn't stand to imagine someone having to suffer that for eternity. I am of the same mind. I cannot stand to think of anyone at all having to suffer such. I trust in the wisdom, mercy and goodness of God and I too will do my best to do all I can to help as many as possible. The perfect purposes of my Father in Heaven are my greatest goal and joy. I have simply seen clearly.

I think of this young man and his early end to life on earth. I also think of the incredible promises of God for those who stand as a witness of Him and testify. I pray that the Lord will extend those same blessings to him as his testimony comes out this way. I consistently trust in the goodness and perfection of God. Only then can I glimpse His perfect plan and endless symphony of great love. Only then can I see His hand and how He has guided me in His wisdom, and will ever guide me in His wisdom and love.

A week or so went by and I was talking to her again. I had been trying here and there to interject spiritual guidance in my feeble attempts. I was doing the best I could to be healed and fixed from the experience and basically was constantly doing my best to do the things that kept the Spirit with me.

One evening, I got sort of attacked by her. Her normal kind heart had changed and she had made up her mind that it was all bogus and she didn't want to be affected by me. From her perspective then I just wanted to be right about everything; but from mine, I had been humbled to the dirt, the Lord had shown me the right way, and I wanted to do my best for Him and to make right all that I could.

One blessing of the experience I had is that I could see far clearer how things worked and I could see how and what she was effected by. I have seen it since in others; their mind is clouded, doesn't try to listen, doesn't try to discern, just is led in anger and harshness and wisdom in themselves.

I had to humble myself to what I once felt was wrong, and watch all I thought to be right shatter, and was saved and shown real truth in real love, and now I knew what the truth was. I knew it clearly. And for the sake of everyone around I wanted them to know it too. I think of many prophets or servants of God who have simply wanted to help people see clearly and are attacked for it. I certainly can judge none.

It got to a point where I was just devastated. I did my best to stay calm and help but I had cried plenty in the last while and this was just tearing me apart.

I thought to myself, "Well, I've tried to help you; I'll just have to block you, because I can't handle this harshness."

I went to the screen to block her, and had this overwhelming strong thought. "You, are one of the very few, if not the only one, who can understand what she is going through, and what is happening to her, and what is attacking her. Is there anyone else but you that can care more? Was there anyone else like you so ensnared? Can you blame her? Can you judge her? If you don't help her, who will? If you can't help her, who can?"

I knew clearly, I forgave her. How could I judge? I was as kind as I could be and simply exited the screen to block her. I prayed for her strongly. Something I had been consistently overwhelmed with is proof of how powerful prayer is. I thank our Father in Heaven for it.

Apparently a few days later, she had fallen down from a random seizure. Stopped breathing and someone did CPR on her to bring her back to life. After some time in the hospital they found nothing wrong with her and she went home.

We talked little by little as friends and I was as heartfelt as I could be. I felt I was expected to do my very best at this point and that she was very, very, very important to the Lord, as we all are.

Over time, she would send more and more gospel messages. And through ups and downs would eventually again plant the seed of faith. She too had to go through people around her making fun and making her seem stupid for seeking in truth, but she got stronger and stronger.

I had moved and didn't talk to her much anymore; but I was always grateful and pleased to see that she had grown again a testimony of our Savior and was on the right track. Our Savior had never abandoned her and she could again see Him and be taken better care of by Him. A gift that is so amazing and I am so grateful for, I wish it for all.

Although things working on her clouded her mind at times, as we all have experienced, she broke free, rather the Savior broke her chains as He did mine and guided her back to Him.

Apparently for the last while her family had been putting her name on the prayer roll in many temples. He was aware. He is aware of all of us. The freedom and agency He gives us is very important to Him. He won't ever take us anywhere we wont go willingly. He won't attack us as the adversary, but His arm is always very lovingly outstretched.

As we grab hold in faith, He heals all, makes all right, fixes us, teaches us, comforts us, and gives us the opportunity to help others along the way. He is absolutely perfect love. I will serve Him and praise Him forever.

Chapter 11

RESTORE
See Your Way To Truth

    This chapter has much value for those ensnared in deep 'wisdom' of the world to better see clearly and see how Jesus Christ, our living Savior is necessary. This and the next will help illustrate. I will begin it with an allegory.

    A man learned much. He used his wisdom to scale a mountain. He was guided this way and that and passed pitfalls and misdirection that even the greatest climbers couldn't pass until he finally made it. He was at the highest peak, the pinnacle. He surely was the highest he could go. From up top he could see everything.

    He was above all and 'knew' all because he could see the furthest, infinitely seeming, from the highest point. Surely only the wisest and most skilled climbers could achieve such a height. The absolute pinnacle of height was his goal and he had done it.

    He was proud of the accomplishment and knowledge. So much that he always looked out at everything he could finally see.

    Soon the mountain began to shake, he eventually humbled himself and turned around and for the first time looked up from the pinnacle that he had thought he could only look down from.

    It was then he realized. He was not on the pinnacle, nor was he wise. He had had his back turned to God and was distracted by pride. God in His love had provided a staircase back to Him and to the greater things in Him.

    The mountain was no mountain but it was the very first step on the vast staircase. He humbled himself more and could finally hear the voice that he always just thought was the wind. For so long he only heard the voices praising him for getting up so high and being able to see so much and telling him to keep looking. But finally he could hear the quiet voice that always seemed on the wind.

    He continued to humble himself as he saw the infiniteness of the beautiful staircase of light and how low he was on it. As he humbled himself calm, quiet and peaceful voices became louder.

    A voice far up in the light of the staircase called down, "I went the same way as you; you were lost and now are found. Our Father is reaching down to you! Be deceived no longer brother, He lives! He is the way! The simplicity in faith, the weak things confound the wise. Faith in our Savior, Jesus Christ."

Voices shouted back from behind him begging him to look back in pride at where the man had made it to. Voices telling him to turn back around and remember how he is the greatest climber. But the mountain shook more and the man humbled himself more.

As he humbled himself more he heard more. He left his pride and wisdom behind and humbled himself. He sought faith and guidance as the voice from up the staircase was apparently perfect, peaceful and full of clearer and clearer profound truth. He couldn't turn away, especially as his mountain was crumbling.

A calm voice almost pierced through him, it came from what seemed like the very top of the infinite staircase, where the very glory and beauty and light shone.

"Yes! You finally see! Oh how I've missed you! I was the one who you called ignorant that day. I was climbing the small hill to see the beauty of the Lord and I didn't know what I was doing. Remember, I told you we need to trust the only perfect climber, our Savior. You scoffed and told me you had to become a master ourselves but I knew I could never do it. I was right, we can't do it! Our perfect master climber is the only one and he has built a bridge for us! Remember? I told you, he built the bridge and we just had to keep listening and doing our best. You saw me falling down and pointed out my weak climbing skill and didn't listen. But it was my weak climbing skill and trust in Him that led me to find the bridge! He built it for us! I knew it then and I know it now. I tried to help you but you thought I didn't understand because my wisdom wasn't of the world but in faith in my Savior. I have been doing all I can to get you to see, to help you hear! And you finally see! Come home, listen to him! Humble yourself!"

The climber began to see the impossibility of the climb that was made. He couldn't make it. It was simply impossible for anyone less than perfect. He humbled himself harder and humbly called out to God to help him.

The mountain was shaking and cracking and crumbling. He wanted off of it, how wrong he had been. He knew he needed help. He knelt and called out with everything to be saved from the crumbling mountain he was on.

He felt peace and calm. He opened his eyes and saw himself vastly farther up the steps, moved up by a bright and beautiful shining bridge. Everything was so peaceful. He looked back and saw many trying to climb the mountain with their back turned to the staircase and to their Father in Heaven.

A calm and peaceful voice pierced in absolute power through Him.

"I'm so happy you're back. Now you know! My son, I have missed you. Trust in me and be humble before me so I can help you make it to the top. You are safe now. You are finally out of that deep deception that kept your back turned from me. Help all of them that you can. I love you all dearly."

The voice gestured to the side of the high step he was on. On the side was the bridge built by the master climber, the Savior. All those on the ground could come up to that vast height through faith on Him.

He saw people coming up the bridge, he could tell a very high price was paid for him to be able to walk up such, people he would have called ignorant in the path, people making it by faith on the Savior, they listened humbly and were guided all the higher. As things were crumbling below they were safe.

"We are so happy we found Him and you did too! We are in His light now; lets keep going up! Let's help those that think they are wise of themselves down there looking down on everyone from the mountain, let's help them see the way; their back is turned! Sure they are harsh to us at times and think we are ignorant because we are unlearned but we must help them see the truth."

The once prideful climber was so happy to be around such a humble people. As he humbled himself he heard more. He wanted to help, he realized his divinity more and how much of a child he was. He wanted to show the truth to others more and help them to humble themselves to hear more. All the while he sought with his whole desire single to the glory of his Father in Heaven and His Savior who saved Him. He wanted to do everything to walk in the Holy Spirit.

He looked down from a height he could have never before even comprehended. He could see more clearly than he ever thought possible. And this time, the vastness humbled him instead of making him feel like he was on top.

He could see so much more looking down now. He saw the voices go down from above, he yelled himself, some humbly listened, and others listened to the other voice.

He could now see an opposite wind coming up from incredibly deep. The below wind came up, and with it there was a chain on the high mountain, ready to be pulled down at any moment. The wind built everyone up in pride and pushed them to keep walking to all places where they could be pulled down or pull down others.

He was able to watch himself in the past, talking with the person who tried to help him to the bridge. There was a wind from above, "Listen! Just because you can climb well doesn't mean anything, you cannot make it yourself, please listen! Don't listen to the other wind!"

104

He saw that he didn't listen to the person's actual words nor would he hear the words in the wind, he was too prideful and listened to the wind that came from below. "You are the greatest climber. This person is an amateur climber and will never understand climbing and wisdom like you. They don't understand what the 'bridge' is and they can't even understand the symbolism all over the place. One day this poor climber will get it."

He watched his past and was saddened by his weakness and so thankful to the only perfect and master climber who he could now see walked with him every step, letting him make his own mistakes, ready to reach out and save him when he called out for help. He knew he had listened to deception and he knew how deep it was.

He realized everyone up there wanted to help those below, but he knew there were those that thought themselves 'wise' or 'master climbers' and because of that they were in a deeper deception. Their 'wisdom' was twisted in such a way that it was a great stumbling block to truth. He knew how they had thought.

He saw the path he walked and the turn to the bridge was wrongly discerned by him as simply a symbol to go the opposite way to him, his 'wisdom' was of greatest value to him. He saw the true right way to the bridge as something to scoff at and saw as foolishness. He couldn't humble himself to see it. It was a stumbling block for it was twisted and kept him from seeing clearly.

He had compassion on the 'wise' in their own eyes, he prayed humbly that he could help them see the right way. He knew that his experience of the same could help them see clearly. He called down to them loudly. "Humble yourselves. Look, I went this way."

He again asked to understand humbly and walked the way he was told was safe to walk, not by the edge of the stairs but in the middle, in obedience, in safety. As he humbled himself he was guided and blessed with understanding of all things and went up the stairs.

The love grew and he could see how much he was loved and cared bout, because of this his desire greatly grew to love all and help those seeing so wrong, his brothers and sisters who were blinded by pride and 'wisdom.'

It was all real after all. God Almighty indeed created all things, the Savior Jesus Christ was utterly necessary and the Holy Spirit bore witness to all the humble hearts and guided perfectly.

Before I move on entirely from the partial topic of the 'wisdom,' I will use the next few chapters to sum this up in a sense, and show any ensnared how to properly see and extrapolate to necessary truth that is Jesus Christ.

There is opportunity for pragmatic discernment out of the stumbling block and to realization that Jesus Christ is necessary and the way, the truth and the life. This may be confusing to some, though still worthwhile I believe for all. Then I'll move on to matters centered on the rock of truth and further some personal story as well.

I will quickly describe importance of commandments and quickly extrapolate truth. I will also extrapolate the importance of understanding it in relation to the "wisdom" of the world.

This will be better understood by those with specific understanding in 'wisdom' with the intent to show them clearly the right way; a removal of the stumbling block. I believe it will still be beneficial in a sense for anyone although it may seem confusing. Remember, faith in Christ is the truth and pure wisdom, don't look beyond the mark.

Commandments can seem difficult to some, but when He shows you truth, we suddenly change from seeing the simple things the world thinks are 'no big deal' to "Wow, how could I have been so deceived and naïve? The world is so fallen into iniquity."

Commandments are a guardrail. They can be easily discerned as important by one understanding. There are two overall philosophies in opposite of each other. One: that there is a grand purpose, and everything matters perfectly and infinitely (importance of love discerned). Two: that there is no purpose, and nothing matters.

If there is deception there is truth in opposite. They must have an opposite for us to discern either. Therefore if truth exists, and singular truth exists, as it does, in the opposite there must be seemingly endless possibilities that resemble infinite variable truths based on the specific observer, endless deception. Singular truth, and endless deception in opposite.

If nothing matters, and no one path is right and no one path is wrong, and there is no real defined purpose, what does sin matter? Sadly this is the viewpoint of those with 'knowledge' of the world in the common stumbling block view of understanding it. Although many have good intentions and love and want good, although deceived, many have the thought of, 'In this infinity why does anything matter? It doesn't.' and thus they are led into sin and in their own 'wisdom' deceive themselves and ensnare themselves.

The 'ditto' of personal surrounding pertaining to our earnest expectations becomes an endless deception for those who cannot see clearly that such is their inherent blessing of agency and freedom given to all by our Father in Heaven.

As a radio enjoying tuning to all frequency and seeking things for and of themselves, not realizing lies on every station, for their

106

perspective is such of pointlessness or pride. They can only perceive the lies and deception; when they 'tune' in humility, they then can see clearly what they couldn't before. They see how the pride kept them tuned to all deception. They see above themselves finally, where they couldn't before look, and see the strait and narrow path of singular truth that they can now have faith in and tune to singular truth in opposition to their endless deception.

Extrapolation of self-centered may seem vast in 'wisdom' until humble faith is exercised to find our Father in Heaven; when He is seen in truth as center and originator and creator we can come to see His incredible and utterly vast and endless glorious symphony. This is far grander than we can yet imagine and even glimpsing His glory is utterly incredible and amazing. Seeing clearly we come to see the plan He has always had for us, His little child.

We will get deeper and clearer. Those few in 'wisdom' will gain much here and be set right in clarity as we go along. Those without, remember true wisdom is given from our Father in Heaven; skim through, don't get too deep if you don't want. There is more for everyone in the next chapters.

I don't judge, been there; I just wish to help. I will use many angles to show the same things.

Those in 'wisdom' don't perceive the truth that if there is endless possibilities and paths and nothing is singular truth, that their 'truth' is that all paths are individual truth, and that there is no, 'specific definite truth;' they don't understand that for that to be, there must be in the opposite one singular path defined and true truth.

With that discerned then one can see that understanding the 'wisdom' without being humble before God at the center, they are in a sense building their own prisons of endless deception. Deception wars against truth, and guides in all paths that lead away from singular truth. Continuously deception is manifested and one is prideful in their wisdom. If we are not walking in the Spirit of God, made possible by being clean through faith in our Savior Jesus Christ and His atonement, (I will explain this more soon) then we are prone to the opposite ever pecking spirit of deception.

One analogy is this. They are in a big city with a wall around it. They are subtly, unwittingly controlled. They are prideful in the fact that they have a car to drive around the vast and endless city; one that few have. They look at people walking around and think themselves better and wiser; they have a car after all. The roads go all over where those who walk rarely see them and don't understand. They can drive anywhere, there are endless roads and they can get anywhere they want.

107

However, the only small, strait and narrow path out of the endless, yet walled, city is a small walking path through the single gate out of the city, far from any roads.

The humble and meek, still few among those without the cars, including those few wise enough to get out of their cars and seek humbly, those few find the small and humble walking path.

Most don't have a car, most walk, and are yet taken away from even the belief that there is a single gate that they truly can be led to the Kingdom of God through. They scoff.

Many in their car look down at all those walking thinking, "One day they will walk off the walking paths and see there are cars then they will be wise like us."

They are deceived. Even if this 'car' can fly, even if it can travel through all space and time, and seemingly understand the next 'dimension(s)', they are unwittingly encamped with walls in a fallen state. Their perceived wisdom takes them everywhere possible but the road they cannot go in a car. They are ensnared and miss the narrow path to truth which requires humility to find. Jesus Christ is necessary.

Those walking in the 'wisdom' of the world, which greatly confounds and comes to nothing, are victims of themselves. They drive around and exercise their great pride in wisdom, scoffing at those walking. Thinking of the few that get out of the car that they don't quite 'get it' all; maybe they didn't learn all the cool features of the car, and they continue driving around thinking themselves wise. The more they drive the deeper deception of darkness guides generally.

Few ever perceiving that they are in a grand test and undergoing teaching, awaiting those qualified to humbly walk out in truth, back home, to where God is by trusting the God of all, their very Father in Heaven. Trusting He who came down to the city to save us, who had broken down the wall Himself and built the only gate out. In perfect wisdom. He prepared the way Himself, and only He can lead you out, humbly.

We are as children in a day care with double sided glass, learning; our Father and Holy 'adults' looking in, helping us as we seek it.

Only by walking and seeking in faith will we find the humble and strait and narrow path to without the walls, to freedom. Humility; how are we to act before our very Father, the one who created us and all things? Humbly. We must resonate in truth to find it. And humble we must be to be cleansed through our loving Savior and His atonement for us, His blood that He gave, in His perfection, for us.

Much can be learned and seen from this analogy.

Commandments then can be discerned as walking in deception or truth. Singular truth that all matters infinitely with infinite purpose we can suddenly see that the things that seem simple to the world become sacred; simply through seeing we are here for a perfect and vast purpose. Families, pro creation, the way we treat others, etc. We can discern that looking to our grand exemplar even Jesus Christ, is the only and right way.

We can thus appreciate commandments and see that they are a guardrail to keep us as we must be. For walking as though nothing matters and that all is non-purpose is walking in deception, for He who has created all things has done it in a perfect and grand symphony. We can see how sacred things are then twisted and sin that keeps us from the strait and narrow path can become a social norm. As we lose the eternal perspective in truth, our perspective is skewed to view in deception and we are lulled away captive.

Matthew 7:13-14 "Enter ye in the strait gate: for wide is the gate, and broad is the way, that leadeth to destruction, and many there be which go in thereat: Because strait is the gate, and narrow is the way, which leadeth unto life, and few there be that find it."

Furthermore, let me extrapolate the necessity of Christ to many in a slight mantle, and a more clear help to those who walk in deception in 'wisdom.'

Let me begin by pointing out E=mc2. It is simply another way of showing that all things are made up of energy. This is simple, this is known. The scriptures accurately show that all things are made of the Light of Christ. All things are in fact God's and He rules all things.

E=mc2 is that matter, or things or substance, multiplied by the speed of light squared, a very, very large number, is the amount of energy within. I wont get into the proper understanding of this, but I sought simply to use a famous equation of Einstein. This shows us that all is energy, and lots of it. From a physical understanding, all matter is very tightly condensed energy in a sense. Again, I'm speaking in temporal understanding. The point here is to see that all is made up of the same thing, energy, the Light of Christ as referred to in scripture and is truth.

Some see this incorrectly that we are all one vast energy pointlessly and endlessly playing with itself. One in this view simply doesn't understand the vastness of eternity. The perfect kingdom is. God is. Truth is that He is and has created all things. We will get into this. Keep on.

109

All things are of God, the Light of Christ is the perfect way to understand, His eternal light is within us. We are further told above this in scripture that all is spirit and spirit is matter, a very fine and less dense version thereof. Some look at this that all is mind; whether clearly or in deception. All is God's. Of Him. This is of help in trying to help get a spiritual understating across in a physical way for those of the world to better get an idea. Any who truly seek wisdom of the subjects at hand, seek in truth, in the scriptures and revelations from God. The best wisdom here to start would be that all is His.

Doctrine and Covenants 88:41 "He comprehendeth all things, and all things are before him, and all things are round about him; and he is above all things, and in all things, and is through all things, and is round about all things; and all things are by him, and of him, even God, forever and ever."

A father who is a professional boxer, the greatest ever, he has never been beaten has a son. Should the son ever say, "I am just as my father is in every way, I have fists and look I can understand the rules of boxing." Should the toddler think such things and get into the ring with boxers far bigger than he can imagine or yet understand? This child sees his similarity to his father, after all he is of him. He will still not clearly understand how perfect of a boxer his dad is. He must see that he is a child. Though he can grow up, he will never be his father. He is his son. Though he is in a sense a drop of his father and can become a better boxer he cannot be what created him in terms of being.

The son can walk on his own and learn about boxing himself and become a good boxer, but he will never receive all his father, the greatest ever, has for him. But if he is humble to his father, he can teach him much more, he can teach him everything, the right way. If he says, "I don't need your help, I have fists and know how to box," simply because all the boxers he yet sees are weaker than him, does the kid have any understanding?

This is a very rough way to understand a greater concept. Some experience the same on a vastly, vastly, vastly incomprehensible scale. For how can we understand our endless Father in Heaven entirely? All is His. Everywhere you step, think, walk, is within His creation, even you, are His creation and His child. He simply allows us to learn as we will in complete freedom.

We experience opposition in all things to learn vital lessons here and be able to comprehend joy. We are children. Children. We left the Kingdom and palace that upon return we may appreciate it and endlessly

110

grow in joy for His glory; for we will know His utter never ending perfection. All is in His perfect wisdom. We must be humble and choose Him. We must seek; the promise is that we will find.

I will continue to that of main importance for this area. Christ is essential.

One rather famous smooth voice of the deep 'wisdom,' understood in part and in deception (particularly eastern 'enlightenment') would be that of the famous philosopher Alan Watts. His perspective would be that our own consciousness is 'creating' even God. It is a wrong understanding of eternity and whence things are. This is a terrible incorrect extrapolation in the most wrong areas to continue in the pride of the 'wisdom' he holds, keeping him from the truth, thinking himself to know of himself. One can see the deception of the adversary in pride.

Watts' perspective shatters quickly and in many extrapolations. Though it is the perspective he holds for he can only see through his wisdom with himself centered. It confounds.

Again, remember, I judge none, neither can I. I guide to real truth. If I hadn't been and seen and know how can I guide?

Weigh that what is outside of time is outside of time, all is, and what can even be imagined to be, or 'created,' as Watts would put it, is. Therefore if we can only imagine God, He is still 'before' us, the beginning and the end and creator of all things and we have our 'consciousness' and light in Him; the Light of Christ after all is how we abound and we are of Him.

Timeless Extrapolation in "Time"

This can be better extrapolated even to the realization of entire truth through the infinite ends of opposites.

I will now illustrate this and there is fruit here for those who will consider it clearly. Interestingly we can only see the full picture after we have faith in God, or at least humble ourselves to see the clear picture.

Let us imagine for a moment. If one puts themselves at the center of all things, a perspective of them in eternity, they have all imaginable infinitely all around them, 'spherically.'

All imaginations of what is infinitely become placed all around. All things imaginable that are good and of love are above; and that which is opposite and of fear and darkness below. And all things that are of other things, the gray area thoughts and things at the sides, etc. We can discern this forever and ever in every direction.

The point we are at currently is learning and experiencing the opposites, so it is as if we are at the centerline. Our perspective in this

111

thought extrapolation is centrically such, infinity is all things continuing forever infinitely round about. Again, as we extrapolate this we can come to discern that all things above and below us, good and bad to simplify, extend infinitely.

As we cannot properly discern 'all things' lets see that infinitely 'up' we eventually come to a never ending infinitely glorified God of light and goodness and love, even the originator and endless source of all good, (which we will further extrapolate to truth of such). He is endless and by Him all things must have been created as He is light and one in perfect power above all in goodness that is endless. Therefore, in law, let us understand that the opposite is true, endless darkness and the powers that be there, endlessly below. The Bible calls it the pit. By law alone we can discern that these things can and do exist, and if they can, at that level of power, they do; eternity is infinite and the opposites are clear for existence. There are ultimately two pinnacle powers in infinites. Our perfect Father in Heaven, light; and the adversary of truth, darkness. Darkness is because of light.

Is infinity an even number? 0. In which is all things. Our Father in Heaven being from everlasting to everlasting by Him which all things are. (We will extrapolate to even this.)

On God's side of infinite never-ending goodness and purity and light, we can discern that He is the creator of all things. He is the source of all things good. He is the source of love, light, life itself! He is life; He is love.

In opposite, as we perceive in this existence, darkness comes to existence, hate, darkness, death, and you don't want to be there.

How can such be? In nothingness there is simply nothing. But when there is light, suddenly in it's opposite there is darkness; it must be for light to be discerned. +1-1. By light we have the sudden perception of both sides. Light creates darkness.

One cannot pour out darkness and create light. One shines light and darkness is discerned outside of such, darkness leaves. One cannot throw darkness at light. But light removes darkness. He is light, and the darkness comprehends not.

In the physical fallen realm, where we are now, we experience both light and dark. God is the originator; light is the originator. (We will further extrapolate such soon.) We are here learning opposites, which is really the only way to understand anything, and thereby we learn even direction.

Between influences of darkness pecking at us and our inherent nature of light within us, (guidance from the source of light, even our Father,) between such we have our being. Between these two infinite influences 'working on' us, if you will, we have our being and learn, it is

112

as sides of a ladder we go up and learn by our own experience. We eventually choose a side. We are free. Light and love or darkness.

"In your head they are fighting."

Jesus Christ saves us from the war and the brokenness of the law. He fulfills it. We will get into it more.

Time is irrelevant; it is all simply His. Eternity is, God lives. We experience physical 'life' here because we have physical 'death' in opposite. All is eternal. Our spirit is eternal and we are made by God our Father. We are of Him; we are His children.

It is hard for us who live in 'time' to try to recognize that it is not and the true viewpoint is that of consistent eternity in the infinite present. Thinking often on the subject will make it easier to understand, especially as we prayerfully ask for revelation and understanding from God, though I think most will be content as they are.

I will try to quickly show yet another quick extrapolation to better show some of this and help those to understand it in a perspective of 'time.'

(This is probably rather poorly done but when considered you can probably get a much better idea. After all I am trying to reach a wide variety of different thinkers. Regardless, there is value.)

I do still believe there is very much fruit here for those ensnared in 'wisdom' to see their way out. Humbly and prayerfully consider it.

"In the beginning," if you will, there was nothing. There is nothing. Yet what is nothing? In fact there cannot be nothing without something, as they cancel each other out and make nothing. For nothing is something. Rather there cannot be nothing without everything or at least a conscious observer recognizing the nothing, that observer will soon realize what is within itself in opposite, if it is the first observer, our Father, or what is in opposite to the nothing pertaining to whom is observing and where they truly fit in humility.

This is going to be extrapolated as though time is, though it is not. So it isn't fully correct but will give our small understandings a way of comprehension.

As we get into what that 'something' is in opposite of the 'nothing' it cannot be an inanimate physical object. For one all 'physical,' in a physical sense, is still simply densely compacted 'energy.'

For 2 we cannot have anything unless it is perceived or consciously observed. Nothing cannot perceive the 'physical' something and the 'physical something' cannot perceive itself or the nothing. So

113

there is nothing 'physical.' A dead rock or inanimate object cannot be the only thing in opposition to nothing. For what comprehends either.

When we get down to it, there simply must have been a first observer of the nothing; speaking in terms of time here.

The only thing then that there can be in this true nothing, as we can understand it, is nothing and the perception or perceiver of it. That perception being a single 'consciousness' or spirit which would be able to perceive it, the nothing. We can come to the fact that essentially it 'started' with a single consciousness perceive itself.

We therefore have the opposition of nothing and something, that something being the beginning of true creation (as we think in terms of time) and that something is a consciousness or Spirit.

This will become, (out of time,) everything and nothing. Similar to 0's and 1's of computers, eventually extrapolating to all things, in time, by things so simple. Imagine consistent eternity.

Though both are a something in this sense 1's and 0's, unlike nothing. It is the thing that makes sense of it, 1's and 0's, and understands it and perceives it and makes and creates and perceives that is of vital important. The 'consciousness,' spirit of the 'beginning,' God.

We must continue the extrapolation of eternity to get to the truth and necessity of Christ.

As we go back to the 'beginning' and seek to understand this through the lens of "time," this Spirit can therefore perceive the 'nothing' as it is in opposite of itself. And it can perceive itself as it is in opposite of the nothing.

What we come to is nothing, other then the perception of it. Therefore, there is one in the beginning and that one perceives. There is singular consciousness.

These few things is where many in 'wisdom' can stumble and be led in deception as one can eventually come to base 'laws' and understandings therein, though most often are come to in vast deception. I judge none. The circles within circles are endless and they see the same to themselves and comprehend not the infinitely larger circle they are a tiny part of; not extrapolating to the endlessness of what is, thereby finding God our Father in Heaven and necessity of our Savior to get home. (We will continue.)

Oh how big our Father in Heaven!

For anyone to assume that a physical big bang of something physical is the beginning of all things and that eventually led to gaining 'consciousness' is a sheer lack of understanding even the deeper laws that later become confounded. There must be consciousness, there must be observation, nothing is nothing if it cannot perceive itself, which it cannot as it is nothing.

114

Nothing cannot be of itself, for it to truly exist there must be something, otherwise it cannot be known or perceived. It cannot be perceived without an observer even if there were something in the opposite; if there was nothing and a pea of something there would be nothing still. Consciousness, or spirit, is the 'beginning.' Time still is nothing but this will help us get there.

As we go back to 'the beginning,' we now have nothing, we have one to perceive that nothing as it is in opposite to it, for it is something or at least it can perceive what is, self, nothing. We then really only have the one who perceives. The nothing cannot think, it cannot discern, it cannot be anything. It is infinitely nothing.

The perception of God, if you will in this crude representation, realizes (in time) that 'He' is the opposite of that infinite nothing and that He is infinitely something. Something infinitely. Within Him is infinitely nothing as well as infinitely everything. (When we take away time, which is not, we have the beginning and the end right away, which is that there is nothing, but there is also everything, but we will get there the right way in time.)

In time He realizes He is infinite. Something infinitely. The perception of that infinite nothing and the opposite that He is infinite grows, as does perception.

Soon we come to understanding, "Let there be light." The thoughts and perceptions of God in 'time' can be thought as potentials by us of what there could be in the infinitely something. He does what He does and comprehends vast concepts, which appear vast to us simply because we have a perspective that is far smaller. He is light. (Remember we are thinking 'in time,' He is and always has been infinitely all things, the beginning and the end, one eternal round.)

There is everything and nothing now and already and always. He is unchanging and infinite. Forever growing in perfection and glory and goodness and love. Forever infinitely upward to all eternal glory.

As we go along, thinking in 'time' to understand. The "Let there be light," comprehension emits light from His infinite something. He therefore becomes the light. And as He becomes the light He comes to know the opposite immediately, darkness. For without understanding darkness, how can He perceive the light? Darkness is an inevitability of light. For Him to know and comprehend light, He also must comprehend darkness. And He comprehendeth all things. For what is, is of Him.

One cannot take light away by 'throwing' darkness at it, but light shines and dispels darkness; but darkness is created to perceive the light. The opposite is necessary to understand each other. Therefore there still is always nothing, and in the opposite of 'nothing' to truly have nothing, everything. "The light shineth in darkness, and the darkness comprehendeth it not;"

As we continue to extrapolate 'in time,' we can then come to a relative discernment of the spiritual equivalent of Eve being created from the rib of Adam.

God, who is infinitely something (as well as nothing because all 'cancel out' if you will, yet is for He discerns such; best to just say, 'He infinitely is,') and can eventually create all things, thinking in 'time,' by comprehending something within His infiniteness.

Thinking in time, He eventually creates a consciousness like Him from the bosom of His eternal self. This is the beginning of an eternal family that continues. Hereby comes love, and all the good things of light. For those that are of Him, His offspring, in His bosom of infiniteness are loved perfectly as they are all one in love. That of God is living, and lives forever, as eternity is what we are of and time is not. He is life.

Love then is perceived by perceiving the opposite that is created outside of Him in the once nothingness that is now, darkness. That which used to be 'nothing' in opposition of Him who could comprehend it, is now become also hate and darkness. For He is now, (thinking in 'time,') light and love. In this 'nothing' in opposite to Him who is everything, this nothing now is darkness and in it now we have hate.

Keep in mind, He must know both sides to understand.

God our Father in Heaven, has a family, more of himself, more Spirit children. He is love and creates love. His children filled with and in the love, yet not fully being able to perceive it as they don't know the opposite. They are within Him and His love thus far.

He is perfect as He is the light. He determines the opposite of all things that are and created of Him. The principles of agency and freedom for His vast children are vastly important for He is perfect, love and freedom.

Eventually some of His kids learn and become wiser, He gives opportunities for such and guides as much as they will trust Him and hear Him; and as they are of Him who is infinite, and there is no time, truly, they too are infinite.

One of these later thinks itself wise and attempts to take over and deceive many, seeking own glory at any cost.

Eventually this becomes so disrupted that God casts this one out of His Kingdom and into the darkness, into the infinite opposite of His infinite light. Where now there is no light, only the opposite of all the good things that are in opposition to all the good our Father is and 'in time,' has become.

In such area of darkness is lost the very ties to the infinite source of all light and goodness. The branch cannot do anything of itself unless it is connected to the vine, the infinite source, God. This thought can help us come a big step closer to realizing the importance of being on His side and the importance of Christ.

1/3 it is said followed the deception of darkness and became living in what is called outer darkness.

God's purposes are infinite and love and eternal families grow. He wants His children taught well and to continue in the family business of love and joy. How can His beloved children know joy unless they have the perspective of the opposite of joy to see it? How can His children know the great blessing of the kingdom if they cannot understand and perceive love and all the goodness? They cannot understand it unless they should experience the opposite.

So then a great teaching opportunity becomes necessary. They are to understand opposites by going to a fallen world. Fallen because it is out of perfection of God alone. Instead it is perfectly set up in oppositions of all things. There is physical death, and therefore physical life. There is happiness and sadness, pain and pleasure, love and hate and all things in opposite.

There is singular truth and the small and narrow path of truth to it, furthermore not pushed upon us as truth and light honors freedom; and in opposition, sadly, there is a wide path of deception and loud shouted lies that will, in opposite, shout and jab and not honor our freedom to keep us away from that path of light and truth.

It becomes a great blessing then that light can dispel all darkness; the infinite wisdom of God, all is His design.

These things seem harsh and difficult but without coming here to receive a physical body, in relative opposite of spirit, we wouldn't come to understand all the things necessary for us to gain direction and thereby know happiness and joy. We would be not able to discern or understand things. We can infinitely seek love and joy. How we are children in understanding and children before Him forever.

After we are 'fallen' how can we ever get back into the presence of our Father? He is perfect. We have defiled ourselves in sin and in the opposite of perfect love and sacred purpose, we have acted as though nothing mattered, we have done things that take us away from the perfection we once were.

We are greatly blessed. God our Father, in His great love, sent His only begotten Son, Jesus Christ, to come down, be the only one who would and could stay perfect, and show us the perfect way. He then suffered the atonement which caused even God to tremble because of pain for our sins, though He Himself did not deserve to suffer. He did this for us and paid the price of us.

He suffered the significant pains of opposition and the powers that are infinitely there in opposite of our Father, that we would not have to. We can be made glorious through faith, through Him. We are clean through humble faith in repentance in Him.

Through exercising faith in Him we choose to exercise our infinite freedom, that we are given in agency, in truth. And in seeking truth we choose to seek He who is the author of truth, God, who has prepared the way for us and He can then help us get back to Him. His plan is perfect.

And as we seek we will find. He will then be able to guide, because we choose to seek. As we faithfully trust Him and seek Him and allow it we can be guided to all truth as we resonate in it through childlike humble faith.

We are then brought back into the kingdom of God, by His grace and our Savior Jesus Christ who brought back all power again and forever to the light.

Jesus Christ has fallen and gone through all darkness for us, He comprehends all things and has the keys of all things for all things are His. His infinite atonement was and is eternally important for us in more ways than one. (Remember time again is irrelevant.)

We have been able to understand eternity because we could understand the opposite of time.

Really, in the 'beginning,' there was nothing and the perceiver, who is everything. There is everything and nothing.

There was no time, and it is hard for us to understand but really there is nothing and there is God. And in Him there are all things and all things are by and for Him.

So from a true and eternal perspective, in the beginning there is God and in Him there is everything already. The perfect kingdom already, the opposites, all things and His discernment of it; in this can be further discerned the necessity of the atonement of our Savior. All is right then and right there. There becomes an infinite present, which becomes quite deep. True wisdom is for God to teach when we are ready. The milk of the word is perfect. The simple is made wise and even wiser than the wisdom of the wise.

Psalm 19:7 "The law of the Lord is perfect, converting the soul: the testimony of the Lord is sure, making wise the simple."

We must be fully perfect as our Father in Heaven is, he cannot defile himself and He is infinitely good and love, even the source of

118

such. How can we resonate with Him as we are not perfect? We must be perfect by exercising our path and direction, even our faith in our Savior Jesus Christ. Thereby choosing Him, our Savior that we need.

He was perfect and innocent and didn't deserve it, yet He took our suffering, all suffering, upon Him, that we may become righteousness in Him. Glimpsing this in the smallest degree brings me to utter awe and longing to eternally praise and serve Him. How blessed we are!

Within 0 is then everything. Is God. We come to God, by which all is and we are. All is His, by Him and of Him. His wisdom is significantly, (a word doesn't exist to convey significance) beyond us. And will ever be so, for He created all things, even us. All is of Him and His! He is the Great I Am. He is.

We are children. Just as Moses realized, 'Man is nothing.' Yet we are so loved with perfect purpose.

Many may come to deeper and deeper personal 'wisdoms' and more 'Ah ha!''s and think them selves more and more wise, exalting themselves and digging a deception trench of pride. It will all collapse and the true wisdom of humility before God should be seen now and not after the full and very deep circle. Oh be wise, what can I say more.

Many can extrapolate the same types of things and come to the famous, "I think therefore I am." Thinking themselves to be wise; they are a drop of God made out of the eternity that is our Father. There are scriptures in Isaiah warning people who say "I am, and none else beside me," it is not true wisdom and the 'wisdom' of the wise and of the world perishes. Humility before our Father in Heaven is wisdom.

If we see ourselves at the pinnacle per say, in pride, we can only perceive what is below us and what is below will effect and guide in deception. Our back is turned to the greater and even the source, our home, our Father in Heaven.

In the opposite, if we see ourselves abased and at the bottom we then can perceive what is above and beyond us, we are humbled, then that which is good and above leads and guides as we seek Him to guide us.

Luke 14:11 "For whosoever exalteth himself shall be abased; and he that humbleth himself shall be exalted.

If one chooses to continue in such a way in the 'wisdom' as the world sees, they will eventually come to see by what they are led and how they are in vast deception from the strait and narrow path of true truth. I wish this upon none. The best these can see is all things without

119

glory, they are cut off from the source of light, in darkness and sadly it seems many go ways of dark things. I have perceived some in such areas eventually seeing grander things through fallen eyes as 'magic' or occult lenses or yet deeper deceptions, even becoming slaves to darkness and taken over by such. Deception truly takes over. Restore.

Those who humble themselves and choose the 'foolish' things, by the world's standard, even humble faith in Jesus Christ, and seek the guidance of our Father in Heaven, will come to significant and great revelation. The 'wisdom' of the wise becomes laughably small as all things are magnified and made honorable for His righteous children walking in His ways. All is our Father in Heaven's. The meek inherit.

We who walk in humble faith are on the way back home and resonate with our Father in Heaven. We have the source of all light and goodness and become light in the world. Shining the Kingdom of our true home from within us out into the world. We come to gain a perspective of His infinitely perfect and continuously purposeful, even vastly full of infinite wisdom, plan. We see Him moving in His perfect glory, majesty and power.

We become brought up high into the light of the staircase, seeing below those thinking of themselves wise walking in such endless deception. Alas, all things are done by wisdom of Him who knows all things. And it is the time that He is reaching out for those to see and hear, to be humble and receive and come home. How grateful I am for His perfection and goodness. The way is prepared. The law of Jesus Christ supersedes all things. He truly is the way, the truth and the life.

Doctrine and Covenants 112:13 "And after their temptations, and much tribulation, behold, I, the Lord, will feel after them, and if they harden not their hearts, and stiffen not their necks against me, they shall be converted, and I will heal them."

Many see in simplicity and say, 'It's all good man, we are all one,' this doesn't change the opposition that is and the very real powers of deception. Scriptures that speak of the adversary 'lulling away' into 'carnal security' come to mind.

2 Nephi 28:21 "And others will he pacify, and lull them away into carnal security, that they will say: All is well in Zion; yea, Zion prospereth, all is well – and thus the devil cheateth their souls, and leadeth them away carefully down to hell.

22 And behold, others he flattereth away, and telleth them there is no hell; and he saith unto them: I am no devil, for there is none – and

thus he whispereth in their ears, until he grasps them with his awful chains, from whence there is no deliverance.

27 Yea, wo be unto him that saith: We have received, and we need no more!

28 And in fine, wo unto all those who tremble, and are angry because of the truth of God! For behold, he that is built upon the rock receiveth it with gladness; and he that is built upon the sandy foundation trembleth lest he shall fall.

29 Wo be unto him that shall say: We have received the word of God, and we need no more of the word of God, for we have enough!

30 For behold, thus saith the Lord God: I will give unto the children of men line upon line, precept upon precept, here a little and there a little; and blessed are those who hearken unto my precepts, and lend an ear unto my counsel, for they shall learn wisdom; for unto him that receiveth I will give more; and from them that shall say, We have enough, from them shall be taken away even that which they have.

31 Cursed is he that putteth his trust in man, or maketh flesh his arm, or shall hearken unto the precepts of men, save their precepts shall be given by the power of the Holy Ghost.

32 Wo be unto the Gentiles, saith the Lord God of Hosts! For notwithstanding I shall lengthen out mine arm unto them from day to day, they will deny me; nevertheless, I will be merciful unto them, saith the Lord God, if they will repent and come unto me; for mine arm is lengthened out all the day long, saith the Lord God of Hosts."

We must be careful and see things clearly. He is ever present and guiding, as much as we will hear, back to Him. Let us hear Him. At certain points light shines bright for us to see, may we hold onto light and seek that we may find. There is a deceptive power at work. I can judge none. I am so thankful for Him.

Sacred geometry and such was interesting to me and when I came to see the truth and vast deception I was in I was throwing away sri yantras and other things depicting a simple deep law that I thought myself wise in. So wrongly and incorrectly understood. How deceived. How thankful I am to my Father in Heaven.

I thought of such things 'cooly' only simply depicting a deep law in deep ways, how silly the wisdom of the world, and I later found scripture. Not that I was worshipping anything, but I saw it as a simple law and was led in deception and the wrong way in it. But I was saved and proved truth in God, the 'wisdom' confounded. I saw things in ancient scripture depicted; talking of first how essentially the wisdom of Egypt will fail and they continued on.

121

Isaiah 30:22 "Ye shall defile also the covering of thy graven images of silver, and the ornament of thy molten images of gold: thou shalt cast them away as a menstruous cloth; thou shalt say unto it, Get thee hence."

I wanted nothing to do with anything that wasn't first and foremost God, my Father in Heaven; He who created all things.

We are living in the spiritual equivalent of the Lord rescuing His children from Egypt, spiritual Egypt. We are living in the gathering of Israel.

Truly the wisdom of the wise perishes and the 'foolish' things of the world confound the mighty.

I had no real understanding of what was though I was deep in 'knowledge' and thought myself so wise, and I understood much very deep. The wisdom of the wise truly perishes, just as the Bible says. And that written thousands of years ago will depict your exact steps then tell you how you were told before that you would know. Alas, He is so merciful and good.

Alma 37:7 "And the Lord God doth work by means to bring about his great and eternal purposes; and by very small means the Lord doth confound the wise and bringeth about the salvation of many souls."

OH BE WISE, WHAT CAN I SAY MORE!? And yet still I will get deeper into helping see clearly and out of the stumbling block that is 'wisdom' in error and deception. True wisdom is humble faith before our good and loving Father. He will teach us all things in truth as we seek humbly. Jesus Christ is the way, the truth and the life. We need Him. Faith in Him is the way for He is the way.

John 1:17 "For the law was given by Moses, but grace and truth came by Jesus Christ."

Don't forget God is eternal. He is the originator. All things really are His. It comes down to 'spiritual level,' for lack of better words to come to mind. And His level is infinite for all is His. We are babies mentally; the wisest in the world, babies.

Though we can learn much of eternity, and significantly more as we are taught by Him we will ever be children in His eyes as He is in and through all things and all things are by Him and of Him, this simply is. We are blessed to be a part of Him and be His children.

We are babies and there are many that are SO significantly past us in understanding. We are in time and started at basically nothing so

122

we could have the opposite of something; though we lived with Him before we were here. All in His perfect wisdom. The Plan of Salvation is depicted perfectly.

Furthermore, there are 'infinite consciousness' or minds that are opposites on the infinite never ending 'ends' of eternity; one of light, God, and the opposite, darkness, where fallen things are. These sum up our situation.

1 Corinthians 3:20 "And again, The Lord knoweth the thoughts of the wise, that they are vain."

It really comes down to, in this physical realm in which we now are, that there is an angel on one shoulder and a devil on the other, just as depicted in cartoons. These infinite powers, one of love and truth, and one of deception are about us, almost whispering in our ears. We choose which we will obey.

The lines are drawn; the perfect kingdom exists; in our heads they are fighting in a sense. We must choose love. We must choose love. We choose love.

Commandments become imperative to stay on God's side and to keep His Spirit with us. We must have faith in our Savior who has made the path easy for us.

Oh be wise.

We are here, learning, standing as light in the world. Learning, coming back home, and having joy forever. "Men are that they might have joy." The war has been won. We are of the grandest possible heritage and the victory is sure and secured. Let us choose light and ever walk in it.

God is significantly beyond us. 'Furthermost,' all things are of Him! Nothing can be without Him, He is the light that is within us. Otherwise we could not be.

Doctrine and Covenants 88:50 "Then shall ye know that ye have seen me, that I am, and that I am the true light that is in you, and that you are in me; otherwise ye could not abound."

This rough and crude story of time I am giving of what is is given to help give a picture for us to better attempt to understand that all is His and of Him. Granted it is nowhere near perfect and is basically a baby child's attempt at helping to understand His vast glory that I am far too weak to convey. But we still get across many important points. He created us. All is His.

123

We are a part of His incredible and glorious symphony and we are in a vital part being here on this world. Choose love, choose God our Father in Heaven. Leave the world and worldly behind. Love Him and all of our brothers and sisters; this is a blink in eternity. Leave the things of the world behind. Follow His commandments, let Him heal and guide you. He is perfect. Truly. Infinitely perfect.

Even the tiniest glimpses of His glory are overwhelming joyful sights of His incredible symphony of love for His children. His perfect designs and plans. Worlds without end! It is a perfect symphony! Far more beautiful and complex and incredible than I can imagine or even attempt to convey.

Remember this is just a way to help. All is His. All is His to give. True wisdom comes from Him. Seek His guidance and council. "But to be learned is good if they hearken unto the councils of God."

Perceive here the freedom we are all given. There are scriptures how if one doesn't hearken to the councils of God they will be 'cut off' from His presence. Recognize this is generally self done. Those who think themselves wise will walk in all paths of deception, cutting themselves off of Him. And deception is a horrible thing to be guiding; Restore! Leave pride, leave 'wisdom,' be humble.

Humility, humble faith, is the way to Him. He is so significantly beyond us; we are babies and we always will always be His babies. Let us walk to Him, to truth, earnestly, His arm is outstretched for us to simply grab. Seek Him in faith, humble as a child.

1 Corinthians 3:18 "Let no man deceive himself. If any man among you seemeth to be wise in this world, let him become a fool, that he may be wise. For the wisdom of the world is foolishnesss with God."

Though this extrapolation of 'time' is rough we can extrapolate much and see the necessity of Jesus Christ; we can even then extrapolate and see the wisdom in the ordinances of the Church, in His power, in our path back and the depth of wisdom that must be in all things of God. The greatest gift of all of this is that it gives us the faith to exercise faith in Him, and then all the real blessings come.

Do not be of them that understand in part and are led deeply by deception of 'wisdom,' never actually being able to see the truth. Do not think yourself wise. Follow Him. Light can prove light. He is the source of all truth and all love and light and in Him there is no darkness.

Christ told us the greatest in the Kingdom of Heaven is he who humbles himself as a little child. And so it is. True wisdom is utter faith and trust in God. In Him our Father, to lead and guide us and teach us perfectly!

His work and His glory is to bring to pass the immortality and eternal life of man, His babies. We are nothing before God, yet we are everything to Him!

All things are made by Him in His infinite perfect wisdom and purpose. His symphony of glorious goodness is amazing! How blessed we are to be His children! Let us seek Him and His glory always!

2 Nephi chapter 2 does a great job at extrapolating this. I recommend reading it. I also recommend always praying that He will give understanding to us by His Spirit, the portion that is wisdom in Him that we should gain. We can also read and understand further the true word of God of the 'beginning' Biblically in Genesis 1 of the Bible. It is also iterated well in the Book of Moses in the Pearl of Great price.

His Great Love and Mercy

The perfect Kingdom exists and has. It is our home. We are children of light and are alive and have the breath of life within us. It is imperative we get out of here on His side, in perfect, clean and glorious light. How grateful we are for His love in sending our loving Savior. How grateful we are for our Father in Heaven, our Savior Jesus Christ, and the Holy Spirit of God to lead us in truth. He is just and merciful and graceful. Oh that men would praise Him!

Alas, we see divine purpose in our existence; we are here to gain a perspective of opposition. How could we ever learn the importance of love if we never experienced a lack of it and the opposite, even hate? How could we understand happiness if we didn't know sadness? We cannot even understand something unless there is a point relative to understand it. Opposites must be. How we need Christ.

If a kid was born with riches and his first car is a Lamborghini how can he know to appreciate the small things? There are kids like me who had beater cars and were exceedingly grateful. Those brought up in the palace cannot properly appreciate the palace, if opposition never existed. How then can we discern anything? It is our great purpose here to learn. Again, 2 Nephi chapter 2 does a great job at further illustrating this point. I recommend reading it.

In this existence we experience both sides. Sure there are some gray areas, but it is because there are two infinite never-ending sides. The never ending pit of darkness and the never ending glory of the goodness and light of God. He who created all things. We want to be with Him.

Again, We are here to learn, yet the way back is strait and narrow.

I will poorly quote from memory a quote from a great mind, Nikola Tesla, probably adding my own spin on it to make it more

125

understandable. 'All things are energy and frequency thereof; therefore resonance is what matters.'

This comes down to the exceedingly grand principle of faith. I will continue to extrapolate the necessity of our loving Savior as well as bring to better understand the principle of faith and the importance thereof.

How are we to properly resonate with utter perfection, utter glory, utter love? We are in a fallen state? We have all already sinned. We can never of ourselves become as He is, thereby resonating with Him perfectly. We can pretend we are perfect all we want, but the glimpse of His perfection and glory will show us we are nowhere near, we cannot fake it before He who created all things. He is perfect.

We must become as He is, perfect. He took care of this for us.

He sent His only begotten Son, In His great love for all of His children.

His Son, Jesus Christ, and His atonement are entirely necessary. He lived an entirely spotless and perfect life of pure love. He is our grand exemplar. And He paid the price for all of us.

His atonement is vital. He took upon Himself, even perfection, all the sins of the world, for of all of us. He paid physically and spiritually and suffered for the opposite that is required by the very nature of existence. That which is in opposition to the pure view of truth, the sacredness and pure purpose that this existence is. He physically suffered what we would have to as we could not resonate with God in perfection because of our sins. He placed them on Himself and bore them and bled from every pore. He experienced all darkness and even went below all things. Pain so serious even God trembled in pain.

This life becomes a university of learning, and a probation period to choose God, to be saved. He wants His beloved children taught well, and He reaches out to all in their time and season. Yet He compels none. I pray you will see the truth of these things and turn your eyes and heart toward our Father in Heaven.

In scripture Jesus asked our Father in Heaven if the significantly bitter cup could be taken from Him. God knowing the need, and I'm sure in tears, gave us His only begotten Son that we too may be saved.

He bled from every pore and His agony is scripturally said to be so terrible that it caused, "even God, the greatest of all, to tremble because of pain, and to bleed at every pore, and to suffer both body and spirit – and would that I might not drink the bitter the cup, and shrink- Nevertheless, glory be to the Father, and I partook and finished my preparations unto the children of men." Doctrine and Covenants 19:18-19

How incredibly blessed we are. I testify to you of the truth of this. He lives.

He is so pure and perfect. He has no sin, the only one ever without. He did the will of the Father perfectly, in love, for God and for us. "Glory be to the Father," let us never forget His work and His glory is to bring to pass the immortality and eternal life of man, even His beloved children, us.

Because He was perfect, there was no claim of sin on Him and He entered into the kingdom of God, having paid for all of us.

Perfect light, even the source, lights His infinite light in the kingdom of darkness, even below all. He destroys it and takes it out of place. He suffers for us and takes our place, He can come back as there is no claim on Him, He is perfect, and thereby we can become His perfection. He suffers death to break the bands of it and be resurrected in His light. His perfect light fully fills such and those held by darkness are made new in Him. He breaks every chain. Let us let Him! Thus through Him and His blood and sacrifice we can be made new and be 'born of God' and through our faith be saved.

He paid the price we would have had to pay. He can heal us perfectly, we can resonate in perfection with our Father in Heaven and because our Father in Heaven is just, our Savior for us suffered for our debt so we wouldn't have to. It is a truly incredible free gift. Because of Him our Father is just, and merciful. All things in wisdom of Him!

Because He descended below all for us He could also be with us and by our side through all things. All things become subject to Him. Truly by Him alone can we come to our perfect Father. He is the way the truth and the life. He is the only way to our Father in Heaven. He has suffered for us that we don't have to. When you glimpse this incredible vast love you will want to serve and praise Him forever.

All things in heaven and earth point to Him. Of course we would center our societies counting of time on His life and of course our grandest holiday would celebrate His birth. Regardless of darkness and pagan attempts to over shadow, all is His and His love confounds and fulfills! He is simply so above all. Dude, He's so big and so perfect! Oh that men would praise HIM!

Of course so many things would constantly point us to truth just as springtime is celebrated by Easter and His resurrection.

I think of even China, a place that is seemingly not Christian, though truth is growing rapidly there. Their most ancient roots that are tied to their writing and everything are based on the worship of a single supreme being, Shang Di which when studied is as our Father in Heaven of the Bible. They were worshipping our Father in Heaven.

Much writing was developed during these same periods and is evolved pictographs that contain meaning. And more complex meanings or words are simply multiple simpler pictographs put together. Not much is thought into this as these are very ancient, 4000 years ago, yet this ancient writing points to Christianity.

Very many of the words have the story of Jesus and Biblical history, or now history, prophesied right into the writing. I will not get into this but I say seek and ye shall find! There are many videos showing this clearly and it is quite amazing. I highly suggest even a youtube search on the manner. Seek. There is so much. All is His.

The Lord is like this in seemingly everything. The Spirit can reveal the things the Lord is doing in everything that man may have thought they were originators of. His messages will get through for those with eyes to see.

All things are simply our Father in Heaven's and all things point to our Savior, our way back to Him. If we would only look we would see. Seek and ye shall find. See above. See Him.

Faith

Faith is the 'vehicle' of our agency. It is better to see it as a tuner. Agency is our God given perfect freedom. We can believe and go wherever we choose; however the greatest blessing is exercising that faith in truth.

Faith is our choice. A famous scripture is thus,

John 3:16, "For God so love the world, that he gave his only begotten Son, that whosoever, believeth in him should not perish, but have everlasting life."

Why then is our belief so important? Why is our faith in Him so important? We have agency, to choose as we will. Just as a tuner of a radio can resonate the frequency, if you will, of a specific station, so can we, with our faith, tune to truth. Truth requires a special switch, that of humility, to resonate proper with truth. For what are we before Him who gave us life, created us and all things.

Therefore, as we choose to exercise faith in Christ we are aligned then with Him, and with truth. So very important. Our tuner is being tuned to the only correct station. We are aligned and by our agency, He can then bless us, and we walk in perfect unity with truth.

We tune our frequency of agency of faith just like an FM tuner. We can tune to many stations. Many can think themselves wise tuning

128

into many stations, but it is the humble that can tune to truth. Humility is required to properly resonate and tune to truth.

Yet again, we cannot resonate with truth unless we humble ourselves. For what are we before God? And His Son our Lord and Savior who has given us all things? We are lost without Him. We must place ourselves in our true place before Him. Otherwise we cannot resonate with truth. This place is humility, without it we will not resonate and we cannot see clearly.

The window to look and see is simply at kneeling height. We must look from the correct perspective, humility.

Faith in the Savior and humility before Him confounds all 'wisdom' and becomes the grandest true wisdom there is.

Luke 14:11, "For whosoever exalteth himself shall be abased; and he that humbleth himself shall be exalted."

As we resonate with truth, by having faith therein, exercising our agency in law toward truth we confound worldly 'wisdom' and by faith walk in and are guided by the Spirit of God.

Romans 8:14-16 "For as many as are led by the Spirit of God, they are the sons of God. For ye have not received the spirit of bondage again to fear; but ye have received the Spirit of adoption, whereby we cry, Abba, Father. The Spirit itself beareth witness with our spirit, that we are the children of God:"

And He works in true wisdom, giving these words to you now, and others in their time and season desiring all of His children to come to Him and be saved. The field is white and the sun is going down.

29 "For whom he did foreknow, he also did predestinate to be conformed to the image of his Son, that he might be the firstborn among many brethren."

32 "He that spared not his own Son, but delivered him up for us all, how shall he not with him also freely give us all things?"

His guidance becomes continuous and incredible. He's our Dad!

Romans 8 is worth reading the whole chapter; all the scriptures, read them, seek true wisdom. It's true. He lives. I cannot possibly overstate that He is so good and can infinitely give us all things we need and teach us incredibly beyond what we have thought possible; as we seek humbly and rely on Him as a child to their Father.

129

Resonating in faith and humility with God and Christ is the beginning. Light can utterly prove light. In Him is no darkness, as it is all for love and all for you. The opposite is in paths of selfishness and pride. If you count yourself wise, "Let him become a fool, that he may be wise."

It becomes quickly apparent that though we are in the world, we should not be of it, for true wisdom is different than the world would think. "He that humbleth himself shall be exalted." The meek truly inherit.

We must 'die' to this world and the things thereof, pride in the grandest sense. I think of the man Christ asked to forsake his riches, sell all to give to the poor and follow Him. He didn't because he had great riches.

What is gold to He who can feed thousands? What are wordly riches to He who pays His taxes by money brought forth from the mouth of a fish? He who holds to the world cannot live in His Spirit.

Doctrine and Covenants 6:7 "Seek not for riches but for wisdom, and behold, the mysteries of God shall be unfolded unto you, and then shall you be made rich. Behold, he that hath eternal life is rich."

Again and again we can see that becoming as Christ is, our grand exemplar and Savior, becoming as He is, is the grand key to everything. Perfect love and unselfishness, fully seeking to glorify our perfect Father in Heaven; seeking His will in all things.

We will see that the ways of God are utterly perfect. He will heal us, He will show us the way and our eye will become single to His glory, as His glory is love spread to all, even saving His children. We will become partners with Him, and we will see our place has always been in His kingdom, our true home, bringing the light thereof into this world and all over, the light of truth and love.

Through repentance and essentially faithfully becoming humble before Him and denying ourselves of all ungodliness and walking for His glory, as He would have us, we are washed through the blood of our Savior. Our faith grows in what He has done; we can see more clearly His amazing grace and wondrous love. We can see how we need Him and we can better appreciate His sacrifice for us.

We come to love Him dearly, and see how incredibly we are loved. When we see this we see how much He loves each of His children. It becomes easier to love them too, for He loves them so much. We can become more and more like Him, perfecting ourselves, in and through love as it, as He, grows within us. And His Spirit can ever be with us, guiding us in love.

We do not become full of charity, (the pure love of Christ.) Rather, we become swallowed up in Him who is perfect love and charity. We seek to surrender to perfect love and become swallowed up in Him and His love the best we can. We simply must die to our old selves and live in Him.

This world then becomes a great learning place, with a strait and narrow pathway out of here back to Him. It becomes only those who become truly hardened against Him that become lost, yet there are still sadly many that don't hear, yet He will not forsake us and is ever for us and I am forever grateful. We are in a great university of learning, yet with a strait and narrow pathway.

How are we to find the strait and narrow path? The answer is, is anything to hard for God? I look at my full circle path of deep deception and see the utter wisdom in Him. I can help others and I was able to learn in a way that I needed, I was utterly saved and guided in true truth.

He is pure freedom and allows such, He gives us enough to know that when the route of cause and effect takes place that we will eventually need Him and eventually see clearly if we are willing to, if we are humbled. It is perfectly set up by Him, we are all learning ourselves and He reaches out at times; His arms are always stretched out, calling to us.

We can see that our faith will take us toward, resonating in truth, bringing us to finally see the plain truth. Through humbling ourselves and denying all ungodliness, loving God, trusting in the atonement and His saving grace, in effect repenting the best we can, we rid ourselves from our past and are made entirely new and clean through Jesus Christ our Savior. He has done it! Oh that men would praise Him!

We can see His plan, He knew we would stumble, He sent His only begotten Son for us; now that we are clean we can achieve the things we were meant for. We can live for Him, our perfect Father. We can labor and seek for good, the good that saved us in love.

Thus, after godly sorrow and seeking His will with a contrite heart the mercy and grace of God has come to pass for us. Thus we are clean and through amazing grace we are clean and pure, even pure as God is. He is MIGHTY to save. He has done it perfectly. It simply is incredible mercy. We don't deserve it of ourselves and He is to be praised forever for what He has done for us. As He says we deserve it, we do. He paid for it for us. He says we are a new creation. In Him we are perfect, for each whip He took He says we are a new creation in Him.

I will praise Him forever! We simply owe Him everything! We very simply owe Him everything.

For the first time, in many cases, we can finally properly resonate with God and receive revelation from Him as we exercise our Faith and tune to the frequency of truth that is Him.

Many seek revelation in life, yet don't see it clearly, why is that? A lack of faith in short; in the atonement of our Savior to clean us, that we can resonate with God and be one in Him and walk in His Spirit. Also, a lack of faith in Him, that He will provide and guide. The greatest antidote for all of this is simple and it is this. Be humble, meek, submissive, loving, even as Christ, even as His child.

Christ taught this simply,

"Whosoever therefore shall humble himself as this little child, the same is the greatest in the kingdom of heaven." Matthew 18:4

This will help us resonate with truth in ourselves. We are His babies. In this world we see through a glass darkly. But the truth is He loves us, dearly. He is not mad, He simply will do all He can to make us see truth and come back to happiness and joy in Him and eventually return to Him and His Kingdom, our home.

John 3:16 "For God so loved the world, that he gave his only begotten Son, that whosoever believeth in him should not perish, but have everlasting life.

17 For God sent not his Son into the world to condemn the world; but that the world through him might be saved."

The grand key is to wholly and fully trust Him, even as a child, His child. Trusting Him wholly becomes power. Walking as best as we can as He would have us.

I am not perfect, but we all get better as we diligently do our best and seek His help.

Remember the perfection of God. He is also perfectly just. Does His mercy that we away from His perfect justice? Not at all. For Christ actually paid for it. He actually took it upon Himself. And in that end, God is pleased and all is right. All is perfect for His children are well taught, and back in His loving arms.

1 Corinthians 1:18 "For the preaching of the cross is to them that perish foolishness; but unto us which are saved it is the power of God.

19 For it is written, I will destroy the wisdom of the wise, and will bring to nothing the understanding of the prudent."

23 "But we preach Christ crucified, unto the Jews a stubmlingblock, and unto the Greeks foolishness;

24 But unto them which are called, both Jews and Greeks, Christ the power of God, and the wisdom of God.

25 Because the foolishness of God is wiser than men; and the weakness of God is stronger than men."

27 "But God hath chosen the foolish things of the world to confound the wise; and God hath chosen the weak things of the world to confound the things which are mighty;

28 And base things of the world, and things which are despised, hath God chosen, yea, and things which are not, to bring to nought things that are:

29 That no flesh should glory in His presence.

30 But of Him are ye in Christ Jesus, who of God is made unto us wisdom, and righteousness, and sanctification, and redemption:

31 That, according as it is written, He that glorieth, let him glory in the Lord."

The truth of our Savior the physical Jesus Christ confounds all wisdom. He truly is the way, the truth and the life. He is the only way.

Doctrine and Covenants 132:22-25 "For strait is the gate, and narrow the way that leadeth unto the exaltation and continuation of the lives, and few there be that find it, because ye receive me not in the world neither do ye know me. But if ye receive me in the world then shall ye know me, and shall receive your exaltation; that where I am ye shall be also. This is eternal lives – to know the only wise and true God, and Jesus Christ, whom he hath sent, I am he. Receive ye, therefore, my law.

Broad is the gate, and wide the way that leadeth to the deaths; and many there are that go inthereat, because they receive me not, neither do they abide in my law."

Psalm 19:7 "The law of the Lord is perfect, converting the soul: the testimony of the Lord is sure, making wise the simple."

Ether 6:17 "And they were taught to walk humbly before the Lord; and they were also taught from on high."

Whether you are one of the few just stepping out of the car and into faith exercised in truth, or of the many who walk around unsure what path to go, exercise faith in the way, the truth and the life, Jesus Christ, our Savior. Plant the seed of faith, it will grow, nourish it, it will become a strong tree that brings forth fruit. Alma chapter 32 gives great wisdom on such.

Seek and you will find, and the Savior will lead you on the strait and narrow path that leads to the gate to Him. He will carry you through. We will see His vast goodness and we will all praise Him forever. Rely on Him.

Soon you will come to see the perfect, necessary, glorious and perfect rock that our Savior is. He lives. I am forever grateful.

1 Corinthians 2:5 "That your faith should not stand in the wisdom of men, but in the power of God."

Chapter 12

THE LAW IS FULFILLED IN CHRIST
Of Further Depth and Importance; Entertainment, etc.

There are a few things that I feel deserve clarification. Is the law or 'wisdom' destroyed in that it is gone? No. It is simply perfectly fulfilled and confounded by Jesus Christ by His atonement and who He is. It becomes fulfilled and faith in Him becomes the paramount true wisdom. The law is fulfilled in Jesus Christ. He supersedes.

3 Nephi 15:4-5 "Behold, I say unto you that the law is fulfilled that was given unto Moses. Behold, I am he that gave the law, and I am he who covenanted with my people Israel; therefore, the law in me is fulfilled, for I have come to fulfill the law; therefore it hath an end."

There may be those who 'walk' in the 'wisdom' thinking themselves wise for a 'thousand years' or a long while before seeing things clearly and the need for our Savior and His perfection in what He has done for us.

There is simply a singular avenue of truth and it is not in deception of 'wisdom' in the ways it steers most. Faith in that singular avenue of truth, Jesus Christ, is key. From a spiritual aspect the law is confounded perfectly. Faith in Him becomes the grandest wisdom and leads to the higher things.

By humble faith in Him the 'wisdom' of the world, the base 'laws' of the Spirit become utilized perfectly and correctly in truth in the "strait and narrow path" Christ. We simply are blessed with perfect agency, to learn for ourselves and to be given as we seek, as well as it being our choice to go back home to Him. We all have our times and seasons.

I used to look at some eastern religions and ways of understanding and enlightenment and think they were so interesting and wise in the way they 'understood' much of the 'wisdom.' Now that I look back with a much clearer picture I see how significantly further Christianity is ahead.

Christianity left behind what becomes of no essential value, as it is 'broken,' and follow God in faith. The 'foolish and weak' things of God, by the world's standard, confound the things of the wise and mighty. They are so much a higher wisdom than many yet perceive and it grows and grows. All things are God's!

Not only considering the fact that God sent His only begotten Son and all is wisdom in Him, and just as scripture says, even the

135

foolishness of God is greater than the wisdom of man. Christianity saw the law and wisdom confounded perfectly, saw the right way and left it behind entirely. Seeing that faith in the truth trumped all things. Regardless of where we are, we all need Christ and His atonement. And humble faith in Him and in truth is the deepest wisdom.

Hebrews 7:19 "For the law made nothing perfect, but the bringing in of a better hope did; by the which we draw nigh unto God."

Oh the day when you can perceive even a little more of our Father in Heaven's infinite and perfect symphony!

Romans 3:30-31 "Seeing it is one God, which shall justify the circumcision by faith, and uncircumcision through faith. Do we then make void the law through faith? God forbid: yea, we establish the law."

The law, this 'wisdom,' as I perceive and is profitable in areas to understand in this manner, is and was given by God for many reasons some of which are mercy for those in wickedness and to be a schoolmaster for those ensnared to come to Christ. Do not forget that the way it is pushed in the world right now is often pushed by the adversary as it leads us away from the truth of our Father in Heaven, He who created all things. Spiritually, walking in truth, Jesus Christ, in faith, is the grandest wisdom and is essential.

I have given scripture in previous chapters, and will further on, of the just and the free by the promise of God that we are they who walk in faith. In the next chapter I will get into some of the deep scriptural symbolism behind this as the Lord provided. Understand it is all given by Him and all is His, we can soon come to see He simply requires humility, for we cannot even come to Him or find Him without it. One can even discern this in the law. Let us be wise and humble children.

We are justified by Jesus Christ alone as we exercise faith in Him; for the law requires it; He fulfills, confounds and supersedes. God is just and merciful; Christ has paid our debt. He fulfills the law perfectly. All is His.

Truth is of faith that it might be by grace in Jesus Christ, who is perfection and the only one who could have prepared the way for us. We are ever indebted to Him.

Remember also in scripture, that the words of God in scripture are living and have deep meanings that are seemingly endless. In a spiritual sense can refer to one thing of vast importance and in a physical a different thing. Oh the symphony of God our Father.

Galatians 5:6 "For in Jesus Christ neither circumcision availeth any thing, nor uncircumcision; but faith which worketh by love."

Jesus Christ simply fulfills the law. We are lost without Him. He is the only way out and up from it, and therefore confounds it. Again and again, deeper and deeper; all things are His. He is the only way for us to get home to the kingdom of our Father in Heaven. There really are powers of deception that are strong if we are outside of His kingdom. How we need our Savior Jesus Christ. I am so thankful for Him.

Again let me quickly re-iterate. I will not explain the 'wisdom or the law.' Even if I did all can only understand from their level of perception. Things are to be learned in our own time and the things of this world are nothing compared to the true wisdom that comes from our Father in Heaven through faith on His Son, Jesus Christ. I explain very, very vaguely this way that those who are in it may recognize it and see past the stumbling block to truth and walk in it. We walk in truth, in Jesus Christ.

The law of Jesus Christ supersedes the law of Moses, the spiritual law, for all things are His. The law of Jesus Christ, in and through actual Jesus Christ who died for us vastly supersedes all else. Truly through Him is the way. Humbly.

Matthew 23:12 "And whosoever shall exalt himself shall be abased; and he that shall humble himself shall be exalted."

In Him is the fullness and the blessings. He fulfills and supersedes all. All is wisdom in our Father in Heaven for He has been given the fullness of our Father in Heaven.

Hebrews 5:4 "And no man taketh this honour unto himself, but he that is called of God, as was Aaron.

5 So also Christ glorified not himself to be made an high priest; be he that said unto him, Thou art my Son, to day have I begotten thee.

6 As he saith also in another place, Thou art a priest for ever after the order of Melchisedec."

10 "Called of God an high priest after the order of Melchisedec.

11 Of whom we have many things to say, and hard to be uttered, seeing ye are dull of hearing.

12 For when the time ye out to be teachers, ye have need that one teach you again which be the first principles of the oracles of God; and are become such as have need of milk, and not of strong meat."

Hebrews 7:12 "For the priesthood being changed, there is made of necessity a change also of the law. "

Humble faith is the way. Jesus Christ is the way, the truth and the life. Humble yourself that you may hear. The Church of Jesus Christ of Latter-day Saints is the Biblically promised everlasting gospel, truly. Alas, still it is the Holy Spirit that will be your teacher, as you are humble and seek wholly to serve Him. There is much showing the truth of the everlasting gospel in the history discourse chapter. Do not think you know wisdom of yourself or from the arm of flesh, rely on revelation from our Father in Heaven.

For those in this 'wisdom,' the 'law' or base 'spiritual law' can be thought of as recognizing you are in great endless place, free to choose where to go, and no one can tell you what is truth because you can define it yourself, for your 'truth' is yours. So one can go along until they realize that true joy is the goal and that there is an actual source of all joy and love, which is God. Then one can see that though there is seemingly endless paths and 'no specific truth,' or paths, (because of our infinite God given agency) that still there is only one way back to that perfect joy and love to resonate with our Father in Heaven. One can perceive the things beyond us behind veils of darkness that have kept us in deception, through pride and other things and that 'non specific truth' "wisdom" was all along a deception keeping us from our one and only Savior Jesus Christ; for there is a singular path of singular truth. There is a strait and narrow path.

Matthew 7:14 "Because strait is the gate, and narrow is the way, which leadeth unto life, and few there be that find it."

When we come to Him we exercise our faith perfectly in Him and are justified by Him and His grace in true faith. It will be tested and made strong and as we get closer to Him and seek our Father in Heaven we become stronger. Humility is a grand necessity and then the greater things are given as we seek earnestly and OH HOW SMALL the "wisdom of the world" then becomes. Oh how vast the wisdom and glory and goodness and understanding from on high, from God our Father. Oh how ALL THINGS are wisdom in Him and the greater things are truly hid from the wise and prudent and are given unto babes.

Early on in the Church's restoration there were many who were Freemasons. I am certainly not one but they seem clearly to give the 'wisdom.' I don't give it as true wisdom is faith in Christ and meat comes in the right season to the humble from on high in a way that will not be a stumbling block if given from God (which from Him is so far

138

grander anyway.) To so many who receive of the world in such a wrong manner, what a stumbling block it is. Seek humbly wisdom from God for all in Him is much, much grander and for His glory. How good our Father is.

Anyway, some of them were freemasons. When they went to the temple to receive their Endowment, (a gift from on high for those close to God seeking wisdom from Him and to who make holy and sacred covenants with Him,) there were many who saw this same thing, that even the greatest 'wisdom' of the world was simply just a step to get closer to God, and in Him is where true wisdom is. How he guides us.

Joseph Fielding, An endowed Latter-day Saint and a Mason noted in his journal that Masonry "seems to have been a stepping stone or preparation for something else," referring to the endowment.

It was Joseph Smith's and others take that this 'wisdom' that had been passed down through years was a very basic and highly worldly degenerated bit of what was once far greater and holy when it was perfect and given specifically of God.

From my perspective, it took holy things and twisted them to be tools of the adversary as they are mainly twisted and nit picked to be used for self aggrandizing. Of course I judge none and do not for a moment say that all in such are wrong or evil. I simply point out that in such ways powers of deception can cause one to walk prideful and can all to easily deceive. We see many walking in deep 'wisdom' touting esoteric things and putting themselves above others. I again, judge none. Restore.

Remember, all is in true wisdom of our Father in Heaven. Without humility we ensnare ourselves. Very clearly, the Lord's ways are vastly higher and holier, taught us by His Holy Spirit and made perfect and possible through our Savior Jesus Christ who has prepared the way. He simply is the only way.

This 'wisdom,' seen the wrong way can be understood by the analogy shared earlier. It is as though one is led to sit atop a high mountain, looking out and 'seeing' more than any, and 'knowing,' more than any because they can see everything from the highest pinnacle. They see themselves at the utter pinnacle. Until they turn around from the pride that has their attention and look behind them in humility, then they finally see they have had their back to God and they are standing on top of the first step of an infinitely seeming staircase. Now they can see Him and they are humble. They can soon see all the many steps walked right up by the meek and humble by the bridge the Savior built, and the only way up is by the bridge. As they further humble themselves the steps will be taken as true wisdom from God comes through faith and in the merits of our Savior.

139

It truly is in a wrong way and those not humble to be led by Him will be led by darkness that doesn't care about our agency and freedom as God does. We must be humble before our Father, it is the only way and if we are not we are open to guidance by power of deception in pride; we must not be distracted from the way, the truth and the life. The greater things of Him simply cannot come from His Spirit by any ways of man. Humility before Him is such a key.

I can attest to this. The vastly grander things are the Lord's alone. Put again on the earth as promised in the fullness of times to the humble and meek. The meek will inherit. God Almighty owns all things and all is His. He restored His everlasting gospel and the covenants and ordinances thereof. In the ordinances godliness is manifest. All receive by His Spirit for those who are ready and proven, only from on high, to those who are covenant keepers. From on high for His purposes, to His servants and His children are the greater things given and made manifest. Even to those children who prove themselves.

Alma 12:9 "And now Alma began to expound these things unto him, saying: It is given unto many to know the mysteries of God; nevertheless they are laid under a strict command that they shall not impart only according to the portion of his word which he doth grant unto the children of men, according to the heed and diligence which they give unto him.

10 And therefore, he that will harden his heart, the same receiveth the lesser portion of the word; and he that will not harden his heart, to him is given the greater portion of the word, until it is given unto him to know the mysteries of God until he know them in full."

Alma 5:28 "Behold, are ye stripped of pride? I say unto you, if ye are not ye are not prepared to meet God. Behold ye must prepare quickly; for the kingdom of heaven is soon at hand, and such an one hath not eternal life."

Truly we must come unto Christ who can perfect us. We can do nothing of ourselves.

Those outside of His kingdom who walk in 'wisdom' may be able to have a portion of goodness as they walk in love, (which is the rays of our Father,) and other things but the truly grander things and fullness of joy are only even possible to have in Him. We are so weak. We are nothing compared to Him. He loves us, we must be humble we must seek Him and we must come in through the gate that is Jesus Christ.

140

Any in 'wisdom' should first consider all the depth of analogies I have thus far given and in simplicity should just see it as a testament that there simply are far grander things so beyond the physical; and before it becomes a stumbling block, simply allow it to give you greater nourishment to the seed of faith in Christ that you choose to plant. For it will grow into a mighty tree and graft into a tree grander than comprehension.

1 Nephi 15:15 "And then at that day will they not rejoice and give praise unto their everlasting God, their rock and their salvation? Yea, at that day, will they not receive the strength and nourishment form the true vine? Yea, will they not come unto the true fold of God?

16 Behold, I say unto you, Yea; they shall be remembered again among the house of Israel; they shall be grafted in, being a natural branch of the olive-tree, into the true olive-tree."

Do not let the 'wisdom' become a stumbling block. Do not grow faster than your roots of faith. Plant the roots of faith deep. Nourish and water. He is the way. Faith, faith, faith; in Him, in truth.

Any who ignorantly continue in their 'wisdom' and pride for length perhaps eventually come up other ways and are turned back by cherubim placed by our loving Father that we may come up the right way, that we may be made righteous through Christ and find our Father, who will lead us to infinitely greater things for His glory. We must choose Him. Our Father in Heaven is pleading with us to come up to safety. Do not be outside of His kingdom when things of the world end. He alone is the source of light and life. Do not be lulled away into destruction. Hear Him; seek Him.

Our eyes must become single to His glory; it becomes easy to do when we become close to Him and see how perfect He and His ways are. Those who persist in the wrong ways inherit only darkness and become slaves to it; things become a sad situation for all without Christ.

Chirst is the only way. There are many people without faith in Christ who die and have near death experiences and they come to experience part of the 'wisdom' as they see the 'law'. I will do a section within the history discourse more on NDE's further on, but I'll touch on it briefly now.

Many become confused and wonder why in not all NDE cases Christ is present. We are all to learn of ourselves. God is a perfect teacher. As we are lead in truth and accept that truth in faith we are then given more truth, and as we harden our hearts against it we lose even that

141

we have had; agency is given us. There are many scriptures that speak of this and I will get into it more later.

The deeper understanding of the revelation of the degrees of glory and kingdoms of God make this more easily understood.

There may be some who die without knowledge and swim in the law outside of the kingdom alone with love poured out per our Father's desires; how important faith is to guide, and how important it is exercised in truth. Those who lead into captivity surely go there; we all have sinned, we all need our Savior and His saving grace.

How good our Father in Heaven is in all cases as He teaches us and guides us all in perfect goodness and patience. How merciful He is to all of His children. All things are of God, and if one cannot perceive that yet then they are a help in our means to reach Him; or, for the hard hearted, our eventual need for Him. The understanding of The Church of Jesus Christ of Latter-day Saints is perfect to understand every type of NDE.

There is a man who made a video about himself; I will share more later. He studied near death experiences deeply as well as many religions. And eventually found that The Church of Jesus Christ of Latter-day Saints had the only model that fit. He studied the church and didn't want anything to do with it at first; he had been told many lies about it and had developed a harsh opinion. As he kept studying he got to a point where he could no longer deny it and found out the lies the world spreads of the Church are indeed lies. The truth is fought hardest against by the deception in the world, as it always has. A war of principalities and powers, we overcome thanks to our Savior.

Outer darkness is a place outside of the kingdom of God, and God is infinitely fair and teaches all of us. I've heard it also said, that if we could see the glory and goodness of even a lower kingdom we would want so badly to be there.

Understanding NDE's is something I had to prayerfully consider before coming to an understanding of. These truths remain. He wants us to learn for ourselves the best we can, and there is singular and absolute truth. True wisdom is humbly seeking His guidance.

Understand that the law is. It is no different than in the analogy I used of the infinite city. Yet there is one way to God, one path of truth, for He is the truth, He is the source of all good and all truth. Faith is the way to Him and through the strait and narrow path.

His plan upholds the law as it works with it, and His wisdom therein confounds and fulfills even the law, 'wisdom.' Jesus Christ simply vastly supersedes such. To put very simply, all things are His and done in His perfect wisdom. The meek will inherit. He loves His children so much. He truly prepared the perfect way. And the meek and humble will inherit. "Blessed are the meek: for they shall inherit the earth."

A quick interjection. Remember, it is not all bad to understand certain things, it is simply true wisdom to seek being taught from on high by our Father in Heaven; and I still will not yet get into any such 'wisdom' as faith in Christ is still the way we are to go and is true wisdom. As long as they are understood in the correct way; which is to be cautioned that it is almost never seen in the correct way and almost always in pride and not with God at the center. The reason for this is that many are snared entirely as it can become a GREAT stumbling block for those who receive such anywhere but of God directly. Still if any hold such, and have the Lord at the center they can see how faith in Him is and becomes incredibly vast true wisdom.

We must never place ourselves at the center, we may understand how things are from a personal standpoint but God must be at the center and we must be humble. I will get more into it in further chapters but remember this,

2 Nephi 9:29 "But to be learned is good if they hearken unto the counsels of God."

Saying it is not 'all bad' is still not saying, 'go seek meat,' not in the slightest. For through humble faith we can be taught from ON HIGH. THIS IS OF GREATEST VALUE, revelation from our Father in Heaven is given us! And how great it is. And quickly the 'wisdom' the way the world has it comes to nothing and we can reason with our Father in Heaven and be taught perfectly. All is His. We must be humble as a child.

Isaiah 42:21 "The Lord is well pleased for his righteousness' sake; he will magnify the law, and make it honourable."

The wisdom of this world is made honorable through faith in Jesus Christ, for the very deep 'wisdom' is fulfilled in and confounded by and vastly superseded and made perfect by the law of our Savior, Jesus Christ. Then the greater things are made known to all those who serve Him and seek His revelation. And more and more to those who have an eye single to His glory. I will get more into this in further chapters. But know this thing; the deep wisdoms of the world become so insignificant before the wisdom of God obtained in humility before Him. We must be humble.

Humility before God becomes the grandest wisdom and the simplicity thereof comes to a point where it destroys the 'wisdom of the wise.' Just as is said all over scripture; much in Isaiah, as well as the first few chapters of Corinthians and many places throughout, Romans, "The just shall live by faith." And so it is.

The wisdom of the world is greatly confounded even in the simplicity and 'foolishness' of God. We are significantly less than babies in comparison. Any who choose to continually walk in 'wisdom' are walking the wrong way. It may seem like wisdom but it is putting yourself out of the kingdom of God. When you no longer are within His realm and have His influence then the light leaves, and then are subject to the opposite power; and thus a grand deception has taken place and lulled many away in 'wisdom'. Oh be wise.

Recognize this. For the adversary will deceive in hope we don't see God. But any who can properly extrapolate the 'wisdom' and law, as I have tried to do previously here, can see that both by the law, God is, and that the creation thereof and of all things was given of Him. All things are His. He gives life and light and all goodness. Do not leave that goodness.

2 Nephi 2:5 "And men are instructed sufficiently that they know good from evil. And the law is given unto men. And by the law no flesh is justified; or, by the law men are cut off. Yea, by the temporal law they were cut off; and also, by the spiritual law they perish from that which is good forever."

Do not perish from that which is good forever. All good is from Him, He is the eternal light and eternal source thereof. There really is only one way that doesn't lead to eternal misery and that is through Jesus Christ. God is rich in mercy and just and I rest in this. He will give all the proper chance and perhaps any who is stuck in such is reading this now, as it is wisdom in Him. How grateful I am for His longsuffering and love.

Do not be outside of His kingdom. Darkness exists and we are all small. The 'law' and 'wisdom' and the way it is pushed by the adversary makes all seem so chill and life is just all good and cool and chill and many sit back and think how cool it is that consciousness is growing and that everything is good and it's not the way the world makes it and that worrying itself, by the law, creates reasons to do so, and so on. How the adversary will lead you and lull you in carnal security. Do not buy it. We are actually in a serious situation. And Jesus Christ came to save us.

See, Hear

There are many in music and in books and movies that will quietly show the 'wisdom' and give esoteric symbolism toward it, thinking themselves wise or for art. I have seen it stated, "When you realize your favorite bands, or writers or movies, have been trying to 'wake you up' for years." And they go on thinking themselves as wise, as they are finally among those who "know" in the world. Oh the twisting and deception.

Remember I judge none. How can I? The Lord has shown me truth and I simply wish to share to help bring others to the saving grace of Jesus Christ; His glory is my sole purpose.

2 Nephi 9:28 "O that cunning plan of the evil one! O the vainness, and the frailties, and the foolishness of men! When they are learned they think they are wise, and they hearken not unto the counsel of God, for they set it aside, supposing they know of themselves, wherefore, their wisdom is foolishness and it profiteth them not. And they shall perish.

29 But to be learned is good if they hearken unto the counsels of God."

Let me interject, there are relatively few, in the general sense, who have a full knowledge of this 'wisdom', but I am compelled to write all of this because it will be pushed more and is pushed more. Deception should be quelled as much as possible.

There are many who walk in the 'wisdom' and even many leaders very high up in the world. Sadly, I perceive some walk in darkness. Many think they get it, they are not convinced of truth, they think they have it; their understanding being that there is no specific singular truth and the understandings therein. Yet there is singular truth, it IS Jesus Christ.

They are as it says in Isaiah 42 "a people robbed and spoiled; they are all of them snared in holes, and they are hid in prison houses: they are for a prey, and none delivereth; for a spoil and none saith, Restore."

"Hear, ye dear; and look, ye blind, that ye may see."

They think they have the 'secret truth;' they 'know.' They are ensnared.

You relatively few and still many who "know," and what you know is a law in such a twisted and wrong way that you will ever build and be led in a continuing deception of chains, as long as you hold your own wisdom in any pride. Until perhaps you come to see the brokenness thereof and the necessity of our Savior to fulfill such. Or perhaps until you make it to a point and see your folly in a later thankful manner made clear, potentially made possible by the sword of the cherubim, finally being able to see what has been guiding you in deception. Or you will go endlessly from deception to deception, never being able to find truth. By the spiritual law becoming miserable forever.

2 Timothy 3:7 "Ever learning, and never able to come to the knowledge of the truth."

Our Father in Heaven alone can reveal all things. And truly, He can and does. Again,

2 Nephi 2:5 "And men are instructed sufficiently that they know good from evil. And the law is given unto men. And by the law no flesh is justified; or, by the law men are cut off. Yea, by the temporal law they were cut off; and also, by the spiritual law they perish from that which is good forever."

I pray none of you have to see that or go the ignorant way. I pray you'll humble yourself now and have the Lord show you true wisdom.
Restore my brothers and sisters, the children of God! He is making up His jewels!
I testify to you, these seemingly deep 'wisdoms' become small compared to the immensity that our Father will reveal to His humble children! To say the least! All is His! Seek, humble yourself as a child. We have a home! Don't be taken from it.

Doctrine and Covenants 128:18 "…And not only this, but those things which never have been revealed from the foundation of the world, but have been kept hid from the wise and prudent, shall be revealed unto babes and sucklings in this, the dispensation of the fullness of times."

Matthew 11:25 "At that time Jesus answered and said, I thank thee, O Father, Lord of heaven and earth, because thou hast hid these things form the wise and prudent, and hast revealed them unto babes."

Again in Isaiah 42, after the Lord guides them the right way and doesn't forsake them, and they are changed and see the error of their ways and are turned back, His word says this deepness, "The Lord is well pleased for his righteousness sake; he will magnify the law, and make it honorable."

146

Confounds, reveals real truth, fulfills, makes honorable, magnifies; whatever the wording, faith in Him is the way and not the works of the 'wordly wisdom.' All is His and His purposes are incredibly vast.

Let the kings of the world see that which has not been shown them. Let the Lord restore those whom He calls. Let them allow the bands that hold them to be broken. Let them return to their Father who loves them. Let them be made new; our Savior has already paid for them.

Isaiah 47:10-11 "For thou hast trusted in thy wickedness: thou hast said, None seeth me. Thy wisdom and thy knowledge, it hath perverted thee; and thou hast said in in thine heart, I am, and none else beside me."

"Therefor shall evil come upon thee; thou shalt not know from whence it riseth: . . ."

Isaiah 29:14 "Therefore, behold, I will proceed to do a marvelous work among this people, even a marvelous work, and a wonder: for the wisdom of their wise men shall perish and the understanding of their prudent men shall be hid.

16 Surely your turning of things upside down shall be esteemed as the potter's clay: for shall the work say of him that made it, He made me not? Or shall the thing framed say of him that framed it, He had no understanding?"

18 "And in that day shall the deaf hear the words of the book, and the eyes of the blind shall see out of obscurity, and out of darkness.

19 The meek also shall increase their joy in the Lord, and the poor among men shall rejoice in the Holy One of Israel.

23 But when he seeth his children, the work of mine hands, in the midst of him, they shall sanctify my name, and sanctify the Holy One of Jacob, and shall fear the God of Israel.

24 They also that erred in spirit shall come to understanding, and they that murmured shall learn doctrine."

Here it is given you. A highway; the perfect path in our Savior Jesus Christ.

Entertainment

This next few pages will sadly touch on a few things in the world. This is done lightly to help people ensnared be able to see clearly. Though I am not a fan of such it must be stressed the deception that is

147

about and by knowing it we can be better prepared to stay on the rock of Christ. All will be able to see clearer.

I want to quickly provide a word of caution as I see this paraded in society in places.

Remember that magic and sorcery and such things are an abomination and sin before God. It is a shame to speak of those things done in darkness so I simply provide scripture.

Deuteronomy 18:9-12 "When thou art come into the land which the Lord thy God giveth thee, thou shalt not learn to do after the abomination of those nations. There shall not be found among you any one that maketh his son or daughter to pass through the fire, or that useth divination, or and observer of times, or an enchanter, or a witch, or a charmer, or a consulter with familiar spirits, or a wizard, or a necromancer. For all that do these things are an abomination unto the Lord: and because of these abominations the Lord thy God doth drive them out from before thee."

These things are paraded even in kids movies and shows, I find myself turning off so many things that most would seem innocent that are sad to see.

Those who lead into captivity are leading themselves into captivity. Even that many don't see. Oh how foolish those that think they are wise because they of themselves understand much compared to average man. Oh how small they are and how small their understanding. Restore.

Furthermore, let me say, any of those who choose to walk in such are walking in the most minute tiny 'power' and 'wisdom' that shatters at the very glance of even the foolishness of God. How confounded it all is.

Do not be silly; do not be deceived. Oh be wise. Turn to our Savior. The foolishness of God, even the first bits of humble wisdom to His humble children from on high, destroy all things of and had in the world; all is His. Praise be to our Father and our God. Let us ever walk humbly before Him seeking His glory. Oh how good our Father in Heaven is.

It may take those walking in pride in 'wisdom' 1000 years to see how essential and perfect Christ is in every way and to see that the way He walked was the way we should all walk for perfectness in freedom; as well as the necessity of Him for us. Choose to see this now.

Understand if you are walking away and leaving this behind that there will probably be things working against you, pray for protection

148

and guidance. He is mighty to save. Don't see yourself far gone, rely on Him. He will run out to you with tears in His eyes. Oh the day you glimpse His love!

Oh be wise. The path of obedience leads to freedom. The highway of God is of love; He has made it strait. The guardrails of commandments are set not to take away but to keep us on the path and protected; there is freedom.

Isaiah 35:10 "And the ransomed of the Lord shall return, and come to Zion with songs and everlasting joy upon their heads: they shall obtain joy and gladness and sorrow and sighing shall flee away."

The Lord is gathering Israel. He is gathering us, His children. He is gathering you. To be saved in His vast and perfect kingdom, with Him forever. He has restored His gospel for all of us, to give us a fullness of blessings that we may be able to be glorified with Him thanks to our perfect Savior. This is given of love, and we have done nothing of ourselves, but it is the pure gift of God in His love, mercy and grace. All we have to do is look, come unto Him, and follow Him.

Alma 37:46 "O my son, do not let us be slothful because of the easiness of the way; for so was it with our fathers; for so was it prepared for them, that if they would look they might live; even so it is with us. The way is prepared, and if we will look we may live forever.

47 And now, my son, see that ye take are of these sacred things, yea see that ye look to God and live. Go unto this people and declare the word, and be sober. ..."

A quick mention of the confounding experience.

Among those that are ensnared, there are also those that have experienced the confounding; the similar experience I had. They know what is there, in opposition of God.

Many can see in true wisdom and are or become Christian. Like the many with the 'wisdom' who write books and music and give esoteric and other type symbolism there are still some who have seen beyond such and have experienced the 'confounding' I did. It wasn't just me who had it. The Lord is merciful.

Though many see there way out in these confounding moments, there are also those who experience it and cannot see clearly beyond it. Deception takes hold. I can't blame them, I simply feel for them and point the way out. Our Father in Heaven is breaking chains.

They fail to see they are in a fallen state and see darkness as all there is. I sadly have seen this is the case of some and they fail to see the

149

strait and narrow path that is in Jesus Christ that will get them to again resonate with our true home and Father in Heaven; where there is all goodness, love and light as well as perfect guidance for the humble who seek.

There are many large books and movies and music that get deep into it on both sides; either seeing clearly in Christianity or in manners of deception.

For instance, one night bowling I heard song lyrics that said something to the effect; "You think you have it all figured out, you think you've broke the code; well I came to warn you the devil is in the next room."

This is one example of many and it is rather prevalent. I will give a few more.

There is a song that says something in context to that of playing with magic, and that it is a dark horse, and what you find, there is no going back. Then to later see the singer, in true wisdom, following Jesus again.

These are just a couple of many examples and some examples get incredibly detailed too. For instance. The Lord of the Rings by JRR Tolkien is an allegory for all of it. Finding the 'power,' in the story, and seeing what is behind it. Finally destroying it and the eagles saving them after it is destroyed; with much symbolism throughout of the same allegory. The author was a strong Christian.

Sadly many will hold their deep 'wisdom' in pride as "precious;" most entirely unaware of what is really controlling and guiding them, some sadly aware. They can hold onto it incorrectly and be destroyed or humbly destroy their pride in wisdom and become humble and seek in faith and let the eagles, even the power and goodness of God, take care of them.

Someone like CS Lewis who went from atheist to devout Christian wrote many books and one of which is a series of the Chronicles of Narnia. There is deep symbolism here as well. He certainly had wisdom and understanding and probably experienced the same. He thankfully came to truth in Christ and became a bold proponent for our Savior.

The books are filled with much deep symbolism. One of which, one boy is taken by the wicked witch; he is lost. And a lion Savior loving figure, who is of great power and worth, trades himself for the one boy and he is killed. Afterward he comes to life and it is said that he knew an even deeper "magic" than the witch.

Consider also a monkey putting on the skin of the lion. Or fables of the past of an ass in a lions skin; fallacies of those thinking themselves wise.

Magic is wholly the wrong word to use but in the story is an allegory of that which is of God, symbolizing power generically. Magic is a perversion of things of God, we are to walk uprightly and He knows all things. I digress, but the stories are full of deeper and deeper symbolism and he gave much of it.

I had always loved a very famous book serious about a magical society and would wait in line to get them right when they came out and I read them all. Now I won't touch one. I am well aware of the debate whether it is that of occult symbolism or harmless or whatever. There is much deep symbolism there and in a sense the author did an incredible job of explaining much of what really is. Reality is stranger than fiction and praise God for giving us an easy and perfect way. The author is in fact Christian. And she clearly knows some stuff and I wouldn't be surprised if she experienced the same.

The book is replete with symbolism both of that which is dark stuff and that which is concealed, perhaps, valuable information to help in cases and give better understanding. I do not think it is good to glamourize magic in anyway; and what used to be harmless things of fantasy to me are now realized as something I personally want to stay away from.

Now all this being said might sound harsh and I will lighten the punch with this. Sure, there are some dark principles, but also some light principles; are the things given in an inappropriate way through the idea of and normalizing 'magic'? Sure. But so are many other books as there often isn't a better way to explain things and a better word to use. So I give the author a break in that, though there is much that I think shouldn't be glamourized, I digress.

And this last bit I will say for it, there is SO much dark symbolism and dark things before our very eyes all the time and most of us are totally unwitting toward all of it; a ridiculous amount actually, in your very face. It is actually utterly wild to really see just how much there is. So for one to simply try to open our eyes a little in interesting ways to it might not be so terrible entirely. Alas we should keep our focus on light and love. I for one simply want to focus on the good of the world and the things of light and of God. The author is Christian.

One thing to note in a newer movie of the same, (I saw before my experience that brought me back to truth in our Savior.) One of the characters who understands 'magic' is caught slipping saying something to the effect of, 'because you don't yet know the knowledge that we do,' when that character is taught to believe he is simply born different and cannot attain to such. Little things like this is why I for one will not watch or have such around. This 'wisdom' is being increasingly pushed

151

more and more and people will glamourize all that is wrong in the wrong ways away from God. Do not let it happen. Stay on the rock of Christ.

I will again bring to remembrance the story I related early in the book of the famous philosopher Friedrich Wilhelm Nietzsche. A very famous philosopher, who said, "You have your way. I have my way. As for the right way, the correct way, and the only way, it does not exist."

This is again considered clear 'understanding' of part of such 'wisdom.' Remember this man lost all mental function at the age of 44. Do not think yourselves wise in 'wisdom.' We are children with very real danger outside of our Father's protection.

For this man's 'truth' to exist, in opposite, a singular correct way, right way, perfect and only way must also. The strait and narrow path that is our Savior Jesus Christ.

We absolutely utterly need our Savior Jesus Christ. He is the only way. We must learn this. We must be humble. We simply must learn this. Our Father will give chance after chance but eventually we must learn to seek Him and rely on Him in faith.

He is mighty to save. Don't let any other voices or such tell you otherwise. Call to Him.

Realistically a vast majority of books, famous movies, and stories are based in some part or another on all of this, many in deception. You can see how far along some writers are in the understanding of things; those who become Christian and see the 'wisdom' collapse and praise and thank God have the grandest understanding and Jesus Christ is the way, the truth and the life.

I see movies where some who can't see clearly make fun of people worshipping 'god' or 'gods.' Either seeing 'wisdom' in the twisted darkness around them or scoffing at truth because they think they know of themselves. Some allude to the end how they, gods, just want to destroy; as well as push the point that we aren't all really 'real.'

Many cannot see they are in a fallen state and that darkness is about deceiving. I perceive many didn't come to the knowledge themselves and perhaps had it given them, therefore it becomes vastly harder to extrapolate as one would find necessary to get to such understanding in the first place, to then at that point begin to see what must be; then to find and extrapolate to real truth. In some cases I think some didn't get to 'wisdom' themselves so when such darkness is thrown on them they don't have the 'tools' that one would have to come to, in a sense, to help them see their way out.

Regardless there is so much deception and many getting to all differing forms of it. I truly cannot blame any, I just want people to see clearly the way home! We simply cannot think ourselves wise or that we know of ourselves. Come unto Christ!

I certainly don't intend to make myself seem any form of wise in the statement or at all, for my Father in Heaven truly saved me out of serious ignorance that I could do nothing of myself. I am forever thankful. I am utterly weak. He is utterly strong. All good and strong of me is the bits of Him and His goodness He has given me and I am forever thankful!

For those who see this incorrect way after such a confounding, that cannot see the fallen state they are in, if you aren't resonating with God you're finding things masquerading as such and if it's not through Jesus Christ, the very way, truth and life, even the light, alone, then there is deception aplenty.

I can see how people get stuck in these areas and see only darkness; it is another reason I wanted to write this, for those to see, learn truth, and humble themselves to see it and be saved and healed by our Father and His amazing grace.

Just as I had thoughts to reach out to my friends about the truth of Christ, knowing that for some, I was the only one who could understand their situation, I have the same feeling here. I see, just as it says in Isaiah, beloved children of God our Father in Heaven, snared and for a spoil. None is helping them. Who will help them? Who can help them? Who even understands the snare?

I have been saved out of it, blessed abundantly and shown clearly. I must do the little I can. I know my Father can make my weakness strong. If it helps one, it is so very worth it. For I was once the one and I am forever thankful to my Savior for saving me.

Restore! Come join the song of all the redeemed! We will rejoice forever!

I could go on all day but the simple point is this stuff is everywhere. Even in the Lion King the allegories are replete, which is such an awesome movie. The elephant graveyard for one part of it, elephants symbolizing wisdom, saved by his father. I digress and as I said, one can see how far along they are in the understanding of the fullness of truth, which is Jesus Christ, our living Savior.

A quick random thought that comes to mind, to show and help understand the love of God. After the experience I had, being utterly saved and shown the right path, the scene after Simba is saved from serious situation with the hyenas. Simba says he thinks they were even more scared of his dad. His dad laughs and says, "nobody messes with your dad." This is the intimate closeness and love and power of our literal Father who is God Almighty. We are more blessed than we can yet

153

see; it is up to us to seek Him. Seek and ye shall find. We are children of Almighty God! It is so much bigger a deal than you can yet see. Become as a little child. Love.

There are many books, songs, movies, etc. from people who have gotten past the confounding and have seen truth. Most are Christian; and some are still deceived in pride in wisdom. Some are far along; some are far back. I cannot blame them as what they experience will deceive and deceive and many probably don't want to change their life to be able to try the test of faith and resonate with God and have Him show them. Regardless I do my best to reach out with the way to our Savior. It is such a stumbling block, but the Lord is mighty indeed.

I urge all to try faith. Humble yourself and leave 'wisdom,' it can at least show you that your choice in what you have faith in and resonate with will guide you there. Then light will prove light and you will see how all is His, God Almighty, our Father in Heaven. You will begin to understand more clearly and then rejoice and leave behind the small things that we thought were so big.

We can see how Eastern "enlightenment" was tossed and left so far behind for true wisdom by Christianity, the truth in actual Jesus Christ.

All things in heaven and earth point to our Savior when one sees in truth. Do not see that all things point to your own pride. The such 'wisdom' you hold that increases your pride.

I perceive this is a reason why many books, movies, songs, etc. come with such 'wisdom;' everyone within the pride of the 'wisdom,' those who 'know' becomes further aggrandized in themselves by it. Seeing the esoteric symbolism, thinking themselves better than any other. I judge none; deception is deep. Restore. Light destroys darkness. Humility before our Father in Heaven is true wisdom.

All is of Him; Jesus Christ lives. He is the light in each one of us. He is necessary. Seek and ye shall find, ask and it shall be given, knock and it shall be open.

As we seek to follow our Savior and humbly seek His will, boy, will we learn true wisdom in Him. We need Him.

True Wisdom is Humility

Ether 4:13 "Come unto me, O ye Gentiles, and I will show unto you the greater things, the knowledge which is hid up because of unbelief.

14 Come unto me, O ye house of Israel, and it shall be made manifest unto you how great things the Father hath laid up for you, from

154

the foundation of the world; and it hath not come unto you, because of unbelief.

15 Behold, when ye shall rend that veil of unbelief which doth cause you to remain in our awful state of wickedness, and hardness of heart, and blindness of mind, then shall the great and marvelous things which have been hid up from the foundation of the world from you - yea, when ye shall call upon the Father in my name, with a broken heart and a contrite spirit, then shall ye know that the Father hath remembered the covenant which he made unto your fathers, O house of Israel."

The Lord has promised to gather scattered Israel, and so He is. Oh thank you for your perfect goodness Father! Oh that men would praise Him! We will, forever, in such joy!

I have seen people who came to 'wisdom' not of their own but through secret societies or others teaching them, and then go through confounding experience, and come out thinking all manner of things. Either that the pearly gates are suddenly no more, or that darkness is all that there is, or that they are aliens alone and all is a type of physical pertinence, and one of the worst I have seen is that all is magic, not perceiving the fallen state we are in.

One of the grandest deceptions, always twisting a truth, is that there is endless gods and man. They don't perceive the actual war between light and dark which is real, they perceive demonic things and dark forces as a type of god and that is the higher end of things, and they are all lumped into that category. Deception abounds.

The 'magic' viewpoint is of high deception. I've seen it said even Joseph Smith experienced all he did because of magic alone and all things that are greatly perverted from the truth. All things discerned because they cannot see we are in a fallen state. I judge none.

If you are not humble to resonate with God and try faith and tune to truth and not lies, you will not see truth and you will ever see deception. The things of God are vastly above and pure. We are in a fallen realm. We must be humble and seek Him.

1 Corinthians 3:18 "Let no man deceive himself. If any man among you seemeth to be wise in this world, let him become a fool, that he may be wise."

'And none sayeth restore.'

Isaiah 42:22-23 "But this is a people robbed and spoiled; they are all of them snared in holes, and they are hid in prison houses: they are for a prey and none delivereth; for a spoil, and none saith, Restore.

23 Who among you will give ear to this? Who will hearken and hear for the time to come?"

Restore! See true wisdom. Jesus Christ is the way, the truth, the life. He is not to be stood on what is twisted and seen as simply a level of understanding. I have dropped a great amount of truth for those who want to be led in it. And I will continue to. The prideful and hardhearted will be led in deception; the humble will see truth. Humility before God is the greatest wisdom.

How great the wisdom in Christ when He explained that He will build His church on the rock of revelation from God;

Matthew 16: 13-18 ". . . Whom do men say that I the Son of man am? And they said, Some say that thou art John the Baptist: some, Elias; and others, Jeremias, or one of the prophets. He saith unto them, But whom say ye that I am? And Simon Peter answered and said, Thou art the Christ, the Son of the living God. And Jesus answered and said unto him, Blessed art thou, Simon Bar-jona: for flesh and blood hath not revealed it unto thee, but my Father which is in heaven. And I say also unto thee, That thou art Peter, and upon this rock I will build my church; and the gates of hell shall not prevail against it."

We don't have to stumble at the arm of flesh but can be shown by Him as Peter was, and His Spirit that shows all truth. Light can surely prove light.

There are also those, who get to the end and see the confounding and what is and by deception or anything or one reason or another they choose wrong and choose the wrong side, perhaps seeing no other way out or in a deception. They choose the very wrong path.

I wont say much here. But I will say this; Jesus Christ is MIGHTY to save. He has overcome it all, and has done it for you. Do NOT be deceived by deception and lies that you aren't good enough or that He can't yet cleanse you and heal you; He can do all things, and He does all things well. He is MIGHTY to save.

Ephesians 5:10-13 "Proving what is acceptable unto the Lord. And have no fellowship with the unfruitful works of darkness, but rather reprove them. For it is a shame even to speak of those things which are done of them in secret."

156

Isaiah 59:1 "Behold the Lord's hand is not shortened, that it cannot save; neither his ear heavy, that it cannot hear:"

Exercise faith in Christ, pray to Him and let His mighty hand guide to get your life on track, He will help us greatly and make all perfect as we humbly seek His guidance. We simply all need Him! He loves you and will guide you perfectly.

Commandments are not grievous to be borne. Commandments are a guardrail that a loving Father in Heaven has given to His beloved children so that they don't stumble and that they can make it back to Him. Though I do not and cannot judge, the world is truly wicked. He has made the way simple. Christ has done all of the serious heavy lifting. He has done it all. We simply must choose faith and follow Him humbly. As we humbly repent and renew our minds and come unto Him He truly makes weak things become strong. Oh how He loves us.

Jump on the road that has been now graciously given you out of the pit; that prior to many couldn't perceive. Walk no more in pride and ignorance. God, our Father, reigns.

Here is the way out. Here is the way to truth and salvation, faith on Jesus Christ our Savior.

1 Corinthians 1:20 "Where is the wise? Where is the scribe? Where is the disputer of the world? Hath not God made foolish the wisdom of the world?

21 For after that in the wisdom of God the world by wisdom knew not God, it pleased God by the foolishness of preaching to save them that believe."

25 "Because the foolishness of God is wiser than men; and the weakness of God is stronger than men."

27 "But God hath chosen the foolish things of the world to confound the wise; and God hath choses the weak things of the world to confound the things which are mighty;

28 And base things of the world, and things which are despised, hath God Chosen, yea, and things which are not, to bring to nought things that are:

29 That no flesh should glory in his presence.

30 But of him are ye in Christ Jesus, who of God is made unto us wisdom, and righteousness, and sanctification, and redemption:

31 That, according as it is written; He that glorieth let him glory in the Lord."

True wisdom is humbly trusting Him in Faith. Don't look beyond the mark of Christ, for He is the way the truth and the light, and it is so.

Jacob 4:14 "But behold, the Jews were a stiffnecked people; and they despised the words of plainness, and killed the prophets, and sought for things that they could not understand. Wherefore, because of their blindness, which blindness came by looking beyond the mark, they must needs fall; for God hath taken away his plainness from them, and delivered unto them many things which they cannot understand, because they desired it. And because they desired it God hath done it, that they may stumble."

Those who think they understand in 'wisdom' without God are doing themself a disservice. This 'wisdom' of deception is growing and deceiving many.

We are but a drop; we are His children, we are so small in even the grandest thoughts of our mind, He is infinite. Don't perceive incorrectly; don't be led in deception. Again, don't be led in deception. Don't walk in pride. Walk humbly, or be humbled. I suggest making the choice to walk humbly and seeking to get better at it.

Though the law stands it is superseded vastly by the law of Jesus Christ who has fulfilled and confounded such. The law as perceived by many in the world, as it is given incorrectly, spiritually in deception, leading away from truth of God, will do nothing but enslave you and take you from that which is good. He is the source of all good. The 'foolishness' of God is greater, far greater than the deepest wisdoms of man. Oh be wise, what can I say more?

The milk is perfect. The greater things must be given from Him, from on high. The 'greater things' of mans 'wisdom' can become a great stumbling block.

Revelation from Him then, how great and good they are, and how small all other 'wisdom,' even the vastest man seems to have, becomes. Truly the grandest things have been hidden from the wise and prudent and are given to babes.

Trust Him. Have faith in Him. Be led humbly by Him. Humbly trusting Him is the greatest wisdom in truth.

Doctrine and Covenants 136:32 "Let him that is ignorant learn wisdom by humbling himself and calling upon the Lord his God, that his eyes may be opened that he may see, and his ears opened that he may hear;

158

33 For my Spirit is sent forth into the world to enlighten the humble and contrite and to the condemnation of the ungodly."

Doctrine and Covenants 112:10 "Be thou humble; and the Lord thy God shall lead thee by the hand, and give thee answer to thy prayers."

Matthew 18:4 "Whosoever therefore shall humble himself as this little child, the same is greatest in the kingdom of heaven."

1 Peter 5:5-7 ". . . and be clothed with humility: for God resisteth the proud, and giveth grace to the humble. Humble yourselves therefore under the mighty hand of God, that he may exalt you in due time: Casting all your care upon him; for he careth for you."

Leave pride forever, including pride in wisdom. Humble yourself. Humility before God our Father in Heaven is a grand key and deep wisdom in truth. The judgments of Him are in love to help us become humble and see clearly. He doesn't want to lose any of His beloved children. He just wants us back. He lives. I testify it is true.
I judge none; I seek to help all; that they may know the love I know. And be saved in Him. He is the source of love, goodness and righteousness. Humble yourself that you may find and hear.
Seek the way, the truth and the life. For he that seeketh findeth. Even Jesus Christ. Seek His guidance. He will guide and show all truth to the meek and humble.

2 Nephi 28:30 "For behold, thus saith the Lord God: I will give unto the children of men line upon line, precept upon precept, here a little and there a little; and blessed are those who hearken unto my precepts, and lend an ear unto my counsel, for they shall learn wisdom; for unto him that receiveth I will give more; and from them that shall say, We have enough, from them shall be taken away even that which they have.
31 Cursed is he that putteth his trust in man, or maketh flesh his arm, or shall hearken unto the precepts of men, save their precepts shall be given by the power of the Holy Ghost.
32 Wo be unto the Gentiles, saith the Lord God of Hosts! For nothwithstanding I shall lengthen out mine arm unto them from day to day, they will deny me; nevertheless, I will be merciful unto them, saith the Lord God, if they will repent and come unto me; for mine arm is lengthened out all the day long, saith the Lord God of Hosts."

Chapter 13

THE LOVE OF OUR SAVIOR

After the experience my life had really changed. The things that mattered before suddenly meant next to nothing. My entire focus of life was on learning real truth. My whole focus was on the will of the Lord. I was amazed at His saving grace and love and long-suffering; over time I would learn more and more.

There were things I needed to better understand and sought revelation on and each time I just wanted to serve Him better. I was being healed and still needed healing and as I was being healed I was being taught all the more.

There are scriptures that applied to my whole situation. It was incredible to learn and see the further confounding and fulfillment of His words, the infinite wisdom of God. It was even deeper to see how much true wisdom and continual wisdom was given in scripture. Truly the words of God are living and have more and more insight to give on more than one level of understanding. Glimpsing His infinite wisdom is truly amazing.

I had need of being healed in so many ways. He began to heal my backsliding as I began my best to walk in the commandments of the Lord; it got easier and easier and all the necessary revelation to understand was given. There were times early on, I would go back into a worldly view and the Lord would basically step in and keep me on the right path. He basically entirely changed me and my perception to understand how perfect His is in a short amount of time. And the understanding provided was significant. Light can prove light.

I also had to be healed of now knowing what was truly plaguing the world. It couldn't be explained to anyone, I would wish no one to have such an understanding; but know it is real. It really affected me and no one around could have any clue or could help, I relied on Him, and He healed me more and more over time. Each step was a grand lesson; the grandest overall lesson, trust Him.

It truly is for us in this existence just like it is in cartoons, a devil on one shoulder and an angel on the other. I had thought at times in life that an adversary is a cop out and wasn't real, it is not a cop out. Oh be wise, what can I say more?

Remember, the one will peck and peck and peck at you, and the other, in the opposite, is an arm outstretched. An arm respecting our freedom, always ready to help, able to help just as much as we are walking in a path that it can best help us. Awaiting our earnest desires and reliance on Him. Our thoughts come from two sources, and it becomes imperative to have the Spirit of the Lord with us and stay on His side of the guardrail.

I became much more aware of what thoughts were from where most of the time and had a strong need to always have the Spirit with me. I stopped listening to any music other than Christian music and hymns. I stopped watching movies that had dark themes that often seemed no biggie to the world. There are so many hidden things and I could finally see much of it and what was behind it. All I wanted to see was the glory of God.

I read scriptures a lot. I had to have the Spirit always with me, if I didn't I could really notice a difference and it would get more and more drastic. This too healed over time, and it healed because the presence of the Lord could be with me. His Spirit was and is essential to keep with us all the time. After that experience it was exceedingly so, and well noticed.

It became a great comfort in many of the early months to be able to pray for the Spirit and immediately feel the Spirit and the comfort. The Lord certainly was there for me in a huge way and every time I have really needed Him He was immediately there. He is always immediately there.

I had to overcome many different things and would eventually really learn to entirely trust in God and His omniscience. Trusting in Him I would learn is the greatest strength, for I truly had none of myself.

Ether 12:27 "And if men come unto me I will show unto them their weakness, I give unto men weakness that they may be humble; and my grace is sufficient for all men that humble themselves before me; for if they humble themselves before me, and have faith in me, then will I make weak things become strong unto them."

It was a great blessing that I had such an interest in learning. The zeal I had for learning before was even more magnified as I finally KNEW what was true and the scriptures weren't something that they were early in my life; they had become much more. They were real people, called of God Almighty to give important words strait to me. They became so much more to me. The scriptures and words of the leaders of the Church through conference talks and others were in constant study as they were given in the Spirit of the Lord; they still are in constant study and the Spirit teaches continually as I seek.

I am utterly amazed at how the Lord teaches by His Spirit. Two people can hear the same talk, or read the same verse, and both learn an incredibly deep and new truth to them depending on whatever level of learning they are on. All roads leading to become as the Savior is. He truly is the grand key. We owe Him everything.

I could begin to learn a lot, and see that many messages alluded to deeper messages. "Eyes to see and ears to hear," really became of strong meaning. When one is taught in faith, seeking in prayer, and having the Spirit, the Spirit is then the teacher and the Lord really can teach.

I've perceived it as running as fast as I'm able to understand. Sometimes deeper things would take me a while to learn; others I would jump to the next and the next. I was amazed at how the Lord could teach. Always wisdom in Him.

I understood what it means to be "quickened in the Spirit." The 'wisdom' that confounded simply became an understanding of how certain things worked. I was able to understand how certain things worked in the ability to exercise faith. The deepest wisdom truly is humility before God, and trusting Him. Being led by Him is the key. Faith in Him confounded the 'wisdom' and became paramount and true deep wisdom and knowledge came from Him. All was His, given and created by Him. As faith was exercised in truth much was open to me.

When "quickened" we are realizing and exercising faith in the truth that all things are His. And we are seeking revelation and it is like the doors are blown off. He can speak intimately through all things in His Spirit as we resonate with our faith and agency in truth.

These types of things I will not deeply and in detail explain. Exceedingly much of what I was taught by God is to be taught by Him to you. Exercise faith, all is His. Seek and find. We are all being taught and will come to things in our time and season. Furthermore, we are all designed for incredibly different things; we truly all have specific missions. And never forget, that greater than all wisdom, even of prophesying, is charity.

Our greatest and most important calling is to love and become as our Savior is. That is true wisdom. The greatest missions are generally the humblest seeming ones. The small acts of love have some of the grandest ripple effects. Though the small things are important, if we seek diligently and in faith, we will find.

I simply want to illustrate the fact that the Lord is always there for us, to teach us and give us as much as we can bear. I was taught and came to understand incredible amount of things. Many things that are so sacred I will keep personal. The teaching never seems to stop for those that seek. We can truly come to know all things, and every grand step seems another beginning. We must seek to be close with Him.

One thing that I will share however, is this. The greatest lesson that I want everyone to know.

162

One night, praying over and over for a long time, in tears, repenting for the many missteps and wrongs I had in the past. Having seen the perspective of the Lord more clearly on the seeming 'no biggie' things of the world, I was essentially brought into deep despair and sadness and regret. Above all things, I just wanted His forgiveness. I wanted Him to know that if He would forgive me I would do everything He ever needed as best as my often weak self could. When we see any sin, even seemingly light ones through the perspective of God we can see clearly why it is sin and the pain it causes. Alas, He has gone through all that we may be healed.

I recognized clearly I could be of no help to Him while wallowing in the past. For a while I continually unwittingly received the wrong spirit, seeing myself in such a low light. My heart breaking, I kept calling out to Him to forgive me and to heal me.

Eventually, I went from the thought of sadness of myself to the thought of what the Savior had done for me and all of us, the Atonement. I recognized He didn't suffer all things, pure pain and agony for me to suffer for them again.

As my mind seemingly caught hold of this the spirit about me and my thoughts changed. The Spirit of God grew about me as my faith began to better be exercised in my Savior and what He had done for me. I began to see more clearly what He had done for me. This horrible weight, He took for me. He paid for it. I began to see his 'Amazing Grace'.

I began to be overwhelmed by this. In praying earnestly as His Spirit and love was finally with me again that night. I was spoken lovingly through many things, gently. It became harder to say sorry, and easier to say, 'Thank You,' through tears.

I began to better understand the 'wonders of His love.' Then I remembered something. I had been praying earnestly to understand His love, and overwhelmingly now I was seeing it.

Later I would come to understand far deeper how to discern the Spirit and things of God, and the greatest key that I found was that the things of the Spirit lead one to glorify and to serve Him and to love Him, and it brings such joy. If there ever was a moment where I was led to love Him and serve Him and glorify Him, it was that moment. I was and am so eternally grateful. He loves us so much. SO much.

The next day I was led to an amazing talk by Elder Jeffery R. Holland. In it he speaks strongly in the Spirit about leaving behind our past, letting it go and forgiving ourselves; that the Lord cares most about who we are now and who we are becoming. It hit me hard.

I have always been hard on myself, and I have been told this same thing by many people. I am always grateful to hear it because at times it was hard. I believe this further lesson can help others learn more about the Saviors atonement.

The adversary continued to work on me, taking my focus toward things that would make me feel bad and deeper into darkness of sadness and I would again find myself praying to have such feelings taken away and to be forgiven.

I must interject, the amount that I learned of the goodness of God in coming to Him in supplication, He wants all of His children to always rely on Him and trust Him and in turn become closer to Him and always grow closer.

Another night I was on my knees again praying. I was in the process of being healed more and more. My thoughts would get on sadness often and the Lord continually led me to better trust and rely on Him in faith and not in fear. Each further push to trust in Him would heal me more.

I was praying and begging to be fixed and healed and forgiven, and one of the biggest lessons came then. I had this thought. "This is not yours to bear, give it to me."

I thought to myself, 'No, I couldn't ever give you this, I can bear this, I can overcome this, I don't want you to have to, you've done so much, I'll get over it, just help me.'

The thought of giving all of this to Him seemed unfair, He had given me so much already and done so much.

The thought came again, "This is not yours to bear, give it to me." I continued pondering in tears. "I love you, I have done this for you, don't fear, this is what I have done for you, it's my job, I love you, give it to me."

The thoughts in my head made me break down more. He truly didn't deserve any of this. He simply wants to heal us, His incredibly broken children. His family. He simply loves us so much and has borne it all for us.

I physically reached to my chest, and mentally grabbed all of my pain and heartache and hurt, and reached out and handed it to Him. Metaphorically and symbolically in the physical, but very real in the Spirit.

This was the greatest lesson of the Atonement I could have. In my weakness I couldn't bear it. I was broken and destroyed in my weakness. All who see sin from the perspective of God, I feel, will see it the same way. We will see our foolishness and weakness and we will have such sadness at our past mistakes. But we will learn.

The lesson was that I couldn't bear it alone. The crippling weakness of myself was immense. I couldn't bare the thought of being lost. I couldn't bare the thought of having to carry such burdens. And He

164

came and said, "Give them to me." He has done nothing wrong, but everything right.

From above, He looked down, He saw our agony and sadness and pains and in His love He came down and paid for them all great and small. He didn't deserve them, He is perfect, so perfect that He loves us too much to see us in sorrow. In His great love and perfection, He would rather bear all of our infirmities and sorrow and pain so that He can see us in happiness and joy and newness, being born of Him and His Spirit.

Reaching in and pulling out all that hurts or destroys us, shame, sorrows, whatever it is, He is waiting eagerly for it. After all, He has already paid for them. It becomes wisdom in Him then in this that He already has paid for all of them, even for those that wont take advantage of what He has done.

Upon even the slightest recognition of this I break down and just praise Him forever. Upon seeing Him or gaining even a slightly better understanding of what He has done, and His love, will bring the deepest and most humble serious admiration and love. I am forever grateful.

He did this so that in the days like I had, I can see clearly, "Yes, you can give them to me, I have already paid for them. I know you don't want me to suffer. Don't worry I already have for you. Give them to me. I have paid already. I have borne all of this for you already. Be new now. My joy is full in your joy. Oh how I love you."

Alma 26:16 "Therefore, let us glory, yea, we will glory in the Lord; yea we will rejoice, for our joy is full; yea we will praise our God forever. Behold who can glory too much in the Lord? Yea, who can say too much of His great power and of His mercy, and of His long-suffering towards the children of men? Behold, I say unto you, I cannot say the smallest part which I feel."

I tear up writing it. I love Him and serve Him forever. I cannot say the smallest part.

Chapter 14

SYMBOLISM

The Bible is replete with infinite symbolism. Many incorrectly think when they liken one spiritually learned thing to themselves that they have figured it out and it's not this way but another, depending on what they learn. They fail to see the vastness of Almighty God, a common mistake, for He is infinite and beyond our capabilities to comprehend.

His words are never ending.

His teaching is endless and are circles within circles within circles. If one gains a 'deeper' understanding and becomes prideful, their teaching is postponed until they again humble themselves. The greatest in the kingdom of heaven is he who humbles himself as a little child.

What happened physically before can teach a spiritual deep lesson now, and still will lead to the physical grander thing, to yet a grander spiritual understanding and so on.

The Old Testament speaks symbolically of the necessity and coming of Jesus Christ our Savior. He teaches us spiritually many things; some through physical stories and aspects played out, others through spiritual things played out. They have incredibly deep and continuous and perfectly complex spiritual teachings and necessities. And one leads to yet another, and to more understanding and all will come to the very return of Jesus Christ. Oh the endless glorious symphony of God.

Remember, that of God is living. His Kingdom is of the living. And His words are living. One can read a scripture and gain a certain level of understanding. Another can read the same and be significantly ahead yet gain a far deeper yet just as important to them spiritual understanding. His Spirit quickeneth. All leading us to become more like our Lord and Savior, perfectly loving and meek.

Remember always the way to gain such is that all is God's. All wisdom, all things, are His, our very existence is of Him. When we are reverent to this truth, He can teach us. As He teaches us we see more and more His perfection, perfectly and deeply explained in pure freedom, and we want ever more to serve Him for His glory.

Proverbs 3:5-6 "Trust in the Lord with all thing heart; and lean not unto thine own understanding. In all thy ways acknowledge him, and he shall direct thy paths."

1 Corinthians 3:18 "Let no man deceive himself. If any man among you seemeth to be wise in this world, let him become a fool, that he may be wise."

Two great scriptures of truth here. Eventually He will give us understanding of all things as we seek.

The symbolism of and within scripture is vast to say the least. I wish to touch on just some symbolism pertaining to 'wisdom' and other important things. There is so much symbolism and so much can be learned. I will touch on just a tiny bit.

There is walking in the 'wisdom' of the world and there is walking in faith, faith is the way the Father intends and it is the way. This is spoken of deeply in scripture; Oh how God can teach.

The blessings of the Kingdom of God come through the vital covenant with Abraham. We are grafted in as one of the twelve tribes of Israel by and through our Savior Jesus Christ.

Covenants are vital to the workings of God. To show His trust and love of God, Abraham was willing to sacrifice his son Isaac; showing he would give the Lord all things he would require. This is a similitude of God, in His love, sending His Son, Jesus Christ, to save us. We know Isaac was saved and the Lord knew Abraham would honor his covenant. Abraham knew all was the Lord's; even Isaac was given by Him in a miraculous manner. Everything is our Father in Heaven teaching us little by little to better trust in Him that we can be blessed all the more.

The covenant with God to Abraham went through the line of his son Isaac. Why is all of this important?

Abraham couldn't have children with his first wife Sarah, at first. She gave her Egyptian handmaiden Hagar to Abraham so that he could have a child. He did.

Later, in Abraham and Sarah's very old age the Lord promised they would have a child. This promise took strong faith and didn't happen immediately. They were very old and by all worldly standards this seemed ridiculous. Yet they had faith and trusted in the Lord.

Isaac was born. Finally as son of he and his wife, Abraham was tested and trusted Isaac to God entirely. He fulfilled much symbolism and God promised him and covenanted with the seed of Abraham, through Isaac, through that of the free and not of the bondwoman of Egypt.

This is one of very many uses of symbolism toward truth, to help us see clear, Oh the depth of much of it.

167

Galatians 4:21-26 "Tell me, ye that desire to be under the law, do ye not hear the law? For it is written, that Abraham had two sons, the one by the bondmaid, and the other by the freewoman. But he who was of the bondwoman was born after the flesh; but he of the freewoman was by promise. Which things are an allegory: for these are the two covenants; the one from the mount Sinai, which genereth to bondage, which is Agar. For this Agar is mount Sinai in Arabia, and answereth to Jerusalem which now is, and is in bondage with her children. But Jerusalem which is above is free, which is the mother of us all."

There is far more symbolism here than I care to share. So much of the experience I had that I will leave out and not described.

Among much of this symbolism see that truly, the 'wisdom' of the world as it is pushed is truly bondage, that 'wisdom' of Egypt. I have done my best to properly convey this, in the non-descriptive ways that I think are best. Freedom is through faith. I hope those ensnared can no longer be so, but be free in faith in Christ, being led in truth.

One can choose bondage through pride in living in the 'wisdom' of man. This is deception and not true wisdom. This is similar to being a son of the bondwoman, unmarried, rather married to death for she is not married to life. Such becomes a child of a widow, a child with no inheritance, a child of bondage, of "Egypt."

One should choose the "foolishness," by world standard, which is the power of God; it is meek and humble faith in our Savior Jesus Christ who has fulfilled the law. The promises, covenants and inheritance are given through Him; He is the source of life and light. We are children of the covenant, of the free for we are made new by Him, by life and light.

Fear not, come unto Christ; He is compassionate and has history of healing and giving life again to widows dead children through Him, Luke 7:11-17. Life is in Him.

Galatians 4:28-29 "Now we, brethren, as Isaac was, are the children of promise. But as then he that was born after the flesh persecuted him that was born after the Spirit, even so it is now."

31 "So then, brethren, we are not children of the bondwoman, but of the free."

Galatians 5:6 "For in Jesus Christ neither circumcision availeth any thing, nor uncircumcision; but faith which worketh by love."

The prophets of old were far wiser than we can see. The Word of God is living. His symphony is endless. And much more symbolism is

168

there. In short, we must, to be free, live by faith in Jesus Christ and His saving grace; we must walk as He would have us and be led by Him.

2 Corinthians 5:17- "Therefore if any man be in Christ, he is a new creature: old things are passed away; behold, all things are become new. And all things are of God, who hath reconciled us to himself by Jesus Christ, and hath given to us the ministry of reconciliation."

Another story I love with deep symbolism of Christ is that of Joseph being sold into Egypt. Joseph has many similitudes of Christ. He was sold into Egypt to be a servant. He was in bondage for nothing that he did wrong. He was saved by the grace of God and plan of God. He became a ruler and second to Pharaoh in Egypt.

He saved the kingdom in wisdom given by God. His brothers came to him not knowing it was their brother Joseph. He eventually showed himself, and as his brothers sought forgiveness he forgave them, and took care of them and gave them that which they needed.

It is interesting to note that Joseph's father is Jacob, the son of Isaac, who the covenant of God is through. Joseph having two sons that the blessing went through; as well as the other sons of Jacob.

In Genesis Jacob, who's name was changed to Israel by the Lord, gives his children some interesting prophetic blessings before his death. Symbolically promising Judah that through his loins Christ should come and that the scepter and lawgiving shouldn't depart from him. Christ coming through the tribe of Judah. And Joseph is also very interesting, "Joseph is a fruitful bough, even a fruitful bough by a well; whose branches run over the wall."

There is symbolic similitude of Christ in Joseph's incredible prophetic blessing. One in that he was a similitude of Christ, how true that prophecy is of Christ. Also that the decedents of Joseph, even that of Ephraim, becomes the Gentiles, who took the reigns of the gospel after the Jews hardened their hearts to Christ. The deep level of symbolism throughout all of this is more than I could ever convey and probably more than I could know of myself.

The similitude of Egypt and Joseph being sold into Egypt is a strong similitude. In their ignorance they were taken care of and God took care of His child and made Joseph a ruler, and helped and forgave His brothers. His brothers repented and he forgave them and said it was the design of God that by him many would be saved.

Genesis 45:5 "Now therefore be not grieved, nor angry with yourselves, that ye sold me hither: for God did send me before you to preserve life."

Though Judah and his brothers sold him,

Genesis 50:20 "But as for you, ye thought evil against me; but God meant it unto good, to bring to pass, as it is this day, to save much people alive.
21 Now therefore fear ye not: I will nourish you, and your little ones. And he comforted them, and spake kindly unto them."

Their loving Savior was the one they harmed and persecuted, even their brother.

Joseph died telling that the Lord would eventually bring them out of the land of Egypt in the land of promise.

Genesis 50:24 "And Joseph said unto his brethren, I die: and God will surely visit you, and bring you out of this land unto the land which he sware to Abraham, to Isaac, and to Jacob."

Moses was a descendent of the covenant. He was called to free those of the covenant of God from the bond of the Egyptians. A new Pharaoh had arisen to power and persecuted the people of the Lord. By the 'wisdom' of Egypt some of the people of the Pharaoh then were able to do some of the smaller miracles as Moses did. This was wisdom in God, and God soon began doing strong and mighty miracles. He continuously warned the Egyptians and they didn't listen.
On the night that became symbolized as the Passover, the first born of all Egyptians were slain, all firstborn were slain except those that placed lambs blood on their door, a similitude of what Christ and His blood has done for us. He is the firstborn and through Him we become of the Church of the Firstborn as we are sealed through faith, the way prepared by His blood. "Behold the Lamb of God, which taketh away the sin of the world." John 1:29
Moses ended up leading the children of Israel out of Egypt and parted the Red Sea. God saved those who were enslaved in Egypt.
I perceive this is a similitude also of 'spiritual Egypt,' those many that are enslaved and think themselves wise in the 'wisdom' of Egypt, they don't place God at the center as they ought and they think they see clearly, but they are ensnared and have truly a great stumbling block. Again I judge none and neither can I. None sayeth restore.
"Restore."
In these last days many will think themselves wise in them, I have seen it myself, and I have seen others entrenched in them. Let Him

170

lead you out of slavery into truth and faith in Him, stand on the rock of truth, Jesus Christ.

Go from the child of the bondwoman to the children of promise, of the free, through faith in Jesus Christ, who has fulfilled the law, saved us and brought us home. The Lord is breaking chains. He is always freeing the captive. He is mighty to save. He has done all. His arm is outstretched.

God lives and Jesus Christ is the way, the truth, the life and the light.

Today is truly the 'Gathering of Israel.' It has long since been prophesied and happens prior to the return of Christ. I am one that has been saved, and am one of the last in the work of our Savior to do my best to show the vital truth to as many as I can.

Recognize this; be converted and come into the field for the harvest is great. There are many who you alone have been prepared for.

John 9:39 "And Jesus said, For judgment I am come into this world, that they which see not might see; and that they which see might be made blind."

2 Nephi 2:5 "And men are instructed sufficiently that they know good from evil. And the law is given unto men. And by the law no flesh is justified; or, by the law men are cut off. Yea, by the temporal law they were cut off; and also, by the spiritual law they perish from that which is good forever."

Christ has told us there would be strong deception in the last days, that if it were possible, the elect could be deceived.

Matthew 24:24 "For there shall arise false Christs, and false prophets, and shall shew great signs and wonders; insomuch that, if it were possible, they shall deceive the very elect."

25 "Behold, I have told you before."

See what the truth is my friends. Jesus Christ is the way, the truth and the life and He confounds even the deepest of 'wisdom.' All is His, and He has done all for us. Let us be faithful in Him, let us trust Him, and allow Him to break the bands in sunder which have held us bound; freedom is in Him alone.

Symbolism's Hand in Revelation

Finally in this part, let us recognize the importance of symbolism in how the Lord teaches us in faith, especially in that of ordinances.

We can discern the importance of baptism and the symbolism. The Lord can teach us much from this. In one sense is that of repentance that we are changed and born again through our Savior to walk as the Lord would have us, in His commandments.

The Lord gives us pure freedom. Therefore we are given the opportunity to entirely choose Him and choose to make covenants with Him by our own choice, recognizing our need for Him. We choose to follow Him and keep His commandments; whatever we give, we are blessed all the more. All things are for us to better rely on Him, come closer to Him, and receive His blessings by giving all we are to Him who created us, our Father in Heaven. It is the way back to Him.

Even Christ who was perfect was baptized to 'fulfill all righteousness.' He set the perfect example to follow at every step, pointing the way back to our Father in Heaven and showing He would give all for our Father in Heaven. There is symbolism after He came up out of the water of the dove descending on Him, showing the Spirit descending on Him after the covenant.

In like manner, once we make such a covenant with our Father in Heaven to follow Him and His ways we are cleansed by our Savior and choose to rely on Him, we then can be blessed with His Holy Spirit to be with us. We are clean through the Savior and His sacrifice, we resonate with the perfection of God as we walk as He would have us, we are able to have His constant presence with us and be taught by Him.

As we remember Him, have faith in Him and keep His commandments we can have His Spirit to be with us; His peace, comfort, guidance and enlightenment and teaching.

In the ordinance of baptism we make a vital covenant with Him. He teaches us greatly and deep herein; we will take His name upon us and do our best to follow His example and He will cleanse us and make us new, even through the reception of His Spirit, to then lead us the more and more perfectly.

Remember this scripture as it comes to ordinances, covenants and the promises of God.

Romans 8:32 "He that spared not his own Son, but delivered him up for us all, how shall he not with him also freely give us all things?"

Our Father loves us. He wants to continually teach us in His Spirit that which is of His Spirit. Furthermore, He teaches us in true wisdom and with covenants. We are royal children in an important classroom to learn to become as our Savior. He is our Savior and grand exemplar.

Christ, in Doctrine and Covenants, has said that whosoever repents and comes unto Him is His Church. This is open to many in the world; the works of God are vast. Though the fullness of the everlasting gospel is restored, His Church is vast. He needs good people in many areas of the world and our callings are varied. Whatsoever is good is of God.

Regardless, He has restored the fullness of His gospel that is in continuous revelation and by His organization. It is The Church of Jesus Christ of Latter-day Saints. Above all the Spirit of God bears witness and we can know truth. (I will get much more into this in the revelation and historical discourses. Ch. 18 & 19.)

As promised Biblically, Christ has brought about the fullness of His gospel again. The gathering of Israel is now. The further ordinances in The Church of Jesus Christ of Latter-day Saints are of Him and teach all the more as we are guided on the path of our Savior. They are as they have always been, in symbolism and covenant. He teaches us significantly more that we may be prepared to receive 'all things' as we truly seek His glory. The symbolism and covenants teach us.

The ordinances are real. They are of Heaven and the Spirit beareth witness to the humble earnest seeker.

The Bible talks much of the tabernacle of the Lord being present in the last days, the everlasting covenant and even of important oaths regarding the ways of Christ. We are simply free and choose for ourselves. Christ shows us the way back home.

The Church of Jesus Christ of Latter-day Saints is a church of great revelation, personal revelation and guiding revelation to leaders. The Spirit truly beareth witness to all truth.

Many churches say they are perfect or right by history or by the word or by other things of man, the true fullness of the everlasting gospel, The Church of Jesus Christ of Latter-day Saints makes this much simpler. We rely entirely and wholly upon the revelation from God and His Spirit. And by His Spirit we truly can know the truth of all things. Light proves light. It is His Church.

Christ Himself gave the perfect example of how He would establish His church in Matthew 16.

13-18 ". . . Whom do men say that I the Son of man am? And they said, Some say that thou art John the Baptist: some, Elias; and others, Jeremias, or one of the prophets. He saith unto them, But whom say ye that I am? And Simon Peter Answered and said, Thou art the Christ, the Son of the living God. And Jesus answered and said unto him,

Blessed art thou, Simon Bar-jona: for flesh and blood hath not revealed it unto thee, but my Father which is in heaven."

"And I say also unto thee, that thou art Peter, and upon this rock I will build my church; and the gates of hell shall not prevail against it."

Our Lord and Savior Jesus Christ has taught us that He will build His Church on the rock of revelation. The Spirit is what shows us truth and teaches us.

1 Corinthians 2:14 "But the natural man receiveth not the things of the Spirit of God: for they are foolishness unto him: neither can he know them, because they are spiritually discerned."

In the back of The Book of Mormon, which is simply another testament of Jesus Christ, we are given the following promise.

Moroni 10:4-5 "And when ye shall receive these things, I would exhort you that ye would ask God, the Eternal Father, in the name of Christ, if these things are not true; and if ye shall ask with a sincere heart, with real intent, having faith in Christ, he will manifest the truth of it unto you, by the power of the Holy Ghost. And by the power of the Holy Ghost ye may know the truth of all things."

I once was told by a friend I should be careful in trusting 'feelings.' I probably would have said the same at a time earlier in life, but I felt sad for him. He is a Christian, but it is not a feeling, it is the very presence of our Father in Heaven. I felt sad that he must not have ever felt it, otherwise he would know it. I know by far more even than this, by serious revelation and experience.

He who receiveth and will not harden their heart but keep seeking in faith will receive more until they know all things.

Seek in truth, and in faith. Do all necessary to receive the Spirit of God, walking humbly and meekly to receive correct guidance of God and not of man.

Joseph Smith was His prophet and restored His gospel. Where there are grander blessings and revelations of God, there is a greater requirement of humility and faith to receive them; then are the windows of Heaven open. The grander things are protected by humble and meek faith and diligent seeking.

Even writing these things, the Spirit bears witness. A great blessing.

Unto him that receives in faith, to him more is given. He who hardens their heart against things of truth will receive no more and lose

174

that even which they had gained. We are free to hear the Spirit or harden our heart. Scriptures all over have given many examples of this.

3 Nephi 26:9-10 "And when they shall have received this, which is expedient that they should have first, to try their faith, and if it shall so be that they shall believe these things then shall the greater things be made manifest unto them.

And if it so be that they will not believe these things, then shall the greater things be withheld form them, unto their condemnation."

Friends, I have been on both sides of this and I judge none. I have hardened my heart earlier in life and lost much truth for a time. And I have since exercised great faith in seeking and have learned deep and incredible truths. The Church is true I testify. Let the Spirit show you as well. Seek, humbly and earnestly, in meekness, not being wise in yourself or of words of others; let our Father in Heaven show you. The faith and revelation discourse chapters will provide more guidance for these areas.

Many have left the Church and some have had all of what they hardened their hearts against taken away, by their own choice. Some only harden their hearts against some and regress into a gospel of Christ with less vital truths, although having the truth of Christ alone is an exceedingly great thing to have. The point here, is that as we have God show us, in pure humility and meekness we can be led in truth to more and more truth.

On one end, we can truly become those who "KNOW" the gospel is true, as I do, and have real and serious revelation till we 'know all things.' And on the other hand we can scoff and harden our heart at those who say they 'know' the gospel is true and think that there is no way they could know such things, as I had done in the past. Though some say they 'know' in hope, there are many who know truly, by every vast concept or experience one could ever need to truly know.

In the end we can walk faithful, or harden our hearts.

I testify to you in truth and in the name of our Lord Jesus Christ that if you stay faithful and diligently seek the Lord to teach you in humility and meekness, greater things will truly be made manifest to you, you will be guided by Him and become closer to Him. We simply must be meek, humble, and diligently seek, as His children before our perfect Father.

I will get more into such things, revelation in more detail, not too deeply, but in ways that will help.

"Oh, there is so much more that your Father in Heaven wants you to know." – President Russel M. Nelson

175

2 Nephi 9:42 "And whoso knocketh, to him will he open; and the wise, and the learned, and they that are rich, who are puffed up because of their learning, and their wisdom, and their riches – yea, they are they whom he despiseth; and save they shall cast these things away, and consider themselves fools before God, and come down in the depths of humility, he will not open unto them.

43 But the things of the wise and the prudent shall be hid from them forever – yea, that happiness which is prepared for the saints."

Be humble before Him. Knock, He will open. Let Him change you and heal you and bless you.

I say and do my best to show these many things, in hopes there are some who may be ensnared who read and see their error and are saved. And also, as the growing deceptions of the last days have come amongst us that none will be swayed from the rock of Jesus Christ.

In these last days, as deception grows, this twisted 'wisdom' may even be pushed as a singular and 'end all' 'world religion;' pushing away from the rock of Christ. Seeming to those ensnared to confound all faith and a lie that there is 'no specific truth' simply because all may be experienced. But there is singular truth and it is the 'wisdom' of the flesh that will be confounded.

Jesus Christ is the specific, singular and endless truth. The 'wisdom' of the world is confounded. He has fulfilled all. He is the light. Do not leave the rock of Jesus Christ. He is truly the way the truth and the life.

Matthew 24:24"For there shall arise false Christs, and false prophets, and shall shew great signs and wonders; insomuch that, if it were possible, they shall deceive the very elect,"

25 "Behold, I have told you before."

Christ told us before it happens.

I can tell you myself, from personal experience, that the deception is vast and appears to be absolute wisdom; it is not as there IS singular truth in Christ. It makes sense it is called a stumbling block. Without God at the center we cast ourselves off unless we come around to true truth. Oh be wise.

Many who dabble in "consciousness" understanding don't get the very ends of it fully to the 'wisdom,' and of those who do even fewer are able to extrapolate it in truth to the truth and necessity of the

176

Atonement and saving grace of Jesus Christ our Lord and Savior. Oh how blessed we are to be so loved by Him. He has done it all and made the path clear and easy.

1 Corinthians 1:19 "For it is written, I will destroy the wisdom of the wise, and will bring to nothing the understanding of the prudent."

The words are true.

Don't leave the rock; don't look beyond the mark of Jesus Christ. He is absolutely necessary. The worst deceptions are bits of truth skewed hard. Jesus Christ lives. Do not leave the rock and do not forget it. Be not deceived. Oh be wise.

Keep God at the center and be taught by Him. Light can prove light. Serious revelation is real and at the grasp of those prepared properly in humility to receive it.

The end of wisdom is humbly, meekly and entirely trusting God our Father, as His child. We are His beloved children and we are babies in comparison.

I will get more into this as we go along. The Church of Jesus Christ of Latter-day Saints is the fullness of the restored everlasting gospel of Jesus Christ and revelation continues; personally and by His leaders of the Church. The Spirit bears witness.

He ever teaches us, as we seek so in faith. Many who join the Church find much humbling required; and they can perceive how much it is fought against. Alas, it is true! Deception fights hardest against Truth, just as in the days of Christ. Praise God for His guidance and love.

Jesus Christ is the center and all who have Him in their lives are greatly blessed. I am blessed and forever grateful and will forever serve Him.

Oh when you can even glimpse the incredible and deep symphony of our loving Father in Heaven! A fullness of joy is realizing His perfection and vastness and that we are even the beloved children of Him; Perfection, Love, God Almighty! I will praise Him forever! He has done all for us!

Chapter 15

WHERE YOUR HEART IS

I became centered on my Father in Heaven and became new in life, following the gospel and Jesus Christ the best I could.

I had moved because the decision was the only one that would be entirely for the gospel and following the will of God. I spent tons of time praying and tons of time reading scriptures. The zeal that I had for riding and then learning all transferred into studying scripture. After all I had finally known that it was true and the very word of God.

I spent hours a day reading and had a strong desire to learn and understand everything I could. I watched talks and was amazed to see how deep the Spirit could teach.

Among all of this I had a strong desire to do my absolute best to become like my Savior. "Be ye therefore perfect even as your Father which is in Heaven is perfect." We are told to be perfect, a large task but one that started with earnestly trying.

Each day I would sort of ask myself this, and over time I started getting uncomfortable about one thing.

My main sponsor was Monster Energy Drink. I had ridden for them for a few years and had recently re-signed a new contract with them. They were super great people and really supported my career. Not only that, they paid my bills. I got paid monthly by them, had travel to contest and hotels covered by them, and received incentives based on how well I did in contests. It was a great sponsor and they treated me overall well.

In BMX energy drinks are basically the 'end all' large sponsor. In a sense they take the place of having many other ones. They want a larger spot on your helmet, and they want you wearing their hat all the time. They pay the most and are a great achievement in the industry.

That specific brand also had the largest influence. They were the main sponsor of so many things, and basically everything for us. X Games is our super bowl and they are a main sponsor. They do a large amount financially for the industry and more opportunities come because of it. I had basically ridden for the best brand from strictly a BMX professional monetary standpoint. The support was by far the greatest.

Every time I would analyze myself, 'be ye therefore perfect,' the thought of my sponsor would come into mind. Though it was offseason and I didn't have events for a few months I eventually came to a big decision. I was going to be the first dude to choose to quit such a sponsor.

I had been greatly changed. I saw many of the modes of advertising as no longer appropriate. I absolutely had one goal for the rest of my life and that was to do my best for God and do the things I feel would best glorify Him; to walk as He would have me. Though I was nowhere near perfect, I began to feel more strongly about this decision.

The decision wasn't simple and light, but it became much more when the eternal picture was there. I had wrecked, as I said, in the main contests of the season earlier that year. I needed to do well and I had a business that I put a bunch of money into that was not doing well. I am grateful for it all as whatever is wisdom in God to bring me to Him I am grateful for. The income I relied on was the monthly support from this large sponsor.

In BMX you work and build your career and name to the point of getting your break, which for us is a big energy drink contract. They support you and generally stay with you for a long time. My perceptions were changing.

When I say all of this I judge none. I made the personal decision best for me. From my perspective, the brand advertised in ways that I was seeing more and more as inappropriate in different ways, they were advertising to the world in worldly ways for one.

The final bit that really kept getting to me was an irreverence for things of God. Seemingly making a show in a 'no big deal' attitude of things of darkness and of the adversary of this world. To me it lightly mocked the things of God. I cannot judge for from one perspective it is no big deal, but to me I had come to know better.

From their perspective I'm sure it is harmless advertising and different things are probably 'witty' ideas of the marketing guys. This type of stuff is all over the world and most don't bat an eye or care. But I knew all too well. And I knew how through the little 'no big deal' things, what was actually pushing those types of agendas that made light of such things.

I had simply come to understand and see a lot of what most wouldn't normally see or care about. Further even in the experience I had.

Realizing this I stopped wearing the hat, took logos off my bike, emailed the team manager that I couldn't be a part of it or have it on me anymore. I wanted nothing more to do with the brand. I couldn't be a part of it; I couldn't be seen with it. I wanted to be far from it and close only to the things of God. All else meant nothing.

It was regrettable that seemingly such 'small' things as specific advertising and logos had to be a reason to part. The edgy marketing was simply too edgy in areas that were too real for me and didn't fit in my new life.

I had worked hard riding for so long, doing well and doing things no one else did in big ways to get to such a good sponsor and was letting it go.

Surprisingly the decision was easier than I thought. I had seen clearly how all is God's and I trusted Him. All I wanted and all I still want is Him to be happy with me and the opinions of others doesn't matter.

There are athletes that are Christians that still ride for them and that is their own decision. They haven't been through what I have and I know for myself the path that is right for me personally. I judge none and many look at it as simply a drink that helps them as a sponsor. My experiences made me see differently for myself.

I was happy to witness to God that He is first in all things. I trusted God that I would be taken care of financially, I trust Him for everything. I had already fallen into His arms and needed Him in the deepest and most real need ever. I was blessed to see clear that all was His and I know I can trust Him fully. I wanted to do whatever He wanted me to.

Matthew 6:19-22 "Lay not up for yourselves treasures upon earth, where moth and rust doth corrupt, and where thieves break through and steal:

20 But lay up for yourselves treasures in heaven, where neither moth nor rust doth corrupt, and where thieves do not break through nor steal:

21 For where your treasure is, there will your heart be also.

22 The light of the body is the eye: if therefore thine eye be single, thy whole body shall be full of light."

I very simply wanted to do everything my Father in Heaven would have me do. And I want to do anything that brings Him glory. He has done all for me.

I look back and laugh to myself regarding the email I sent to my team manager. I was very frank and straightforward and just said exactly how I felt and why. That I couldn't wear the brand or logo anymore and that I wouldn't and didn't want to even have the perception of evil about me. He, seeming non religious, must have been like, 'What the. . .. '

For a while I got no reply, they had to consult the higher up dudes. He told me other guys on the team were Christian, I explained my firmness to him. Thankfully they were very cool about it and signed a quick end of contract for me.

I was in the midst of a new contract to represent the brand and products riding BMX. My contract gave me some outs, basically because no one would ever seem to just desire to walk away from the finances, but I didn't care. I was still prepared to be done with BMX if it came to that. I simply couldn't be a part; it was that simple. I was glad they were understanding and signed a mutual end to the contract.

I told the team manager that I was very sorry for any inconvenience and I'm sure it must be weird from his perspective. His reply was along the lines of, "Just when you thought you've heard it all, but I'm not one to judge." I had a decent relationship and he was always kind so I laughed it off and said that not long ago I would have agreed. I was blessed to see truth, no matter what others thought of it.

The sponsorship ended quickly and easily and like that I didn't have finances and I didn't have a sponsor. I let them even keep payments due for travel for their trouble. Yet I felt much better.

When I asked myself if I was doing all I could to be perfect and doing all I could to be as the Lord would have me, I could answer yes. I could answer, "Lord, at any cost, I am yours forever." And I was blessed with knowing that His will was always good toward me and would always bring the most happiness.

There is a more of a main BMX website that publishes much of BMX including sponsor changes. I wrote an explanation to the dude there that I had known for years, he had always been kind.

I sent it to him at the website and him alone. From there it went many places. I declined every interview and everyone that called me and instead they all drew from the comments I made. I didn't want to come off as self-righteous or draw attention to myself, though many thought giving up my main form of income was that anyway. I just wanted to say it once, not parade it, and make the decision for myself. If anyone cared to know why, I gave them the thing that really matters, 'Our Savior lives.'

I will put it here. In a sense I wanted to say, I left this sponsor and glory be to God! I went a little in, but I felt passionate and still do and want to help people see truth. It is real. God is real. If I wanted others to see anything it was that I was like-minded to many in that I had dealt with many of the same doubts but that indeed God lives. Our loving Savior is real; He lives!

Two things that are very uncommon in the BMX world - leaving energy drink sponsors by choice and doing anything in the name of religion. This story has both.

Colton Satterfield has decided to leave Monster Energy due to "personal religious reasons." Here's his official statement -

"I want to thank everyone at Monster for all they have done and do for action sports. I have chosen to part ways for personal religious reasons. Some of the marketing and logos that are meant to be edgy simply are edgy in areas that I personally could no longer support. I wish all the great people there the absolute very best and I thank them for their kind understanding.
This was not a decision I made lightly. Getting such an energy drink sponsor is a big achieving step in action sports; they provide more than just financially, they help their athletes in many ways. The decision was not a light one by any means. I regret something seemingly so small, to some, as logos and various marketing, has to divide us; but I know it is the correct decision for me."

While many will disagree with or not understand Colton's viewpoint here, you've gotta give him credit for putting his personal morals above a paycheck. Colton is a one-of-a-kind individual and puts a lot of thought into every decision he makes. He also does double flairs on giant quarterpipes.

Colton sent this over to follow up on his initial statement -

"I can imagine some non religious people thinking this is wild or crazy, and not that long ago I would have been one of those people. Previously I had been a far too logical person in life to go deeply into religion and still am that logical minded person. But I had a strait up real and wildly profound experience that shockingly confirmed serious religious truth to me. I had always been one to learn as much as I can. This experience was at the end of a knowledge or a deep world wisdom, most don't find, that seemingly discounted it; then that 'wisdom' was confounded as the bible describes and had my eyes opened in a real profound way. Some perceived 'wisdom' of the world is certainly a stumbling block that ensnares if one is not careful. There is an actual dark side of things that deceives. Most who find this 'knowledge' sit in their pride of having it and don't actually step back and analyze it and can be pulled down into darkness; those who analyze it fully are already - or then become - Christians. My experience was profound. Whole countries don't allow missionaries or other religions because their leaders trust this false or highly partial wisdom so hard. It is also wild to later read prophets of old, like Paul and many many others, who were wise dudes that essentially described every step of this knowledge that leads 'wise men'

away and then describes each step up to the confounding and true light for those who seek. These were real, and actual very wise dudes of old. So for me, I do my best to walk uprightly before a very real and good God and, with some of their marketing and logos, it just wasn't something I could keep supporting. God is very real, Christ in actual reality lives. That's from a dude who has to logically understand things all the way around. Christianity is actually totally real. I was furthermore blown away to see the LDS religion understands literally everything in a very clear way. I know them to have the entire fullness of the gospel of Christ. It is His church. Something not long ago I would have sadly laughed at. But it is in actual true reality. God can show you this far better and more profound than even logically getting it. The highest form of wisdom is being humble before God. Everything else falls. It's true. A truth that is sadly scoffed at by many before ever given a fair shake. A truth too precious not to share. Love is what's up. It's real."

Other than people simply watching me ride I don't like being in the spotlight. And this went wild fast. Many news places picked it up, I suppose it's a rare occurrence. I turned them all down and felt I had said the best I could, all that I cared to share. They all took from the BMX website source of what I shared and many shared it.

Comments and messages and posts and all of that sort were not in short supply. As a professional you are used to hearing peoples opinions good and bad, it doesn't matter to me, I try not to judge. This got pretty wild.

There were a few nice comments and things of people reaching out saying how grateful they were to have such an example and there were many people reaching out saying all kinds of harsh things.

I wont go too deep into much of the negative, who wants to waste time there? Let's just say there was a fair amount. I was surprised to see the amount of people giving crap over the Church, Christians reaching out to "save me" from the Church, while deep in the spirit of contention. And many people just having all kind of harsh and mean things to say.

I remember having a couple of thoughts clearly.

My first thought was, "Wow, imagine how Joseph Smith must have felt! I'm so glad he was man enough cuz I sure don't know if I could have handled that."

This thought was wild to me. For I knew, I actually knew that God was real and Christ was essential and that His Church was true and all I wanted to do was shout it and help everyone. And they scoffed and laughed and most didn't for one second consider anything. They believed

183

in what they already felt they knew and wouldn't for a moment look into anything but bashed instead.

How would Joseph Smith have felt? He had seen in the physical Jesus Christ and God. Angels were ministering to him and others and teaching him all the time and all that he wanted to do was help everyone. It was a wild feeling to understand how he must have felt. Especially now that I had seen both sides.

My second thought was that even when the most harsh and unkind things were said, my thoughts jumped to, "Well, I probably at very least thought that in the past in some form, how can I judge them?"

How could I judge those who were deceived and saw serious things just in a light and joking sense? I couldn't. I simply really felt for them.

I again looked at the wisdom of my Father in Heaven in the way He brought me back to His fold. It wasn't just that I chose not to judge them, but I couldn't. I felt for them. I knew what was real and I could see their snare. I had been there, perhaps I wouldn't have been so harsh but I told my own mother she was deceived and church was pointless; now I would give anything to that very true Church of Jesus Christ and to my Saviors purposes, my most merciful, gracious and loving Savior. I am so happy to call myself a member of His Church.

I looked at all of them in a bit of sadness. A few times I tried to reach out and help many. I truly gave time and in wisdom trying to show them where they erred; most times for no immediate reason. I really felt for them and wanted to help show what I actually knew was true.

I could see how deeply ensnared many were. Light-mindedness, trust in ones own wisdom or wisdom they had been taught, essentially a lack in humility. Very few actually considered my words and it was eye opening to see. I could judge none but I began to realize the predicament many were in.

Because of the experiences that I had had, and that I had been through I could see others better, judging them less; seeing myself as unable to. Even though many were harsher than I would be, I could see how silly it was to compare such things.

From a perspective of a person I may have previously affected, who am I to say that I didn't absolutely crush someone emotionally by my words of trying to 'help?' Even in words that seemed like no big deal to me. It breaks my heart to think. I truly could not judge them.

Sure we needed people to humbly seek, to not think themselves wise but to actually care about these things. But did I care before? I guess I did greatly, but how easily I was deceived as well.

In striving to be like my Savior I began to be further taught by Him. I began to see how love was that perfect answer. It was more than a cliché.

Chapter 16

IMPORTANCE OF LOVE

Most of this harshness happened shortly after dropping my sponsor, but one time a while after that, a story worth sharing happened.

My Instagram quickly went from BMX to purely Christ and scripture. I lost a bunch of followers and gained some that care. I've never cared much about social media but I wanted to share what matters.

One day on one post of a Bible verse some kid wrote an incredibly harsh comment against 'Mormons' and The Book of Mormon. I knew he didn't know what was up as it was a Bible verse and not from The Book of Mormon but again, I couldn't judge him.

I decided to private message him. I told him that I understand how people may think the way he did in his comment. But that I wanted to assure him that it is actually true. I told him I used to think similarly to him but it is indeed true.

He wrote back some harsh things at first explaining why he unfollowed me, then gave me props for being a good rider, then telling me how 'anti Mormon' he is and then he got down to the real issue. He was in The Church of Jesus Christ of Latter-day Saints up to 9th grade. He said he was treated horribly and he 'knows how to deal with it.'

He then said that he had tried reaching out to many other pros, "just to have a friend and a homie," then he said, "not one of them cares so I won't." "Thanks for PMing me." All this before I could reply.

I saw the real problem. One that plagues all of us at one time or another; a lack of love. Namely insecurity this time, which manifested after a lack of receiving love.

Insecurity can cause a lot of acting out, people place their inner emotions of how they feel others feel about themselves and put it onto others. Essentially how they truly feel about themselves is pushed on others. We can only give what we have. He stated clearly, 'not one cares so I wont.' This comes from a lack of receiving love.

Love is essential; pride and insecurity are the great destroyers of love. God can heal both of these; He is the source of love. Pride is a lack of giving love and insecurity comes from a lack of receiving it. And insecurity can create pride.

Every problem of the world very simply comes from a lack of love; from insecurity or pride.

If we are not loved it becomes harder to love ourselves. If we do not love ourselves in that we are not content wholly with ourselves, (which only comes through Christ fully,) we cannot love others well.

Essentially, if we are not loved we become insecure; we need more love within us. As we are insecure we become cut off from others and love others less and become prideful, an unfruitful act of trying to love ourselves. We then tear the love down in others trying to build ourselves up in an unfruitful manner.

This cycle is only broken by loving even those that are hard to love. We must above all choose to be kind and understanding. We are simply all a victim of one thing, a lack of love.

We must choose to live at a certain level of love, and no matter what is said, what unkind things are tossed our way, we must choose to not be persuaded off the high rock of love. "That's fine you feel that way, but I'm going to love you. That's cool if you keep throwing insults, I'm not going to love myself less or you any less. I am simply full of love."

This is a challenge to master but it is what we must do. It comes easy when we realize and glimpse the infinite love of the source of all love, our Father in Heaven and our Savior Jesus Christ; oh how the Holy Spirit can convey this amazingly.

When we see ourselves even a little of how our Father in Heaven sees us we can truly love ourselves and love others and stay up on the high rock of love no matter what is thrown.

We simply have to not judge others. We would all make the same mistakes given the same cards. We have no idea how difficult things are for others. We should choose compassion, empathy and understanding.

We are of the Kingdom. We are of the light. We must only shine light and heal those afflicted by darkness. Starting with ourselves. The Savior in our lives will surely powerfully do this and bring love out in amazing ways.

Here was a son of God writing me, greatly beloved by the King of Kings, acting out and saying things that are harsh because all he wants and needs is someone to care. Memories from the past that are harsh made him harden his heart to the truth that those people of the Church knew. The lack of love was turning to hate occasionally and the actions of others and lack of care was taking its toll on a kid who just needs some love in his life.

Let us not forget that hardening his heart and focusing on such harshness makes more apt to the adversary pushing his focus onto the negative things around him, to judge it harsher and to hurt himself more. Truly forgiveness is a great blessing to learn for ourselves.

This was a great lesson. Many of us will get upset at the surface thing someone says without understanding why they said it. If we understood people perfectly we would learn that if we were in their shoes, and born to the same family and experienced the same experiences we would have likely made all the same decisions.

A deeper analysis of this is that we are all inherently the same. More money and more wisdom are given us from God, not gained only by us, we cannot judge those with more or less and we cannot judge any.

We cannot be quick to judge surface things said. I was in a place where I saw this comment with compassion, as I could clearly see where he must be coming from. And then I saw more clearly.

Let us be compassionate first, that we don't have to learn compassion by walking in the very shoes to then learn it.

Regardless, those who have gone through rough things, how pure their love, how compassionate their heart. How brave they must have been coming here knowing the Lord would use them as such a light of love to shine in the world. Sadly at times this compassion can come through things endured. But the Lord will use all things for our good and for His glory.

Doctrine and Covenants 98:3 "… and all things wherewith you have been afflicted shall work together for your good, and to my name's glory, saith the Lord."

Sometimes things of light can only be understood by the wisdom gained in darkness. As we choose the light we can be magnified in it. How good our Father in Heaven is that even in our hardships He can consecrate them for our good and His glory. How amazing His love!

I spent the next 4 paragraphs giving a heartfelt testimony of truth as I feel he might listen to. I ended with "I reply to even a harsh thing you say because I have compassion as I was similar to you and I know how difficult it is. So hear my words homie. Much love. Your Father in Heaven loves you more than you know."

He wrote back, "Thanks man. Much obliged."

I don't say this to parade myself as a saint; I blocked many with unkind comments. I am not perfect, though I strive to be better always. I say this to illustrate the similarities of all of us. There is a reason in 1 Corinthians 13, all throughout the Bible, and Book of Mormon it says that above all things love and charity are of the most value. What better way to spread the Spirit of God then through love? God is the originator and source of love. God is love. All that is good is of God.

If we carry the banner of love we carry our Father in Heaven. Even a tiny ray of love is a vast opportunity for our Father in Heaven to do much good. The tiniest drop in the water makes a fast ripple all around it, ever growing.

I think many of us will be surprised to find that a vast majority of the problems of this world can be solved with real love, and teaching others to really love. Doing away with pride can do this; which is a lack of giving love. Real love is charity, the pure love of Christ. It starts with ourselves, knowing how much we are loved by our Father in Heaven, loving ourselves, and loving others.

Relieving ourselves of our insecurities by trusting in God and His love for us will help us love ourselves. We will come to be filled with His love, love ourselves and in turn love others. When one comes to the realization of just how much our Father in Heaven loves you, you will want to serve Him forever and ever and a smile will hardly leave your face.

If you were a person with no worries, plenty of money and everything that made one stress free about the cares of the world, also everyone in the entire world loved you dearly and gave you every compliment in the world at the very glance of you. You could not be told any more often how much you were loved and how awesome you were. You would begin to believe it, you would feel full of happiness and well being. Imagine how you would then treat others. You would want to give and lift them up and help them and let them know they are also loved.

Vastly grander than this analogy our Father in Heaven, God Almighty truly does love you and each of His children more than one can imagine. It's actually so very true and amazing. He gave us our attributes and we are divine. We can totally rely on Him. He built us perfectly in His image and has built us for perfect purposes. He loves us dearly. Pray to see this love. When we do we will love ourselves and love others because He is so good, and He loves them too.

Let's walk in love! It heals. It is far deeper than we know. In the physical world even it vibrates on a very high and healing frequency. Keep in mind fear is in the opposite, which is the same as stress and vibrates on a very low frequency. Keep in mind that stress can cause all manner of disease and lowers our immune function. Remember what spirit causes such and do all things to keep the Spirit of the Lord about us always.

Isn't it interesting to see what influences are constantly thrown in our faces? "Fear this, stress about that." It is as though, (well. . . ,) we are culturally programmed to look for things to fear or be bummed about. Fear is in opposite of faith and can take us away from the healing of love and the Spirit of God. Faith and love will change the world. God is far bigger than all, He created all; let Him heal.

What then is the antidote? Love! Accept love. Love yourself! If you don't start with yourself how can you spread love? Pray to know how much God loves you, He will show you more and more. The small glimpses I have seen are enormous and a small ray of that love, when you can see yourself as God sees you will make you love yourself and see yourself so much better. We can become better and better at being powerhouses of His love filling us all the time. This takes practice, but the best things do. We are aiming to become even as our perfect Savior Jesus Christ. Perfect love.

Furthermore let us focus on all we are grateful for and blessed with, that our hearts will be ever filled with love and gratitude, the high frequency of love. As we maintain it we maintain the avenue in resonance for the Lord to continue to bless us with such. He can bring light and love from His Kingdom through us, out to the world.

We are what we are created to be. He can bless us significantly more as we walk in His commandments and on His side of the guardrail. Seek His Spirit and walk in love.

Charity is the pure love of Christ. God is the very source thereof. It heals all and is what we should do above all.

Doctrine and Covenants 88:125 "And above all things, clothe yourselves with the bond of charity, as with a mantle, which is the bond of perfectness and peace."

What a scripture!

When famous minds say, "Love is the answer." It is not some ridiculous and lovey cliché. It is real. It has profound and measurable effects even in the physical temporal realm. It is the very Spirit and Light of Christ reaching out into the world. It is the greatest and the grand point of all of this! Becoming as Christ is becomes the absolute key to all good things and blessings. And loving as He loves is of the greatest importance and use.

Love!

K-Rob

One man who did a great job at being kind and loving to others was one of my friends and mentors Kevin Robinson. Growing up I had posters of him on my wall. He was an absolute BMX legend.

He was the first guy ever to double flair BMX. He's the only guy to do it on vert. He gave me pointers on the trick over the year I was training for it on the Big Air quarter pipe at X Games. He had tried it once before on the Big Air quarter pipe and had a big fall that he got out of luckily. He gave me the pointers I needed to figure it out. He was one of the first people I talked to when I figured it out.

190

He was the guy that got me on the Big Air ramp. I traveled the world with him and he was always the kindest most motivating guy. I was blessed to ride many times with him and I was blessed to ride the event he retired at.

I was further blessed to have him be one of the TV announcers at the moment I landed the first double flair on the Big Air ramp and won X Games again.

He was always a kind, loving and supportive guy. While some guys would go out and act wild he would be chilling and having conversations with everyone and making everyone feel valued and cared about.

After retiring he started the K-Rob Foundation. They raised money to pay for kids to be in sports in the community for families that couldn't afford such. This always resonated with me as I was a kid who grew up in a like family and seen many families that would have really been appreciative of such. He spoke at schools all over the east coast and talked to kids about bullying and motivation. He even did a Ted talk on it. Kevin was a really good guy and is incredibly respected by BMX.

After comments started getting heated after I chose to drop my sponsor Kevin took to an instagram of the BMX site that posted about the initial story. Comments were going wild with all sorts of negative and this is some of the comment he posted.

"Just a note. I'll defend Colton until the death. That is no exaggeration. I'm proud of him for standing for his beliefs. Something very few people do anymore."

He told everyone with negative comments basically to look at how I chased a passion up to the pinnacle point and that I was traveling the world riding a bike for a living. He ended with the hashtag #faithisstrongerthananyhuman.

This may sound small, but it was big. I was handling all the negativity just fine. Though it wasn't the most fun, the Lord and His Spirit was with me, I had all I needed. But it was a big legend and friend that everyone respected that chose to stand up in defense in a big way.

I was taught a lesson here. To have a real friend stand up with you and for you when you could use it, such a friend that they will defend you until death. It was big to realize how much even one standing up could have a bold effect. Granted he was a big and respected legend. At the very least, it made me even less worried about the opinions of people. Every ray of light, love and every helping hand, no matter how small is what help the most in the long run. They are often what mean the most.

Only a few weeks later I went to the temple for the first time. It was incredible and I was amazed at the strong presence of the Lord and His Spirit there. I was so grateful to be there.

I was with family afterward and learned that Kevin had died from an unexpected stroke. He was young, in his 40s, with a great wife and family. He was like a super dad and one of the most genuine people one could imagine.

I pondered this from a personal standpoint. He had been a light to me, guided me and helped me so much. He had always wanted the best for me and for others. He defended me and was a great example throughout years of travel. He was sincere and always focused on the things that mattered most. I had been greatly blessed by the light he carried.

He had unknowingly guided me little by little. In my career, and supporting me in choices of a spiritual nature, even defending me.

I recognized that even though Kevin wasn't a member of the church or outwardly religious he had always been a profound light to me personally. What was it? It was that he always walked in love.

He has become a great example to me of the power of love and kindness and he kept the promise that he made in defending me.

I look on his example and so many have genuinely great experiences with him. For instance, the guy at the BMX website was once on a trip early in his career. And lucky for him he got to go eat with Kevin Robinson and some other big named guys. The dinner was expensive and he didn't have much money, but he wanted to be there with such a legend. When it came time to pay Kevin paid for him, surely understanding his need.

These are the types of people that make a difference. There is a reason love and charity are the greatest things that we should choose to share with all we can. Love is of Christ. Love is from God our Father, the source of love. In love for others we treat them more as the Savior would, and through that love we make a greater impact.

Him dying on that specific day made me personally reflect and see, that even he had a small hand in that sacred day for me in going through the temple.

God could work little by little through every ray of love that he brought to the world. Each time he was genuinely caring and loving and kind I could look back later and see how it actually would lead to grand effects on me, simply by being who he was.

He helped me see the good, he helped me treat others kindly. When I wanted to wear a shirt at X Games that said 'love' and do it again it had become a part of me, and I knew it was valued with a legend and not just myself.

192

I saw the value of the bigger things through the good example of a legend. I saw continual examples that kindness was cool and subconsciously I emulated them and wanted to give more to others as he did.

I really saw that the small things that we don't pay attention to are not small things. But the small little things of love around us indeed have the greatest ripple effects. I never made a conscious decision to care about others or want to inspire others, it came naturally; it was all influenced by good around me. It was a norm from the people I respected.

The day I won X Games with the double flair, I said on TV that I grew up watching legends like Kevin on TV and I wanted now to inspire the kids watching to do something awesome with their lives.

I can now say this on a bigger and better scale. I grew up watching a good legend with love in his heart for others, defend and have compassion for the small, seeing the best in everyone, genuinely wanting all to succeed, choosing to see the best in others. He spread love as a norm and cared about those around him. That example inspired me and I could see the true wisdom of this. I want to carry that torch and love and care about those around me and lift others to their potential. And I hope that they will be lifted and see the effect of love and for themselves want to naturally love others and grow love and be part of the grandest snowball of inspiration. I hope we all can receive love and be inspired to love.

I think way back to this moment in Chile with Kevin. One of the first times we traveled together; I was blessed to be there. We were signing autographs and I had sunglasses on. He came up to me saying, "You should take those off, these kids love to see you and the eye contact and engaging with them can mean so much."

My very first reaction and thought was prideful. 'Um do what? I'm not taking these off thanks.' I quickly suppressed the thought and took off my glasses. Thinking to myself then that at very least I would oblige a legend that I had respected for a long time. I later took the advice to heart from someone I genuinely respected and tried to better engage with the people that were excited to see us.

Over time I went from the inward reaction of hard heartedness to seeing that he genuinely cared about the kids who were seeing their heroes. He genuinely came to Chile to effect people in a positive way. Over time I saw this more and more and my first reaction changed slowly to that more of compassion and genuine care of others.

He had large goals in riding so that he could effect the more for the better. This is evident when looking at what he did when he retired. He simply wanted to bring love to many.

193

I now think back on this and think of how at the event we put on, "Ramp Riot," we did autographs at halftime and as long as it took after the show. The kids probably would never get anything of the sort, only this chance and although we stayed for hours and braved a long line, we cared and stayed as long as it took. We valued their joy. The small little things would last.

This had become a genuine instilled piece of me, and it came through experiencing that genuine example. It was his example, and most importantly that his example was genuine love. That changed me. It was something I wanted to emulate.

That day after the temple I could see how even the tiny slivers of light that God sends to us are a big deal. Everything has some sort of ripple effect. Negative emotions are no fun to be around. But when love is spread, the ripple effects are magnified and God can work through that love. All good is from Him. He can change people for the better in little ways that will lead to big changes. He can slowly make changes on and heal a hard heart. Love is the way.

One thought that just struck me now. I started riding BMX more on street and park. Those that I looked up to that rode street and park weren't that kind to me. (I don't blame them I was probably annoying.) Those that rode dirt were super nice and super kind. Even in contests all the dirt guys were always very cool, laid back and kind. I naturally gravitated toward dirt. I felt comfortable doing it. My friends were all dirt riders and that's where I thrived.

I loved riding all types of things, dirt just felt the most comfortable. In park guys were centrally focused and more serious, many of them were nice but I felt comfortable in dirt. Dirt became the main focus. All the guys on the deck were always super relaxed and kind and supportive.

Older guys and legends rode vert. They respected everyone and were stoked for anyone to take on vert because it was so hard to become good at new guys wouldn't do it much. They were kind and supportive and stoked for you. I naturally gravitated toward that also.

The very first time I rode Big Air was the only open event ever and Kevin hosted it for BMX. I was terrified; the speed was no joke. It was such a ridiculous level of BMX. I remember sending a 360 backflip, one of my biggest tricks then over one of the bigger gaps, and somehow pulled it.

I remember hearing Kevin announcing say something to the effect of, "I love that kid!" I was then the only dude then since Dave Mirra, a huge legendary name I looked up since a kid, to ever 360 backflip the Mega Ramp. I pushed myself and it was recognized and encouraged. I felt genuine love. And I naturally gravitated toward Mega.

194

Riding that ramp, everyone is so kind, you have to be, it's so gnarly and we have all been beat up. Kevin's genuine loving and motivating influence was there.

I remember it taking me a long time to go high on the quarter pipe. I would do a 10 foot air and he would be so genuinely stoked for me and help every step of the way. I was gravitated again toward what made me feel comfortable. Toward love. I didn't give up, I kept working until the ramp was comfortable. Furthermore, he always spoke in knowing it would all come. Encouragement for everyone, keep going you'll get it.

The very reason I chose action sports even is that I didn't like being yelled at by coaches and that I could be free with my friends. I didn't ever feel like I wasn't doing good enough or needed to work harder.

In action sports I never felt that influence from anyone but me personally. Everyone who did it did it for the love of it. Everyone experienced injuries and were humble because of it. Every time we would learn a new trick we would be mobbed by our friends, they would be so excited for us, even if they learned it years ago. We knew the elation of learning something ourselves and loved that we could be a part of someone else's.

Love led my life. Though I couldn't see it in the moment I can look back now and see how God guided me.

That day Kevin left a great lesson was taught me. Although it is a very sad loss, he lived 100 lives in one and affected so many for good. From my perspective it was, "Well I've done my small part in your life, you're on the right track now and you'll be fine without me."

Although there is no perfect way to view a sad death, this perspective does provide some amazing insight for me. Each ray of light of love God can work through and guide more and more. It has allowed me to see the ripple effects of love. And how at the very core we all just want to feel closer to home, the Kingdom of God, and closer to our true nature, Love.

When we recognize this we can help perceive others more clearly. We can love others more. Love heals and blesses us and the people we love. We can see the importance in defending in love. Each little kind word or standing up in the right direction, every stand in love will have a great impact even from a small ripple effect.

We can learn to love more openly, and to defend that which is of love, even the source of love, Jesus Christ and His gospel.

Love is the grandest thing, the grand point of everything. We gravitate toward our nature. Love is our true nature; we are children of

God. Love is our home; and it has such a larger impact, even in small doses, than we can imagine.

I am forever grateful for those rays of the love of my Father in Heaven, given me through such incredible examples around me. He magnifies those rays of His love. The things of God are living, the ripples continue.

Moroni 7:47 "But charity is the pure love of Christ, and it endureth forever; and whoso is found possessed of it at the last day, it shall be well with him."

Chapter 17

FAITH DISCOURSE

I have briefly touched on the necessity of faith and will touch on it quite a bit more in this discourse on faith.

Remember that agency, our personal freedom of choice, is very important to God. He is pure freedom; in the opposite we have basically slavery.

In love and within the guardrail of safety of the commandments we are guided to be able to perceive the right choices but are given each choice to be made on our own.

In opposition, as wrong choices are made darkness takes the lead. For example things that were once just random bits of anger become ensnared into personality and grow, things can become addictions; our freedom of choice on God's side become compulsion and control on the other. Often times they are things and ways the world simply perceives as normal.

This is one area that we can see how God and His side of the line will always care about our agency. This is of great importance to God.

When it comes to our faith we can exercise it any way we choose. It becomes important how we choose to direct our agency.

I have talked without giving detail, for good reason, about the 'wisdom' of the world. Faith in the things of God greatly confounds the 'wisdom' of the world, and faith is of paramount, paramount, paramount importance.

Faith is like an FM tuner. We can tune it all over the place. A tuner 'tunes' in to a specific frequency. It resonates with that specific frequency. As we tune to the frequency of truth we can receive and transmit, this requires humility to resonate. It is as though there is a hidden switch of humility on a radio, by which then we can find the single station of perfect truth.

God is always there and always with us, yet we can only perceive Him when we are properly tuned it. It may be that as we become in tune, through faith, that we can look back in our lives and see the bigger picture and truly those times He has carried us.

Many in 'wisdom' come to understand this without an option of truth; they cannot see it without faith and humility. For them it can become a stumbling block and relatively a deep level of deception. Many are incredibly ignorantly and dangerously led away from all true truth.

I have touched on this somewhat deeply. Many simply have it and are led in deception by it, thinking there is no singular truth. Deception is bad when it steers away from our home and Father in

Heaven. There are portions that are potentially good to understand, inherent nature of certain things, but most are led in vast deception. It truly can be a vast stumbling block and hard to see out of. They miss truth and explore vast deception, with ever growing iron bars. After all faith in Christ is the way. The truth of Christ can break them.

I see many in life lately ignorantly getting to even small understanding like the 'law of attraction.' It has been popular in the modern culture as of late. Be careful of pursuing such things as they can lead down and down and down and down if one is not keeping God at the center in faith. Thinking man's 'wisdom' avails much can lead to deception. Let us reason with Him and have Him show us all things we seek. Things of Him are far, far greater.

Take care how you hear and what you take to heart, especially in what way. We are His children. All is God's; keep Him at the center. Wisdom is in Him. The way the world pushes things can be utterly great distortion. Simply keep Him at the center; every good and perfect gift is from above. Much today is twisted by the adversary to steer us away from God; be not ensnared. Remember,

2 Nephi 9:29 "But to be learned is good if they hearken unto the counsels of God."

Keep Him and faith and reliance on Him at the center. Leave the things of the world and cleave to Him.

Doctrine and Covenants 6:7 "Seek not for riches but for wisdom, and behold, the mysteries of God shall be unfolded unto you, and then shall you be made rich. Behold, he that hath eternal life is rich."

Doctrine and Covenants 136:32 "Let him that is ignorant learn wisdom by humbling himself and calling upon the Lord his God, that his eyes may be opened that he may see, and his ears opened that he may hear;
33 For my Spirit is sent forth into the world to enlighten the humble and contrite, and to the condemnation of the ungodly."

Remember, the greatest wisdom IS humility before God, unwavering FAITH and trusting in Him, even as a child trusts.
Let me repeat.
REMEMBER, the greatest wisdom IS humility before God, unwavering FAITH and trusting in Him, even as His humble child. True wisdom is trusting Him in faith, praying in faith, and letting Him guide

us to all truth. His truths are FAR grander and not even comparable to the twisted bits the world will give; all is our Father in Heaven's.

I will delve more into this in the discourse on revelation. Keep and grow your faith in truth and in He who created all things. Remember He is real, and all these things are real, and believe and know you will experience and behold.

Hold to the faith that this physical reality will 'pass away' in a sense, and God and His Spirit is the grandest reality, then one see how greatly things can change. This faith may take some mental and spiritual preparation. As the Brother of Jared in The Book of Mormon was at first scared to see the finger of God then later received great revelation and even saw Him perfectly, we must be ready and close to Him to bear the greater things and become who we are meant to be.

Joseph Smith eventually got more used to the glory of God while Sidney Rigdon was limp on the ground overcome with the power and glory on one occasion, "Sidney is not used to it as I am."

We must prepare ourselves in faith for the grander things that we may be better children and servants of our Father in Heaven. We must get closer to Him. For all things are by faith. We must be able to hope, to anticipate and fully expect the greater things. Diligently seeking and believing in faith. If we seek we can be more normalized to the grand things to be able to bear grander things and be greater servants blessed with all that we need for His work.

Paul teaches us in Hebrews that by faith the universe was formed by God's command. What a powerful lesson then we are learning on this earth. Faith is powerful, especially when we are seeking even God Almighty our Father in Heaven. And all things are His in His power.

Consider this scripture when wondering why faith?

1 Peter 1:7 "That the trial of your faith, being much more precious than of gold that perisheth, though it be tried with fire, might be found unto the praise and honour and glory at the appearing of Jesus Christ:"

Faith can be hard. It will be tried with fire. But is greater than gold.

Doctrine and Covenants 88:118 "And as all have not faith, seek ye diligently and teach one another words of wisdom; yea, seek ye out of the best books words of wisdom; seek learning, even by study and also by faith."

As all things require an opposite we must overcome doubt with faith for it to be perceived, understood and grown. It will be tried with fire but as we hold faithful it will be of significant eternal value. He lives.

Mormon 9:25 "And whosoever shall believe in my name, doubting nothing, unto him will I confirm all my words, even unto the ends of the earth."

When we resonate with Him through faith He can teach us and guide. Faith is knowing the sun will rise.

Faith can seem blind at times, yet the Spirit guides us and shows us truth in ways that we know that we know, depending on our specific needs. I was one who has needed to deeply understand, and eventually as I have sought in faith, diligence and patience, I have come to understand. Not only to know, but to understand. Seek diligently and we will find. Truly we should be led by the Spirit and do all to keep the Spirit and our Father in Heaven's influence. He simply must be of greatest importance to us.

Eventually we will gain powerful revelation and eventually will have overcome. Each thing we chose to overcome by faith will have greatly strengthened us and will turn to fruit. I understand the difficulty for some as it was for me in my youth. I am so thankful that now I can know and understand the depth of faith. To keep and grow it comes as a matter of priority and focus.

Remember that which is of God is living. Water the seed. Read scriptures, pray, seek; it will grow and become a mighty tree. Alma chapter 32 provides very great wisdom on the subject of nourishing faith. Pray for understanding and much is given.

After coming back to the fold, I had many times where I wasn't sure about certain things, even times when doubt would creep in as certain other things would make sense and my mind would be distracted. What did I do? I exercised faith, and waited patiently on God, knowing that He would make known to me that which I needed to know.

Sometimes I had to wait a while, other times it was quick. But each and every time I was proved in a big way with an understanding that absolutely confounded any specific questions and such doubt. These things would happen until I got to a point where no small doubts could even linger for I had destroyed them all with deep and perfect understanding, rather my Father in Heaven gave me wisdom that my faith and understanding grew and doubt was destroyed. The understanding I was gaining from God was deep and vast.

Each time I saw where the doubt originated and how it had come up. Each time I would learn more, rely on Him more, and become closer to my Father in Heaven.

I will interject. Our thoughts are so vastly important, even of greatest importance. All things are spirit. That said, our mind and thoughts are like a fish swimming in water with hooks. Swimming in dangerous waters of thought, in doubt and other things will give us many hooks. What we seek will be given, so be careful what we seek; humility and meekness becomes such a powerful principle and security.

A seemingly innocent thought can be a hook. We can bite the hook and take hold of the thought, thinking it no big deal, just a thought. Next we are led to another thought, and another and another and soon we are angry and upset and doubting truth. It is up to us to discern the spirit that is about us and behind each thought, and if necessary cut off our thoughts and jump to something good. It becomes wise to be able to discern a spirit of peace and comfort and that that steals peace and comfort.

Swim in good waters. I used to ignorantly think harshly of many that didn't think critically and chose faith over critical thinking, now I know what is out there and I know what truth is. I am so thankful forever to my Father in Heaven. Remember even that little thought of judging others are a hook to lead to deeper pride and thereby deeper deception. The commandments are a guardrail. Love for God and all is the way.

What spirit and thoughts you choose to exercise your agency and your faith in will lead you that way as you persist. You are given freedom to go wherever you want. It's an endless pond, but only the way of the Savior will lead you to freedom, to the pond of Living Water, with God, where no hooks exist, and it is true. We must seek faith, promote faith, and swim toward faith, truth and peace in our Savior and Father in Heaven by His Holy Spirit. As we do diligently we will swim to glorious waters where all such good abounds greatly and we are home. Be humble and meek, love and trust in God as His child with reverence for His guidance is important.

We must recognize as He is, loving, perfect, kind, merciful and have faith in that. Keep that faith strong until the day that by that faith we realize we greatly underestimated all of His perfect attributes and our faith is greatly strengthened and we are with Him.

If you are unsure about anything, tune your tuner of faith to the only frequency we should be on, the station of truth, faith in Jesus Christ. For that station of truth when we are exercising faithfully will absolutely prove all truth and is significantly above all things. Recognize the perfect love, what He chose to do for us.

Absolute truth and utterly serious revelation can come to us often as we need and desire it, though it takes practice in humbling. It is important we walk in the Holy Spirit and keep our thoughts away from all contention and meekly and humbly in His love. We must keep our thoughts in the greatest love we can imagine. As we become humble as His children we will realize humility is the key to seeing in truth.

I will get more into this in the revelation chapter.

Some are blessed with strong faith. Some have to go through the refining trials, for your faith is more precious than that of gold. God is wise and knows all things. He knows what He is doing. Pray and trust Him to settle all that you need settled.

Each time I have gained a glimpse at the power of prayer, especially faithful prayer, I pray longer and longer. It is a great and vast blessing. This should be re-read and re-iterated. Prayer is powerful. Be open with our Father in Heaven. We are His children. Prayer is powerful.

Pray to be kept strong in faith and against difficulties of the world. Pray to be kept strong with Him. Be totally open with Him, every tiny thought, He knows it deeper than you can imagine, you're His child. Upon recognizing this clearer and paying attention to our thoughts we can begin to have real conversations, which is the beginning of amazing.

Faith in God and in truth, and as we walk as He walks, serious miracles can begin to happen. There are significant promises given to all those of the world with faith in Jesus Christ.

Faith in Jesus Christ is the beginning of very deep wisdom, very large revelation, miracles and all joy. Read that over 10 times. He has done it all for us. He has prepared the way.

Especially as we also become like Him. He is the way, the truth and the light. We must go through Him. He is center of the strait and narrow path; He is the gate.

For those who are out of the gospel currently, place your faith first in Jesus Christ. Every person's faith will grow as we read The Book of Mormon and the Bible and all the word of God for His Spirit will testify to us of the truth. Pray often and in faith, earnestly, from the heart. We can discern the truth as it testifies of Jesus Christ as our Savior, we can see the fruits thereof and above all the Spirit can testify to us incredibly.

Walk humbly and meekly and let the Spirit attend you. We will be taught. I seek to get better at this myself, but over time and as we diligently try and seek, we get better.

Our humility before God get us in 'tune' and resonance with truth and we are able to receive the things of God, we can feel the Spirit and our faith will grow. As our faith grows we can receive more and more and grow more. We are blessed by and through our faith, it is strengthened all the more, and we are blessed all the more. These grand blessings give us the genuine desire to be more like our Savior and walk in love like Him and as we do this we grow much more and are blessed all the more.

For those who are new to such things, it may be odd at first, but the peace that passeth all understanding will soon have you wanting to feel and be guided by the Spirit of God all the time.

I suggest reading Alma chapter 32 for this part. You are planting a seed of faith, in a well-intentioned experiment. As we humbly and meekly in hope and faith grow this seed it grows into a strong tree over time. And boy does that tree of faith in the Spirit bear fruit. Our Father in Heaven is so abundantly good my friends.

I will add the last couple scriptures of the chapter to give you an idea; their value is great. Note that a whole recipe is provided. Seek. Open your heart and let Him guide in love.

Alma 32:41-43 "But if ye will nourish the word, yea, nourish the tree as it beginneth to grow, by your faith with great diligence, and with patience, looking forward to the fruit thereof, it shall take root; and behold it shall be a tree springing up unto everlasting life. And because of your diligence and your faith and your patience with the word in nourishing it, that it may take root in you, behold, by and by ye shall pluck the fruit thereof, which is most precious, which is sweet above all that is sweet, and which is white above all that is white, yea, and pure above all that is pure; and ye shall feast upon this fruit even until ye are filled, that ye hunger not, neither shall ye thirst. Then, my brethren, ye shall reap the rewards of your faith, and your diligence, and patience, and long-suffering, waiting for the tree to bring forth fruit unto you."

This recipe works for receiving many things of the Spirit, revelation included.

Before we get into revelation let us remember the very first thing we should have faith in, the first and most important reason why. That is in Jesus Christ and that is to be clean through His blood, His sacrifice for us, the Atonement.

He has already paid for all we have done wrong, He suffered exceedingly. It caused Him to bleed from every pore and caused, even God the greatest of all, to tremble in exceeding pain. It is important to always remember what He has done for us because of His great love. We needed it; we couldn't have done it ourselves. Without Him, we are lost. With Him, we are saved. I have explained this further back.

Exercising faith in Him and His Atonement for us will cause us to see clearly, be repentant and change our heart; we are reborn and born of the Spirit, He cleanses us from our sin. This must be one from a humble and contrite heart. As we truly repent we become humble before Him and really recognize what He did for us. Our hearts are penitent and contrite. Our heartfelt and true 'sorry' turns to 'thank you.' I explained a bit of my process of this earlier on and it is real. He truly heals us.

Moroni 8:26 "And the remission of sins bringeth meekness, and lowliness of heart; and because of meekness and lowliness of heart cometh the visitation of the Holy Ghost, which Comforter filleth with hope and perfect love, which love endureth by diligence unto prayer, until the end shall come, when all the saints shall dwell with God."

It is important that we have faith in Him and rid ourselves of sins that we can have His Spirit to be with us. With His presence in His Spirit, our faith will grow and we can partake of the many amazing fruits and blessings of God.

"If you have felt the influence of the Holy Ghost today, you may take it as evidence that the atonement is the working in your life." – Henry B. Eyring

What at amazing quote from an apostle of the Lord that provides great understanding to us. We can be clean and pure and 'resonate' again with God. Christ has done it all for us. How incredibly blessed we are.
As we trust and have faith in Him He will change us. We will want to be more like Him. He is the grand key, our grand exemplar. We will recognize it is Him who strengthens us.
It is important for us to keep His Spirit with us always. I try to only read good things that are spiritual, listen to good music that is spiritual and avoid places, thoughts and all things where the Spirit won't dwell.
The Holy Ghost is a member of the Godhead. It is the very presence of God! Why would we not do all necessary to keep Him around us? I had to learn this lesson out of necessity, until I was more fully healed by the Lord, and then it is a lesson that stuck. The Spirit is important to keep with me always; it is a priority and of paramount importance to me.

"We must never let the noise of the world overpower and overwhelm that still small voice." - L. Tom Perry

When we have faith in Him and remember Him and are cleansed by Him through faith, we can have then have His Spirit with us. As we strive to grow that and do and be better, becoming more like our Savior, that influence will grow and real revelation and guidance and teaching will come. Our Spiritual eyes and ears will begin to develop and will grow as we diligently seek them to. I will speak more in the next revelation chapter.

It all starts with faith, it is essential, it is real; you can tune it all over, tune it to truth. It becomes of vital importance where and how we tune it. We must tune it in faith of truth, and that requires humility.

How are we to discern faith?

I once saw a news header that went something like this. "How do I handle defeat when I pray for a loved one's healing when I know they wont be healed?"

This is a sad story and this headline really alarmed me. We are told, "Ask and ye shall receive." We are also told to "upbraideth not." We are to not doubt but count the Lord and His promises as true and tune our faith to that truth. Peculiar by wordly standards, but God has made us a 'peculiar people.' We are blessed greatly.

This person had faith enough to try a prayer, and then immediately negated that prayer by 'knowing they wont be healed.' Where is the faith placed? In the prayer or that which they KNOW?

They chose to put the large and exceeding portion of their faith into great strength in the opposite of their desire, they made it knowledge to them. They trusted the physical, which is below the power of God instead of Him, they 'knew' that person wouldn't be healed. They came to know and fully expect the worst outcome. They put their faith in the opposite of their hope. Oh the trial of our faith.

Mormon 9:20 "And the reason why he ceaseth to do miracles among the children of men is because they dwindle in unbelief, and depart from the right way, and know not the God in whom they should trust.

21 Behold, I say unto you that whoso believeth in Christ, doubting nothing, whatsoever he shall ask the Father in the name of Christ it shall be granted him; and this promise is unto all, even unto the ends of the earth."

25 "And whosoever shall believe in my name, doubting nothing, unto him will I confirm all my words, even unto the ends of the earth."

What did these people do wrong in this sad story? For one I cannot blame them as I have gone through the same lessons, the truth is, the blessings do come after faith. We simply must overcome the physical and the world and have faith in our Father in Heaven.

205

It becomes of vital importance to watch our thoughts and keep them on faith, rebuking any doubt. In many a sense our personal world experience is a looking glass of our thoughts. Faith is active all the time, whether we put it in that we shouldn't and expect fear or that we keep our faith strong and overcome fear with faith in our Father in Heaven. This is where we get the continual push throughout this book to, "tune our faith to truth in Him and to have a humble childlike trust in our Father in Heaven, thereby resonating in truth." It is from this place that He can teach us greatly and does. All is His; we are His children.

As we pursue in faith and choose to overcome with faith in Him we learn a great deal seeking His teaching. In the Epistle of James we are taught,

James 1:5 "If any of you lack wisdom, let him ask of God, that giveth to all men liberally, and upbraideth not; and it shall be given him.

6 But let him ask in faith, nothing wavering. For he that wavereth is like a wave of the sea driven with the wind and tossed.

7For let not that man think that he shall receive any thing of the Lord.

8 A double minded man is unstable in all his ways.

I have learned mastering this comes more over time. But we are told we cannot upbraid. Basically we cannot think both ways, we cannot doubt. We must garnish our thoughts unceasingly and wholly rely on Him and faith in Him. We must leave the thoughts of doubt and darkness that will peck at us and say, 'listen to what the Dr. said, this is silly,' and all things of this world that will cause us to doubt. We must overcome doubt by faith. We must have faith that destroys all fear. Then is our faith made perfect in perfect love and abounds to miracles. We are a peculiar people, a royal priesthood; we are to hold out faithful just as one waits for the sun to rise.

Anytime all physical signs may show one way, we have 'died' to the physical and are born of the Spirit and live above in faith in our Father in Heaven. We live anew and above, we come to know what the Savior meant when He said, "the flesh profiteth nothing."

There are many Christians in many sects including The Church of Jesus Christ of Latter-day Saints that have all manner of astounding glorious miracles made possible by the promises of faith on our Savior. One simply must seek, there are many. Even on youtube many are there, incredible ones. The promises of faith in our Savior are vast! I personally have been a part of them, and I personally have had experience that helped me to strengthen my faith. The world becomes less and less physical all the time as our faith grows. Faith is both diligently obtained and a gift from our Father in Heaven.

In the restored everlasting gospel in The Church of Jesus Christ of Latter-day Saints the very Priesthood of our Savior has been restored and this is a very immense magnification of all things pertaining to the power of our Father in Heaven. I will not get much into it in this book but seek and ye shall find.

We are being taught faith. As I said it is a tuner. Even those in 'wisdom' understand this in a way, though most are led in deception and kept from the truth and glory and power and right way that is in our actual living Savior Jesus Christ.

Remember, He is the singular avenue of truth, the strait and narrow path in opposition to endless deception where there is no singular truth; He is the way, the truth and the life. The law of our living Savior Jesus Christ supersedes all and all things are His.

This scripture also does a great job at helping us understand faith as in this situation. It is a description of the Liahona, a compass-like guide given by the Lord.

Alma 37:40 "And it did work for them according to their faith in God; therefore, if they had faith to believe that God could cause that those spindles should point the way they should go, behold it was done; therefore they had this miracle, and also many other miracles wrought by the power of God, day by day.

41 Nevertheless, because those miracles were worked by small means it did show unto them marvelous works. They were slothful and forgot to exercise their faith, and diligence and then those marvelous works ceased, and they did not progress in their journey;"

This is edifying even to me personally now. We will progress as we have faith. Consider a few points here, "if they had faith to believe that God could. . .," "behold it was done;"

We must have like faith. It is a small seeming thing but by the small means marvelous works are shown. I have had utter immense things happen by a physical standard that if I wrote would probably be not believed by many, but it came through recognizing that "God could," and that all is His.

We all have agency to tune our faith wherever we will. Brothers and sisters keep it tuned to truth, to faith and not to fear. If you tune to a station full of fear, what station will you hear?

"The future is as bright as your faith." – President Thomas S. Monson

Place your faith in sunny days, praising God in joy, glorifying Him. Do not place it in fear and sadness. Do not change the quote to, '…as dismal as your faith.' Take heart. See and hear. He lives. Our future is bright in Him.

He is the way, the truth and the life. Stay tuned to Him. His promises are vast.

John 10:9 "I am the door: by me if any man enter in, he shall be saved, and shall go in and out, and find pasture.

10 The thief cometh not, but for to steal, and to kill, and to destroy: I am come that they might have life, and that they might have it more abundantly.

11 I am the good shepherd: the good shepherd giveth his life for the sheep."

Many, many, times we are told throughout scripture and even commanded to 'fear not.'

2 Timothy 1:7 "For God hath not given us the spirit of fear; but of power, and of love, and of a sound mind."

It is up to us, by our agency, to tune our faith to truth. Even those walking in truth at times place their faith in the areas of fear, we mustn't. See the calm love and utter trust of God.

We will all learn eventually to let go and trust our Father in Heaven. We will recognize our weakness and He will make us strong for He is strength.

We are to overcome fear entirely and always count the Lord faithful and tune our faith to that. As we tune our faith in truth and rely on the Lord entirely we are then attuned to see such miracles provided by Him in our life.

The world around us today will put all manner of fear into us to look at and naturally and subconsciously put our faith in. Is it any wonder that we are counseled to and even profess to the world that, "If there is anything virtuous, lovely, or of good report or praiseworthy, we seek after these things."

We are to have our mind affixed in the trust of God and follow His commandment to fear not. We are to focus on in faith the good things of the world and walk in the fruit of the Spirit: love, joy, peace, longsuffering, gentleness, goodness, faith, meekness, and temperance.

208

If the world screamed to always tune the radio to a frequency of constant fear, doubt and terrible music would we? Yet we unwittingly do and often focus on the harsh and trivial. Instead we must choose to tune to truth and good things and listen to uplifting stations. Our station becomes our world.

Thus again and in another way many stumble vastly as they never see singular truth in our Savior Jesus Christ and are not humble to see. It is as though humility and humbly relying in faith on Him suddenly gives the option to hear the station.

Fear can dictate much. To the point of anxiety to where some only know and see the fearful outcome and not that of faith. I for one had to be healed of such, and He healed me.

Choose instead to believe as the world does not. Choose to earnestly believe in and have faith in good outcomes. Choose to pray and hope and let your faith become a knowing just as knowing the sun will rise. Choose to trust and wait upon the Lord in faith for His promises to be fulfilled and praise Him all the while. We are different from the world; we are not of the world. Christ was far different and not of the world and He did great miracles in love. Let us boldly be different and live in faith.

1 Peter 2:9 "But ye are a chosen generation, a royal priesthood, an holy nation, a peculiar people; that ye should shew forth the praises of him who hath called you out of darkness into his marvelous light:"

Remember the vast agency we have been given. It is the reason that there is a strait and narrow path of truth and a wide way to destruction; many tune to all things but truth. We must always keep our tuner on our Father in Heaven.

Humbly trusting in Him becomes power. As we keep our faith tuned properly we can resonate with Him, be guided in truth by His Spirit, receive revelation and grow to rely on and trust in Him more.

Just as Abraham and Sarah were very elderly and the Lord promised them a child, he didn't stagger at the large promises of God that seemed outlandish by a worldly standard.

Romans 4:18-22 "Who against hope believe in hope, that he might become the father of many nations, according to that which was spoken, So shall thy seed be, And being not weak in faith, he considered not his own body now dead, when he was about an hundred years old, neither yet the deadness of Sara's womb: He staggered not at the promise of God through unbelief; but was strong in faith, giving glory to God;

And being fully persuaded that, what he had promised, he was able also to perform. And therefore it was imputed to him for righteousness."

It was this miracle that led to the promise and the children of Israel.

Let us remember to against hope believe in hope, and stagger not at the promises of God. Let us be fully persuaded that what is promised the Lord is able to perform. Let us not consider the flesh but be strong in faith. If the world thinks you are crazy then yay, you are on the right track. The Lord designs us to be a 'peculiar people.' We do not stagger at His promises to perform, we choose to maintain faith though it be tried with fire, and it will be imputed to us for righteousness as well.

By faith alone we can change the world, rather God can change the world and we can accept and see His blessings through our faithfulness. By faith we can open up our eyes to His grand symphony before us. Humbly trusting Him is powerful.

Remember our agency is huge to Him; our faith must be reconciled to Him. We must overcome the temporal understanding with faith. We must see God clearly, His vastness that we may trust Him. All is His, He is above all and nothing is hard for Him.

Humility, meekness and trusting Him as a child becomes the key to try faith. The folly of many in the world now is coming to see the vastness of the stations and tuning ability. They see it all so vast that they become prideful in it. Finding the station of singular truth requires vast humbling and meekness to tune to it properly. To tune properly to truth we must act in all truth and place ourselves in the proper place before Him, truly humbled.

Moroni 7:43 "And again, behold I say unto you that he cannot have faith and hope, save he shall be meek, and lowly of heart."

If we cannot resonate with truth, and what we truly are before God Almighty we will never be able to see truth. The incredibly grand things of God are perfectly protected by meekness, humility and faith. Many in the world cannot yet realize a total transformation and reliance on God that is needed to finally see truth. Therefore they walk in 'wisdom' keeping themselves prideful in it, unwittingly building a deeper prison of deception for themselves. Get out of the car and humble yourself, for it is faith we need. We are made perfect through faith in our Savior Jesus Christ.

We must resonate in faith in truth, and keep our faith tuned to truth in God. And as we are humble we will be lifted up.

Matthew 23:12 "And whosoever shall exalt himself shall be abased; and he that shall humble himself shall be exalted."

Be humble and trust Him. Let our loving Father fight our battles, bless and heal. He does all things well.

Choosing to become as Christ is, in all aspects, is the grandest key; walking in overpowering, perfect, unconditional love, even charity, the pure love of Christ.

Faith Analogy Story

I will explain much more but I have one analogy that, though quite long, I think may help people with understanding faith. For me growing my faith came by getting a little bit more revelation and more learning and understanding of faith. Little by little exercising it more and more it grew. I would learn things that would strengthen it and I could exercise more the next time. Soon it became exponential growth. Revelation in humbly and meekly sought guidance of the Spirit became a thankful expectation.

Truly those who learn by humble faith and don't harden their hearts are given the greater things by the Holy Spirit. Those who harden their hearts, the greater things are withheld.

Here is a little story and analogy that I think will help understand faith; and I have found it rather accurate as pertaining to myself.

Imagine a large group of people. A teacher comes to that group and says, the essential answers to everything and where their eternal home lies is in a palace in the middle of a vast and endless forest. And that it actually exists. Furthermore, that eventually they would all need to make it there, for where they were would pass away.

Of the many who are told this only a very small percentage take it seriously and don't scoff at it as silly. 3 boys decide that maybe it was true and they would search for the palace. They felt something in the words of the teacher.

They inquire of the teacher more. The teacher tells them they need to follow the bright blue pebbles scattered throughout the forest and that if they followed them, they would come to the palace in the forest, their loving home.

The 3 boys came to the edge of the vast forest and began searching all over the ground for the bright blue pebbles. They searched and searched and began to doubt as they couldn't seem to find any.

The teacher came again and said, "The way is true boys. Take heart and seek and believe. Your home and answers truly are there to be

211

found." The words pierced the hearts of the boys and they felt the power and a familiar comfort in the words.

All 3 of them lifted their hearts and sought diligently. Each kept looking for the bright blue pebbles to show them the way.

One of the boys eventually decided that he had searched long enough. He had overturned many rocks and with each one he allowed his heart to feel let down. The encouragement the teacher gave him was gone and his heart was hardening.

In despair he told the other two looking for the pebbles, "We have been misled; we should have stayed with the others and not gone on this fools journey. There is not a blue rock anywhere."

The one boy left and went back feeling foolish. He was upset that he wasted his time. To make matters worse as he was leaving he tripped and fell in the rocks. He angrily picked a pebble up, threw it, and left.

When he got back he told all in the group that the whole thing was ridiculous and nonsense just like the other nonsense around them and cautioned them against listening to the teacher, even though he had felt deeply the words were true.

The other 2 boys kept up their hearts and trusted the teacher.

"I just know this must be true, I feel it and I felt it." The boys said and agreed; but they had been searching for quite some time.

They grew weary but again they chose to take heart, "I know it must be true." They said as they picked up another rock and looked at it. They must have picked up the very rock before but this time it felt different. There was a very, very small speck on the pebble. It looked kind of blue.

"Well its not bright blue but this little speck here looks sort of blue. We must have checked every rock here, lets follow this one." The other boy was unsure if the speck meant anything but he agreed to faithfully follow the direction. After all they had been searching for some time.

They picked up the rock with the tiny blue speck, trusted the words of the teacher, and followed the direction it led into the forest.

They began walking in the direction the pebble led through the dense forest, scouring the ground for a blue pebble. They walked and walked and the forest got denser and denser. They would look for a long time occasionally finding somewhat of a blue speck on a pebble, and they would follow in that direction deeper into the forest. As they went on the specs seemed to become slightly larger. Their faith grew each little bit.

Soon the boys came to a deep stream that they needed to cross. 1 of the 2 boys looked at it and sighed. He realized crossing it would ruin his shoes and soak his clothes. After all they were just following normal looking rocks with some specks of bluish on them.

"I don't know about this, we have been searching for so long and maybe we are just going in circles. Maybe we should go back. We are getting lost. If we cross and ruin our clothes and shoes everyone will make fun of us all the more when we get back."

Just then the teacher happened to be walking by.

"Oh hello. Are you guys following the bright blue pebbles? Just follow them and take heart and believe. The palace is there waiting for you I assure you." The teacher encouraged the boys smiling kindly at them. "It is all worth it for the palace boys. Take heart."

The boys could again feel the power and comfort in the teacher's words, they could feel the truth in them. Although they were only finding tiny yet ever growing specks of blue on pebbles the teacher's words gave them strength to keep looking. They would have seen bright blue rocks; they were looking diligently at each one.

The teacher walked away in an important seeming rush; the comfort carried them and they began walking through the stream. Their shoes were soaked and sinking into the mud. Their clothes were getting wet but they kept walking until they got to the other side.

They climbed out of the stream on the other side, soaking wet, their shoes covered in mud. They laughed it off as their spirits were greatly lifted by the teacher, they continued searching for the blue pebbles.

They immediately found one with an even larger speck of blue on it. Taking heart they smiled and followed its direction. They came to another pebble that had a larger speck of blue; they started to feel they were on the right path.

Soon after the stream the path led right into a rocky hillside that was very sharp, tall and hard to climb. The boys quickly realized they couldn't climb it with the slick mud all over their shoes and they weren't about to sacrifice their shoes, though they were muddy and becoming ruined already. If they sacrificed their shoes the only way up would be by their feet and they would surely become cut and tattered and ruined. It wasn't an option; the hillside was too vast and had no end in sight.

They decided to try to go around the rocky hillside instead, and keep their shoes; after all they had already made the sacrifice of their shoes becoming ruined and were searching and doing their best. They eagerly wanted to get to the promised palace.

They eventually found pebbles with smaller again specks of blue on it and followed them. They followed and followed and continued in their muddy shoes. The path got rougher and harder and it became harder to find new pebbles. Trying not to despair they kept heart and kept searching until they found some.

The boys were getting very tired but kept looking and following. Their shoes were becoming tattered, their clothes ruined, they were tired and exhausted. They kept going.

Soon the boys realized something big. They were back at the very stream they had first crossed. They had gone in a very big circle and circled back to where they first exited the stream.

The boys were devastated. What was going wrong? They had given their all. They sacrificed where it was required and did all they could and kept going amidst everything.

They looked down at their tattered muddy shoes, thinking back to the rocky hillside that the larger speck of blue pebbles pointed to. The shoes were too muddy and slick and tattered and would only hinder the climb, and there was no way their bare feet could handle the large climb. It was too rocky and sharp; they couldn't do it.

One of the boys had had enough. His shoes were ruined; He had wasted so much time. He had looked and looked and followed all the instructions given. He believed in the palace, he believed it was home, he believed the teacher and sacrificed for the promise. But, he thought, it was all for nothing. He felt it was all nonsense and that he was wasting his time. He had given his all; there was nothing more he could do.

"Remember the power and comfort of the words of the teacher, the palace is real, it's home." The other boy tried to keep him from leaving.

"There is a logical explanation for that, we have been deceived and I am leaving. I should have left before." The boy said.

He took a step away from the rocky hillside again toward the stream and as he stepped forward his tattered and failing shoes got stuck in the deep mud. His foot flew out of his shoe and he took a step to catch himself with his bare foot in the mud.

"Great! As if all of this wasn't enough! My shoes are ruined; I've wasted my time. I'm going back. And I'm taking what is left of my shoes with me! I refuse to waste another thing."

He stopped, pulled his shoe out of the mud, put it back on, and angrily trudged back through the stream and back toward where he started.

He went back and told everyone how ridiculous the whole thing was. They were led here and there and couldn't find anything of substance, and worse, he thought, they made him sacrifice so much for something that was total nonsense. The feelings, he thought, surely were nothing but his mind wandering.

214

The now lone boy pondered after his friend left. He had felt so strongly that the words of the teacher were true. Was he really wrong? After all they had given their all. He had felt so strongly that the palace was real. He could feel it in the words and the power of his voice, it gave him such comfort and he could feel at such a peace. He so wanted the palace to be real.

Was it all just a figment of his imagination? Could it all be explained in some other way? He sat down and pondered deeply and began to cry.

"It's real, I know its real." He cried looking down, longing again to feel the peace and the words that would draw him to the palace.

"It just must be real, I feel it. The teacher said to believe. There have been false teachers in the past, but this was different, I felt something, I know I did! I'm going to the palace!"

The boy lifted himself up and wiped his tears.

"I don't care what anyone else says, the palace is real. I am going."

He took his muddy shoes off and started walking toward the rocky hillside. He knew the muddy tattered shoes would make the climb impossible.

As he got closer to the rocky hillside he looked up and realized something he hadn't seen before. This was the first time he looked at it really wanting to climb it. It went steeper and steeper and became a mountain, and it looked very sharp and treacherous.

He knew that was the way the brightest blue pebbles directed him but it was just impossible, he knew he physically wouldn't be able to do it. He sat down and began to sob. What was he to do? He had tried everything. He simply couldn't climb something so treacherous.

The boy sat and cried, helpless and hopeless. "What should I do?" He thought amid his sobs. "I just want to be at the palace more than anything. I don't care what people think. I have given up everything for the palace and I will do whatever to get there. I have felt that it is true. I must keep going."

The boy thought again, "I thought it was my home and that my true Father loved me and prepared the way for me. If he's doing this all for me, if he loves me and prepared the way for me and is so big and I'm his child why is this so hard?"

The next thought struck him like lightning. "Wait, if that's truly all true, and I really feel it is, then he is doing it all perfectly for me. And I'm just not seeing it clearly. I just have to trust him."

Suddenly the boys eyes grew wider as his faith shifted and began to realize just how vast and how big his Father must be. It must be true. The way must be perfect. "I simply must realize it!"

The boy got up and looked again at the rocky hillside, he looked up further at how it became a mountain. At one point it where it was already beyond reach it went into the clouds. It was treacherous.

He stood up, and with determination in his heart turned with bare feet to the rocky hillside and began walking toward it. He was going to fully trust the vastness and perfection of his father. He knew it must be true, he felt it, he knew he must be loved. He would give everything he had for as far as he could and not give up.

As he began trudging through the mud he thought of how he would have to take his shirt off to wipe off the mud from his feet before his first step on the rocks.

Suddenly his bare foot hit something hard under the mud just before the base of the mountain. He must have stepped on it before, but with his shoes on, he couldn't feel it.

He reached down into the mud and grabbed a bright blue rock. He noticed it pointed in the exact opposite direction around the rocky hillside than they had walked. He looked and saw thick trees and rough looking ground.

In his elation of finding the brightest yet blue rock he immediately stepped into the rough looking ground and began walking quickly. To his surprise the ground was very soft and as he walked it got softer. He brushed some of the debris away from the ground to find that there was perfect soft grass planted under it.

The further he walked the softer the ground got and the comfort increased beyond what he ever though possible. The path had more and more blue rocks lining the way, they became brighter and brighter, the pathway became more and more beautiful with flowers and trees on the sides.

Eventually he got to a beautifully hewn tunnel that went right through the mountain. Covered in ever softer grass, in the tunnel it became yet softer carpet and within the tunnel that tunneled through the mountain was now beautiful glowing bright shining pebbles lighting it.

The boy began to be filled with that beautiful peace and joy that he felt when the teacher spoke. It grew larger and larger. He soon reached the end of the beautiful tunnel and it opened up to an even more beautiful valley.

Beautiful green trees were everywhere, over top of perfect plush green grass. Waterfalls were all over the place. He had never known such beauty.

He looked back at the mountainside and to his surprise the mountain that he was going to try climbing was taller than he ever imagined and on the other side was a steep cliff, he would never have made it.

216

He was so grateful. He looked around and found a path with a beautiful bridge over a beautiful stream. Each step was more comfortable and glorious to his bare feet. He couldn't have ever imagined the beauty and the comfort.

He rounded a corner of trees and there it was. The most beautiful palace he could ever imagine. It was grander than he could imagine; the beauty was overwhelming.

It was real! He had made it! Tears filled his eyes as the overwhelming peace and joy filled his heart.

As he started toward the beautiful palace he noticed a figure sitting nearby the door. The moment he noticed he saw the beautiful figure in white stand up and beginning running toward him. His mind raced wondering who it was, his heart swelled with love, admiration and excitement.

He could make out that it was a man. He was running eagerly toward him as fast as he could.

"Son!" The man yelled out as he began running faster toward him. The love swelled in the boys chest and the comfort and peace was beyond comprehension. The boy kept walking toward him slightly perplexed.

"My Son!" The man yelled again and was excitedly running faster, pulling up the bottom of his white robes to run faster. The boy was still confused but as the man got closer the beauty of the place became brighter, and the love he felt was growing powerfully.

"My boy!" The man was getting closer and the boy could tell he was sobbing. He was yelling through sobs of tears and running as quickly as he could. He got closer and he could just see the tears down his face into his beard. The feeling of love and comfort grew greatly.

As the man was finally nearing him the boy thought how oddly familiar the face of the man seemed to him. As he kept running and getting closer the boy was overcome with love.

The man ran into him with his arms wide and grabbed him and picked him up. The boy had never felt such an immense sense of love, joy and comfort come over him.

"MY SON!" The man said again through sobs; the boy looked into his face full of tears and an instant explosion happened. The love was so strong that it exploded and filled everything.

The boy suddenly remembered everything! He remembered his Father and who his Father was. He remembered who he was and where he was from. He remembered his Father's face, his love. He remembered everything. He was home!

217

He couldn't believe it! He felt finally back in his rightful place. He looked into his Father's eyes with tears and remembered, "Daddy," the boy said in tears.

The Father and son both sobbed. The Father held the boy close and began walking toward the palace, laughing and crying in absolute joy. "Oh my boy," the Father's voice to the boy was in the same comforting absolute power that he could now remember.

Every major question the boy had always had was answered immediately. He could again see and remember the eternal glorious symphony of his perfect Father who created all things in perfect purpose. He was finally back with his Daddy. He was finally home.

As they got back to the palace the boy noticed his fathers feet and hands were bleeding wrapped in bandages. He had just run with bandaged bleeding feet. What was wrong he thought?

Before he could ask his Father said, "I had to bring you back home son, no matter what, I need you forever, I love you so much son." The boy was filled with love as his Father spoke through tears.

"I came down and climbed up over the rocky hillside and the rocky mountain, I climbed and climbed and my feet were torn up. I climbed and climbed until I finally made it. It hurt and at times it was unbearable, but son I had to save you, I kept going. I got to the top and I fell down the cliff. Son I just couldn't see you go through that on your own so I picked up that pick over there." He gestured to a mining pickaxe with the handle covered in blood. "I got up and went right to that mountainside and began hacking away and making a path right through it for you to get here to be with me. I just couldn't imagine you having to walk up that mountain and I know you just wouldn't have been able to take the fall, I couldn't bear seeing you go through that son."

"I worked and finally finished the tunnel through the mountain to the palace so you could get here too. It beat my hands up a little and I'm ok; it reminds me of how much I love you."

"Ever since then I have been making it smooth and soft for you. I planted grass on the trail, and worked to make everything beautiful. Son, I even built you a mansion here, just over there. I have been waiting eagerly for you to get here; I just wanted it all to be perfect for you. I am so happy you're here and I love you so much!"

The boy was overwhelmed as he came to realize all his Father had gone through to get him there. It was more than he could comprehend or understand.

"I knew it would be hard to find son, because you're free to choose however you want, so I sent you your teacher, and I marked the path for you. And I made sure you could tell that it was true. All you had to do was trust me and I was always there for you to guide you and bring you here."

The boy was amazed and full of gratitude. How much he was loved was overwhelming, he was so grateful.

"Now you know that I have always been with you son, now you can finally see clearly that I'm right there, right inside of you, always with you, always doing all I can for you to be happy. You finally know."

As this was said the boy gained a revelation. His Father truly was always there, in his lack of vision and lack of faith he hadn't been able to see him.

The boy thought back to when the teacher first spoke to him and he saw his Father, right beside him, lovingly rubbing his back like a baby. He was rubbing everyone's back there. Many were focused on other things and many wouldn't feel it and many who did feel it discounted it and hardened their heart.

The boy looked back and saw how much he loved each one of them. He saw himself and the 2 other boys walking at first to search. He saw the first leave and as he tripped he saw his Father with tears in his eyes trying to stop him. He was trying to keep him looking; he loved him so much and wanted him to find Him. He was speaking lovingly to his other child to stay but he wasn't listening.

The first boy that left, when he fell down his Father placed a bright blue rock right in his face and in his sight. He was doing everything he could to keep his sons trying to walk to him in faith. He even picked it up, but in his anger and hard heartedness he threw it and left. With his eyes as they were, full of doubt, he couldn't even see a speck of blue on a bright blue rock.

The boy sat on the steps of the palace with his Father as he was shown again how his Father was always there. He saw him speaking calm loving words in the ears of him and the second boy as he rubbed their backs, comforting them and keeping them on the path, he even sent the teacher again.

When the second boy quit he could see his Father again in tears, pleading with him to just keep going. But he wouldn't hear it. He loved his shoes more than the palace. And had lost his faith in it. When the boy got stuck in the mud his Father caught his shoe in the mud so that he would be able to feel the pebble he stepped right on in the mud. But he was too angry to feel it; he was too upset to see it. But in tears his Father put it right where he could see it. He listened to the voice of anger and not of peace.

His Father loved them all so much, he always put their freedom first, and let them make their decisions with faith, he had always

219

promised to honor their freedom and agency; he loved them so much. He wanted it to be their choice.

In tears he begged his son that was now on his lap to keep going. He watched him as he fell in tears. He cried with him.

"Just take your shoes off, leave those behind! You aren't going to want that stuff that matters so much in that world here! If you only see things of that world you wont be able to see the greater things. I've prepared the way, I love you." The boy heard a little then and took his shoes off before he faced the mountain, seeking the palace above all.

The boy was in his Father's arms still and he looked up into his eyes again, both filled with tears. "You just wouldn't want those things you think you need there here. You just wouldn't want those shoes here. I worked so hard to make everything so soft and comfortable and I just have wanted you to be as happy as you possibly could! The things that make you happy there will only get in the way of the true happiness here! You can't imagine and see the way if you hold onto that there."

The boy could see clearly. The goodness of his father was absolutely amazing. He remembered he was truly the most blessed and a part of the best family in existence, with the best Father ever.

The boy looked up and saw his Father again crying and perceived His pain. He could see Him so happy that His son was back with Him and how badly still He wanted all of His children back. He could feel the pain of the two sons that didn't come, that fell off the path, and how hard he worked to keep them on it, but He respected their decisions. He wanted them happy so badly.

When the boy realized this he said, "Daddy, I'm going back, I'm going to get them for us."

His Father looked down and smiled through His tears. "Son, that would make me so happy. I love them so much. I love you all so so much."

"And son, before when I wasn't there, you couldn't see me, but now you will. You'll know I'm always right there and I'll be able to help you so much, because you know that I am right there."

"Son, tell them to follow the path and believe and they will make it. I need them back."

He hugged his Father and filled with his love could feel the love for His children; he had to do his best to let everyone know that the palace was real. He remembered why he had been there; he was from His Father's Kingdom and sent to help bring His children back to Him. To bring others to feel and know His love how he knows it. He remembered his purpose.

On his walk back everything felt comfortable, the path was easy and as he looked back at all the lightly marked blue-specked pebbles, they now glowed brightly. He saw the path clearly and could help others; it was brightly marked now.

The boy thought within, "Why are they bright and easy to see now and before was so hard?"

He heard the quiet and now discernable voice of His Father answering immediately within; "Son, when you change the way you look at things, the things you look at change. Have faith in Me son. You can see clearly now."

The boy was puzzled at first and humbly pondered faithfully on the answer given him, holding to it in faith as if it was a rock with a speck; trusting in his Almighty Father.

As he faithfully pondered on His Father's answer the fullness of the answer was suddenly given and understood all at once.

"You are so free. The way you look at things will change the way you see it and even what you see. To see truth you must have faith in truth and walk in truth; to see truth requires humility son for I have made all things. If you want to see truth you have to act in truth and believe in truth. Truth requires humility. It is protected. Humbly trust me, for you are my son, I love you. Walk in truth to see truth. Rely on me son. I am always here guiding you. When you're humble you can see it. My symphony is endless. How can you see something so big unless you are humble enough to let me show you? You see now, help all see. I love you."

The story will continue a bit but the direct allegories can be discerned. From an overall gospel perspective with the end goal to be with our Father in Heaven forever we can see each pebble as a vital ordinance starting with faith and baptism, to receiving the gift of the Holy Ghost and ultimately being guided thereby. That gift is paramount as we aren't walking blindly, we can rely on the guiding hand of God. Each time we trust in faith, we are guided by our faith to a grander waypoint closer to Him.

This is also a great allegory for receiving guidance by the Spirit of any kind. Revelation requires faith to see it. I will get more into it in the revelation discourse. Those small seeming things lead to bigger things when we trust in faith. When we trust fully and know He is guiding us, we are led by Him.

Soon we can trust in His love and eternal and unfathomable perfection and 'size;' in this we will finally see His utterly immense, ever growing, perfectly beautiful symphony. For all things are His and we are loved so much, in such that a way that this symphony that we can finally see is for us.

221

The going through the river can be discerned as any wordly sacrifice that we must give with an eye single to God. We must want His kingdom more than anything. Being willing to kick of the shoes is the more important part, it is us being personally and truly eagerly willing to leave all things we see important of this world behind. We must, as Paul, be willing to count all things but loss for the excellency of the knowledge of our Savior.

We must truly desire to give up whatever is necessary to gain the kingdom; this makes us humble enough to leave the world for the things of God, and to be able to constantly see clearly. Furthermore, we must kick off anything of this world that mud clings to. We must simply leave the things we think mean anything in this world behind. This prepares us for the kingdom and for the joys prepared for us. The humble and meek with an eye truly single to the glory of God throw off their shoes the moment they see the need with an eye single to and entirely trusting our Father in Heaven.

Furthermore, we must trust Him and His perfect goodness in all of our sacrifices. When we feel we are called to climb a treacherous mountain without preparation, we must trust in Him, His love, and His mercy. And as we do so, always walking in entire trust with a 'thy will be done' attitude it allows us to resonate with faith in His will, and it provides us with that will. We will realize that he simply has wanted us to trust Him in faith and rely on Him all along.

Every time I have experienced this I realize that He has prepared the way and already taken care of the hard things. His mercy and loving path has been established.

A faithful dying widow gave the prophet Elijah her last bit of food during a great famine in the Old Testament. Her son and her were going to eat their last meal and die. The Lord sent a hungry prophet to her. One who could provide her with what she needed, but her faith was required for her to align with what the Lord had lovingly prepared for her in her need. She needed to trust the Lord and His love.

She was asked to feed the prophet with the last of her food, a hard choice. She chose to, and the Lord gave her the miracle of her food containers overflowing, and they continued to be full till after the famine. Not only that but her son was so bad off from starvation he died and the prophet raised him from the dead.

The Lord knew His beloved daughter was suffering and would suffer if she didn't have anyone but a prophet of God to help her. He sent his hungry prophet to her and the Lord took care of both of His children. She received it in faith. If she had held onto that little bit that was wordly, the last of her food, would it have been wise? Surely not, for the Lord provided and saved her son.

The greater things are protected by humble trust and faith in God. He will bless us incredibly if we continually maintain that childlike trust.

Friends, I would submit that if we feel we are being asked to climb the rocky mountain to change our perspective. We cannot imagine or fathom what God has already done for us. When things seem horrible, perhaps we are simply only walking in circles. Often we are clinging too hard to the world view to take off our shoes and trust the path God has given us, that He will take perfect care of us.

It is choosing between the two perspectives.

1. "This is so hard, I thought you would make this easy for me, I thought you could do anything and you loved me and wanted me happy." This perspective is a lack of faith.

2. "Oh ya, why am I worrying, you are so much bigger than I can imagine, and I am your beloved child and I just need to simply rely on you and all will be awesome!" This is faith and you will be able to find your way to what He so graciously gives and has given.

A grand lesson then is; how can we walk on the soft ground God has prepared if we can't trust His path for us enough to even try it? If we don't try in faith we will not find it. Let go of the world, don't blow the problems out of proportion, have an eternal perspective and praise God who has done all the hard work for us. I of course can judge none and have offered many prayers in tears.

Another way to look at this story of faith is that of direct personal revelation. Are we receiving something from God or is it our thoughts? Or is it just a speck? Will we choose to see His ever present immensity and love, and hear Him in and by faith? I will continue the story a bit regarding the humble and the wise but there is more to understand now.

When we truly trust Him in faith then He can lead us; we are weak. Trust Him, our perfect Father. When we come to a point of having to humble ourselves, throw the shoes off with a big smile and simply thank God the whole time, in hope and waiting for the soft grass. We rely on His strength in our weakness. Then His strength is made perfect in us.

Soon we will gather all the pebbles, and we will see how each one perfectly answered our prayers as we allow the faith and hope to continue. Trust He is leading us, beyond feeling silly of gathering small tiny rocks with barely a message. Soon we will see that our entire prayer is answered.

After we do this a few times it becomes easier and more direct as our faith grows and we can see clearer. We get to a point to where the pebbles are glowing bright as we are familiar with the path and trust Him in faith entirely, we can become quickened in His Spirit and see how close He is.

Many times I have had random thoughts come at seeming random times and I am suddenly amazed, 'Wow this random thought is a perfect answer to what I asked.' Then when analyzing my thought I can see how it was a product of many other thoughts that were tried in faith and guided me. Even these final thoughts grow together with earlier 'revelation' and the grander answers become a tiny speck of truth in them leading to even larger grander ones.

The perfect symphony of God is seen as we fully humbly trust Him.

I will get more into revelation in the next chapter.

I will continue on with the story to make a few important things clear. The boy leaves the palace and kingdom and his Father to go tell everyone it is real. He begins telling one young child who receives it with all of his heart; he is meek and humble.

This boy is very young, very humble and very excited. He knew within himself that His Father in Heaven loved him, he knew that the path was true, he knew that His Father was so big and so good that He would just guide him so perfectly. The boy believed it all humbly.

The young boy couldn't wait; the other boy who now became teacher was following him trying to guide him to the palace.

Outside of the forest where all of the rocks were the humble young child picked up a pebble and in meek excitement pointed to it and said, "Some blue! I'm coming Dad!" The now teacher boy wanted to say something to maybe look closer but he knew enough to simply be amazed at the boy. He walked after him. Though he had made it, he was being taught still.

Soon they were in the forest and the young boy was picking up pebbles in excitement, pointing to little bits of blue and excited to see his Father.

Soon they got to the river and the young child jumped in with both feet and laughed as he splashed. He walked out of the river and his muddy shoes were stuck to the ground so much that his little legs could barely take another step. The young child laughed aloud again and said, "You're funny Daddy!" He recognized the vastness of his Father. He was meek, and humble, and he knew it was true.

He stepped right out of his muddy shoes, laughing at his Father's guidance and kept running in excitement. He stepped barefoot right on the pebble in the mud and laughed again in his childlike laugh in the direction the bright blue pebble pointed toward the grassy path.

The boy ran in joy down the grassy path, through the hewn out tunnel with bright blue pebbles into the kingdom, and into his loving Fathers arms.

The teacher boy who had made the path so much harder looked at the young child and marveled at the ease of the way for him. He simply entirely trusted His perfect Father.

They all embraced and with tears in His eyes the Father thanked the boy now turned teacher for bringing back one of His humble children who could hear His voice so well, but just needed to be told the way.

Both of the boys went back in search of others to bring to their loving Father. They were again in the pebbles just outside of the vast forest when a group of men came out.

These men were wise and had high ranks in the world and done many things by the world's standard.

The first of the wise men spoke, "We have been in the forest for a long time and thought ourselves very wise. We have long since learned the nature of many things. We have scoffed at you guys and your kind who believe in such things for a long time. We scoffed because we simply felt we understood more knowledge."

"We have explored all the depths of the forest. We were led wherever we wanted to go by believing we would be led there. We would go from a colored pebble to the next until we got where we wanted to go. We always scoffed at you guys because we thought you didn't understand how colored pebbles worked."

"Over time, we realized we had gone all over the depths of the forest and we couldn't get over the mountain. We simply cannot get to the source of all joy and happiness and we just want to go home, we believe now we must have a home. We walk in our wisdom trying to get there but we are taken everywhere we desire but there."

The men gestured down to their nice shoes that they walked in, the word 'wisdom' was on their very nice shoes. They had walked long in their prided wisdom.

"We have realized that there must be yet more and that though we can go seemingly everywhere, we cannot go where we need and most desire. Every time we seek in our wisdom to get there we end up here, and each time we get a little more humble. Today we have ran into you."

"It used to be below us to ask for help or think others may know better, but will you help us?"

The boy turned teacher marveled at the many men who walked in 'wisdom.' Though they could go many places their wisdom was a snare to keep them away from the single right way, where the humble were prepared to go until they were humble to be guided there. The Father was simply above all.

The boy turned teacher replied filled with a strong desire to help his loving Father. Being filled with love for the men, the words of deeper wisdom than he knew poured out of his mouth in loving help.

"Of course I will help you. You have walked thinking you know better and you have seen no clear singular path, thinking that there could be no singular truth. I don't judge you; I want to help you. Deception has guided you in your pride; there is a singular true and real path and it is to our Father in Heaven who truly lives, who created us and all things and has prepared the way for us."

The men walking in wisdom replied, "We can see now that this must be and that we have walked in deception as we prided the things of the world and man. Show us the way. Please."

The boy turned teacher gestured to the young humble child at his side, "Follow him, and go as he goes."

One of the men walking in wisdom piped up, "This is a child! He is ignorant and will lead us all over the place, he doesn't even understand wisdom or how the pebbles work!"

The boy turned teacher looked at the man in compassion and replied, "Unless you humble yourself as this child, you will never see the kingdom."

The young child looked up and smiled at the man. He grabbed his hand and said, "Come on guys! Our Dad is going to be so happy to see you! I saw you before and Dad said to pray for them, so I asked Him to help you and now you're here! Let's go!"

The boy laughed excitedly seeing the vastness of His Father and knowing the excitement He and his children would have, pulling the men into the forest. "I hope you guys don't like your shoes too much!"

Our Father in Heaven is big. All is His. The greatest in the kingdom of heaven is truly he who humbles himself as a little child. It is the easiest way simply relying on our loving Father in Heaven who has given all to get us back. All is done in His perfect wisdom.

Matthew 18:1 "At the same time came the disciples unto Jesus, saying, Who is the greatest in the kingdom of heaven?

2 And Jesus called a little child unto him, and set him in the midst of them,

3 And said, Verily I say unto you, Except ye be converted, and become as little children, ye shall not enter into the kingdom of heaven.

4 Whosoever therefore shall humble himself as this little child, the same is greatest in the kingdom of heaven.

5 And whoso shall receive one such little child in my name receiveth me.

10 Take heed that ye despise not one of these little ones; for I say unto you, That in heaven their angels do always behold the face of my Father which is in heaven.

11 For the Son of man is come to save that which was lost.

"Your future is as bright as your faith." – Thomas S. Monson

Our Father in Heaven has prepared the way and done all the heavy lifting. The big lessons for us to learn then are as follows.

1. Leave the things of the world behind and have our eyes on things of importance. Money and other worldly fears or stresses should mean nothing to us and we should be willing to sacrifice all things for our Father in Heaven. We must come to humbly rely on Him and trust Him in childlike faith. He always has something far better to bless us with. As we cling to things of lesser importance we take the opportunities for the greater blessings away from ourselves and put them on hold until we are humble enough to see in faith the greater plan.

2. Humility and meekness before God. Humbly walking as He would have us. Recognizing our position before Him and that He wont allow us to be steered wrong as long as we are faithful and meek and seeking His will. We are His beloved children. These characteristics including perfect trust become powerful keys. We must be humble for He will teach and guide us many different ways, all gained by humbly trusting Him in faith.

3. Absolute trust. This is probably the grandest key. Totally and wholly trusting Him to guide us. Soon we will recognize that nothing is too hard for God and that is saying the least, all is His. We should not trust the flesh or wisdom of ourselves but the revelation of our Father in Heaven. This goes along with humility and cannot be understated. As we have full trust that He alone is perfect wisdom we can expect and receive His perfect guidance, protection and love. Constant revelation and guidance is available. The greatest in the kingdom of heaven is he who humbles himself as a little child.

4. Seek always the guidance of His Spirit. This comes as we do the above things. We should keep an eternal focus, not of this world but above; we must be humble and seek his guidance, not thinking man knows better or we know better; we must absolutely trust Him and see His utter vastness. He is smiling down and all around us, guiding us ever closer if we will let Him and trust in him.

If we do not have faith in how big and how good our Father in Heaven is we will cling to our muddy shoes and miss the perfect way prepared. We must have faith, and see how perfectly He loves us and how utterly immense He is. The very hairs of our heads are numbered.

Leave behind the mud and the shoes, with joy and rejoicing thank Him for cleansing us and preparing the way.

I want you to look at me as though I am holding your hand, and we are at the river. I am telling you, 'I have been here before, trust me.' He has done everything for us; we just have to go the way He has said. When we get to the other side of this sacrifice, we are going to throw off our shoes and trust Him entirely, and watch Him take care of us.

"A religion that does not require the sacrifice of all things never has power sufficient to produce the faith necessary unto life and salvation; for, from the first existence of man, the faith necessary unto the enjoyment of life and salvation never could be obtained without the sacrifice of all earthly things. It was through this sacrifice, and this only, that God has ordained that men should enjoy eternal life."

-    Joseph Smith, Lectures on Faith, 69

Faith in Jesus Christ's Saving and Healing Ability Through Him Because of His Atonement

The first thing we must do is to get past the past. After all, why would we pay for something that has already been paid for by our precious loving Savior Jesus Christ?

As I have spoken previously, 'resonance' with God in His perfection is our necessity. We were once innocent, now once fallen and in sin we can only be clean through Jesus Christ for He alone has paid for our sins, He alone lived perfectly; He is the way.

It is through our true faith on Him, in His healing ability, and in His saving grace that we can be properly aligned to Him and be healed and cleansed, which He longs to do for us all. We must become entirely humble with a contrite heart and it takes absolute utter reliance on Him; recognizing we can do nothing of ourselves. We truly need Him. How blessed we are.

In the Garden of Eden when Adam and Eve first partook of the fruit they were told they were naked, and they were told to go and hide because they were naked. They were ashamed and hid themselves from the Lord. This happened right after their first sin.

Because they fell, some can see this as a harsh judgment that they were cast out of the presence of God and became in a fallen state, where this world is. But because of the nature of the law of God it became necessary. He is simply perfection.

228

Notice that it was not God who ran away from His children. Rather it was his children, who crossed the guardrail of sin, they then became subject to the adversary and suddenly were told they should be ashamed and that they should hide from God their Father. They listened to voices that they shouldn't and hid themselves from their loving Father, too ashamed to look Him in the face.

Because of the sin they fell out of the presence of God our Father, which is Holy and perfect and without sin whatsoever.

Right when this happened our Father already had a plan to get His children back. Though He gave His children agency and they chose wrong and sinned, He loved them dearly, He prepared a Savior in His Son Jesus Christ to come down and atone for us and prepare the way for us.

Though we came here for a test and to learn and gain much we all have sinned and we can of ourselves do nothing to be able to come back into the presence of God. We absolutely need Christ.

We must choose to exercise faith in Him and what He has done for us that we may be healed.

As our faith grows and we humble ourselves with a penitent and contrite heart He heals us and takes the guilt from us. Sometimes we have to exercise strong faith and not allow negative thoughts to creep in, to move on. The Lord must heal us, He wants to heal us, He suffered to heal us, if we are not healed how can we help others?

Hebrews 9:13-14 "For if the blood of bulls and of goats, and the ashes of an heifer sprinkling the unclean, sanctifieth to the purifying of the flesh: How much more shall the blood of Christ, who through the eternal Spirit offered himself without spot to God, purge your conscience from dead works to serve the living God?"

This is a great scripture. It shows in similitude and symbolic foreshadowing of what Jesus would do for the world, people sacrificed animals to leave sin behind before Christ; it is Christ's atonement symbolized and what Christ would come to do for us all, before and after Him.

How much more should the very blood of the perfect Son of God given willingly on our behalf rid our consciousness of guilt. Leave it in the past; don't let Him suffer for nothing. He suffered it all so you don't have to.

Through the gracious and merciful atonement our Father in Heaven is both entirely just, and entirely merciful. He is perfect and perfect love, love at even the highest cost. He loves us dearly.

229

A quick story interjection to help illustrate this point; my wife told me this one.

A seminary class had donuts. A buff and tough dude was in the class and was known for being able to do a lot of push-ups. He was to do 10 for each person, and for every 10 pushups done by him that person received a donut.

He did 10 for the first couple, they got a donut; then the next and next and next. Soon he had done 60 and only 6 people got donuts. Then 100 and only 10 people sat with a donut. Soon he began to be in agony and sweat was dripping like crazy, each pushup would be insanely harder. By the time he got to 150 he would collapse after each 10.

The teacher went up to the next student and said, "Do you want a donut?" The person was about to say no, they didn't want to see him collapse like that again and grunt and strain in agony just so they could have a donut. But before they could say no he got up and had already started doing the pushups. He collapsed again.

The next people said no, but regardless he did them anyway and collapsed, and how could they then refuse the donut he had paid for? It was placed on their desk and they could eat it if they wanted, it was paid for.

Soon he was really struggling to even do one, but he was a determined and tough kid and the teacher knew he could trust him to finish the pushups.

He had done well over 200 pushups and 10 pushups would take a much longer time. Sometimes he would collapse and have to get up and keep going, one by one. His sweat was dripping and pouring.

After seeing how difficult and serious he suffered to do the pushups the donut was placed on the desk, and although the next and next student couldn't imagine him doing that for them and for a donut for them they felt the need to accept it after it was done, the cost was too great.

Soon the whole class had a donut and he collapsed trying to breathe, having done more pushups than he had ever done.

The teacher came to him, "There are 7 donuts left in this box, I can give them to some kids in the other class or in the hall if you want to do the pushups."

The kid could barely breathe, but he got up and spent all the effort that he didn't know he had. The class was getting the lesson. The kid didn't complain or murmur. He was far past his record and limit, but he would do as the teacher needed.

The kids in the class started to cheer him on with each pushup that seemed impossible, realizing he would stop at nothing. Soon, somehow, he finished them all. Everyone cheered in disbelief.

The teacher stood up and cheered the kid on after he had finished. It was an incredible feat. Everyone ate their donut, the cost was so great. He didn't need to do it, he could earn his own, but no one else could, so he did it for them.

Now take this story to heart. Christ suffered far more than pushups; we will never be able to fully comprehend it. But his atonement was absolutely essential. We can purge our conscience through him healing us through what He has done, by His loving grace we are forgiven and healed.

If we do not resonate with this in faith we cannot align and receive it. Faith is a deep and large principle. Remember also that God is just, and there was payment required. He sent his Son to suffer on our behalf that He could be both just and merciful and eternally graceful. Truly perfect love.

How blessed we are! As we exercise faith in this we begin to better recognize it. Recognizing this truly brings us to the depths of humility and our heart becomes contrite and we gain a deep appreciation, we needed it and couldn't do it ourselves. Accept what has been given us! Be new!

Alma 33:16 "For behold, he said: Thou art angry, O Lord, with this people, because they will not understand thy mercies which thou hast bestowed upon them because of thy Son."

This scripture makes me think of how the teacher would react if someone still didn't eat the donut. Especially if that donut was absolutely necessary.

This can be understood more clearly when the atonement of Christ is NECESSARY for us, and our Father in Heaven had to watch His only begotten suffer beyond what any of us can imagine. And He of all didn't deserve it. Of course He wants us to accept healing that is freely given!

At the Waters of Bethesda Christ came to heal a man. He came to him and asked, "Will you be made whole this day?" Quite a question.

After all, all the power is His. He has paid for it all. All we have to do is meekly and humbly receive in faith in order to receive; it truly is the recipe and conduit to be able to receive.

Christ healed the man at the waters and said, "Thy faith hath made thee whole."

The very same words were used many times. One time they were used was in the Book of Enos in the Book of Mormon.

Enos went into the mountains and prayed all day long and into the night to the Lord for remission of his sins. Eventually a voice came to him saying that his sins were forgiven and he will be blessed. Enos asked how it was done. And he was told, "because of thy faith in Christ, whom thou hast never before heard or seen." "wherefore, go to, they faith hath made thee whole."

It is our faith in Christ that heals us, I have needed real healing and He has been there always, I have relied on Him entirely in real need.

He either lives and can heal and cleanse us, or we are lost and in ruin. How grateful I am that He truly lives and truly has done all for us.

I think of the lyrics of a hymn, "I'll strengthen thee, help thee, and cause thee to stand. Upheld by my righteous omnipotent hand."

In Matthew 8 a man with leprosy speaks to Christ, "if thou wilt, thou canst make me clean,"

This mans comes to Christ in faith. He knows full well and has faith that Christ can heal him. He even declares that he can do it, if only He will. He has the ability to do all things.

When we see clearly His character and exercise faith in the truth, with an earnest humble contrite heart, we will realize that His answer to us will always be just as it was to the man with leprosy, "I will, be thou clean."

We are all beggars before God; luckily for us, He loves us perfectly and sent His Son in love so that He could always heal us and bless us.

Christ's atonement is more powerful than we can imagine. In the Bible in Isaiah as well as again reiterated in The Book of Mormon we can read that, "even the lawful captive are delivered."

When Christ was cast into prison he was found that he had done nothing wrong. The tradition of that time was to set free a prisoner, instead of Christ an actual criminal named Barabbas was set free instead.

This story is not only of historical significance that fulfills prophecy but is symbolism of what Christ has done for all of us. We are all captive; we have all sinned and desperately need our Savior. Furthermore the symbolism of the name Barabbas; it means Son of Father, or of Father.

Romans 8:13-14 "For ye have not received the spirit of bondage again to fear; but ye have received the Spirit of adoption, whereby we cry, Abba, Father. The Spirit itself beareth witness with our spirit, that we are the children of God:"

Doctrine and Covenants 88:33 "For what doth is profit a man if a gift is bestowed upon him, and he receive not the gift? Behold, he rejoices not in that which is given unto him, neither rejoices in him who is the giver of the gift."

Humility is of great importance. We must recognize that we can of ourselves do nothing. We must forgive all others as we ourselves are no better than others; we all must utterly rely on Christ.

Mosiah 29:20 "But behold, he did deliver them because they did humble themselves before him; and because they cried mightily unto him he did deliver them out of bondage; and thus doth the Lord work with His power in all cases among the children of men, extending the arm of mercy towards them that put their trust in him."

The grand key is to remember ourselves, we are His children, but also remember that we are children, and we utterly rely on Him. He will always be there when we can exercise our faith in this, so much that we have our mind set in truth, in humility and meekness, even as a child.

Doctrine and Covenants 6:36 "Look unto me in every thought; doubt not, fear not. Behold the wounds which pierced my side, and also the prints of the nails in my hands and feet; be faithful, keep my commandments, and ye shall inherit the kingdom of heaven. Amen."

The first step of faith for us is to be healed by our Savior. In this He will not only heal us from our past mistakes, but He will make us new. He will make us see things clearly and as we strive to be like Him He will bless us and give us more and more. We truly will be reborn; Born of God and of the Spirit.

"The Atonement leaves no tracks, no traces. What it fixes is fixed. . . .It just heals, and what it heals stays healed." – Boyd K. Packer

As soon as we can move on and every day say, "thank you," in gratitude we are healed and He has saved us, then we are ready to come even closer to Him. We ever keep His commandments and His Spirit can ever be with us, a truly incredibly grand blessing. Our faith becomes stronger and we are clean before God. Revelation becomes our privilege and we can move on to bigger and better things that He has always intended for us.

Many are continually pushed with thoughts from the past even after the Lord has accepted of our humility and contrite heart and granted

233

us forgiveness, as He always will. The adversary can push and push and these things can keep us from focusing on the next things of spiritual importance and personal growth. This can be a hindrance, and we must do all we can to forgive ourselves and forgive others.

For this I would give two quick points.

Point 1. Revelation 12:10 "And I heard a loud voice saying in heaven, Now is come salvation, and strength, and the kingdom of our God, and the power of His Christ: for the accuser of our brethren is cast down, which accused them before our God day and night.

And they overcame him by the blood of the Lamb, and by the word of their testimony; and they loved not their lives unto death."

This scripture has much depth, historical and spiritual. Remember the things of our Father in Heaven are living. We can liken this scripture to ourselves and see the 'heaven' of our thoughts many are constantly, accused before God. In this, learning to perceive the Spirit of God as opposed to the opposite that is the adversary is of great importance. Whatsoever is good is of God, and it will lead us to have joy in Him and want to praise Him and love Him and serve Him.

As we recognize what thoughts are not of God, soon we can see the other side, His side, as we pray mightily. We can 'cast out' the dark influences in our thoughts that hold us back, pay no heed to, rebuke and chase away darkness and wholly rely on the 'blood of the Lamb'.

The mental word, 'rebuke' has, on occasion, become of great use. Anytime any thought or mental hook comes in, I simply mentally rebuke that thought and hold to that which is good. Soon enough the thoughts are gone; we can always pray for whatever we stand in need of.

I use this same tactic when someone cuts me off in traffic and a negative thought may arise; in these instances I change rebuke to, 'blessings and love', and mentally my mind can jump to the light and the side of God; the negative spirit of contention is stopped and the Spirit of God stays and love abounds. Recognizing how easily we can allow the spirit we don't want is important. We must choose love and kindness always.

We must utterly rely on Him, and have our faith sure. He doesn't want us held back any longer. There is a reason He did what He did for us, and that is so that we don't have to bear it. He will. He has.

Humble and penitent hearts, that of His child, will always be graciously and mercifully consoled. I have been incredibly blessed to see this. I am forever grateful. I am weak, He is strong. Anything strong of myself is a gift from Him.

234

When we see this and rely on Him we can kick out such thoughts and "Now is come salvation, and strength and the kingdom of our God." Put on the whole armor of God.

2. For the second point I will again illustrate our childlike and utter reliance on our Savior.

Ether 12:27-28 "And if men come unto me I will show unto them their weakness. I give unto men weakness that they may be humble; and my grace is sufficient for all men that humble themselves before me; for if they humble themselves before me, and have faith in me, then will I make weak things become strong unto them. Behold, I will show unto the Gentiles their weakness, and I will show unto them that faith, hope and charity bringeth unto me – the fountain of all righteousness."

What an incredible scripture. We of ourselves can do nothing. Strength is not ours, it is His. We must rely on Him for it.

Note a few things. Our faith is important, and our humility is important; so much that we recognize our absolute utter weakness before Him. When we meet the requirements of humbly coming unto Him in faith, trusting in His grace, then He will make weak things strong. He made us.

His healing power is abundant. He will change us and make us new. The world for us becomes, choose to be humble or later be humbled to the dust. I would choose the first but at times certainly was humbled to the dust and utterly relied on Him and His grace and mercy.

We cannot see truth unless we are humble. Those who walk in pride of 'wisdom' or any other type are keeping themselves from finding truth and resonating in it. He resists the proud, it is by our own doing, and we simply cannot resonate with Him in a false way. We must be humble.

I have seen many "seek" somewhat, but not in a humble and a meek way; and they don't find because they don't truly seek. If we seek truly, we become humble to what and whom it is we seek. Humility becomes a grand key that goes hand in hand with faith. We exercise our faith in truth to find truth. It is no wonder that Christ told us the greatest in the kingdom of heaven is the one humble as a child. For we are His children and small at that. Humble, meek and submissive. Then we can be greatly blessed. We are children.

The importance of faith cannot be overstated. The importance of faith cannot be overstated. The importance of faith cannot be overstated.

235

Doctrine and Covenants 8:1 "...even so surely shall you receive a knowledge of whatsoever things you shall ask in faith, with an honest heart, believing that you shall receive a knowledge . . ."

Mark 11:22-25 "And Jesus answering saith unto them, Have faith in God. For verily I say unto you, That whosoever shall say unto this mountain, Be thou removed, and be thou cast into the sea; and shall not doubt in his heart, but shall believe that those things which he saith shall come to pass; he shall have whatsoever he saith. Therefore I say unto you, What things soever ye desire, when ye pray, believe that ye receive them, and ye shall have them. And when ye stand praying forgive, if ye have ought against any: that your Father also which is in heaven may forgive you your trespasses."

Doctrine and Covenants 8:10 "Remember that without faith you can do nothing; therefore ask in faith. Trifle not with these things; do not ask for that which you ought not."

Doctrine and Covenants 11:14 "And then shall ye know, or by this shall you know, all things whatsoever you desire of me, which are pertaining unto things of righteousness, in faith believing in me that you shall receive."

Ether 12:12 "For if there be no faith among the children of men God can do no miracle among them; wherefore, he showed not himself until after their faith."

Ether 12:28 "Behold, I will show unto the Gentiles their weakness, and I will show unto them that faith, hope and charity bringeth unto me – the fountain of all righteousness.

29 And I, Moroni having heard these words, was comforted, and said: O Lord, thy righteousness will be done, for I know that thou workest unto the children of men according to their faith;"

We should maintain in remembrance the parable of the Prodigal Son. He left home, sinned and chose to come home after coming to himself. He walked back to his father's house and when he was still a great way off his father saw him and 'had compassion on him' and ran to him. The son simply wanted to be his servant to have food, his father instead killed the fatted calf to eat and make merry and gave him a coat and a ring and called him his son. When this meekness and humility

236

abounds we can see His love, which is so infinitely more than I can describe. He is more our Father than our fathers on earth.

I have come back to Him with a penitent heart, sad and broken, hoping and praying He would accept me at least as His servant. He picked me up like a baby, saved me, washed me, healed me, taught me, blessed me, poured out love and showed me the incredible, important and perfect son that He had destined me to be. I called out to Him and a great way off He saved me. I begged to be a servant but He helped me stand taller and called me His Son. When we are His Son, the 'S' is capitalized. He paid a great price. He loves us infinitely. He helped me see the grand picture. Helped me see who He calls me to be, and gives me all to stand as what He sees, His beloved Son. And the celebration of His love, goodness and making merry continues. His arm is outstretched to all of His children.

As we truly become more and more like our Savior, more meek and submissive to our good Father; and above all seeking all things for His glory, putting away old things and aligning our desires with His, He will bless us with deeper knowledge and insight and our faith will become exceedingly strengthened. We will become mighty instruments and strong children in His hands, even as much as our faith.

Galatians 2:20 "I am crucified with Christ: nevertheless I live; yet not I, but Christ liveth in me: and the life which I now live in the flesh I live by the faith of the Son of God, who loved me, and gave himself for me."

1 Peter 1:7 "That the trial of your faith, being much more precious than of gold that perisheth, though it be tried with fire, might be found unto the praise and honour and glory at the appearing of Jesus Christ:"

To see the more we must have faith in what we have received. As we walk in faith of all things we can resonate with and have the Spirit of God confirm things of truth. I will get into this in the next section. The good things of God are protected perfectly by humility and by faith.

Keep in mind, faith is like a muscle; the things of God are living. It can only pass the test it is strong enough to pass; much like a weight lifter lifting a weight. We can only gain the higher revelation with grander faith, and we can only survive such attacks as our faith is strong enough. Constant prayer and scripture study, nourishing ourselves with the Spirit, will increase it.

Trying and nourishing the seed of faith will grow into a mighty tree that will bear the greatest fruit, despite any voices of the contrary. As we are diligent it will graft into the tree of God and in Him we will become mighty and strong and with Him forever.

Faith is precious; it is grand. When exercised fully in truth it becomes exceedingly precious, much more than that of gold. We are then prepared to receive much good. Be humble, even as a little child. We are His little children.

Chapter 18

REVELATION DISCOURSE

The faith chapter was very long but there is much there and it is the building block for revelation; as well as the very foundation, faith on our Savior.

Note that God is the teacher. Most large things of deep learning are to be taught from on high. We must be properly tuned to receive.

Doctrine and Covenants 136:32-33 "Let him that is ignorant learn wisdom by humbling himself and calling upon the Lord his God, that his eyes may be opened that he may see, and his ears opened that he may hear; For my Spirit is sent forth into the world to enlighten the humble and contrite, and to the condemnation of the ungodly."

When one desires revelation let them look at that scripture. Faith is a prerequisite, humility and utter meekness becomes the key. Humility before God is truly the deepest singular wisdom, as we can receive all things thereby. All things are His.

Doctrine and Covenants 42:61 "If thou shalt ask, thou shalt receive revelation upon revelation, knowledge upon knowledge, that thou mayest know the mysteries and peacable thing – that which bringeth joy, that which bringeth life eternal."

I will go over many scriptures in this and each one has deep knowledge for those who will inquire of the Lord to help you. I aim to help everyone hereafter be able to know how to conduct themselves to be able to receive that which God desires to give. He is our teacher.

"Oh, there is so much more that your Father in Heaven wants you to know. As Elder Neal A. Maxwell taught, 'To those who have eyes to see and ears to hear, it is clear that the Father and the Son are giving away the secrets of the universe!'"

This was a quote given by the Prophet Russel M. Nelson in April of 2018 of General Conference. I can attest to the truthfulness of this.

It is as though the Lord is waiting for His children to have the faith to exercise it to receive revelation from Him. He is awaiting us all to seek the deeper things and have our eyes and minds focused on the things of eternity more than the things of the world. I obviously can judge none, but He is truly right there willing to bless us incredibly.

Those few who may be reading this that walked in or understand such 'wisdom' as the world does, know that the things that the Lord teaches are vastly beyond such things in true wisdom. Wisdom is in Him and comes as we walk in faith. It is up to Him to teach us properly, those who seek wisdom of themselves do not find true wisdom. He is the teacher of truth; He is the source of truth. He is the truth. Remember always the importance of humility.

For Him to be our teacher we must be taught by the Spirit, we must be able to keep the Spirit with us always, discern the Spirit better and seek with an eye single to His glory. To do this we must truly ever strive to be and become as He would have us. We must truly strive to become as our Savior. We must truly be willing to sacrifice the things of the world for the things of eternity.

We must do our best to walk as our Savior and in the Holy Spirit bearing its fruit in us.

Galatians 5:22-23 "But the fruit of the Spirit is love, joy, peace, longsuffering, gentleness, goodness, faith, Meekness, temperance: against such there is no law."

The first step is to have a genuine desire to walk 100% as the Lord would have us. For myself this was many different things. One of which was quitting a well paying sponsor and being willing to trust that the Lord would take care of me. Utterly relying on Him. Over time I would learn that trusting in Him entirely is a very, very grand key.

Furthermore, we must be willing to do those things the Spirit directs us to do, with a genuine desire to be of help for good.

John 14:31 "But that the world may know that I love the Father; and as the Father gave me commandment, even so I do. Arise, let us go hence."

We must be willing to live by every word that proceeds from the mouth of God. In my experience there were things that I didn't particularly want to do but that I kept being prompted to and kept feeling like they would be good and help others. Be sure to discern the spirit; that which is good is of God.

Moroni chapter 7 gives more detailed guidance on this as well as Doctrine and Covenants section 11. But to sum it up simply it is as stated all throughout all scripture. What is of love is of God, what is good is of God, and what testifies of Christ is of God. What brings us to believe in Him and glorify Him and praise and serve Him is by Him.

Moroni 7:13 "But behold, that which is of God inviteth and enticeth to do good continually; wherefore, every things which inviteth and enticeth to do good, and to love God, and to serve him, is inspired of God."

My process in following this was a teaching opportunity of its own. For instance I began to see others who were ensnared by this 'wisdom' or trusted in their own wisdom. I really felt for them. I knew how deep that was and how easily it ensnared deeply.

The thought was laid over and over again in my heart just as it was with my prompting to help my friend earlier on, "If you don't help them, who will? If you don't say something to them, who else can? Who else understands as you do? If you say nothing they will have no help."

These thoughts worked on me. My instagram turned from BMX to gospel messages and scriptures and many times would try to expound things in captions. This wasn't enough. I had studied many things deeply and if someone would choose to listen intently and humbly I could help them. If one in the stumbling block of deep 'wisdom' would humbly listen, I could show them the way out.

After more time with the prompting coming I finally came to a conclusion. I would spend the next 2 weeks compiling video of myself speaking and editing it into a video. I would do my best to explain, track down scriptures necessary and I would find supporting videos that would help those who were true seekers. I did this.

This was a bold step, I normally would loathe sitting in front of a camera talking. It is not something I would ever want to do, but I saw the importance and even if a few would gain something out of it, it would be worth it to the Lord.

I experienced something through this process that I pray each one of you will come to; I absolutely did not care about the opinion of anyone but God alone. I let every single thought of anyone else or any harsh thought or judgment of myself and instead said, "Thy will be done Father, guide me to do it well and by thy Spirit."

I said um a lot, had to redo a lot, wasn't perfect to say the least, but I learned just as Ether learned in the scriptures. Ether thought that his writing was weak and that he couldn't write mightily as people in the past. At first Ether feared he would be mocked. The Lords reply was thus, "Fools mock, but they shall mourn; and my grace is sufficient for the meek that they shall take no advantage of your weakness;"

The Lord's words in this case are something that I had learned every part of. I was taught a great lesson. Nothing else matters at all to me but the opinion of my Father in Heaven. I was able to set aside a bunch of time and do that which He wanted me to.

241

Over time this became easier and easier and I soon could see that as my eye became more single to the glory of God that our views were the same, we wanted the same things. Our goals were the same and His views and goals were perfect. His work and glory is that of love for His children, to bring to pass the immortality and eternal life of man. He wants His beloved children home. We were walking in the same path; I was walking in His path clearer. He is not just my Father and my God, but my partner in the same cause, for His glory.

The video was nearly 3 hours long. If any seek it, it is under the channel 'Herein Is Truth.' I certainly didn't do it perfectly, but I did my best. Regardless I have heard stories of people who watched it many times and were helped greatly by it. The worth of a soul is great in the eyes of God.

I soon recognized the vast worth of every good prompting; although I was nowhere near perfect, I determined to at very least try my best.

I heard of and became inspired by a story of a young man who made it his goal and focus to do the work of the Lord. He would pray earnestly for what use the Lord could use him for that day. He would receive a prompting and do it. After that he would pray again earnestly, receive a prompting and do it. Though it started hard to discern his thoughts and the Spirit he followed that which was good and over time it became clearer.

This young man found over time that as he followed the promptings they became easier and easier to discern, it was as though he could hear the voice of God more clearly. Each time he would go and do whatever he felt prompted to do. Sometimes they were easy things, sometimes harder but each time he wanted to be a better and more profitable servant of God.

One day he went to the temple to receive inspiration on what the Lord would have Him do. He heard the words, something like, "My son, you can rest now. Thank you for your earnest desire to serve me."

This story made an impact on me. I began, in my own search, to later realize that such things were a right way of understanding. We must put forth our ears in earnest faith to hear. As we follow each prompting we become much closer to God and He trusts us more and more, and we can believe and trust in ourselves more and more.

I got to the point where if I felt prompted to do something it would sit in my mind and be sole focus day in and day out until it was accomplished. It was hard to think of things past it until I completed them. It is the way as well with me writing this.

Although I am not perfect, I began to be more and more focused to be a more profitable servant. All I genuinely wanted and want forever and cared about and care now about is my Father in Heaven's opinion of me and to be of service to the cause that is so perfect and it is mine as well.

I will share a quick story on another valuable lesson that I've learned.

Doctrine and Covenants 58:26-30 "For behold, it is not meet that I should command in all things; for he that is compelled in all things, the same is a slothful and not a wise servant; wherefore he receiveth no reward. Verily I say, men should be anxiously engaged in a good cause, and do many things of their own free will, and bring to pass much righteousness; For the power is in them, wherein thy are agents unto themselves. And inasmuch as men do good they shall in nowise lose their reward. But he that doeth not anything until he is commanded, and receiveth a commandment with doubtful heart, and keepeth it with slothfulness, the same is damned."

Our overall grand goal of our existence is to become just as our Savior Jesus Christ. We are to leave behind our old selves, see what the perfect path is and genuinely of ourselves want to be as He is.

With this comes the importance to walk in and be led by His Spirit. The center of this is love obviously; it is also choosing to bring the truth of our Savior to others. All good is of God. We must desire to walk in the fruit of the Spirit and bring about good things.

Galatians 5:22-23 "But the fruit of the Spirit is love, joy, peace, longsuffering, gentleness, goodness, faith, Meekness, temperance: against such there is no law"

Doctrine and Covenants 88:125 "And above all things, clothe yourselves with the bond of charity, as with a mantle, which is the bond of perfectness and peace."

Our goal is to desire to become as He is and work to become such. We are to do this by doing our best to act as He acted. To see the pinnacle importance of the gospel and share it to the world as best we can in love. This involves learning ourselves to be better.

A quick story; I went to a place in Southern California where we train. I have many friends that work there and are there year round, including Christian friends.

On my way there I decided to go to Deseret Book and I bought 8 Book of Mormons. I decided I would give them to them and encourage

243

them to read them. I only had a few in mind, and I prayed to have the right opportunity and words to say.

I gave them to a few friends with varying opinions. One friend had been in my mind and I decided to give one to him as he had been listening for a while to a conversation with another friend about the truth of the book. I gave one to him also.

I didn't think much of it over the next little while, other than praying that they would read it and come to a knowledge of it's truthfulness. I knew if they read it in a spirit of meekness, not judging, but relying on God with an open heart to show them the truth, they would come to know of its truthfulness.

A few days later, I received a message from a couple of sister missionaries that were in that area. They said they had been teaching that friends mother and they thanked me for giving him the Book of Mormon.

Of course I had been guided here and there in who and where to give the books to, the lesson however was that the Lord didn't command me outright to do anything. Instead He was able to use my effort perfectly anyway as I did my best to walk in the Spirit and did my best to have my mind fixed on the things that mattered most. He magnified the effort.

Doctrine and Covenants 100:5-8 "Therefore, verily I say unto you, lift up your voices unto this people; speak the thoughts that I shall put into your hearts, and you shall not be confounded before men; For it shall be given you in the very hour, yea, in the very moment, what ye shall say. But a commandment I give unto you, that ye shall declare whatsoever thing ye declare in my name, in solemnity of heart, in the spirit of meekness, in all things. And I give unto you this promise, that inasmuch as ye do this the Holy Ghost shall be shed forth in bearing record unto all things whatsoever ye shall say."

As we put forth such efforts of ourselves, the Lord can perfectly use such efforts. As we walk in the fruit of His Spirit, He works perfectly. As we strive to ask ourselves what Jesus would do in every situation, He works perfectly and magnifies our efforts.

I think back again to my friend Kevin Robinson I spoke of earlier in the book. He wasn't outspokenly religious but each one of his acts of love the Lord could magnify and work through little by little. The Lord grew us through love through each ray of it.

Whatsoever good is of God. He is the source of all good.

As we continue speaking of revelation there are things of value that are of absolute importance. These things are humility, meekness, earnestness desire, diligence, and faith. We must not let our preconceptions get in the way of what the Lord will teach us. We must trust Him to teach us. We must put forth diligence to receive. And all must be done in faith.

Moroni 7:42 "And again, behold I say unto you that he cannot have faith and hope, save he shall be meek, and lowly of heart."

Doctrine and Covenants 112:10 "Be thou humble; and the Lord thy God shall lead thee by the hand, and give thee answers to thy prayers."

Matthew 23:12 "And whosoever shall exalt himself shall be abased; and he that shall humble himself shall be exalted."

1 Peter 5:5-6 "Likewise, ye younger, submit yourselves unto the elder. Yea, all of you be subject one to another, and be clothed with humility: For God resisteth the proud, and giveth grace to the humble. Humble yourselves therefore under the mighty hand of God, that he may exalt you in due time."

Remember the proud are resisted. There is one way to receive, humility; even as a child. Our greatest faith is childlike trust in Him, to rely on Him for everything. All things are His.

Relying on Him and accounting Him as faithful to His promises is vital. We are promised that through obedience and humility and faith and seeking, asking in faith, earnestly seeking that we will receive.

We must remember that Jesus Christ also learned grace for grace, line upon line precept upon precept. He is our perfect example, our grand exemplar. We must seek to glorify our Father as He does, and seek to walk as He does, for the reasons He does, for our Father and His love.

Doctrine and Covenants 93:20 "For if you keep my commandments you shall receive of his fullness, and be glorified in me as I am in the Father; therefore, I say unto you, you shall receive grace for grace."

Doctrine and Covenants 93:24-28 "And truth is knowledge of things as they are, and as they were, and as they are to come; The Spirit of truth is of God. I am the Spirit of truth, and John bore record of me, saying: He received a fullness of truth, yea, even of all truth; And no man receiveth a fullness unless he keepeth his commandments. He that keepeth his commandments receiveth truth and light, until he is glorified in truth and knoweth all things."

We must keep His commandments and walk as we know He would have us. We must be set in that and do all in our power to do our best to always be better for Him. Furthermore, we must always acknowledge Him; truly our lives must become entirely centered on Him, for Him, in love, for Him. Remembering the first and second great commandments are to 1. Love God with all our heart, and 2. To love our neighbor as ourselves.

Proverbs 3:5-7 "Trust in the Lord with all thine heart; and lean not unto thine own understanding. In all thy ways acknowledge him, and he shall direct thy paths. Be not wise in thine own eyes: fear the Lord, and depart from evil."

We must recognize we are little children before Him and trust Him to guide us. As we have faith in this, He will teach us incredibly and guide us perfectly. Furthermore, please recognize the importance and vital map the supplied word of God is. Diligently seek and study the scriptures. Guide yourself in prayer and in faith and in His Spirit, read and seek. "Seek and ye shall find."

Have faith in His promises. Consider this thought to increase faith.

Imagine if a bright glorious angel appeared to you, grander than anything you have ever seen and that angel said to you, "Pray to God and He will give you your answer and guide you."

After that we would say 'wow,' and we would know that whatever we prayed we would receive. We would have great faith to receive. Recognize Christ Himself gives the same promises in written form. Have like faith in His words and promises; they are real. The Spirit beareth witness and shows all truth.

John 20:29 "Jesus saith unto him, Thomas because thou hast seen me, thou hast believed: blessed are they that have not seen, and yet have believed."

1 Nephi 15:8 "And I said unto them: Have ye inquired of the Lord?

9 And they said unto me: We have not; for the Lord maketh no such thing known unto us.

10 Behold, I said unto them: How is it that ye do not keep the commandments of the Lord? How is it that ye will perish, because of the hardness of your hearts?

11 Do ye not remember the things which the Lord hath said? – If ye will not harden your hearts, and ask me in faith, believing that ye shall receive, with diligence in keeping my commandments, surely these things shall be made known unto you."

The more we can magnify the childlike trust of our Father in Heaven the better off our faith is. "Thy will be done." Is a great start, the more we believe that in our heart the better off we are. As we come to know within ourselves that He will bless us more than we ever could, and His will is good and for good, then we can better say it with our hearts.

This can further be magnified, as I perceive it, to look at our own will and agency (which is really all that we have) and choose to give it entirely to God. We choose to have our "eye single to His glory;" so much so that we see ourselves as His entirely.

We are to willingly give our all and sacrifice and truly have our motivations single to Him, knowing He will take care of us. "The workman is worthy of hire," a scriptural reference to servants of God; to trust in Him to provide, all is His.

For myself I have gained strength and been blessed with much by doing my best to see myself in a sense as His to do whatever He will with. His will is perfect. I trust Him to guide me to all good and my faith in Him is that of my loving Father. I have found this to be a grand key perception to magnify childlike faith. We are His.

"Strangely enough the key to freedom is obedience." – Boyd K. Packer

If you were a king over a vast kingdom, and had all wisdom to run it perfectly and had a child you were raising to help see their duty in the right way, wouldn't this be the same principle for us?

Moving along, consider these next scriptures as they are of vital importance to understand revelation.

3 Nephi 26:9-10 "And when they shall have received this, which is expedient that they should have first, to try their faith, and if it shall so be that they shall believe these things then shall the greater things be made manifest unto them. And if it so be that they will not believe these

247

things, then shall the greater things be withheld from them, unto their condemnation."

Alma 12:9-10 "And now Alma began to expound these things unto him, saying: It is given unto many to know the mysteries of God; nevertheless they are laid under a strict command that they shall not impart only according to the portion of his word which he doth grant unto the children of men, according to the heed and diligence which they give unto him.
10 And therefore, he that will harden his heart, the same receiveth the lesser portion of the word; and he that will not harden his heart, to him is given the greater portion of the word, until it is given unto him to know the mysteries of God until he know them in full."

These scriptures are true and vital! They are saying, those who receive with faithfulness in all that has been given, will receive more; "the greater things will be made manifest to them." I testify of this truth.
Furthermore, it says, those who will harden their hearts against the truth they receive, "the greater things will be withheld." I can also testify of this as I have seen both sides and am blessed to have seen truth and now know the right way.
Meekness and humility without trusting what you have heard from others or online and trusting in God is paramount. I think of many great Christian friends that will not for a moment think of reading the Book of Mormon though I stand and tell them and declare of its truthfulness. They have, from the arm of flesh, been told all manner of lies about it. They have formulated their own opinion and seek not the revelation of God. I don't judge. If they read a small portion at all they do so with a hard heart and already create their expected outcome. Their heart is not ready to receive the things of the Lord. The greater things are withheld. I do not judge, been there. I simply wish to show truth.
These scriptures are like all scripture of the Book of Mormon; they uphold the truths in the Bible. So too these speak similarly to the parable of the talents. Those who hath will be given more, those who hath not or who were given much yet they don't seek more or to use that which they have, it will be taken away from them that they receive. This can be likened to a few things all-pertaining to being a good servant of the Lord, using what good has been given and seeking more.
Furthermore, to those in the gospel now, there is much revealed truth for we have the fullness of the everlasting gospel. There are those who harden their heart against it, as I did in my youth. The plain truths were hidden then to me. I hardened my heart against them and certainly

couldn't see more if I didn't have the foundation of what I had to stand taller and be shown more.

Likewise many in the Church harden their hearts and lose whatever truth they harden their hearts against. Some only lose some revealed truths, some fall back into other Christian churches and at least still have Christ in their lives. Some harden against all of it and lose it all.

For those of logical mind, I can see how they can see this principle could be applied to any aspect and pushed to accept anything. My answer is this, whosoever is sufficiently humble and meek before God, He will manifest all truth to them. The Holy Ghost manifests all truth. Those who humbly seek DO find. Light can PROVE light. Faith is required. Thus we must be humble to plant the seed and seek, the promises are there and they are true.

The Church of Jesus Christ of Latter-day Saints becomes this, very grand and deep truths that are perfectly protected by faith, humility and meekness. Where more humility and faith is required, the grander the blessing it is that is protected. He will have a humble people. Much more is even taught only by Him.

His Spirit teaches the grander things and as we learn and accept in faith the greater and greater are taught as we seek to become like our Savior. The vast amounts of truths taught in the Church can become to seem such a small amount compared to the incredible amount the Spirit will teach us. The Church is the perfect vehicle to be guided correctly to our Father in Heaven, giving us all we need by our Father in Heaven, to best be taught all the more by Him, coming all the closer to Him.

Eventually as we seek we can come to understand the words in Alma, "It is given unto many to know the mysteries of God; nevertheless they are laid under a strict command that they shall not impart only according to the portion of his word which he doth grant unto the children of men, according to the heed and diligence which they give unto him."

The things the Lord teaches are grand and confound the 'wisdom' of the wise. True wisdom taught by God is grand and all is His. He has built all things perfectly. The meek shall inherit. I am forever grateful.

Isaiah 29:14 "Therefore, behold, I will proceed to do a marvelous work among this people, even a marvelous work, and a wonder: for the wisdom of their wise men shall perish and the understanding of their prudent men shall be hid.

16 Surely your turning of things upside down shall be esteemed as the potter's clay: for shall the work say of him that made it, He made

me not? Or shall the thing framed say of him that framed it, He had no understanding?

18 And in that day shall the deaf hear the words of the book, and the eyes of the blind shall see out of obscurity, and out of darkness.

19 The meek also shall increase their joy in the Lord, and the poor among men shall rejoice in the Holy One of Israel.

23 But when he seeth his children, the work of mind hands, in the midst of him, they shall sanctify my name, and sanctify the Holy One of Jacob, and shall fear the God of Israel.

24 They also that erred in spirit shall come to understanding, and they that murmured shall learn doctrine."

God is unchanging; He teaches more and more as we listen. He is no respecter of persons. If prophets of old could commune with Him in faith and for good, so can we. We must be diligent.

Moroni 10:5 "And by the power of the Holy Ghost ye may know the truth of all things."

"The Holy Ghost is a revelator. . . No man can receive the Holy Ghost without receiving revelations." –Joseph Smith

Before we go on, we must faithfully accept those things. Pray to have that faith turn to knowledge through diligent learning taught by the Spirit, and then we can see the next and the next. As we go on we are truly blessed with utterly grand revelation, all to help us be better servants of our Father, to come closer to Him and bring others to His love.

3 Nephi 19:35-36 "And it came to pass that when Jesus had made an end of praying he came again to the disciples, and said unto them: So great faith have I never seen among all the Jews; wherefore I could not show unto them so great miracles, because of their unbelief. Verily I say unto you, there are none of them that have seen so great things as ye have seen: neither have they heard so great things as ye have heard."

These scriptures will become an individual truth for each of us and the sky is the limit as we diligently seek to become like our Savior and have His attributes. Our loving Father in Heaven has promised us incredible things and I testify they are true.

"And may I say that the only way to gain true religion is to receive it from the Lord. True religion is revealed religion; it is not a creation of man's devising; it comes from God." – Bruce R. McConkie

Truly.

Psalms 84:11 "For the Lord God is a sun and shield: the Lord will give grace and glory: no good thing will he withhold from them that walk uprightly."

Doctrine and Covenants 71:6 "for unto him that receiveth it shall be given more abundantly, even power."

Diligently seek. ALL for His glory.
The Lord's people truly receive revelation.

Joseph Smith taught ". . .God hath not revealed anything to Joseph, but what he will make known unto the twelve, and even the least Saint may know all things as fast as he is able to bear them."

I have found this to be true, some things incredibly and exceptionally deep and upon learning taking a big step back and saying, "Ok Lord, that's a bit much, maybe not yet on that." Many times learning something and then months later learning something else and piecing together something of a grander revelation, all taught in perfection.

The next bit here is important. I will share some scriptures that will help us discern the Spirit of God and why that is absolutely vital as we seek revelation. We should seek it, we should want to seek to be as profitable servants as we can.

1 John 4:2 "Hereby know ye the Spirit of God: Every spirit that confesseth that Jesus Christ is come in the flesh is of God:"

This is a very important scripture of the Bible and a way to discern that which is of God. The spirit that would teach the opposite is not of God. Jesus Christ lives, and is necessary and reigns forever. It is important to note The Book of Mormon, "we talk of Christ, we rejoice in Christ, we preach of Christ, we prophesy of Christ, and we write according to our prophecies, that our children may know to what source they may look for a remission of their sins."

The Bible teaches us that we will know false prophets by their fruits. The Church of Jesus Christ of Latter-day Saints is very good fruit

251

and is the fullness of the everlasting gospel. We can use the keys and tools given in the Bible to be guided by the Lord. However we must remember the Lord's work and love is vast. He uses many in many areas. All that is good is of Him.

The Bible also teaches us the fruit of the Spirit: love, joy, peace, longsuffering, gentleness, goodness, faith, meekness, temperance. These are a great way to perceive what spirit we are carrying and what spirit is about us.

We are furthermore taught in the Bible that God is love and all good is of God.

Furthermore and again The Book of Mormon gives us a deeper look into these things here. These things are grand keys to perceive the Spirit of God.

Moroni 7:13 "But behold, that which is of God inviteth and enticeth to do good continually; wherefore, every thing which inviteth and enticeth to do good, and to love God, and to serve him, is inspired of God.

16 "For behold, the Spirit of Christ is given to every man, that he may know good from evil: wherefore, I show unto you the way to judge; for every thing which inviteth to do good, and to persuade to believe in Christ, is sent forth by the power and gift of Christ; wherefore ye may know with a perfect knowledge it is of God."

I again recommend studying all of Moroni 7. Discerning the Spirit becomes very important, at least it was in my case and I perceive it to be so in most.

Doctrine and Covenants 11:12-14 "And now, verily, verily, I say unto thee, put your trust in that Spirit which leadeth to do good – yea, to do justly, to walk humbly, to judge righteously; and this is my Spirit. Verily, verily, I say unto you, I will impart unto you of my Spirit, which shall enlighten your mind, which shall fill your soul with joy. And then shall ye know, or by this shall you know, all things whatsoever you desire of me, which are pertaining unto things of righteousness, in faith believing in me that you shall receive."

Further deep importance there. The Spirit is our teacher. We are to be taught by God and guided by Him and His Spirit constantly. I testify of the truth of these things. When your faith is such that you know these are the words of God, and the Spirit will testify of this as you seek humbly, and not harden your heart, you cannot help but have joy in the promises and words.

Now why is it so vital that we can perceive what is directly of the Spirit of God? I will answer with a scripture.

Doctrine and Covenants 68:4 "And whatsoever they shall speak when moved upon by the Holy Ghost shall be scripture, shall be the will of the Lord, shall be the mind of the Lord, shall be the word of the Lord, shall be the voice of the Lord, and the power of God unto salvation.

5 Behold, this is the promise of the Lord unto you, O ye my servants."

The Spirit testifies the mind of God. We must be able to discern when it is present and take to heart all that is taught. Through all these above keys we can discern our own thoughts and that of God; we can make it pretty simple by the broad point that, "whatsoever is good is of God," and it is true.

Truly the Holy Ghost is a revelator. As we listen we can become much, much closer to God. As we are diligent we will be led to scriptures and understanding that are opened to our understanding deeper than we could imagine now. I have experienced this.

Another quick addition I would like to add that will help is to garnish your thoughts; recognize God is right there and can see and understand your thoughts far more than you can. It is true. As we do our best to ask for protection from any wrong and unkind thoughts and quickly repent and change our thought process to that of love and of virtue our confidence will wax strong.

Consider the vast and incredible promises of God in this scripture.

Doctrine and Covenants 121:45 "Let thy bowels also be full of charity towards all men, and to the household of faith, and let virtue garnish thy thoughts unceasingly; then shall thy confidence wax strong in the presence of God; and the doctrine of the priesthood shall distil upon thy soul as the dews from heaven.

46 The Holy Ghost shall be thy constant companion, and thy scepter an unchanging scepter of righteousness and truth; and thy dominion shall be an everlasting dominion, and without compulsory means it shall flow unto thee forever and ever."

I testify of the truth of all of this. And tell you the blessings are beyond compare. They are all for the glory of God. The Lord will teach you when you are ready, the greater things, by His Spirit. He has prepared the way in the fullness of His everlasting gospel, The Church of Jesus Christ of Latter-day Saints.

Keep in mind here the ordinances and covenants of the gospel are vital. Up to this point I had received the priesthood, went through the temple, put my eye single to the glory of God, made covenants with Him, and was married in the temple. Each portion of these has incredible and vastly important learning opportunities and blessings. The covenants therein are vital and the ordinances can teach us greatly as we diligently seek and are taught by the Spirit.

The Church of Jesus Christ of Latter-day Saints is the fullness of the gospel on the earth today. I will show more of this in the next section. The Lord does not stop teaching; there is no end to our loving Father in Heaven. The grandest key is for us to become as our Savior is and be filled with His love.

Taught By the Holy Spirit

I will speak now on being taught by the Holy Spirit. After we are diligently seeking and can discern the Spirit and learn to humbly and meekly heed the guidance of our Father in Heaven we can learn and see much more clearly. As we seek in faith the Lord begins to open things to our understanding.

After Joseph Smith and Oliver Cowdery received and had the Aaronic Priesthood restored at the hands of John the Baptist they had the authority given from heaven to baptize each other.

After they were baptized and began studying the scriptures.

Joseph said, "Our minds now being enlightened, we began to have the scriptures laid open to our understandings, and the true meaning and intention of their more mysterious passages revealed unto us in a manner which we never could attain to previously, nor ever before had thought of."

This happens. Scripture that once was perceived to have one meaning, perhaps historical, or some that were too vague and weird to understand, or some that seemed symbolic and spiritual can be opened by the Spirit and bring great depth of understanding.

This comes from diligent seeking and humbly and meekly being taught by the Spirit; for me diligence is an important part.

Begin with prayer, what do you want to know? Seek in faith, humbly, meekly; diligently seek. Sometimes pondering random thoughts I come to realize a vast truth and say, "Oh wow this is what I had prayed to understand."

With each of these one can get to the next amazing truth and the next and revelation becomes exponentially real. The "grander things" are given. Simple things said in simple scripture go deeper to incredibly deep. Our Father in Heaven is amazing!

As the Spirit teaches us the Lord seems to smile and chuckle and lovingly say, "Now you're getting it." We begin to see His utter vastness and perfection. His perfect and incredibly vast symphony of love becomes more evident.

Being taught by the Spirit is important; also, teaching by the Spirit is important. When we are in tune to be taught by the Spirit, especially those things that are of the Spirit we qualify for the phrase, "Eyes to see and ears to hear."

Similar to the scriptures, I have seen conference talks, even very old ones, that I am absolutely floored by the utter depth of wisdom. Wisdom that is not just open to the naked eye but seemingly disguised to the hearer with eyes to see and ears to hear. Deeper levels to find by the Spirit's guide. Much like Jesus taught. "The flesh profiteth nothing."

Remember the things of God are living and endless. If one prepares a talk guided by the Spirit, they are speaking the words of the Lord. And He who hears in the Spirit, taught by the Spirit, hears with Spiritual ears; and the doors are blown off; revelation is received.

I have been amazed to see incredibly humble men of God with such deep wisdom speak it simply and quietly just there for those ready to hear it; just there for when the Spirit is ready to teach His seeking children. Many on many different levels learn what is prepared for them. When we feel the Spirit through any remarks or actions, it is not them but our Father in Heaven blessing us through them; all good is His, all glory is His. There is significant depth for us to hear and learn if we meekly let the Spirit teach us.

"I have made it my regular practice to assume I need heavenly help to understand the meaning and purpose of the words spoken by prophets." – President Henry B. Eyring

What a deep quote that I absolutely relate with. To say the least the Lord will teach us as deep as our faith will allow. It is up to us to diligently strengthen it and then use it to become better for Him.

I have been graciously blessed with much revelation and all of the areas described are of vital importance to me. Whether it is things being opened to my understanding or things perceived through the discernment of the Spirit all of them become vital to understand deeply to gain the full picture. I will quickly try to explain.

One evening I had a very deep and random thought occur to me, it seemed as though it was just a random thought. It was essentially, "God thinks of you this way. . .," I wont get too into it just yet, but was a

255

grand and amazing blessing. My very next thought was "Wow, if that were so I would just literally praise Him and serve Him forever. I just couldn't imagine it."

It was such a grand thought, and at the time I thought of it just as my own thought. It wasn't until later that I recognized the follow up thought, it was a thought that made me want to love and serve God, a key definer of the Spirit of God. Though I couldn't discern it then, the thought seemed too amazing for me to see that it was truly revelation. Later, I discerned it correctly and realized it was from His Spirit.

Throughout that time I had been having scripture unfolded to my understanding and deeper things shown. I had also been quickened in the Spirit and learned much in truly amazing ways many times at this point. I had learned some significant truths.

Note: (Keep in mind I don't say any of this to make myself seem wise or great in any way. I simply am pointing out that these things are open and available to all who recognize their weakness like me and do our best to humbly and faithfully seek His guidance and strength.)

On top of these, at times I would have random thoughts that stuck out to me. For instance one time, right when I had come back to the Church. I went and spoke with my new bishop. The Spirit was incredibly strong in his office. When I left and walked in the parking lot I had a large thought of the vastness of God; it was totally random. The thought accompanied with a visual type, vision perhaps; regardless it was a result of having the Spirit right there.

The thought gave me an incredibly, incredibly deep insight to the experience I had that brought me back to the Church. It made sense of so many things and I began to see the immensity of God more clearly. I could see the Spirit teaching large things. I began to better comprehend things of a vast nature.

Every time I needed the guiding, teaching and revelatory influence of the Spirit I was blessed with it. I was greatly helped. I relied on Him entirely and He kept me in the right path.

Isaiah 30:21 "And thine ears shall hear a word behind thee, saying, This is the way, walk ye in it, when ye turn to the right hand, and when ye turn to the left."

That first thought, the one after the strong Spirit with the Bishop lingered, though I didn't see the total significance of it then. It led to a later help to discern far deeper meaning in scripture as the Spirit taught me. Being taught by the Spirit led to experiences of being quickened in the Spirit which led to being taught many things all the way to discerning the Spirit and all of that together led to utterly vast revelation and understanding. It all works together. Each piece has a part and it is good for us to learn all good things.

The point I am making here is the Spirit is the key part, the Spirit and your diligence. Pure childlike humility, meekness and utter reliance on our Father in Heaven is important. All is His; all must be sought for His glory. He is a perfect teacher.

It becomes valuable at first in this to seek to better understand His love and vastness. After even glimpsing such doing all things for His glory brings great joy.

In revelation, as we hold in faith, we will be led to grander and grander truths; all that lead us to a deeper desire to serve and praise our perfect Father in Heaven as well as strengthening our faith to an infinite pinnacle of knowledge. It begins with faith, longing to serve Him and get humbly on His strait and narrow path. As we seek more in humble faith, for His glory, the blessings are vast. The promises are vast. He is so good.

Doctrine and Covenants 76:51-62 "They are they who received the testimony of Jesus, and believed on his name and were baptized after the manner of his burial, being buried in the water in his name, and this according to the commandment which he has given – That by keeping the commandments they might be washed and cleansed from all their sins, and receive the Holy Spirit by the laying on of the hands of him who is ordained and sealed unto this power; And who overcome by faith, and are sealed by the Holy Spirit of Promise, which the Father sheds forth upon all those who are just and true. They are they who are the church of the Firstborn. They are they into whose hands the Father has given all things- They are they who are priests and kings, who have received of his fullness, and of his glory; And are priests of the Most High, after the order of Melchizedek, which was after the order of Enoch, which was after the order of the Only Begotten Son. Wherefore, as it is written, they are gods, even the sons of God – Wherefore, all things are theirs, whether life or death, or things present, or things to come, all are theirs and they are Christ's, and Christ is God's. And they shall overcome all things. Wherefore, let no man glory in man, but rather let him glory in God, who shall subdue all enemies under his feet. These shall dwell in the presence of God and his Christ forever and ever."

The depth of all of these verses is immense. "And who overcome by faith, and are sealed by the Holy Spirit of promise," is an area worth seeing the importance of faith.

257

I will speak of this part briefly but I will preface it with an assurance and deep urging of vast and grand importance, the Priesthood of God.

As the law and 'wisdom' of the world is confounded greatly by He who created all things, even God our Father, the greatest wisdom becomes humble faith before Him. For we can resonate with Him, be taught by Him, and come to know our Father. He alone is all-powerful, He alone has done all for us and it is up to Him to give all things.

The Priesthood of God is the authority, given by Him, in His Biblically promised restored everlasting gospel, for His servants to act in His name. All things fall before Him, all is His, and He grants His authority to His servants that do their best to honor, follow and glorify Him. He alone has all power; He alone can give whatsoever He will. The promises to His children are great, and they are given and received in proportion to our faith, and as we strive to become even as our Savior is, in the time and order of our Father. The ordinances of the Church become important guides and learning tools as well as vital covenants with our Father in Heaven.

"The Melchizedek Priesthood . . . is the channel through which all knowledge, doctrine, the plan of salvation, and every important matter is revealed from heaven." – Teachings of the Presidents of the Church: Joseph Smith

Those who have not received the ordinances up to the higher priesthood of the Church I say get on the path and stay on the path with an eye single to the glory of God. After it is received one can receive the greater things if serious diligence is applied; the greater things are far greater; all things for His glory.

The covenants of our Father in Heaven are truly amazing. Much revelation can yet be received. However, as I discern it, the utter depths are given after one has learned much and walks the path and fulfills the ordinances and covenants. Each one is another grand teacher.

If you are of the Holy Melchizedek Priesthood and seek to learn, pray to be taught and guided by the Spirit to have revelation given. Keep in mind, all taught is for the glory of God and an eye single to His glory is an honorable pre requisite.

I recommend to those to pray and be led by the Spirit in study of scripture and talks, one talk of great worth is that of an apostle of the Lord, Bruce R. McConkie, titled The Doctrine of the Priesthood given in 1982. I will provide some excerpts.

"To all of you, to all holders of the Aaronic and Melchizedek Priesthoods, I issue this challenge; come, live as befits one who is a servant of the Lord. This doctrine, the doctrine of the priesthood – unknown in the world and but little known even in the Church – cannot be learned out of the scriptures alone. It is not set forth in the sermons and teachings of the prophets and Apostles, except in small measure.

The doctrine of the priesthood is known only by personal revelation. It comes, line upon line and precept upon precept, by the power of the Holy Ghost to those who love and serve God with all their heart, might, mind, and strength."

Elder McConkie speaks of how he sought to convey this and realized he was thinking of how Alma wanted to have a trump and proclaim with a voice to shake the earth. However he realized, just as Alma did, that it is not the way of God. He realized that there is a time and a season for everyone and that his humble delivery would be enough for those who seek.

He says, "And I know that the Lord does not work in this way. His word goes forth by the mouths of his servants as they minister and labor in their weakness. That word is then carried into receptive hearts by the still small voice of the Spirit."

Though we have utterly incredible amounts of knowledge, it is all the Lord's; to be taught by Him in His way. I remember coming back to the Church thinking, "Ah, I can show people logically if they will follow this to this to this etc." Then later realizing, "Ah, I am so silly, the Lord's ways are perfect and I will do only that which He would have me and seek to better understand and walk in the way he would have me."

Yet I can say it is all true. Listen, seek in faith, you will find.

I will not speak much more of this other than to say, He will teach you all things.

I add this sentence of Elder McConkie's talk as I find it glorifying to our mighty and perfect Father in Heaven.

"How else than by the power of the Spirit can any of us ever understand spiritual truths? How does one describe an infinite God in finite terms?"

I will add a scripture that I love that gives a still vague idea of the vastness and glory and perfect symphony of love of our Father in Heaven, the Spirit truly can make this magnified and clearer.

259

Doctrine and Covenants 88:41 "He comprehendeth all things, and all things are before him, and all things are round about him; and he is above all things, and in all things, and is through all things, and is round about all things; and all things are by him, and of him, even God, forever and ever."

As we humbly and meekly seek His guidance, scriptures will be opened to us in ways we could never imagine. As we put first things of eternal importance, willing to sacrifice the temporal, with our eye single to His glory we can grow vastly. His promises are there.

Within the covenant of the Priesthood, we promise to live by every word that proceeds from the mouth of God. We must be diligent and totally set on this if we desire to move forward; which we all should. Keep in mind the Lord uses all of us differently in different ways and has times and seasons for all of us.

As we seek to do all things required, and magnify our calling and are counted faithful we are blessed with all that the Father hath, an incredible covenant given by Him. As we discern this by the Spirit, discern also all of the ordinances of God. We are even blessed with that of eternal marriage, as we become one with our spouse and are blessed all the more. Eternal families with our Father in Heaven.

All things the Lord has, quite immense to say the least and I think we will have eternity to continue to learn the glory of our endless and eternal good Father, thankfully in His presence. I believe we will desire to do all things always more and more for His glory. He is simply incredibly good beyond our current comprehension. How blessed we are to be accounted as His sons and daughters.

Just as Elder McConkie says, the doctrine is little known even in the church. He simply invites and gives guidance on how to receive revelation; he gives more than I have given here so if you are in the Priesthood, seek with eyes to see and ears to hear, if not, seek the humble strait and narrow path to come to the Priesthood and be a blessed servant of our Father. The Lord invites all of His children.

Doctrine and Covenants 50:10-12 "And now come, saith the Lord, by the Spirit, unto the elders of his church, and let us reason together, that ye may understand; Let us reason even as a man reasoneth one with another face to face. Now, when a man reasoneth he is understood of man, because he reasoneth as a man; even so will I, the Lord, reason with you that you may understand."

Doctrine and Covenants 50:21-24 "Therefore, why is it that ye cannot understand and know, that he that receiveth the word by the Spirit of truth receiveth it as it is preached by the Spirit of truth? Wherefore, he that preacheth and he that receiveth, understand one another, and both are edified and rejoice together. And that which doth not edify is not of God, and is darkness. That which is of God is light; and he that receiveth light, and continueth in God, receiveth more light; and that light groweth brighter and brighter until the perfect day."

In seeking revelation from our Father in Heaven, get close to Him, get used to discerning His Spirit and communicating with Him. Do everything to become closer and perceive how close He truly is. Then reason with Him.

Liken scriptures directly to us for He is big. Be honest with Him, our Father who created us. Tell Him everything, liken things to ourselves with an understanding that He would have done it all just for you alone. That much love. See the messages for you. Faith, He is there.

He will edify us and teach us deeply. Recognize that which is of His Spirit edifies and teaches all in their portion perfectly. All are edified and rejoice together.

In the book of Isaiah, the Lord talks about how after he will destroy the wisdom of the wise he magnifies the law for the righteous. Those who are in the 'wisdom' of the world or perceive it the way the world sees it will always be ensnared in it unless they escape through truth, humility and faith in our Savior Jesus Christ. Our Savior will cleanse through faithfulness and we will become humble and contrite. He is utterly necessary.

Isaiah 42:21 "The Lord is well pleased for his righteousness' sake; he will magnify the law, and make it honourable."

This is translated further by the JST but the same message comes out; he simply addresses those who the Lord had to save after their ignorance in verses before first, we are focusing really on the last part.

"The Lord is not well pleased with such a people, but for his righteousness' sake he will magnify the law and make it honorable."

As we are faithful and abide the ordinances given in faith, and are taught from on high we are healed and the Lord blesses us greatly. In the Priesthood as we diligently magnify our calling and seek revelation and gifts of the Spirit we can be taught of all things until we know all things.

Doctrine and Covenants 45:9 "And even so I have sent mine everlasting covenant into the world, to be a light to the world, and to be a

261

standard for my people, and for the Gentiles to seek to it, and to be a messenger before my face to prepare the way before me.

10 Wherefore, come ye unto it, and with him that cometh I will reason as with men in days of old, and I will show unto you my strong reasoning.

11 Wherefore, hearken ye together and let me show unto you even my wisdom – the wisdom of him who ye say is the God of Enoch, and his brethren."

Remember all is the Lord's; He is significantly above all things; all things are by Him. His ways are vast and perfect. Trust Him. We gain salvation through faith. We learn and gain more through faith, eventually all things, as He sees fit.

The law is fulfilled, confounded, made perfect and magnified in faith in God and humility before Him. The wisdom of the wise perishes. In the end all is the Lord's, that which is of promise is also the Lord's; all is simply His. And all is magnified greatly and made honorable. He gives all to His children in perfect truth that none can see or gain without Him.

Oh that the wise of the world would seek true wisdom and humble themselves before their maker, our beloved Father; those that think of themselves that they know when they are blinded, that they would seek Him in faith. I pray many will see their error, as have I, and many have already, our Father is always there in love. His arm is always outstretched. He is mighty to save. I am so grateful.

The world could never perceive the depths of truths of what the Lord will give His humble children. The world, the few of the world yet in the deepest 'wisdom', walk in a 'wisdom' in a very wrong way that is a snare, that his meek and humble children become far, far above and beyond. The meek inherit.

Our Father in Heaven, God Almighty, is ever magnifying His perfect symphony and the meek and humble will see it. And they are with Him, where He is, above all. Trust our good and loving Father. He is our home.

Those walking in the 'wisdom' of the world see things so incorrectly while many of His blessed children sit above in true deep understanding, blessed through the trial of their faith and diligent humble seeking, in His glory, washed through faith on His Son our Savior Jesus Christ.

I praise Him forever. I am forever grateful for the mercy and amazing grace and wondrous love of our Father in Heaven. I pray all ensnared will listen and restore; and all those who seek to be His servants will be guided and led by Him.

I just have to say this as frankly as possible. When you see the goodness of God and how He works diligently to bless His children you will want nothing but to serve Him forever. When you are quickened in the Spirit and see many things by Him all the goodness and love He has and all He has done for us, you will want nothing more than to praise Him forever. I have found myself laughing in rejoicing at times in joy of His perfection, vastness and glory.

Remember how big He is and how much He loves us. We can liken scriptures and all things to us entirely and honestly, He knows all things and all is possible to Him and nothing is too hard for Him. 'Rebuke' the doubt; hold onto faith that has incredible potential. He loves us so amazingly that He would have done all for us if it were us alone. Let us see through that lens, because our Father in Heaven Himself will gladly teach us alone. He wants His children close. He loves us.

In all of this, I seek not to sound self-righteous or anything; I seek but to help. No good is of me but of God alone, all the good of me is His doing; all the good in you, I praise Him for. It is His gifts and I stand as one who, in His mercy, was saved. He has blessed me, and I am truly one who is incredibly blessed and I will serve Him forever, I am blessed to be His son.

I perceive I am one of whom was spoken that, 'the first shall be last and the last shall be first;' in some blessed regards that I am forever thankful for. Furthermore, I see many things that I must declare that surely are wisdom in Him in bringing me the way He has.

My sole goal is to bring all to see the majesty and perfection of our Father and come unto our Savior Jesus Christ and be saved, healed and blessed! HE LIVES!

"When you spiritually stretch beyond anything you have ever done before, then His power will flow into you. And then you will understand the deep meaning of the words we sing in the hymn "The Spirit of God': 'The Lord is extending the Saints' understanding. … The knowledge and power of God are expanding; The veil o'er the earth is beginning to burst.' The gospel of Jesus Christ is filled with His power, which is available to every earnestly seeking daughter or son of God. It is my testimony that when we draw His power into our lives, both He and we will rejoice." – President, then Elder Russel M. Nelson April 2017 General Conference.

Lastly, our eye becoming single to the glory of God is important to seek. Our whole entire being must come to a point where we truly desire to serve Him and put His causes of perfection and love first. This happens over time as we seek and learn and see His perfection. As we get close to Him and go from faith to truly seeing that His ways are perfect we will want nothing more than to serve Him as best we can.

Often we will see blessings come when we are intently focused on serving Him and what we can give Him, when our hearts are on serving Him. Even in these ways we will be taught all the more.

When we see how much He loves us we will see how much we love and forever need Him and how much He, whom we long to please, loves all of His children. Then we strive to love and as we go along we do our best to become as our Savior is, serving our Father, leaving the things of the world and striving for all good that brings glory to Him. Our old selves are no more and we become truly new in Christ.

Doctrine and Covenants 88:67 "And if your eye be single to my glory, your whole bodies shall be filled with light, and there shall be no darkness in you; and that body which is filled with light comprehendeth all thing"

The promises of God are true. We can exercise faith in them and receive them as we meet the requirements. What incredible promises. Oh that men would praise Him!

One day all will see the vast truths of this, some will see their folly in lack of faith and how much was always at their fingertips, even those in the Church will see how much has always been right there. I am so blessed and grateful to have been blessed exceedingly and desire all to see the incredible love and blessings of our incredible Father.

I testify of the truth of these things. As we accept them in faith the greater things will be made manifest. He longs to bless His children and I am so grateful. I have had days where significant understanding came from all angles. I have had scriptures opened to my understanding in deep ways. I have had nights where the blackboard of the Lord to teach me, as it were, was His stars in the sky. I have had experiences too sacred to share; some that many simply probably wouldn't believe.

I am incredibly blessed. And it is nothing that isn't available to each one of us. As we do our best to serve Him and diligently seek revelation, sooner or later we may run out of things that we desire revealed to us and seek His face. Seek always to be led by Him and walk in earnestness in His will. He guides perfectly.

I am a testimony of much of our Father in Heaven's goodness; His amazing grace, infinite mercy, incredible loving sacrifice, His wondrous and redeeming love and never ending willingness to bless all of His children exponentially and greatly. All for His love and His glory. I praise our Father in Heaven forever.

Doctrine and Covenants 88:68 "Therefore, sanctify yourselves that your minds become single to God, and the days will come that you shall see him; for he will unveil his face unto you, and It shall be in his own time, and in his own way, and according to his own will."

I have been blessed greatly. I want all to know, it is true! HE LIVES! This last scripture, I have been greatly blessed in that I can testify to you that this scripture is true. And of all blessings I have ever received, it is the greatest. I am forever grateful. Seek and ye shall find my brothers and sisters. Our Father is so good. HE LIVES!

2 Corinthians 4:6 "For God, who commanded the light to shine out of darkness, hath shined in our hearts, to give the light of the knowledge of the glory of God in the face of Jesus Christ."

Remember, as knowledge is poured out on the world in these last days may we seek true wisdom from Him alone, always walking in the strait and narrow path. Let us not be persuaded away form the rock of Christ. We have been told by Jesus Christ Himself that deception would be great and even miracles would pull many away. We have even been told by prophets throughout history and even modern prophets.

Heber C. Kimball prophesied for our times, "The difficulties will be of such a character that a man or woman who does not possess a personal knowledge or witness will fall. If you have not got this testimony, you must live right and a call upon the Lord, and cease not until you obtain it. Remember these sayings: The time will come when no man or woman will be able to endure on borrowed light."

Compare these words to our modern day prophet's much more recent words,

"In coming days, it will not be possible to survive spiritually without the guiding, directing, comforting, and constant influence of the Holy Ghost." – President Russell M. Nelson

The deception of the adversary is told to come, and it is among. It is strong, and twists truths into a strong deception. Remember, even the weakness of God is far stronger.
Do not leave the rock of Christ; do not look beyond the mark. Gain and maintain a strong testimony. I testify that all the 'wisdom' of

265

the wise of the world falls before the truth of our Savior Jesus Christ. All is His.

Though most who read this will have no such idea about it, and may never, yet there will be those few who need to hear it. Regardless deception will fight in many forms. Regardless it is a warning. I have been full circle. He lives. We need Him.

Heber C. Kimball also prophesied and it has since been re-iterated by Gordon B. Hinckley,

"Look out for the great sieve, for there will be a great sifting time, and many will fall: for I say unto you there is a test, a Test, a TEST coming, and who will be able to stand?"

Seek His guidance by His Spirit! We need our Father in Heaven. He is our ever-present help. Let us be close to Him.

There are many out there that see it all incorrectly; it will be pushed incorrectly. It seems so well understood that it is the 'end all' 'wisdom'. It is not. Jesus Christ is the way, the truth and the life.

Personally understanding somewhat what truly motivates many powers I could see it pushed as a world religion. BE NOT DECEIVED. DO NOT LEAVE THE ROCK OF CHRIST. Remember the words of our Savior. "Behold, I have told you before."

It falls and becomes the tiniest thing in comparison to even the foolishness of God. Humble yourself and see even the wisdom of God, with an single to His glory.

Remember, true wisdom is humility and meekness before God our Father with faith in Him. It is becoming a child in humility and entirely trusting Him in all things. Obedience is the key to freedom; trusting Him is the key to power. All for His glory. Seek His guidance. He loves us dearly. True wisdom is in Him.

As Christ told Peter in Matthew 16, He will build His church upon the rock of revelation. We shouldn't trust in the arm of flesh, but in our Father in Heaven and HIS Spirit. I have shown you how to discern. Whatsoever is good, and declares Jesus Christ is necessary and lives. His Spirit brings joy and gives us the desire to glorify and serve Him.

His Spirit will testify of all truth to us in a way that makes the things and understandings of the world laughable. He has created all things. Furthermore, we can come to know all things through Him; He has promised us this.

Oh be wise, what can I say more?

I testify that as we are taught by the Spirit we will come to greatly strengthen our FAITH and eventually we can come to actually

266

KNOW, which is a big word. Even beyond this, a faith that is now a knowledge, we can come to even eventually entirely UNDERSTAND the things of our Father in Heaven that once we simply accepted and held onto in faith. Grand revelation can become more commonplace and our lives and realities will shift to being able to perceive in truth.

Again, that which was once a testimony by the Spirit in our hearts will become strengthened faith, continuing in faith that faith can grow to strong faith and eventually will come to be knowledge. And if we diligently seek the Spirit to teach us in faith we can come to even understand the vast things of our Father in Heaven. He can truly show us all things, be faithful.

Vast truths that seem incredible and unknowable can be known and furthermore understood well.

John 14:26 "But the Comforter, which is the Holy Ghost, whom the Father will send in my name, he shall teach you all things, and bring all things to your remembrance, whatsoever I have said unto you.

27 Peace I leave with you, my peace I give unto you: not as the world giveth, give I unto you. Let not your heart be troubled, neither let it be afraid."

I testify that we can come to such understanding of all vast things and that such vast understandings come not by 'wisdom' of man but by wisdom in God; humble reliance on Him. The greatest wisdom that will teach the truth of all things as we exercise it correctly is humility before our Father in Heaven.

Again, the greatest wisdom is humility before God Almighty, our Father in Heaven; who made us, and all things. For by humility we can come to know and even understand grand things of Him. He longs to bless us.

We cannot be wise of ourselves, but as His humble children relying on Him.

Proverbs 3:5 "Trust in the Lord with all thine heart; and lean not unto thine own understanding.

6 In all thy ways acknowledge him, and he shall direct thy paths.

7 Be not wise in thine own eyes: fear the Lord, and depart from evil.

13 Happy is the man that findeth wisdom, and the man that getteth understanding."

We gain all wisdom and understanding by not relying on our own wisdom or understanding. We are not to fear and respect man and ourselves over the Lord, for all is His. We are to fear and respect our perfect Father in Heaven alone. This gives us the path to true wisdom, "foolish" by the world standard but oh how incredibly mighty and in true wisdom of the Lord.

1 Corinthians 3:18 "Let no man deceive himself. If any man among you seemeth to be wise in this world, let him become a fool, that he may be wise."

2 Nephi 9:41 "O then, my beloved brethren, come unto the Lord, the Holy One. Remember that his paths are righteous. Behold, the way for man is narrow, but it lieth in a strait course before him, and the keeper of the gate is the Holy One of Israel; and he employeth no servant there; and there is none other way save it be by the gate; for he cannot be deceived, for the Lord God is his name.

42 And whoso knocketh, to him will he open; and the wise, and the learned, and they that are rich, who are puffed up because of their learning, and their wisdom, and their riches – yea, they are they whom he despiseth; and save they shall cast these things away, and consider themselves fools before God, and come down in the depths of humility, he will not open unto them.

43 But the things of the wise and the prudent shall be hid from them forever – yea, that happiness which is prepared for the saints."

By relying humbly upon Him we eventually can come to understanding and wisdom. As we say and mean, "Thy will be done," we will come to see just how perfect and good and kind His will is for us and how perfectly He teaches us. We must remain diligent and faithful and centered in Him and His perfect love.

A final grand key. Remember to always, above all, be filled with love. Charity never faileth. It is the sure fire way to stay in His Spirit and be properly guided. Love is of vast importance.

Most times that grand revelation has come it comes with a grand understanding of how close Him and I are, how much I am loved, and how much I truly am His son. We are children in the best family and of the grandest King! All is His!

Ephesians 3:19 "And to know the love of Christ, which passeth knowledge, that ye might be filled with all the fullness of God."

Seek to be like our Savior. Humble, meek, full of love for all, quick to forgive, always filled with a pure love for all. This is strength. He is our grand exemplar.

In this love the Spirit abounds; we will be taught by the Spirit even as we teach by the Spirit and all will be edified by our Father in Heaven and His immense goodness.

Jacob 4:8 "Behold, great and marvelous are the works of the Lord. How unsearchable are the depths of the mysteries of him; and it is impossible that man should find out all his ways. And no man knoweth of his ways save it be revealed unto him; wherefore, brethren, despise not the revelations of God."

Chapter 19

CHURCH DISCOURSE
Christ Leads, History of the Hand of the Lord

This chapter has much good and will give the humble and meek a clearer understanding.

The Church of Jesus Christ of Latter-day Saints is true. I have come to know this through revelation, through faith, and then pragmatic understanding given through revelation because of faith. I know this truth, not by my own wisdom or that of man, but by the power of our Father in Heaven. The Lord will give us enough for us to try faith, and then He will teach us by and through that faith until we perfectly understand; if we desire it.

John 6:44 "No man can come to me, except the Father which hath sent me draw him: and I will raise him up at the last day.

45 It is written in the prophets, And they shall be taught of God. Every man therefore that hath heard, and hath learned of the Father, cometh unto me."

For me there were many things that I wasn't sure about, but I had been given more than enough to continue to try faith. The more I learned and was taught the more I had questions about; I think we well established my pragmatic mind and needing to understand. Regardless, when questions arose I would wait in faith and call on God for revelation and understanding.

Over time the things that I really didn't fully understand at first led to significant and deep understand of all the things I hadn't previously understood. Not only that, but because of those things I was able to learn and gain so much more that I otherwise would not have; even in the way I came to learn them.

If I would have hardened my heart against things I didn't then understand I would have missed out on serious revelation and understanding. As we talked about in the chapter on revelation, I accepted in faith those things, then the grander things were made manifest and eventually it all made sense. The Lord want's His children to trust Him and exercise faith that He will provide, He teaches us perfectly and even the way and manner He teaches us also teaches us.

Eventually I have been able to understand relatively well all the things I wanted to understand; although there is always much to learn when God Almighty is the teacher and He and His goodness are endless. Not only that, I have been able to see how such things are and why such things are necessary in our learning process here on the earth. As I have said before, pure trust in our Father in Heaven becomes even power.

I bring all of this up because the Church is true, I want to utilize this chapter and discourse to help some come to understand how they can, from any background, better see and try faith to be shown from God for themselves the truth thereof. God truly can make all things known for those who diligently seek in humility and meekness and in the right way.

The Book of Mormon very simply is just a record of a people. There are many lies told about it and about the Church. The Book of Mormon is simply a record of people that also knew about Christ and were visited by Christ after His resurrection. "Other sheep I have which are not of this fold, them also I must bring." God is vast, and cares about all of His children.

The Book of Mormon is another testimony of Jesus Christ. It upholds the same truths in the Bible and does not take away one bit from it; it simply upholds the truth. Anyone who reads it will see this is the case. It is the work of God.

When the Book of Mormon is given to someone, often times some scriptures are cited.

Moroni 10:3-5 "Behold, I would exhort you that when ye shall read these things, if it be wisdom in God that ye should read them, that ye would remember how merciful the Lord hath been unto the children of men, from the creation of Adam even down until the time that ye shall receive these things, and ponder it in your hearts.

4 And when ye shall receive these things, I would exhort you that ye would ask God, the Eternal Father, in the name of Christ, if these things are not true; and if ye shall ask with a sincere heart, with real intent, having faith in Christ, he will manifest the truth of it unto you, by the power of the Holy Ghost.

5 And by the power of the Holy Ghost ye may know the truth of all things."

These scriptures are a charge to prayerfully, humbly and meekly read the book and a promise that if you do so in such a spirit that the Lord will show you the truthfulness of it. This is true.

Before we get too deep into this discourse remember that in the Bible the Lord has promised us wisdom and revelation if we seek it. There are religions in the world that claim they are the only one because of history or other temporal things such as personal perception of the

271

word. Furthermore none can say they know and understand all things, (though much is to be given by the Lord only by His Spirit.)

Remember these scriptural promises. The Lord will give wisdom to all who are humble enough to seek.

Matthew 7:7 "Ask, and it shall be given you; seek, and ye shall find; knock, and it shall be opened unto you:

8 For every one that asketh receiveth; and he that seeketh findeth; and to him that knocketh it shall be opened."

James 1:5 "If any of you lack wisdom, let him ask of God, that giveth to all men liberally, and upbraideth not; and it shall be given him."

These are some incredible promises and are true.

The main difference, as I see it, from the many different sects of Christianity and The Church of Jesus Christ of Latter-day Saints, (which has the Biblically promised fullness of the everlasting gospel,) is that the Church utilizes these promises.

We come to know and understand truth and are guided to and by truth by the revelation from God. We seek to always be guided by His Spirit and be better taught by Him.

Some other sects say it is history, or their perspective of the word that shows they are right; we say fear God alone and seek His guidance; He will give us wisdom and show us all truth if we rely on Him.

If we do not trust in our own wisdom or that of man and instead seek wisdom from God our Father in Heaven alone we will come to know all truth as we are faithful to receive. In this we follow the same path of revelation Christ explained in Matthew 16, to receive of God and not of man.

Though all are on different spiritual levels there are those who receive vast revelation and serious understanding from on high. I can personally testify of this.

As many churches will say they must be the singular correct one remember that these Biblical promises are real. The Holy Spirit will show the humble and meek, who entirely rely on the Lord for guidance, that the Church of Jesus Christ of Latter-day Saints is the restored everlasting gospel. We know it by the Spirit of God and gain further revelation thereby.

I have many Christian friends, that no matter how I testify of the truth of The Book of Mormon they will not read it. They wont even try it. They believe of themselves in their own wisdom that they know what is right and they have heard lies about the Church and The Book of Mormon and they have come to trust in the arm and opinion of flesh.

Granted they have a portion of the truth and that is great, Jesus is the grandest part, but they miss the very fullness of the truth on the earth today; similarly as the Pharisees missed the very Christ they were waiting for as they trusted in their own wisdom.

Keep in mind in all of this; I judge none. I cannot judge any. I had to go the hard and long full circle way and by grace I have come to truth; a truth that at the time I really had to humble myself to be able to receive. I simply seek to help.

One day I was pondering this. I had come to knowledge of the truth and had many amazing experiences because of it. I came to understand the vast importance of this truth. I really had been wanting every one of my friends to know as well and I was absolutely amazed that some of my Christian friends would not read it.

I prayed and asked, "I know this is true, why then are there many of your children that long to serve you and want to do right by you, yet they wont hear truth?"

The answer came, "I lead my Church." At first glance, I wasn't sure what to make of the answer, whether it was an answer or my thoughts, however I was past the point of understanding revelation a bit more and knew how to receive it. I held onto the thought in faith and pondered the words. As I pondered the words in faith everything was opened to me and I understood.

"I lead my Church." Jesus Christ leads His Church. And He leads it in the exact manner He led it early on. Much was made clear to me in a way I hadn't before thought; I will do my best to illustrate some of this.

When Jesus was in His earthly ministry any who followed Him were shunned. They were shunned entirely from the synagogues and basically kicked out from the main church at the time. It required true humility to follow Christ and being willing to lose much.

To follow Christ then you had to believe in something bold at the time, that the old ways were changing and prophecy was being and had been fulfilled, there was more light and knowledge, even the source of that light and knowledge, that Jesus Christ was the Son of God and would fulfill all the religious requirements of the Law of Moses.

Pharisees and the leaders of the churches would not listen to Him; they attacked Him, belittled Him, and spread lies about Him. They put themselves and their own wisdom above the Savior, a truth all would come to need.

273

They would not listen to Him and rather, they could not listen. For it took a truly humble and meek heart to hear.

Christ often spoke in parables. Why? He told His apostles that it is given for them to understand but it is not given for others to understand.

One grand teaching moment of the importance of humbly trusting the Lord and following His meek and humble Spirit to truth is when Christ stated that,

John 6:53-56 "Except ye eat the flesh of the Son of man, and drink his blood, ye have no life in you. Whoso eateth my flesh, and drinketh my blood, hath eternal life; and I will raise him up at the last day. For my flesh is meat indeed, and my blood is drink indeed. He that eateth my flesh, and drinketh my blood, dwelleth in me, and I in Him."

Many of the disciples there said,

60 "this is an hard saying; who can hear it?"

Well from a physical understanding, boy is this a lot to take it. And there were those who left; I'm sure they were thinking, "Wait, what did I sign up for here? This sounds wild, Let's bail." The greater things are protected by humble, meek faith and trust in God. It is the spiritual ears that could hear.

Christ came to His apostles and asked if they would also leave. They said they would stay for He has the words of eternal life. 68

To some it sounded like a hard to hear temporal thing, yet to His apostles they could discern in the Spirit, they were meek and humble, they had the faith to hear.

Christ taught at that time, "It is the spirit that quickeneth; the flesh profiteth nothing: the words that I speak unto you, they are spirit, and they are life."63

Then another very grand teaching comes from Him.

65 "And He said, Therefore said I unto you, that no man can come unto me, except it were given unto him of my Father."

We are told from that day many of His disciples didn't walk with Him anymore. 66

Yet His apostles said after,

274

67 "Then said Jesus unto the twelve, Will ye also go away?

68 Then Simon Peter answered him, Lord, to whom shall we go? Thou hast the words of eternal life.

69 And we believe and are sure that thou art the Christ, the Son of the living God."

They had the ears to hear and eyes to see. They were being taught by the Spirit of God, they were humble and meek to receive.

The Pharisees back then trusted in their traditions. They followed Moses, and even though Moses prophesied of the coming of Jesus it wasn't clear to them. Many of the prophesies of their day that were happening right before their eyes, right within their own scripture couldn't be seen because they weren't bold and in their face, they were as all things of God are, meekly and humbly and Spiritually discerned. Their trust in their own wisdom, that which was taught by the arm of flesh made them miss the very grandeur of our Savior in their midst.

The Pharisees trusted in the wisdom they already had. They already followed God, to their knowledge, and they wouldn't have anyone come in and tell them what they were doing was wrong. They wouldn't for a moment humble themselves to truly listen to and actually humbly consider His words, but at every turn and every word from his mouth they jumped to another reason that He, the very Christ, was wrong. They wouldn't even hear or consider the words from His mouth. They knew the traditions and they 'knew,' of themselves, that they were right. They couldn't see Him.

The Pharisees trusted in their own wisdom, they trusted themselves, and they trusted in the arm of flesh. They loved the things of the world and it was hard for them to humble themselves to see more. They could not see beyond the bit of truth they were given. They knew God was unchanging, yet they didn't realize that He was always giving more to the humble seeker, for they shall find.

Because of their hard heartedness they missed the very Christ that they had been waiting for. They lacked the humility to even try His words or experiment on them. They even discounted His miracles.

Those who may have listened to some of His words may have been scared off by the consequence of following Him. They would be, in a sense, exiled.

In Matthew 16 one of the many grand lessons of our Savior is taught, this is after Christ asks, "Whom do men say that I the Son of man am?"

275

Matthew 16:14-17 "And they said, Some say that thou art John the Baptist: some, Elias; and others, Jeremias, or one of the prophets.

15 He saith unto them, But whom say ye that I am?

16 And Simon Peter answered and said, Thou art the Christ, the Son of the living God.

17 And Jesus answered and said unto him, Blessed art thou, Simon Bar-Jona: for flesh and blood hath not revealed it unto thee, but my Father which is in heaven.

18 And I say also unto thee, That thou art Peter, and upon this rock I will build my church; and the gates of hell shall not prevail against it.

19 And I will give unto thee the keys of the kingdom of heaven: and whatsoever thou shalt bind on earth shall be bound in heaven: and whatsoever thou shalt loose on earth shall be loosed in heaven."

Upon the rock of revelation from God, and not the arm of flesh, Christ told us He will build His Church. What a huge lesson when we see the context of this great lesson.

How could the Pharisees ever believe if they wouldn't humble themselves for even a moment? They wouldn't for a split second even consider that maybe they were wrong, or maybe the wise men around them weren't the wisest or that maybe all they had been taught was great but they should humble themselves to receive more and revelation from God. Pride leads to deception. Oh be wise. I judge none.

They believed so strongly in the wisdom that they had to be all they needed that they missed the very Christ in their midst. They lacked the humility, even the desire to try humility.

When they heard Christ speak, instead of humbly hearing and being able to hear deep and incredible truths from the mouth of God, they instead hardened their hearts and only listened so that they could trip Him up or find things He said to distort and make Him look bad.

They spread all manner of lies about their very Savior and wanted others to see Him as the opposite of the purity He was. They said He was of the devil, that He was a liar, ridiculed where He was from and reasoned that because He was the Son of Joseph that He couldn't be anything special.

"He is a good man: others said, Nay; but he deceiveth the people." Officers didn't arrest Him at times because, "Never man spake like this man." To which the Pharisees replied, "Are ye also deceived?"

The Pharisees received guidance and were told, "Doth our law judge any man before it hear him, and know what he doeth?" The pharisees didn't want to hear or 'judge righteous judgement' and replied with, "Art thou also out of Galilee?" … For out of Galilee ariseth no prophet. After all what good thing can come out of Nazareth?

Christ led His followers, His people, His Church in humility. He spoke in parables so that only those who would humbly hear in the Spirit would hear. He lived in a humble manner and those who followed Him would have had to give up much, and appear weak and despised of the world, to be His disciple.

Matthew 13:10 "And the disciples came, and said unto him, Why speakest thou unto them in parables?

11 He answered and said unto them, Because it is given unto you to know the mysteries of the kingdom of heaven, but to them it is not given.

12 For whosoever hath, to him shall be given, and he shall have more abundance: but whosoever hath not, from him shall be taken away even that he hath.

13 Therefore speak I to them in parables: because they seeing see not; and hearing hey hear not, neither do they understand."

Though his disciples walked humbly, they had the words of eternal life, for they were received by humble and meek ears, therefore they heard the voice of the Spirit and not of the carnal. His disciples walked in love, knowing full well of themselves the truth, they suffered persecution but understood that our Father would draw others in their time, so they walked humbly still, helping the best they could, giving for those who would and could hear.

Christ leads His Church today in the same manner. Don't get me wrong, His kingdom is vast and so is His Church. He uses people in all areas of the world. Even all that which is good is of God. He uses many to bring others to Christ that otherwise would not have found Him, His goodness and mercy is vast. However, there is a sect, that as prophesied and promised, has the fullness of the truth and much more light and truth again is revealed.

Christ leads His Church today just as He did then. Whether they be Christians or any of the world, many scoff at The Church of Jesus Christ of Latter-day Saints, though it is truly the truth.

Many don't read the Book of Mormon, and if they do read some many don't read with a meek and humble heart. They miss the very word of God in their face because it is humbly and meekly received. They feel they know of themselves or have been taught by the arm of flesh of others who seem wise to them and seem to know the workings of God. They fear others reaction or persecution. They have been told many lies and trust in their own wisdom and the arm of flesh. They miss the very fullness of the restored gospel guided by and given by Jesus Christ Himself.

They miss that Christ Himself told us how He would build His Church on the rock of revelation and that we could understand by revelation. By the Spirit we may know the truth of all things.

Many hear or learn things they think they understand and because they hear it with a hard heart they use it to belittle or make to look silly the Church, and they scoff and leave, just as the scoffers of old when there are things spiritually discerned that are there for the meek and humble to gain teaching from the Lord.

Some hear of the humble origins of the prophet of God chosen to restore much truth, Joseph Smith, and say, "Can anything good of God come out of a random small town in New York?"

"Whence hath this man this wisdom, and these mighty works? Is not this the carpenter's son?" Matthew 13:54-55 partial

Some don't have time to hear out everything or even seek the revelation of the Lord before making a judgment. Christ teaches us in the book of John, "Judge not according to the appearance, but judge righteous judgement." What valuable advice when the world is swirling with truths that are attacked and deception is all over. If people didn't heed that then they would listen to the lies of the world and of the Pharisees. And if they don't heed that today they will again wrongly judge by the opinions of flesh and blood and their own wisdom and not be led in truth; they will not even give themselves the chance to consider truth and then take such to the Lord.

Matthew 13: 11 "He answered and said unto them, Because it is given unto you to know the mysteries of the kingdom of heaven, but to them it is not given.

12 For whosoever hath, to him shall be given, and he shall have more abundance: but whosoever hath not, from him shall be taken away even that he hath."

3 Nephi 26:9-10 "And when they shall have received this, which is expedient that they should have first, to try their faith, and if it shall so be that they shall believe these things then shall the greater things be made manifest unto them.

And if it so be that they will not believe these things, then shall the greater things be withheld form them, unto their condemnation."

Remember the promise, ask and ye shall receive, seek and ye shall find. This is repeated many times yet how many don't hear and trust Him to guide us to truth.

In short, few are humble enough to truly rely on revelation from God. And I tell you, He will absolutely reveal truth through His Spirit to those humble and meek before Him.

I judge none as I was very hard hearted early on, it was an utter shock for me to realize that The Church of Jesus Christ of Latter-day Saints was the truth. I really had to eat humble pie. But I had been saved by the Lord, it was His, and I would do whatever He wanted, and I would always seek His guidance. I would give anything for Him and His Church. I have been on both sides of this now and can now see clearly. He does lead to all truth if we humbly meekly trust Him alone. I am forever grateful.

Just like then, many spread all sorts of lies because they didn't understand it was the very Christ in their midst, they couldn't humble themselves to even try to see it. They missed the grand things and greater blessings. So too today many spread many lies and don't discern it is His Church. Many don't see that the vastly growing numbers of His Church are because of revelation of truth from Him. He does reveal truth in perfect love and light. Light can prove light. His Spirit will guide the meek and humble and faithful and testify of all truth.

Jesus Christ leads His Church just like He led it then. The fullness of the everlasting gospel is restored to the earth. It is built upon the rock of revelation and revelation pours out for those who seek it.

It is for the humble and the meek and those earnestly willing to serve God regardless of how the world will look at them. As we faithfully receive, we are given the greater things. As we harden our hearts the greater things are withheld, and taken away.

Alma 12:9-10 "And now Alma began to expound these things unto him, saying: It is given unto many to know the mysteries of God; nevertheless they are laid under a strict command that they shall not impart only according to the portion of his word which he doth grant unto the children of men, according to the heed and diligence which they give unto him.

10 And therefore, he that will harden his heart, the same receiveth the lesser portion of the word; and he that will not harden his heart, to him is given the greater portion of the word, until it is given unto him to know the mysteries of God until he know them in full.

11 And they that will harden their hearts, to them is given the lesser portion of the word until they know nothing concerning his mysteries; and then they are taken captive by the devil, and led by his will down to destruction. Now this is what is meant by the chains of hell."

279

This scripture is true. There are many who know much, yet they are taught from on high and are patient and simply try to help others want to seek in humility for themselves. And though they are ridiculed and told they are stupid for believing as they do, they are in constant contact with God Almighty and His humble and meek Spirit is about them. They bear good fruits of love, service and high standards, and they kindly smile and think of any way to help those who cannot yet see and are not yet in contact with their good Father.

My brother and sisters, there is a giant gate with all manner of very grand blessings given to us by our Father in Heaven within. The world paints the outside of this gate with all manner of lies and deception, just as they 'painted' on Christ. Many don't even look to the gate because every time they do they see the writing and lies from the world that are all over the outside of it. They want no part of it. They are deceived for they fear man and wisdom of flesh instead of seeking humble and meek guidance from the Lord. Deception fights hardest against truth. Deception throws lies then runs the opposite way. Alas, light dispels darkness.

The humble and meek however seek to be led by God and not man, just as Christ taught Peter and told him he was blessed because of it.

The humble and meek hear the voice of the Lord and they discern it for they resonate with His Spirit; meekness and humility are truly a grand key. They are led to the wall, they see the wall and gate and the lies fall off of it, they perceive clearly.

The Spirit teaches them that that which is purest truth is fought hardest against with deception, therefore their meekness and humility is required to see properly and to go in.

They are able to see the purity of the walls of the gate as the lies fall away, and they go in to the place protected by faith and humble meekness.

These humble are blessed with all the blessings therein which are the greatest blessings of the Lord given to His children on the earth. The blessings are so great and so sacred and so utterly incredible that only the truly humble and those truly putting the Lord first can find it.

The greater the blessings of the Lord, the greater the humility, meekness, trust and reliance upon Him required. We must become as our Savior is, doing our best to better be like Him in His perfect attributes and perfect love.

Once inside we can learn so much more, see so much more. We can see the prophecies that are everywhere and the promises that are everywhere and the puzzle becomes so much more complete and everything is discerned with a clearer eye. We can see the very hand of God working in His vast perfect symphony.

Just as the Pharisees, even many Christians of the world cannot pay attention to the prophecies being fulfilled before their very eyes because they cannot discern it or think they have enough or all that is needed. Though they have much truth, the Lord will guide perfectly the meek and humble.

Matthew 13:9-17 "Who hath ears to hear, let him hear. And the disciples came, and said unto him, Why speakest thou unto them in parables? He answered and said unto them, Because it is given unto you to know the mysteries of the kingdom of heaven, but to them it is not given. For whosoever hath, to him shall be given, and he shall have more abundance: but whosoever hath not, from him shall be taken away even that he hath. Therefore speak I to them in parables: because they seeing see not; and hearing they hear not, neither do they understand. And in them is fulfilled the prophecy of Esaias, which saith, By hearing ye shall hear, and shall not understand; and seeing ye shall see, and shall not perceive: For this people's heart is waxed gross, and their ears are dull of hearing, and their eyes they have closed; lest at any time they should see with their eyes, and hear with their ears, and should understand with their heart, and should be converted, and I should heal them. But blessed are your eyes, for they see: and your ears, for they hear. For verily I say unto you, That many prophets and righteous men have desired to see those things which ye see, and have not seen them; and to hear those things which ye hear and have not heard them."

Let me be clear, the promises of faith in Christ stand for all that meet that requirement. Most Christians are incredible people and many understand a lot. Many are incredible people with real faith and real humble hearts. Miracles can happen by faith in Christ. There are many promises of faith. If any take offense to the words I say, I apologize and I love all, there is no one that was as deceived and incorrect as me, so I judge none. But the words I give to you are guidance and if you find yourself feeling upset I would point out to you the spirit of contention that is there and that there is a lack of humility. We all must learn to humble ourselves and be meekly guided by the Lord in His Spirit.

If we find ourselves getting upset or jumping to the things we think we know or have been taught in opposition by the arm of flesh rather than hearing humbly and meekly and trying and genuinely meekly trusting in the Lord for guidance, we will become even as the Pharisees who heard the words of Christ and instead of applying a humble and meek heart to be blessed by those words, they hardened their hearts and

281

chose to be upset. The greater things were withheld, and Christ is necessary. Choose to be humble and seek our Father in Heaven's perfect loving guiding hand.

It is a perfect design of our Father; He leads His Church as He always has. And the meek will inherit. I pray that I can be such.

I have a Christian friend of mine, actually a couple who fall into the same category. One however, I spoke with for a few hours on the subject after giving him a Book of Mormon. He is great dude, incredibly kind, loves Jesus and does well at walking as He would walk. I am sure the Lord looks down on him in absolute delight. He is a great person.

We had a calm and great conversation and both agreed that we are so incredibly blessed and that Jesus deserves every ounce of praise and glory we can muster forever. Of the things we agreed on there were things we didn't.

He brought up to me a few things about the Church that are occasionally heard. These fall into the category of Spiritually discerned. There were things I saw that there was a wrong perspective on what he thought and how he thought we believed certain things and because of this he clung to his beliefs harder and pushed the further light and knowledge away.

If he had been open, he would have come to have what he already believed magnified and understood it deeper. We all have our times and seasons.

As we kept talking, he essentially said that he probably wouldn't read the book. I told him to be careful because if that was, (and it is,) the very word of God in his hands, the One who he wants to serve has given him more. I cautioned him against writing it off but to check it out.

He seemed to let this roll off of him and didn't really seem to take it to heart. He continued to argue certain things and in the end we had a good conversation but anyone could tell that he looked at that sacred book which testifies of our Savior as a work of fiction that God had warned him about. He saw it falsely; he judged it before he heard it and before he counseled with the Lord.

He wasn't able to even attempt to judge a righteous judgment because of the lies written on the outside of the gate. I pray he will yet see and be shown by the Spirit in humble meekness. He is still a great testimony of love as he follows our Savior. Charity is of vast value.

Though I don't compare this representation to my friend, he is very blessed with Christ; still, it causes me to think of Pharisees trusting so strongly in what the Lord had given them up to that point that they could not humble themselves to receive more. Our Father is unchanging.

We can receive revelation from Him. We must seek humbly. We will find.

I still pray that many of my friends will read it with a meek and humble heart and let the Lord show them the truth. The thing is, revelation is very real, His Saints receive it; light can prove light. His Church is led by revelation from Him. There are countless amazing stories of this and His hand in His work.

There is so much more for those who will humble themselves to receive it. The amount of light and blessing is proportional in a way to the amount we are humble and meekly trusting in our Father.

As Christ teaches in Matthew 16, we are not to trust man or the arm of flesh but are to seek revelation from God. If I give anyone a Book of Mormon I say to read and ask God. I point out the scriptures of the promise. He will show the truly humble and it is an incredible blessing and the beginning of more. There is where He will build His Church, revelation from Him.

Too long have we given glory to man and ourselves, and feared man and their judgment of us. We must give glory to God alone, fear Him alone, wholly rely on and trust Him alone. Can we not rely on He who created us and heaven and earth to show us the right way? We can, He has told us we can and told us to do so, we must be humble enough to see and receive.

Things Often Brought Up

I do feel the need to address a couple things often brought up. I have heard many times that at the end of the Book of Revelation how John says, if anyone should take away from the book of the prophecy, that they will be cursed. I have heard many times that this negates the need for any more. This comes from misunderstanding.

The Lord's work never stops; He is endless. He is unchanging. He is also no respecter of persons, He will give to those who seek and He has promised this.

John is referring to the Revelation concerned in the book of Revelation. The very words specify that specific prophecy. There is much deep and incredible symbolism and prophecies therein including many prophecies of the last days. Ones that the Lord wanted to keep for us all. One very cool prophecy worth reading is this,

Revelation 14:6 "And I saw another angel fly in the midst of heaven, having the everlasting gospel to preach unto them that dwell on the earth, and to every nation, and kindred, and tongue, and people,

7 Saying with a loud voice, Fear God, and give glory to him; for the hour of his judgment is come: and worship him that made heaven, and earth, and the sea, and the fountains of waters."

This is one of many great prophesies of the latter-day work of the Lord in the Bible. He told us much of what would come.

Keep in mind that there were other apostles writing other books, including John who wrote more than Revelation only. John is not saying to write no more about our Savior and to share no more truth about Him. He is simply saying that the Lord gave him a great task of that specific and very important prophecy and it wasn't for anyone else to mess with.

This becomes important in the future for things like the Council of Nicaea, where books were compiled. He put the importance of keeping it and not tampering with it as the forefront.

John himself wrote other books that are now in the Bible, and so did other apostles. For one to assume he meant that there could and would be no more given at all fails to recognize the endless truth and endlessness of the glory of God. His apostles were always writing letters of truth and there is always much more deep truth to learn from our Father in Heaven.

I simply touch on that quickly because I have heard it so much and it simply is taken so wrong, prophecy within the book says that the Lord will give more. This prophecy, like all the words of God, are deep and have larger and larger meaning. Oh the symphony and perfection of God.

The second one I occasionally hear about is words of the apostle Paul in,

Galatians 1:9 "As we said before, so say I now again, If any man preach any other gospel unto you than that ye have received let him be accursed."

I have heard this on occasion and here is the answer. It is the very gospel. The exact same. Centered wholly and entirely on Christ for the glory of God. It is simply the fullness of His gospel.

As it is the fullness it gives us all the path to understand as well as gain the fullness of the blessings given through Christ. The Church of Jesus Christ of Latter-day Saints, the fullness of the gospel, gives us revealed knowledge and path to gain even more understanding. Many who have hardened their hearts before as non-denominational or other Christians come to amazement at the depth of understanding they gain of the everlasting gospel of our Savior.

The Apostle Paul had incredible wisdom, as he warned us of

people who would seek for themselves and not for the glory of our Father in Heaven.

Paul gives us the same key in the verses just after these to gain a testimony of truth. It is the same type Jesus Christ gives us in Matthew 16, essentially that we are to not trust man or our own wisdom but to seek the revelation from God.

Paul says,

Galatians 1:10-11 "But I certify you, brethren, that the gospel which was preached of me is not after man. For I neither received it of man, neither was I taught it, but by the revelation of Jesus Christ."

I give my testimony as Paul does. I know the truthfulness and deep truths of the gospel not known or taught by man but by God and the same revelation from Him.

The fullness of the everlasting gospel is simply that, there is much truth in part spread out in many places, there is the restored fullness again on earth as Biblically promised.

The very same Apostle Paul teaches us that we too will eventually need to be taught again of grander things.

In Hebrews 5 Paul talks about Jesus Christ and his divinity as the Son of God. He speaks of the goodness and mercy and compassion of our Savior.

Hebrews 5:4 "And no man taketh this honour unto himself but he that is called of God, as was Aaron."

In this scripture Paul lets us know that Christ was called of God and did not and could not put himself in any position without the call of God. Paul also lets us know that this was the same case with Aaron, Aaronic Priesthood.

Now, much of this chapter is about the Melchizedek Priesthood speaking of Christ.

5 "So also Christ glorified not himself to be made an high priest; but he that said unto him, Thou art my Son, to day have I begotten thee.

6 As he saith also in another place, Thou art a priest for ever after the order of Melchisedec."

Paul goes on about the mission of Christ and how He was an obedient Son.

9 "And being made perfect, he became the author of

285

eternal salvation unto all them that obey him;

10 Called of God an high priest after the order of Melchisedec."

Now, here we have some of the few times the Bible gives us some insight into the Melchizedek Priesthood, which is the Holy Priesthood after the Order of the Son of God.

Paul is next here telling us that though we are well learned and can be teachers for all that he has taught, we need to humble ourselves and be taught by teachers again.

11 "Of whom we have many things to say, and hard to be uttered, seeing ye are dull of hearing.

12 For when for the time ye ought to be teachers, ye have need that one teach you again which be the first principles of the oracles of God; and are become such as have need of milk, and not of strong meat."

*All Biblical scripture unless otherwise noted is KJV

Paul himself is telling us that we need to again have a teacher to teach us. The Church of Jesus Christ of Latter-day Saints has the keys of such priesthood restored again, by the power of God, as promised by Him, in a direct line from our Savior Jesus Christ.

Powerful. And yet another apostle tells us our need to learn and learn humbly at that. If the Bible is the entire fullness, which God is infinite and we can be ever learning and He promises us more in the Bible, why then is Paul telling us that there is a time we will need to learn more about this? And that there are "many things to say, and hard to be uttered," on the subject. Even concluding, "ye are dull of hearing." I of course can judge none.

The NIV translation of the very same verse makes Paul's words even simpler and clearer.

NIV Hebrews 5:10 "and was designated by God to be high priest in the order of Melchizedek."

11 "We have much to say about this, but it is hard to make it clear to you because you no longer try to understand."

12 "In fact, though by this time you ought to be teachers, you need someone to teach you the elementary truths of God's word all over again. You need milk, not solid food!"

I could have reiterated it myself, but this makes it clear enough. Paul tells us, that in the true gospel, you will need another teacher to teach you about this. And though we could pride ourselves as teachers

286

we should humble ourselves to learn even 'elementary truths.' We humbly should seek and try to understand.

The key again is, humble yourself before God. The Church of Jesus Christ of Latter-day Saints has such keys given from heaven and can teach and guide a great deal, then it is up to us to be taught and guided by revelation from the Spirit.

The NIV of verse 7 gives us this same key in the example of Christ, "and he was heard because of his reverent submission." KJV uses "and was heard in that he feared."

Whether it is reverent submission, humble respect, or respectful fear before God, humility is the key to Him teaching us and us being "heard."

Fear and respect Him alone in reverent submission, not the arm of flesh, not our own wisdom but revelation from Him. And if we do not seek, we do not find.

Revelation 14:6 "And I saw another angel fly in the midst of heaven, having the everlasting gospel to preach unto them that dwell on the earth, and to every nation, and kindred, and tongue, and people,

7 Saying with a loud voice, Fear God, and give glory to him; for the hour of his judgment is come: and worship him that made heaven, and earth, and the sea, and the fountains of waters.

Proverbs 15:33 "The fear of the Lord is the instruction of wisdom; and before honour is humility."

Psalms 25:9 "The meek will he guide in judgment: and the meek will he teach his way.

10 All the paths of the Lord are mercy and truth unto such as keep his covenant and his testimonies.

12 What man is he that feareth the Lord? Him shall he teach in the way that he shall choose.

13 His soul shall dwell at ease; and his seed shall inherit the earth.

14 The secret of the Lord is with them that fear him; and he will shew them his covenant."

Humility, meekness, reverence before Him is the way to be guided.

Paul later touches again on the Priesthood lightly in Hebrews and the importance even of the oath of such. The fullness of the everlasting gospel is restored. Seek to it.

Do not make the mistake of hardening your heart before you earnestly seek in meekness and humility then to take it to our Father in Heaven. He will give wisdom. I have been full circle, from hardened heart to seeing clearly and there are incredible and vast blessings there for those humble and meek to seek. I am forever so grateful.

"Oh, there is so much more that your Father in Heaven wants you to know." – President Russel M. Nelson.

How true the statement. He is unchanging and perfect.

Romans 8:32 "He that spared not his own Son, but delivered him up for us all, how shall he not with him also freely give us all things?"

I for one tell you the Holy Priesthood of God is true and real and is given by the Lord in The Church of Jesus Christ of Latter-day Saints; it is again restored to the earth. Praise be to God. How perfect His infinite purposes are.

1 John 4:2 "Hereby know ye the Spirit of God: Every spirit that confesseth that Jesus Christ is come in the flesh is of God:

Let us all focus on this great truth in all things.

1 John 4:7 "Beloved, let us love one another: for love is of God; and every one that loveth is born of God, and knoweth God."

John 7:18 "He that speaketh of himself seeketh his own glory: but he that seeketh his glory that sent him, the same is true, and no unrighteousness is in him."

Christ gives us a clear understanding here. Joseph Smith lived spreading the truth of Jesus Christ and paid for it with His very life, every step of the way testifying of the truth of our Lord and Savior. He sought to build the Lord's kingdom and not himself, he sacrificed everything for our God and our Lord and Savior Jesus Christ. He served Him and testified of Him to the end.

There are many lies out there. Joseph was told by an angel of the Lord that his name would be had for good and for evil. Truly the greater things are protected by meek, humble faith; even the reliance on our Father in Heaven to guide us to and show us truth.

I have heard of a song that gets bashed and misunderstood a lot called 'Praise To The Man.' It is about Joseph Smith and will show that the above scriptures of love and seeking the glory of God is what this man stood for.

We do not praise him at all, we see him as a servant of the Lord who did much good in the Lord's hands. We praise the Father, the Son, and the Spirit in one; the Godhead. We praise and serve God alone.

The song was written by W.W. Phelps. Phelps had left the church angry and through a series of events the prophet was jailed for quite some time over bogus charges.

Joseph suffered greatly with other Church leaders for months. Around the time he was imprisoned horrible atrocities including murder by mobs were happening to Church members, including women and children. As they were held they were fed putrid food and chose to starve often instead. There was suffering all around that was caused.

A while after Joseph was again free and leading the Church again; preaching Jesus Christ to the world and building temples and the kingdom of God.

W.W. Phelps later realized all the wrong he had done and wrong he had caused. He wrote Joseph and begged his forgiveness. These letters can be found and though there was very serious suffering, Joseph frankly forgave Phelps and loved him and accepted him again with open arms. The letter he wrote back is worth finding; it was in great love. Often Joseph was an amazing example of Christ, he recognized what the Savior had done for all of our brothers and sisters and how much they were all loved.

W.W. Phelps wrote the words of the song as a poem after Joseph was martyred. It stood as a strong example of the redeeming power of Jesus Christ our Savior, as well as the amazing power of forgiveness and love. It stood as a strong example of that the love of Christ and His charity within our hearts could heal all.

W.W. Phelps however did write some hymns, the most famous of which is 'The Spirit of God.' It is sung often. The whole song is glory to God and Christ. "Hosanna, hosanna, to God and the Lamb! Let glory to them, in the highest be given, Henceforth and forever, Amen and amen."

The Church later set Phelps' poem of Joseph to music and made it into a hymn to remember. Many see wrong and see that he is one we praise; this is entirely untrue. With the correct context, like every misunderstood thing of the Church, one can see what is really being honored, a Christ like heart that healed much through love and forgiveness, a great servant of God who did much good for the Kingdom of God on earth. A heart that forgave even the most hard to bear things, and a heart that could put the past aside and genuinely love as the Savior would; always with an eye single to Him and serving Him.

Joseph gave everything for the Lord, his very life even. He suffered greatly and many of his children died. When one friend died he adopted their twin children, one of them even died after getting sick a cold night when Joseph was ripped out of his house and tarred and feathered in the street by a mob. They tried to force acid down his throat even.

He was beaten badly and another Church leader was severely beaten and unconscious. He stayed up all night after his wife fainted at his appearance, trying to clean himself up and preached the very next morning, which was the Sabbath. Some members of the mob of the night before were noticed in the congregation, Joseph preached in love and didn't even mention the night before.

Joseph was called of God. An angel of the Lord told him that his name would be used for good and evil alike in the world. I myself have been full circle on this and am so grateful I can see clearly now. He was a prophet called of God.

He also pointed out much scriptures and promises that the Lord would bring to pass through him before the second coming of Christ. The humble and led by the Lord will see he was called of God for they will seek that revelation humbly from God.

A man who preached of Jesus Christ, and although imperfect like all of us, left an incredible example of serving our Father in Heaven with everything we have.

Humbly and meekly seek the revelation from God. If a Jewish person prayed to know who the Messiah was they would not for a moment think it was Jesus. They most likely would harden their heart against what the truth is because of what they were taught and what they have come to believe themselves.

I saw a video of a seeming Jewish leader. In it he was speaking of the coming 'messiah.' He said that, "it wasn't Jesus," and that he would, "rather go back to Auschwitz than accept Him."

What a bold statement. Think about that. He spent his whole life in a deception that the Messiah wasn't Jesus. He had built up such a pride that he was willing to suffer incredibly and go back to horrible situations rather than to humbly accept he was wrong.

How could this man ever pray to our Father in Heaven and receive revelation to know that Jesus Christ is in fact the Messiah? For this man to come to know the truth he would have to be so humble that he could entertain the thought that he was wrong.

Surely when this man sees the perfection of our Savior Jesus Christ and His perfect goodness and how horrible things are without Him he will change his mind.

I have heard and seen many manners of lies about The Church of Jesus Christ of Latter-day Saints from many including other Christians, even my friends. I judge none obviously, I am just so grateful to my Father in Heaven. They harden their hearts because they think they know of themselves or from the arm of flesh.

Who can humble themselves enough even to hear from on high that they were wrong? Such truly was the case with me and I am thankful that I was humbled to see truth that I had previously hardened my heart against, I am so thankful.

I assume there are many who have spoken so harshly and trusted their own wisdom just as this Jewish man did that they would do anything to hold onto that pride and continue to assume lies about the Church. It takes humility. We are children. We must trust the true wisdom from God alone.

We need true meekness and humility, not trusting the arm of flesh or our own wisdom. If we trust our own wisdom or flesh or what we think we know we could be hardening our hearts in a way that will prevent us from seeing truth. Relying on Him is the sure way to be guided correctly. "… and upon this rock I will build my church; and the gates of hell shall not prevail against it."

The Jews have some great truths, Christians have greatly more, The Church of Jesus Christ of Latter-day Saints has yet much more; and those who meekly humbly are led by God have the source of all truth and are led to all truth, wherever it goes.

I want all to know that I contend against none. I just know that the Lord is continuing to pour out light and knowledge and I want all to know. I have seen it full circle and it is real. He lives; revelation is real.

I contend against no church. For anyone who believes in Christ is a brother or sister in Christ, and even all of this world I will love like my brother and sister, for they are and my Father loves them as He does me; regardless of belief.

His Church is vast, He defines it as those who repent and come unto Him. All that is good is of Him. He simply has blessed many with more, much more, even the everlasting gospel, which I can attest is true, not of myself or of man but of revelation from God.

There is a near death experience I heard. This can be found in a video titled "Near Death Experiences and Mormonism" by Mormon

Convert on youtube. This was a man who did many studies of NDE's to finally come to the truth of The Church of Jesus Christ of Latter-day Saints, which he had previously greatly hardened his heart against. He speaks of several peoples NDE's and quotes many, from agnostics and athiests to muslims and non-denominational Christians. He came to see the pure truth of The Church of Jesus Christ of Latter-day Saints.

In one specific NDE he quoted the story from the specific persons book of their NDE, I relate roughly as follows.

The many churches testifying of the truth of Christ were all vehicles, from walking, to horses, to planes and cars that go to the destination at varying speeds. Some were moving slow, some were moving faster, some vehicles were very quick, some stopped and slowed to a crawl at times, and then there was a rocket moving very quickly, the rocket symbolized what the person later found was the restored gospel in The Church of Jesus Christ of Latter-day Saints, the fullness of the everlasting gospel.

The Church of Jesus Christ of Latter-day Saints today is the fullness of His gospel and is led by Him. Furthermore and more importantly His authority is restored and given again to men as it was given to His apostles. The next section will get somewhat into this. There is much more truth revealed and can be found by humbly being led to it and seeking it.

As for me, I have come to see that as I humbly seek revelation from our Father in Heaven that I am simply learning what actually is simply reality. In a sense understanding, remembering and coming to greater knowledge of what actually is. We use the word "truth," but often don't see it simply is the reality of what is. We use the word 'religion' but in fact it is simply a vehicle to show us how things really are, the truth. And Jesus Christ is the way, the truth and the life.

The fullness of truth truly is given in The Church of Jesus Christ of Latter-day Saints. Much is taught, and all is discerned and given from the Spirit as we seek to understand and seek to become like our Savior and walk in His attributes better and better always.

There is much truth in many sects of Christianity, but I testify, the fullness is in The Church of Jesus Christ of Latter-day Saints understood by the Spirit of God teaching us. It takes true humbling and our faith will be tested; in a sense we must be as one drowning seeking air as we seek for truth and understanding from God our Father in Heaven. We must be willing to give all things for Him.

Ones specific 'religion' is simply a vehicle with varied amounts of truth provided depending on each; vehicles moving at varying speeds. We ourselves must come to God and be close with Him. They are simply vehicles for truth. As we come to know those truths the Spirit will bear witness of the truth and we can be guided by the Spirit to be closer to and be taught by Him.

Our personal relationship with Him is so important and we can be very close and very well taught by Him as we maintain humility and walk in the meekness of His Spirit.

Alas, the greatest to do is to love all, to be one in Christ. To love our perfect Father in Heaven with all we have, for He has done all for us; to Him be glory and honor and praises forever!

I simply tell you there is more and there is a great and perfect way of greater things defined and given by Him.

"And above all things, clothe yourselves with the bond of charity, as with a mantle, which is the bond of perfectness and peace."

"Ask and ye shall receive, Seek and ye shall find."

History

I would also like to briefly touch on the history of the world and the grand work of our Father in Heaven.

After Christ died His apostles made a very good run of it. Some ended up killed off themselves after a good work but much good of what they wrote is preserved in the Bible.

Over time masses caught on and Jesus Christ became seen as He should, as the Savior of the world, the Son of God. The church grew and over time it became greatly tied to the state and government. At times those over the church were the most powerful.

Different books were overseen and councils were called early on to see which doctrines were probably the most correct. This was called the Council of Nicaea. I used to look back on these and see them as a sure fire way to make the Bible seem untrustworthy and a method of control. I can look back now in truth, having a better understanding of the immensity of God and how in control He really is.

As the church grew over time the leaders asserted much control over the state and became in some areas as the Pharisees of old, often having much more power.

In my ignorant and logic stage of life, seeing only the vast control of power in the physical, I saw occasionally such as a method of control. God is vast and knows how to honor His children's agency while understanding their pride and worldly ways to be able to get His word to them.

I think that religion in the past was, in certain instances by some, pushed solely for control; also many times for genuine true purposes to serve God. In both still, the word of God came to the meek and humble,

293

though an apostasy would come as told by God Biblically and the common man would soon not be able to hear the words of God.

Soon the amount of power grew out of hand and the church asserted much control over the people in varied ways. One of the ways was that the leaders of the church, then the Roman Catholic Church, alone could have scripture; it was very strictly not available to the people and they took the word of the leaders, which was still often in a language they couldn't understand.

This was hard for many and in the mid to late 1300s finally a man came along who had had enough. John Wycliffe was a man within the Roman Catholic priesthood who dissented as he saw the wrongs that were being done. Wycliffe was not happy with the status of the clergy. The clergy were of a high and privileged status; they lived lives of luxury and wielded a lot of power.

Wycliffe was greatly against this; he was against lifting any man higher up above others. He resonated with the teachings of Christ in this way, that he who is greatest should be servant of all. To say the very least he was very against the inequality, he wanted everyone far more equal before God. He was also against the very office of the pope.

He wanted to translate scripture into the every day man language, at the time called middle English, an early English. He was a learned man who could read the texts.

John Wycliffe did this, he translated scripture into English and for the first time the average man could learn the things of God from someone other than those in power.

This was done however before the printing press and although this had a great effect, it wasn't as explosive as it could be; though it paved the way.

The Lord has promised that He will hasten His work in it's time. And at this time the people were waking up. They themselves wanted to be close to God.

In 1450, shortly after the death of Wycliffe the printing press was invented, by a pious man named Johannes Gutenburg. However, this was a wild time in the world. If anyone was found with a Wycliffe translated Bible in English, since the late 1300s, that person would receive a death penalty. Those who lived in the high class and were more learned and knew other languages could legally have the Bible in other languages such as Latin.

The average man who was under control was not permitted to have such material. I perceive they did not want to put at risk their hierarchy of power. If people didn't have a permit for their scripture, they were put to death.

Wycliffe was so despised by the church that his body was exhumed and burned and his ashes were scattered, so were his beliefs and so would be the word of God.

Another man arose; his name was William Tyndale. He was an English scholar and had like ideals as Wycliffe. He chose to illegally translate the Bible.

In a conversation with a higher up of the Roman Catholic Church it is said that the man told Tyndale that he trusted the word of the Pope over the word of God in scripture.

To this, Tyndale is said to have replied, "I defy the Pope and all his laws; if God spare my life ere many years, I will cause a boy that driveth the plough, shall know more of the Scripture than thou dost."

Tyndale believed the direct word of God to be of grander value than the pope's words. He was a learned man and translated directly from the Hebrew and Greek texts.

The Bible translated in English was the very first English book to make use of the brand new printing press, though it had to run in secret.

Tyndale obviously made a large rift with the Roman Catholic Church as well as England and it's laws. Tyndale was later convicted of heresy and sentenced to be strangled to death and burned at the stake.

His dying prayer was said to be that the king of England would open his eyes. His prayer was heard and two years later the king authorized "The Great Bible" for the new 'Church of England.'

One year before Tyndale's death King Henry VIII was able to, thanks to Tyndale, break away from the Roman Catholic Church and he formed the Church of England.

After Tyndale's death, and his prayer, the Bible would be legalized and the King compiled a Bible in English, based in the majority off of Tyndale's translations, with another translator as well.

The King couldn't get a divorce legally from the church so the King made his own and placed himself at the head. This event is said to have been a 'seismic shift in the power dynamics of Europe.' England had split from Rome.

The Word of God spread and the Lord continued to spread His word, even if it were through the desire of power in men. Prayer is powerful; the Lord's designs go forth.

The sole controlling power which was the Roman Catholic Church, which they had for a very long time had ended its singular control, although still quite strong, not the power it once had, and the Church of England grew.

For years people within the church never even heard scripture in anything but Latin that most could not understand. They relied wholly upon the words of the priests and what they were told to do. The people again had the words of God, this time, it was spreading like wild fire and the printing press kept running.

Wouldn't you know at the same time period in Germany a man named Martin Luther was going through the same issues with the powerful Roman Catholic Church.

Martin Luther had many particular issues and recognized that Jesus Christ himself took all of our sin upon Him. He had a particular issue with the 'indulgences' of the faith. He began to see, just as Tyndale did and at the same time in another part of the world, that the leaders had become similar to the Pharisees of old.

Martin Luther taught that the Bible was the only source of the word of God and not that of the Pope. Luther was also a learned man and also translated the Bible from Hebrew and Greek into the common people language of German. This translation spread quickly thanks to the printing press and is said to have greatly enhanced the creation and perfection of the German language.

Many were burned at the stake by the authority of the church then, either for creating or spreading the Bible or simply having it. They were burned for doing their best to be true Christians. They were burned just as many Christians were shortly after the death of Jesus Christ.

Let us never forget the cost, how great for us to have the truth we have, and how, though it is vast, it all is nothing in comparison to the cost Christ paid for us. Oh that men would praise Him for His goodness!

In 1611, 54 scholars produced the King James Bible. This again drew significantly off of Tyndale translations. Estimates suggests 83% of the modern New Testament was translated by him and 76% of the Old Testament. The requirements for this translation were stringent and much time and resources were used. It is widely spread and used today.

It is said of the printing press, "The sharp increase in literacy broke the monopoly of the literate elite on education and learning and bolstered the emerging middle class."

Johannes Gutenberg was the man to invent, in a sort, and bring the printing press to the modern world. What seemed to be the motivation behind his world changing invention? Remember the time period of his life (1398-1468) and what was happening in the world as we read these quotes of him.

"It is a press, certainly, but a press from which shall flow in inexhaustible streams...Through it, God will spread His Word. A spring of truth shall flow from it: Like a new star it shall scatter the darkness of

ignorance, and cause a light heretofore unknown to shine amongst men."
– Johannes Gutenberg

"Religious truth is captive in a small number of little manuscripts which guard the common treasures, instead of expanding them. Let us break the seal which binds these holy things; let us give wings to the truth that it may fly with the Word, no longer prepared at vast expense, but multitudes everlastingly by a machine which never wearies to every soul which enters life." – Johannes Gutenberg

His whole purpose and view of the invention was for the word of God to be spread. A vastly world changing invention. How much did this man really care?

"God suffers in the multitude of souls whom His word cannot reach." - Johannes Gutenberg.

Gutenberg seemed to be a total man of God; after all his major work was the Bible, known as the Gutenberg Bible.

Oh how the Lord will prepare and use ordinary men to do His great work; even when men use it for control or set it at naught, it is given to the people.

"Behold, I will hasten my work in its time."

As we move along through history the more main powers are again asserted, only now there are a few more. Granted now the people have the scriptures which is a huge jump forward; it also came at a great cost. Even the church that historically had burned people for it's existence would come to have its followers reading in the very works by which they were burned.

I'm grateful we can all learn love from history. Millions came to knowledge of Christ and salvation through the Bible being available and many missionaries with the truth at their fingertips.

Because of this, and the printing press, ideas grow and people began to see for themselves that the overbearing Church of England shouldn't have as much control as it does. People generally wanted the freedom to worship as they pleased.

Christopher Columbus, a very pious man, would leave and find a new land in the late 1400's. And soon after that, many would leave to that land to escape religious persecution.

It seems odd for the time and inspired that Columbus would up and leave with seemingly 'pie in the sky' goals. Yet he found the new land and became the beginning of the next great movement.

What were his motivations?

"It was the Lord who put into my mind (I could feel His hand upon me) the fact that it would be possible to sail from there to the Indies. All who heard of my project rejected it with laughter, ridiculing me. There is no question that the inspiration was from the Holy Spirit, because he comforted me with rays of marvelous illumination from the Holy Scriptures ... encouraging me to continually to press forward and without ceasing for a moment they now encourage me make haste."

This was all written by him in the introduction of his "Book of Prophecies," pertaining to bringing the gospel to coastlands yet unknown; and he goes on.

"It is possible that those who see this book will accuse me of being unlearned in literature, of being a layman and a sailor. I reply with the words of Matt. 11:25, "Lord, because thou has hid these things from the wise and prudent, and hath revealed them unto babes.""

Columbus is a huge figure and surely is a very pious man. He obviously believed that the hand of the Lord was on Him. How much did he understand the incredibly vast role the Lord had for him?

"For the execution of the journey to the Indies I did not make use of intelligence, mathematics or maps. It is simply the fulfillment of what Isaiah had prophesied."

Ok, Columbus, one of the greatest known explorers in our current world, because of him we have our current world, and to find it he trusted it was divine and of God so much that he didn't navigate with any form of mathematics, intelligence or maps. Can we properly weigh the immensity of what he is saying here? He knew it was divine and of God and allowed Him to guide. He knew that he was simply fulfilling prophecy in scripture.

Obviously Columbus understood then how the Lord had been and was continuing to unfold prophecy. Could he see how vast the workings of the Lord up to his day?

"No one should fear to undertake any task in the name of our Savior, if it is just and if the intention is purely for His holy service. The working out of all things has been assigned to each person by our Lord, but it all happens according to His sovereign will even though He gives advice. He lacks nothing that is in the power of men to give Him. Oh what a gracious Lord, who desires that people should perform for Him those things for which He holds Himself responsible! Day and night moment by moment, everyone should express to Him their most devoted gratitude."

Columbus and many leaders of our past knew what is being attacked much in our day today and that is, God is real, He lives, Jesus Christ lived and lives now. They knew this, because their faith was in the right place they saw His hand moving. This is being stolen from us much in the world. Do not let it. He lives.

A new world was found and soon those escaping religious persecution came first to it. They also were led by God, and incredibly pious to say the least.

Soon more came over for the same reasons, for God, and then many more for many reasons. Soon the new found freedom wasn't so free as England came and took possession of all of it.

What would happen next? A Revolutionary War, farmers and pious men of God fought against the greatest military power in the world.

George Washington was an incredibly pious man as were many of the founding fathers. There are many incredible quotes and many incredible miracles that happened and had to happen for the Revolutionary War to be won. Our founding fathers knew it was God who gave the victory.

At one time when the revolution was about to stomped out early, a miracle of 'random' dense fog that came from nowhere covered the retreat of the small force of the revolution; it kept the opposition, that would become America, alive. This is one of many miracles.

Our very nation was established on a covenant of God by incredibly pious men. General Washington would tell soldiers to repent and not to sin and to respect the commandments of God. He knew who was at the helm and knew who was guiding his hand. There are so many quotes of so many of our founding fathers and it suffices to say for writing they were very pious men. Feel free to seek these quotes on your own.

"The man must be bad indeed who can look upon the events of the American Revolution without feeling the warmest gratitude towards the great Author of the Universe whose divine interposition was so frequently manifested on our behalf."
-George Washington's letter to Samuel Langdon, Sept. 28, 1789.

That quote makes it pretty clear how strong General Washington's faith was. These men knew truth.

Did Washington genuinely believe it was God who blessed the nation with the Revolution? Undoubtedly.

"May the same wonder-working Deity, who long since delivering the Hebrews from their Egyptian Oppressors planted them in the promised land – whose Providential Agency has lately been conspicuous in establishing these United States as an independent Nation – still continue to water them with the dews of Heaven and to make the inhabitants of every denomination participate in the temporal and spiritual blessings of that people whose God is Jehovah."
- George Washington, Letter to the Hebrew congregation of Savannah, Georgia

There are so many quotes of George Washington and they are followed with many like quotes from truly and indeed all of our founding fathers. We are not taught about this, but it is true that our founding fathers were incredibly close to God and understood their role.

Did Washington understand the path of the Lord? Could he see those inspired before him which led to him and the cause he championed?

"Whereas it becomes us humbly to approach the throne of Almighty God, with gratitude and praise for the wonders which his goodness has wrought in conducting our fore-fathers to this western world...and above all, that he hath diffused the glorious light of the gospel, whereby, through the merits of our gracious Redeemer, we may become the heirs of His eternal glory."
- Washington's General Orders, November 27, 1779

The scriptures tell us our nation and constitution was the work of the Lord.

I could spend the rest of this book showing the incredible piety of all of our founding fathers.

When Washington was sworn in, he himself added, "So help me God," at the end and those after him followed suit.

When he took the oath of office his left hand was on the Bible, and not just on any page. His hand was on Genesis 49. On the very prophecy and blessing of Jacob to his son Joseph, of the stick of Ephraim. He knew that he was fulfilling prophecy. He knew that the gentiles were the of the "fruitful bough, even a fruitful bough by a well; whose branches run over the wall: The archers have sorely grieved him, and shot at him, and hated him: But his bow abode in strength and the arms of his hands were made strong by the hands of the mighty God of

300

Jacob." It continues and is amazing, I suggest reading it all, "unto the utmost bound of the everlasting hills."

The blessing and prophecy continues and the symphony of God continues fulfilling and preparing the way for the return of His Son our Savior Jesus Christ.

Washington knew how big this was, he knew the God he served. These were deeply intelligent men who had vast wisdom and understanding. They saw the hand of God.

Finally our Father in Heaven had given his children a free nation, a nation that didn't aim to control every single finite detail of their people. The Lord finally had a land that was free. He could restore His Church and pour out the promises and prophecies of the last days.

Any deep look into the history of the Roman Catholic Church one can rightly assume that it did not stay perfect and led by God from the instance it began. One can see the many decisions made and at times the Pope and other leaders in the Roman Catholic Church had more power than kings. It certainly had not been perfectly led by He who said, "My kingdom is not of this world." Any one who takes a look into this can discern this quickly.

Though men surely are imperfect I believe one can clearly discern historically that many rough things happened and much was used for government and control.

Remember what Christ taught in Matthew 16,

17 And Jesus answered and said unto him, Blessed art thou, Simon Bar-Jona: for flesh and blood hath not revealed it unto thee, but my Father which is in heaven.

18 And I say also unto thee, That thou art Peter, and upon this rock I will build my church; and the gates of hell shall not prevail against it.

The Catholic Church will use this same scripture to show that historical descent is what matters above seeking revelation and they claim the keys given Peter in historical succession. They will say he meant that Peter is the rock. Yet any further look into scripture and this one, one can see that Christ was clearly making a point of receiving revelation from the Lord and not from man.

Why was Peter blessed? "Blessed art thou, Simon Bar-Jona: for flesh and blood hath not revealed it unto thee, but my Father which is in heaven."

Consider again all the replete Biblical scripture pushing us to seek wisdom from our Father in Heaven and not from man. This is the rock of revelation and The Church of Jesus Christ of Latter-day Saints stands on it.

The Holy Spirit of the Lord can prove light and truth far beyond comprehension and things of this world in such powerful light. The gates of hell cannot prevail where the light of truth shines and dispels all darkness.

Remember the Lord has told us if we lack wisdom that He will give it to us. We do not serve a dead God, for our God is alive and He reigns forever and will speak with the humble just as He has promised!

James 1:5 "If any of you lack wisdom, let him ask of God, that giveth to all men liberally, and upbraideth not; and it shall be given him.

And truly He will give it to us and show us all truth. This scripture becomes important as this historical account goes on and it is important today. "Seek and ye shall find."

I saw once a video regarding a Catholic man say that if he were not Catholic he would be 'Mormon.' He said this was the case because either the authority of Christ continued down the line and the Catholics still had it, or they had become corrupted and there truly was a need for a restoration of the truth and authority of God in the last days; which The Church of Jesus Christ of Latter-day Saints claim to and does possess.

If the Catholic church was not true, although still playing a great role in keeping people knowing Christ, the actual authority of God then had vanished off of the earth.

The apostles were killed; the keys given to apostles were lost. The authority to lead the church was gone. Although some important truths remained the church was not led perfectly by God and serious incorrect variances made their way in as well as historical abuses came from the controlling hand of power.

The greatest difference: on one side, man and people counseled together to choose doctrine and make changes. On the other side direct revelation was received from God and it was widely proclaimed of speaking with angels and God Himself.

I can personally attest that grand revelation from Him is real. Our Father has Biblically promised wisdom from Him 'liberally' for those who seek HIS guidance in faith. The humble shouldn't have to stumble.

302

If no one made decision by revelation from heaven, and weren't properly prepared to receive such then no leaders could hear His word or be led by Him. This time is referred to as 'The Great Apostasy'.

Though it wasn't perfect, the word and some large truths of God and Christ still made their way into powerful places. Christ was beginning still to be seen in His rightful place, as the Son of God, our Savior. It didn't take too long for the government that killed Jesus to embrace Him as their Lord and Savior. There is still good to be said of any who will carry the banner of truth which is testifying of our Lord and Savior Jesus Christ.

There is much to the history, and I don't intend to get into it fully. However, if one seeks to really find they can see the same; there was a great apostasy.

It took quite some time for the Lord to begin pouring out his spirit in great measure and again giving the word of God to His children.

There are many prophesies of the Lord speaking of scattering Israel and then in the last days gathering Israel. There are the same, in His words, of the apostasy.

Amos 8:11-12 "Behold, the days come, saith the Lord God, that I will send a famine in the land, not a famine of bread, nor a thirst for water, but of hearing the words of the Lord:

12 And they shall wander from sea to sea, and from the north even to the east, they shall run to and fro to seek the word of the Lord, and shall not find it."

After so many years of apostasy and the people not hearing or having the word directly the Lord raised up men. Miracles upon miracles began in the hearts of men moved upon by His Holy Spirit. Again in respect to the much good the Catholic church has done; If the Roman Catholic sect hadn't lost anything and was all aright why would so many be raised up to do so much, even miracles, with such zeal? To the point that members of that sect now had the word, long captive, finally freed and in their hand; contrary to their earlier laws. The Lord was fulfilling prophecy and promises.

The Lord promised to again bring Israel in the last days. He brought forth inventions to hasten His work. He brought forth men who could see that the traditions had faltered from His guidance and they brought His words to the people, many at great cost. Many came to finally know His word, after many for a long time could not hear His word when it was kept from the people, just as prophesied.

He inspired men to travel to new lands. He blessed that land with freedom, in miraculous fashion. He fulfilled many prophecies and promises and would yet fulfill more. He would restore His gospel and lead His Church.

How has the Lord restored or given such imperative truths in the past? He prepares and raises up His children.

When it comes to imperative truths, especially those of great promise and prophecy, He raises up a prophet.

Amos 3:7 "Surely the Lord God will do nothing, but he revealeth his secret unto his servants the prophets."

Restoration of the Everlasting Gospel

A few short decades after the Revolutionary War was won, In the Spring of 1820 a 14-year-old boy had seen the frenzy of different peoples religious opinions growing all over Palmyra New York. The new free country was growing new ideas like crazy and this boy, Joseph Smith, grew up in a very pious home. One day he read in the book of James,

James 1:5 "If any of you lack wisdom, let him ask of God, that giveth to all men liberally, and upbraideth not; and it shall be given him.

6 But let him ask in faith, nothing wavering. For he that wavereth is like a wave of the sea driven with the wind and tossed."

He had been deeply curious on what church to join. Many were pulling him in many different areas. He thought that if at any time man needed wisdom it was now.

He also trusted that God was not a respecter of persons, He loved all of His children. He had the faith that if he were to ask and seek earnestly he would receive an answer just as men of old.

Joseph said of the scripture, "Never did any passage of scripture come with more power to the heart of man than this did at this time to mine. It seemed to enter with great force into every feeling of my heart. I reflected on it again and again, knowing that if any person needed wisdom from God, I did; for how to act I did not know, and unless I could get more wisdom than I had, I would never know; for the teachers of religion of the different sects understood the same passages of scripture so differently as to destroy all confidence in settling the question by an appeal to the Bible."

Joseph humbly sought revelation from God and not of man. He faithfully sought the promise given in the Bible of our Father in Heaven. He went into a grove of trees, prayed, and God and Christ themselves came in a pillar of light and talked to him in the grove. It was though the trees were on fire with glory, and thus began the early and slow beginnings of the restoration, great promises were being fulfilled.

You can find accounts of this whole thing given by Joseph that detail far more than I do in "Joseph Smith History."

I had a similar experience that he had before He saw our Father and our Savior, he was overtaken by darkness, "not to an imaginary ruin, but to the power of some actual being from the unseen world, who had such marvelous power as I had never before felt in any being – just at this moment of great alarm, I saw a pillar of light exactly over my head, above the brightness of the sun," he prayed all the more and in his praying then they came and brought light and love and all manner of goodness and glory. He saw Jesus Christ and God and love and glory filled the sacred grove.

Obviously there is much attacking of Joseph and one of those is that there are a few people who heard him tell the story of his vision and they are all slightly different. I will tell you what I have learned myself for one who has had incredible experiences.

I will probably never give the total and entire full experience in detailed detail. In some situations I have chosen some parts not to say for who is present. In other situations I want to just get a certain part across and get the main idea.

One time my wife said to me after relating it to a church group, "I never heard some of that before," This was surprising to me as I felt I had told the same story. I had chosen to pick certain parts, and many parts I don't want to think about or remember and some parts are so deep that they become pointless and would do no one any good to know.

The fact is, it is a personal experience and I give the necessary and main parts that pertain to the people. I have been blessed to see how this can happen easily. Some things aren't worth sharing, for a while I didn't even want to think of it, as it was fearful. Some parts are too deep for many to understand and in the end I don't want any to have to know it.

Regardless, I have at times felt somewhat what Joseph must have felt. He knew by serious real experience and just wanted to help people, but they wouldn't hear. I can blame none. But now I have the same and I know of the truth and want people to hear, and many don't. I seek simply to do my best.

It becomes imperative to be able to rely on our Father in Heaven and the guidance of His Spirit to give us wisdom and truth.

Hear. Jesus Christ lives, we need Him; it is all real.

Joseph Smith's story is true. He was prepared after that, angels came to him and taught him immensely. He was a true prophet of God.

After time he was guided to the record of a people who knew about and testified of Jesus Christ and was called to translate it by the power of God. This is the Book of Mormon, another testament of the truth of Jesus Christ.

Consider these prophetic scripture as we can see the "stick of Ephraim," the son of Joseph who was sold into Egypt, (which was well known by the nation even George Washington,) which stick in this scripture is The Book of Mormon, and the "stick of Judah" which would be the Bible. These are prophesies for the latter days of Ezekiel about the gathering of Israel.

Ezekiel 37:16 "Moreover, thou son of man, take thee one stick, and write upon it, For Judah, and for the children of Israel his companions: then take another stick, and write upon it, For Joseph, the stick of Ephraim, and for all the house of Israel his companions:

17 And join them one to another into one stick; and they shall become one in thine hand.

18 And when the children of thy people shall speak unto thee, saying, Wilt thou not shew us what thou meanest by these?

19 Say unto them, Thus saith the Lord God; Behold, I will take the stick of Joseph, which is in the hand of Ephraim, and the tribes of Israel his fellows, and will put them with him, even with the stick of Judah, and make them one stick, and they shall be one in mine hand."

These scriptures are fulfilled and being fulfilled.

The Book of Mormon, written for the stick of Ephraim and for all the house of Israel have become one in the hand with the Bible, coming through Judah and then for all the tribes of Israel. The scriptures all testify of Christ, His divinity, atonement, and gospel. Because these become one the people will become one in truth. One of the many roles of the Book of Mormon is to bring the Jewish people to the knowledge of Christ. Many have, and many more will.

As we know these scriptures are deep, and the whole chapter of Ezekiel 37 is very well worth reading. There are many great prophesies therein of great value pertaining to the latter days. For us to recognize first and foremost, that the Lord has promises us a 'great work,' He has promised us much in the latter days as He gathers Israel.

26 "Moreover I will make a covenant of peace with them; it shall be an everlasting covenant with them: and I will place them, and multiply them, and will set my sanctuary in the midst of them for evermore.

27 My tabernacle also shall be with them: yea, I will be their God, and they shall be my people.

28 And the heathen shall know that I the Lord do sanctify Israel, when the sanctuary shall be in the midst of them for evermore."

The Lord's temples and churches dot the whole world and are growing in number. All ordinances and covenants of the Lord within the temple are all thanks to the atonement of our Savior and are grand gifts to bless us yet more. All things in the temple point to Christ. I can testify of the true work within them, including the everlasting covenant. The grandest blessings are within His everlasting gospel.

The work of the Lord is vastly on the world today and growing. The fullness of His gospel is on the earth today. He continues His work and is fulfilling promises. The Book of Mormon, covenants and temples, are all part of that. The Spirit beareth witness.

Joseph was directed by angel Moroni, an angel of the Lord, an ancient prophet to deposited plates that would be translated by the power of God. The Lord truly brought forth things in a way that is for the humble.

I have gathered for myself that the greater blessings are seemingly protected by much more humble and meek faith, trusting in the Lord alone to show truth. One must be truly humble, faithful and spiritually in tune to learn the greater things. It becomes easier as the tree of faith grows strong. Then truly the greater things are made manifest.

Isaiah 29:3 "And thou shalt be brought down, and shalt speak out of the ground, and thy speech shall be low out of the dust, and thy voice shall be, as of one that hath a familiar spirit, out of the ground, and thy speech shall whisper out of the dust.

10 For the Lord hath poured out upon you the spirit of deep sleep, and hath closed your eyes: the prophets and your rulers, the seers hath he covered.

11 And the vision of all is become unto you as the words of a book that is sealed, which men deliver to one that is learned, saying, Read this, I pray thee: and he saith, I cannot; for it is sealed."

In 1828 Charles Anthon, a scholar of Columbia College in New York replied, "I cannot read a sealed book." After seeing some of the characters that were translated he wanted to see the whole book. Martin told him some of it was sealed.

Moroni 10:5 "And by the power of the Holy Ghost ye may know the truth of all things."

Seek and ye shall find, Ask and ye shall receive, knock and it shall be opened unto you.

3 witnesses testify of being shown the plates by an angel of God, 8 witnesses testify that they were shown the plates. Though some left the church all held the truth of those accounts forever. They went out of their way to uphold them.

In some occasions there were rumors flying that they didn't see it; a signed affidavit years later, when such rumors arose, would put such rumors to rest.

The Church would grow quickly amidst incredible and horrible persecution the likes our country had not before see. However temples were built, the Savior came to it, prophets of old came to it and restored keys and promises were fulfilled such as one in Malachi.

Malachi 4:5-6 "Behold, I will send you Elijah the prophet before the coming of the great and dreadful day of the Lord: And he shall turn the heart of the fathers to the children, and the heart of the children to their fathers, lest I come and smite the earth with a curse."

John the Baptist restored the Aaronic Priesthood and authority to baptize. The Melchizedek Priesthood was later restored. Later Elijah himself came to the temple along with other prophets of old and restored priesthood keys.

Now some think that all these things are fake and many were misled and that the few witnesses were simply the only ones. This is a great lack of information.

There were hundreds of early Saints who experienced incredible things, many wrote incredible things in their journals. When the temple was first built, many saw angels; many on the outside of the temple even away from it even saw angels on the roof. Many experienced amazing manifestations of the Holy Spirit and many saw the face of Jesus Christ there in deep vision.

Many who were influential in helping and were meek and faithful were given visitation of angels even. There are a great many experiences and journal accounts of these things being true. I can testify of them to you in a bold way as I myself have experienced incredible things. The Lord leads His church.

The angel Moroni alone visited many different people in different ways.

The mother of one important early figure had him walk up to her and show her the plates and tell her to basically, 'hang in there, its all true.' More would see him specifically in vision, dreams, in glorified personage and in average physical.

A Protestant minister of a large congregation, Zerah Pulsipher spoke of a bright light that came above his head while working in his barn one day. He thought he saw an angel with The Book of Mormon in his hands saying, "This is the great revelation of the last days in which all things spoken of by the prophets must be fulfilled."

Zerah and most of his congregation were baptized. What a humble man. One would have to be willing to leave their way of life of preaching to a congregation you have built and sustains you to go where the Lord wants you to go and lead your congregation to truth.

Zerah became a missionary and baptized Wilford Woodruff, the 4th prophet and president of the Church. There were many experiences like this; the Lord used many great and humble servants that He had.

Speaking of Wilford Woodruff and the grand work of the Lord in calling His prepared children. When Wilford was young he looked everywhere for the right church but found no manifestations of the Holy Spirit.

Soon Wilford was taught by an aged man named Robert Mason who lived in Sainsbury, Connecticut. He was called a prophet by many. By him the sick were healed by him through the laying on of hands in the name of Jesus Christ and devils were cast out.

Robert Mason did not claim to have any authority to officiate in ordinances of the gospel and he didn't believe such authority existed on the earth. He did believe that it was the privilege of any man who had faith in God to fast and pray for the healing of the sick by the laying on of hands. He believed it the right of every honest hearted man or woman to receive revelation by the prayer of faith.

Robert Mason told Wilford Woodruff, (who would be the future prophet and president of the restored everlasting gospel,) that the day was near that the Lord would establish His Church and Kingdom again on the earth with all of its ancient gifts and blessings. He said such a work would commence upon the earth before he died but he wouldn't live to partake of its blessings. He told Woodruff that he would live to do so and that he should become a conspicuous actor in that kingdom.

309

The last time Wilford Woodruff saw the aged Robert Mason he related to him the open vision which he had in his field in open daylight. It is recorded as follows.

"I was carried away in a vision and found myself in the midst of a vast orchard of fruit trees. I became hungry and wandered through this vast orchard searching for fruit to eat, but I found none. While I stood in amazement finding no fruit in the midst of so many trees, they began to fall to the ground as if torn up by a whirlwind. They continued to fall until there was not a tree standing in the whole orchard. I immediately saw thereafter shoots springing up from the roots and forming themselves into young and beautiful trees. These budded, blossomed, and brought forth fruit which ripened and was the most beautiful to look upon of anything my eyes had ever beheld. I stretched forth my hand and plucked some of the fruit. I gazed upon it with delight; but when I was bout to eat of it, the vision closed and I did not taste the fruit."

"At the close of the vision I bowed down in humble prayer and asked the Lord to show me the meaning of the vision. Then the voice of the Lord came to me saying: "Son of man, thou hast sought me diligently to know the truth concerning my Church and Kingdom among men. This is to show you that my Church is not organized among men in the generation to which you belong; but in the days of your children the Church and Kingdom of God shall be made manifest with all the gifts and blessings enjoyed by the Saints in past ages. You shall live to be made acquainted with it, but shall not partake of its blessings before you depart this life. You will be blest of the Lord after death because you have followed the dictation of my Spirit in this life."

Upon telling Wilford Woodruff this vision he said, "Wilford, I shall never partake of this fruit in the flesh, but you will and you will become a conspicuous actor in the new kingdom."

Wilford later marveled at how it was the last time he saw Father Mason and he had never mentioned his vision to him before but felt compelled by the Spirit at that time to relate it to him. He mentions the vision was given to him about the year 1800 and it was 1830 when it was related to Wilford, the very spring the Church was organized.

Three years later Wilford was baptized by Zerah Pulsipher who had received the vision of an angel testifying the divinity of the work. Wilford thought back to Robert Mason and sent him a letter informing him that he had found the true gospel with all it's blessings and that the authority of the Church of Christ had been again restored to the earth just

310

as he had told him it would be. He let him know that he received the ordinances of baptism and the laying on of hands and that "I knew for myself that God had established through Joseph Smith, the Prophet, the Church of Christ upon the earth."

Robert Mason received the letter with joy and read it over and over. It is said he handled it as the fruit in the vision. He died without having the privilege of receiving the ordinances of the gospel at the hands of an elder of the Church. As soon as baptisms for the dead were again revealed Brother Woodruff was baptized for him in the temple font at Nauvoo.

(Quoted portion, Wilford Woodruff – His Life and Labors, p14-15)

Very many had incredible experiences. It is His Church. Miracles and mighty things were and are still very common place today.

I recently saw a video about a man who was a Deacon in the Roman Catholic Church; one night he had a dream. In his dream God told him to, "Follow Christ more closely, follow my servant Joseph who was given the gold plates."

He woke up, was disoriented and had no idea what it was about. Seeking the Bible he found nothing about gold plates. One day flipping through the channels he heard the words gold plates on BYU TV. He listened until he learned it was the 'Mormons' and he basically scoffed it off and changed the channel.

Eventually through a series of events, and realizing real estate he managed was by a temple and LDS bookstore, he went in and got books and researched himself. He was later baptized.

This is obviously one type of many that the Lord reaches out to his children. Many miracles seem to constantly be happening. It seems each person has a few of their own to share. There seem to be endless amounts of incredible stories and I have even some of my own. Seek and ye shall find indeed. How great our Father in Heaven and His perfect work and glory.

In 1840 a young girl, Marie Madeleine Cardon living in Torino Italy. In her own words she shares,

"I was upstairs in bed. A strange feeling came over me. It appeared that I was a young woman instead of a mere child. I thought I was in a small strip of meadow, close to our vineyard, keeping my father's milk cows from the vineyard. It seemed that I was sitting in the grass reading a Sunday school book. I looked up and saw three strangers in front of me. As I looked into their faces I dropped my eyes instantly, being very much frightened. Suddenly the thought came to me that I must look at them that I might remember them in the future. I raised my eyes and looked them straight in the face. One of them seeing that I was afraid said: "Fear not, for we are the servants of God and have come from afar to preach unto the world the everlasting gospel, which has been restored to the earth in these last days, for the redemption of mankind.""

"They told me that God had spoken from the heavens and had revealed his everlasting gospel, to the young boy Joseph Smith. That it would never more be taken from the earth, but that His kingdom would be set up and that all the honest in heart would be gathered together. They told me that I would be the means of bringing my parents and family into this great gathering. Moreover, the day was not far off when we would leave our homes and cross the great ocean. We would travel across the wilderness and go to Zion where we could serve God according to the dictates of our conscience. When they had finished their message to me they said they would return soon and visit us. They took some small books from their pockets and gave them to me, saying. "Read these and learn." Then they disappeared instantly."

Marie told her father everything she had seen and heard. Roughly a decade later after a royal decree had granted their persecuted people freedom, the family moved to Piedmont, Italy.

Marie's father Philipe heard about three strangers preaching the very same doctrine he had heard from his daughter a decade earlier. He immediately left work and got into Sunday dress. He traveled over mountains and valleys and arrived Sunday morning to hear Elder Lorenzo Snow, a future prophet of the Church, preach.

Her father is recorded by her as being happy to hear the pure truth so well and so earnestly. His heart was full of joy. He approached the servants of God and invited them to come to his home where he desired them to make it their headquarters.

Most of her family was converted, she later translated for some of their sermons and the Cardon family immigrated to Utah in 1854. She wrote down and kept the record for her posterity.

"My dear children, I cannot doubt the faith and the principals which I have embraced. My whole soul is filled with joy and thankfulness to God for his regard for me and for you in His manifesting to me the divinity of this great work in so remarkable a manner. How sincere is my prayer that you my children may realize how wonderful and yet how real and true is this, my life's testimony to you."

Since the Church was established the Lord has called His humble children to it. His greatest blessings and fullness of the gospel is there. Many there say they 'know' of its truthfulness, I used to scoff at such.

Now I can see as they see. Though there are some that still have said this without truly knowing, which is a good hope to have and build from, there are many who say it who truly do know. I know of its truthfulness, not of myself, not of the arm of the flesh, but of my Father in Heaven, in so remarkable a manner.

Throughout history there have been many prepared for great things.

Men inspired to give scriptures to the common man in translating the Bible to common language, a man inspired to make a way that those words could be printed to reach many in the printing press, a man inspired to find a new land led by the Lord to fulfill prophecy given in Columbus, those with the now printed Bibles in hand inspired to leave to the new land and establish it, those inspired by Him to free the new land and make it a land of liberty in our founding fathers, and the young boy with the Bible in hand and in the free new nation. He realized, just as the Bible said that the Lord could show Him truth, he was the product of it all, Joseph Smith. And the Lord inspires many and brings about His righteous purposes.

His humble servants are of great use. Even the humblest seeming actors for Him and His truth have had great ripple effects that continue on. May we be humble before Him that we can be taught from on high and guided for His perfect purposes.

President Lincoln even checked out the Book of Mormon for 9 months. He was an incredibly pious man and said he went through a 'period of crystallization' in his presidency.

After all, years later, decades after the death of the prophet, the Civil War started just as prophesied, in the exact place prophesied and in the exact way by Joseph Smith in 1832. And from that, wars should continue, and they sadly do. See Doctrine and Covenants section 87.

The Lord also in 1833 had Joseph go all the way up the ranks of government to those who would be able to stay the hand of mobs and massacres and unfair treatment. He ended up going all the way to the president who couldn't help. At the time the states could decide which rights they would honor in their state; the U.S. President could do nothing.

Doctrine and Covenants 101:89 "And if the president heed them not, then will the Lord arise and come forth out of his hiding place, and in his fury vex the nation;"

It is interesting to look back and see the actions and words of Lincoln.

"The Civil War might be God's punishment on both North and South for the evil of slavery." – Abraham Lincoln

In the very same section of Doctrine and Covenants 101; 79-80,

"Therefore, it is not right that any man should be in bondage one to another. And for this purpose have I established the Constitution of this land, by the hands of wise men whom I raised up unto this very purpose, and redeemed the land by the shedding of blood."

Lincoln worked hard to end slavery and did. The works of the Lord and His goodness are never ending.

I think of the vast plan of the Lord in hastening His work and how He used many ordinary people for great things.

Let us remember that though He rose up a free nation, the first of it's kind, with freedom of religion, the Church seemingly barely survived. The Church suffered serious persecution.

Granted nothing can stop the work of God so it continued and has become a strong Church of millions, but let us not forget the price that was paid and how hard truth was fought against.

Even though the Lord had raised a free nation, men, women and children were killed and massacred and mobs rose against the work of God. Many tribulations were in store and for the first and only time in US history a state, Missouri, even passed an 'extermination order' against the 'Mormons'. Many were killed and most were dispelled out of the state.

It amazes me that though the Lord did so many incredible things, even a new nation, to bring about the fullness of the gospel, that it still was met with so much horrible harshness; most of which out of fear of others. I judge none but simply marvel at the strength of the early saints.

It was truly the one time in history that was prepared to restore the fullness of the gospel and bring about the promised blessings in the last days. In a nation built by Him for freedom it had to survive serious harshness and injustices. Still the Church grew rapidly in the US and abroad, the light and truth of God couldn't be stopped.

Even after the martyrdom of Joseph Smith, the Lord by the prophet had already prophetically set up the kingdom to move forward by revelation. And by revelation it continued.

The saints were continually attacked and mobbed and eventually moved high up in the mountains to Salt Lake City, many walking the whole way with handcarts. Many dying along the way. The pioneers were truly a strong people reserved and preserved by the Lord. A very many miracles upheld and blessed many. Zion was growing.

In all of this the Lord's purposes were fulfilled and His Church was raised up in great strength in the beautiful mountains of Utah. His work moves along guided by Him.

Isaiah 2:2 "And it shall come to pass in the last days, that the mountain of the Lord's house shall be established in the top of the mountains, and shall be exalted above the hills; and all nations shall flow unto it."

In today's age truth is fought against very hard still. Though people generally aren't mobbed and killed as they were in the early days of the Church there is much persecution.

I can watch a church video on youtube and see all the suggested videos on the side often are 'Anti-Mormon' videos full of absolute lies. For one who was incredibly well versed in the supposed 'lies' of the Church, I knew them better than most, most are entirely and totally erroneous and not anywhere near or based on truth. Others take things that can be properly explained and twist and trash and make look bad, many are taken far out of context.

At the end of the day the purest truth is fought hardest against. I was on the wrong side thinking myself wise at times in my life. I judge none. There was a time I thought I had been deceived and lied to since I was a kid because of lies. I thought I knew so much; even when I 'knew' so much 'wisdom' I thought I understood. Oh how perfect God is and I'm so grateful for His mercy and kindness and love.

Regarding the videos of lies and hate on the side; there is a power that is vast and strong, and will lull you away. It is beyond anything worldly imaginable. It will change things and twist things and put whatever lies in your face it can. This is not a joke. I used to think of it as a cop out, it is not. Alas light shines and the darkness cannot comprehend it. Our Father in Heaven has all power.

Jesus Christ is the way, the truth and the life. He is the light. He truly is our Savior and we truly need Him. He has done it all for us. Stay on the rock that is Jesus Christ our Savior.

Do not forget to keep your faith tuned on faith and truth. Do not let the doubt come and creep in. I have studied it all deeper and far more than any should have to, I had to go entirely full circle; congrats, now you don't have to.

315

Use faith, plant the seed, grow the tree, it will bear fruit and that fruit will be far more incredible than is imaginable in the world.

Leave fear behind. Have faith in God and trust His guidance. Let Him show you truth in meekness and humility. His Kingdom is again on earth today.

Our society and world as a whole is being subconsciously coerced away from truth and away from God. Be not of the world.

Matthew 7:7-8 "Ask, and it shall be given you; seek, and ye shall find; knock, and it shall be opened unto you: For every one that asketh receiveth; and he that seeketh findeth; and to him that knocketh it shall be opened."

The amount of stories of this promise being fulfilled is incredible. There are all kinds of incredible stories; people who went to any type of church to pray for guidance and later the same day the Lord sending them missionaries for the first time ever.

There are literally so many examples. The underlying truth is that God is near, He knows our thoughts and our hearts far more than we ever could. He is truly right there.

If you seek there are PLENTY of testimonies of all kind. Even youtube has miracles after miracles. Terminal diseases entirely disappearing. People raised from the dead. Doctors baffled. But we don't look! That and there is a force that keeps us away from it until we are on the Lord's side. There are so many miracles and incredible things happening around us all the time. But we don't have the eyes to see. SEEK AND YE SHALL FIND.

His Goodness

There is a man who studied near death experiences, I mentioned him earlier. Which, there are many of those. There are plenty of amazing stories of people who talked to Christ, were miraculously healed, had angels, all manner, some taken to heaven and many different people who saw the same things, and some that without faith experienced just parts of the understanding of the 'law' and not yet Christ.

There are those who have experienced all manner of horrible darkness, as well as many in deception that later realize what it was, many come back and warn everyone and they preach Christ. There are many plucked out of it by Christ. The most amazing ones are the ones of Christ and I have heard some incredible ones of members of The Church of Jesus Christ of Latter-day Saints as well.

316

Anyone who would ever devalue the truth of the reality of near death experiences doesn't have much of what is available of further understanding. They are looking at it through a lens of physical, which is essentially, non applicable to say it in a nice and frank way.

To anyone back there I would show tons of NDE's where the experiencer experiences and sees things they could not have known or seen or understood. Whether it be something happening miles away with a loved one, seeing what doctors and people did or said throughout the hospital, following loved ones in different areas of the world, learning more informational truths from God or from loved ones on the other side; there are tons of these experiences that simply cannot be from a physical standpoint. Furthermore if you think like this, the physical is not as you think, have faith in God and seek wisdom. All is His!

We are infinite beings. Anyone who argues this, even the non-religious, simply are living in stone ages of what there is to know and understand. Alas, the true path is by faith still.

When it comes to 'Near Death Experiences' one thing is solidified. That is the understanding and revealed knowledge of The Church of Jesus Christ of Latter-day Saints. Even the lower kingdom of glory is said to be so incredible we would not want to come back. The Lord has restored this knowledge.

As I said before, there is a man who did in depth personal studies of NDE's. He came to understand, after strongly doubting and putting aside the faith, that The Church of Jesus Christ of Latter-day Saints is true. You can find a video on youtube he did titled, "CHRISTIAN to "MORMON"-Christian (a near death conversion)" He has some other great study videos as well.

His description is thus. "A long study of Near Death experiences leads my family to rearrange our Christian Beliefs. I was a very knowledgeable and grounded Christian, but scared away from studying the "mormon" faith by "half-truths". The Church of Jesus Christ of Latter-day Saints has the most perfected truths of any other faith that I could find. This church was divinely restored through revelation and I have no doubt about that. Enjoy our conversion story and please share with anyone interested in learning more about the amazing miracle of the restoration."

One quote I like from his video is that, the Church was the "missing puzzle that I almost never found because I hardened my heart and I allowed others to fill my mind with 'half truths' against the faith."

317

He goes on to testify of the truth of the gospel. He starts the video and says that he is, "a very unlikely convert."

Another great quote regarding the Spirit and the Church, "In the end, the reality is the Spirit strongly testified of the truth of this Church. I was stunned at its amazing capacity to relay a pure gospel message of Jesus Christ. It had a unique strength in its teachings on the Atonement of Jesus Christ."

Anyone who truly humbly seeks will find.

There have been atheist Doctors who have done pragmatic searches of the physical life of Christ and the physical record throughout history. Generally to disprove then to come to find that Jesus must be the prophesied Christ; they see the miracle of it all then they became Christians.

We simply must seek! All will find, it is a promise of God; let Him guide.

Today, the 'wisdom' of the world is partially distributed into many wild areas of 'spirit' and 'consciousness'. I later found this area to be relatively referenced as a whole, "New Age," or the "New Age movement."

Most times the people messing with areas of such are thinking themselves wise as 'consciousness' is 'ascending' and they are in all manner of deception. We have been through such in depth in this book. Most times as well the people dabbling in them do not fully understand or 'know' the depths of 'wisdom' but partially they continue in their wisdom; some however, do. All sorts of things are twisted and truly many are led in deception. And many come to understand what is going on, see truth and are saved by Jesus Christ.

If one took 5 minutes on youtube and searched, "New Age to Christianity," one would find tons of stories similar in ways to mine. People dabbling in many different areas, unwittingly twisting 'wisdom', come back and are ashamed; many make videos and warn people away.

It truly is the grand deception of the last days. There are many who dabble in such and it can be perceived as no big deal, 'people simply don't understand,' this is why it is such a grand deception.

There are many, many videos with people who have been led out of darkness to the light of truth. Praise the Lord for His goodness, mercy and great love!

One who made a video correctly stated how this was how the adversary has always worked. Pushing all away from even thinking of God; instead pushing to put ourselves there and all things and perceptions so that we cannot perceive the truth that is God.

318

It is all very dark, especially when we weigh that there IS singular and necessary truth. Jesus Christ is the way the truth and the life. For some though, and myself, I can see how our hard heartedness needed a serious wake up call, so it was truly wisdom in the Lord.

It is amazing to see this prophesied, and even spelt out. Parts of Isaiah spell it out, deeply, in ways I wont get into; and there are vast other parts in scripture that do so as well. The Lord talks about how He would gather many in the last days as well.

I think about all the things I was shown and those things that were confounded before me and then the immense light I was given to understand thereafter. The Lord has been incredibly good to me and I am very blessed.

Doctrine and Covenants 35:25 "And Israel shall be saved in mine own due time; and by the keys which I have given shall they be led, and no more be confounded at all."

We are truly living in the last days and the gathering of Israel is now, the Lord is pouring out His Spirit. I do my best to be a profitable servant and help my Father's perfect causes. The family business is all manner of love and salvation.

Oh how grateful I am for a loving, merciful, gracious and perfectly kind Father. He is by our side in love all the time, giving us all we need to find our way back home to Him. Listen and find the path! I praise Him forever and forever serve Him!

Isaiah 42:16 "And I will bring the blind by a way that they knew not; I will lead them in paths that they have not known: I will make darkness light before the, and crooked things straight. These things will I do unto them, and not forsake them."

I owe Him everything. We all owe Him everything. After all, He created us. Love. Stay on the rock of Christ; be not moved! Do not look beyond the mark!

Again regarding that man's NDE study.

There is a lady named Elane Durham. She was not a member of The Church of Jesus Christ of Latter-day Saints and knew nothing about it. She had a near death experience. In it she asked about the true church. She was told that in old times the church had become diluted by those seeking power and though there were still partial truths that it didn't stay in the way heaven had created it. She was then told some very specific things. She was told there is a true Church, it wasn't the 'right' church

319

but the 'perfect' church. It was composed perfectly and organized perfectly and was given again by heaven. She was not informed which church it was, she was given the opportunity to seek and learn for herself. She was told that Christ's heavenly church is on the earth again today, organized like in the days of old, and that if she desired to find it, she would. She was told she would recognize among the people of the church, the same spirit of peace and joy that she had felt with Jesus and the angels in the higher spiritual realm she was in. She was told it would take her a while to find it. 15-20 years.

One day, 15 years later, she came in contact with missionaries from The Church of Jesus Christ of Latter-day Saints, she recognized the Spirit immediately and all the doctrine made sense to her. She had finally found what she was looking for and she became a member of the "perfect" church.

Her book is entitled, "I Stand All Amazed," and there are excerpts of it in the man's video that I titled just a bit ago about NDE's and his conversion.

The Church of Jesus Christ of Latter-day Saints is the fullness of the gospel. Jesus Christ is the actual head of the Church and He leads it! It is true. You can know it as I know it, by revelation from heaven! Oh that men would praise Him!

For a while I found it hard to describe to people the utterly incredible, amazing and indescribable depths that the powerful Holy Spirit of God can convey. I found this account given by Oliver Cowdery while with Joseph Smith during a heavenly encounter conveys this somewhat.

"I shall not attempt to paint to you the feelings of this heart, nor the majestic beauty and glory which surrounded us on this occasion; but you will believe me when I say, that earth, nor men, with the eloquence of time, cannot begin to clothe language in as interesting and sublime a manner as this holy personage. No; nor has this earth power to give the joy, to bestow the peace, or comprehend the wisdom which was contained in each sentence as they were delivered by the power of the Holy Spirit! Man may deceive his fellow-men, deception may follow deception, and the children of the wicked one may have power to seduce the foolish and untaught, till naught but the fiction feeds the many, and the fruit of falsehood carries in its current the giddy to the grave; but one touch with the finger of His love, yes, one ray of glory from the upper world, or one word from the mouth of the Savior, from the bosom of eternity, strikes it all into insignificance, and blots it forever from the mind." – Oliver Cowdery, Messenger and Advocate, Vol.

Chapter 20

OUR GOOD FATHER
X Games Again, Revelation, Childlike Trust

Upon first returning to the Church I told the Lord I wanted to be brought back as quick as possible. I wanted everything to be aright quickly and I wanted to be on His pathway for me. The Lord blessed me with this, gave me deep understanding of things I needed help with, gave me an incredible drive to learn the things of the gospel and all things, gave me the drive to receive revelation and even put the most perfect and incredible wife in my path.

I think of the scripture,

Malachi 3:10, "Bring ye all the tithes into the storehouse, that there may be meat in mine house, and prove me now herewith, saith the Lord of hosts, if I will not open you the windows of heaven, and pour you out a blessing, that there shall not be room enough to receive it."

I was willing to give up anything I needed to walk as He wanted me to and to be taught by Him and blessed by Him. The windows of heaven were opened and blessings poured out. I received a lot of serious revelation and understanding and got much closer to my Father in Heaven.

The greatest blessing, so large that there shall not be room to receive it, could have been many things. Revelation was certainly that, overflowing as I sought. Healing was also that. To me it was being blessed with my loving wife. Truly the most incredible person I know. I was and am incredibly blessed. And there would be yet more truly incredible blessings.

As I put wordly things completely aside and focused entirely on the Lord's paths for me I was blessed exceedingly. Not with money, or wealth; but things of eternal value that would last forever, the things that really mattered and brought real and pure joy. I was and am very well taken care of and I am forever grateful. The eternal perspective is a blessing that we can see our greatest blessings.

X Games came around again. My life was obviously far different and far more blessed. I was riding now with no major sponsors save my small denim company; the perspective was so much different. I wanted to ride well to the glory of God alone.

I was riding well and felt very confident, I set my eyes on winning and decided to do a double flair really high out of the quarter pipe and lock in the win on the first run.

The week leading up to the live televised final was a great one. In my hotel room I spent time before and after practice studying scripture. I was blessed to understand some more things deeply and have the Spirit teach me. Everything was leading up to have a great weekend.

The weekend came, we were live on TV and it was time to get back on top of the podium. I was confident and would go for the win on run number 1.

It came time for me to drop in for my run. Many were watching, my family was there, and family and friends were watching on TV. I did the trick over the jump perfectly and sent the double flair high on the quarter pipe.

The next thing I know I am in an ambulance being asked questions. I had come very slightly away from the quarter pipe. I had done the trick absolutely perfectly, but because I was a matter of inches out, I fell much further, over rotated, landed sideways, instantly thrown to my head and knocked out. I went roughly 40+ feet to my side and head. Someone filmed it on their phone and posted it to youtube, it was a hard hit.

My head hit so hard on my right side that the ricochet alone of my helmet off the flat of the ramp bounced in to my left collarbone so hard that it broke it. It was the only time in my whole career that I had been knocked out at a contest; though I wasn't the first to be knocked out on that ramp, it was a hard one.

In the ambulance my memory was obviously very vague. I could remember my wife's name and wanted her near me, but couldn't remember we were married. They asked me questions that I could answer and some I couldn't, I couldn't remember what had happened and couldn't remember much but I was very calm and had a strong peace about me.

I utterly relied on the doctors and medical staff and forever am grateful to the guys at ESPN for being so amazing. I was well taken care of, they sent their own doctor to the hospital with me and ensured I would be well taken care of. I had never been in such a vulnerable state physically. It was entirely new. I couldn't help myself at all and utterly needed their help. It was humbling.

My memory of the contest was a weird dream and I had a better idea of where I felt I had actually been, somewhere else.

In the hospital they did test after test and didn't take off the neck brace until they were very sure and multiple checks that there was no breaks.

322

I couldn't remember much. Though many things came to my memory, I knew the date and other things, but I couldn't remember things like that I had come back to church, or my wedding day, I couldn't remember so many things. I remembered that I had been learning large and vast things but I couldn't remember what they were. Granted I had just been knocked out hard.

My step dad was there and he and another friend's dad gave me a blessing. I vaguely remember it and then couldn't remember that I had come back to Church and was so dedicated. I was blessed that I would heal quickly.

After the blessing my memories began to come back slowly then quicker. I was laying in bed with broken in half collar bone, and the right side of my head was hurting terribly bad. They had done some CT scans right when I had arrived and were very quiet about the results.

They wouldn't do anything until it was triple checked. A few people had read the scans and they were waiting on the further opinion of a Neurologist. Finally the ESPN doctor that had thankfully hung around with us for a while came in and spoke to my mother.

He was upset that they wouldn't tell us yet what they knew. He told my mother that that CT scan I received upon arrival showed bruising and bleeding on my brain. Eventually they told us the same.

There was nothing I could do but relax, I was told I would be staying the night and eventually accepted it. My headache slowly went away and my memories began to come back fully.

Though I couldn't remember the wreck or much after it my memories of life were back and again full, I could trust God and remembered how close He was. The vast things I had learned were remembered and a continual comfort was there. I simply waited for the Lord's will and healing.

When they were checking for other injuries, (such as to my back and neck before they would take off the brace, though I was sore and somewhat worried to move at first which worry faded away,) my memories were back. As they came back I remembered to trust. I remembered everything and trusted in Him that nothing was wrong. All those areas kept checking out fine and braces came off.

I experienced calm the whole time. Even when I could remember nothing, telling the ambulance guys some answers but admitting I had no idea what was going on at all, I was calm, I was at peace, I knew all would be well.

Laying in bed with the headache I prayed that it would leave and I trusted God for that blessing and though it didn't leave immediately I trusted that it would leave as He willed it. Soon it began to leave and I could sleep.

Very early in the morning I was woken up and taken to another CT scan. They were worried about the head injury and wanted to make a plan. I had a friend who once had some minor brain bleeding and was in the hospital for a few days. I wasn't worried, my headache was gone, I felt 100% normal and fine and remembered everything but the wreck and the time I was out, remembering some deep dream type thoughts when I was out. I trusted that I was ok.

I went back to the room after the early CT and began to wake up fully from sleeping. My amazing wife and mother was there, my brother came and brought my scriptures and my step dad was there to give me the blessing shortly after first arriving the night before.

That morning I felt really good to go. It was as though nothing happened except a broken collarbone, no big deal I had broken it earlier in the same year anyway. No headache, no memory issue, I felt totally fine. This didn't matter much to doctors though as they go off of the physical data.

Soon the CT scans came back and again we waited for more people to check them out again. Specialists looked at it and again they wanted another opinion of a Neurosurgeon.

Eventually they came in. "So your brain looks really good." Odd to hear compared to the news last night. "The scan shows no bleeding at all and everything looks to be in perfect shape."

They had been confused about these findings and everyone again went back and looked at my original arrival CT scan. "We looked at your previous scan and it seems they must have been read wrong. The scans look totally healthy and fine."

None can stop the Lord Almighty.

Though they had gone through many people to read the first scan and it showed bleeding and bruising, and though I had a severe headache just after, it had all disappeared. "So you fell about 40-45 feet to your head I guess?"

"Ya that's a fair estimate," There was no trace of any head injury, there was however a broken in half collarbone, from the ricochet alone of my head.

This was not the first time though that I had seen 'reality' completely change in an instant. All is God's, I had been given a blessing and I had trusted in Him. I smiled and thanked my Father in Heaven. I am forever grateful.

I was pushing to leave and they were making every effort to make sure I was able. I went through various manners of cognitive tests, physical and mental. I passed all with flying colors as if I had no injury at all. Soon they took out my IV's and discharged me.

324

I left the hospital in socks and shorts; they had cut every bit of clothing off of me. I felt totally fine and perfect. I was and am forever incredibly grateful to my Father in Heaven for taking care of me.

I remembered thinking, after remembering some of 'coming back to consciousness' or 'reality,' after being KO'd' how silly it was than anyone ever worries. Whether it be money or anything else, even about injury. He was always right there to rely on wholly. I am grateful to my Father in Heaven for all of it and all the good involved.

I was and am also very grateful to the medical guys at ESPN and the hospital for taking care of me when I really needed it. I have never experienced such utter necessity and absolute reliance, in very real need, on the medical staff at the event. I had however needed my Father in Heaven in very real need and in absolute reliance before, and this was another testament to relying on Him, He is always there.

A quick note from the hospital that becomes important later on in the story. The morning just before leaving the hospital I wrote a quick note in my phone so that I would remember the way things happened and what I experienced myself. One of the last parts of the note I wrote this, "After coming out of 'gone' state, not knowing memories, asked if I'd been saying Jesus is coming back soon. Mom said, 'You said within 10 days.' I didn't say that, I said to her before I think signs will start. But either way deep thought because something on that side had me thinkin that way."

I had remembered I had been saying something like that and wasn't sure, I for some reason said that and I felt that signs would start then. At the time I felt it would be signs in the world, though many had already started and were being fulfilled. This is something I didn't realize until looking back on the notes after this book was written. This becomes important as the story goes on.

His Perfect Symphony

I left the hospital, and I wanted to figure this out and realize why such happened.

I wanted to and was ready to win X Games, I even had an angel Moroni shirt that I was stoked on. I was ready and a small mistake, by a few inches, caused my very hard wreck.

But why? I fully trusted God and had since entirely trusted myself as His, knowing His will would be perfect. I didn't dispute this but I knew He could have very easily blessed me to win the contest. I wondered and, as humbly as I could, wanted to know why it was wisdom in Him that it would be this way.

I was not worried as He had just easily taken me through what normally would be a hard trial, yet it was smooth and calm and of no worries. I trusted Him fully and wanted to understand. I took comfort at first in that I could trust Him yet more, to take me through hard things in ease, and if I was yet more humble that it would become a good thing.

I still wanted to understand more, I knew well enough that His wisdom was incredibly vast and I couldn't see always the wisdom at first. I wanted to see it. What could be better than me winning and standing as a witness on TV of Him? I knew His wisdom was greater and I sought to know it.

I had two opposing thoughts, "I know enough to know that God could have made me land it if He wanted and I did the trick right, it was inches that caused the wreck, why didn't I win?" and the thought of eternal value, "Clearly there has been great blessings here, and clearly there is more than meets the eye if I will but trust in His purposes that are far grander than I can comprehend."

I had been through much, I was taught much, and it had become easy for me to discern between what is of truth and deception. If I am worrying about things of this world, money, physical etc. my worry is ill placed. If I am concerned of the things of God and of His glory and things of eternity my thoughts are placed well.

I could easily discern what thoughts were of His Spirit, they made me humble to God, and want to serve and praise and love Him.

These opposing thoughts were quickly discerned and I held out in hope and prayer that I would be shown His wisdom in this grand affair. I was furthermore very grateful to have been taken so well care of and healed.

Fireworks

To illustrate this story perfectly I will jump back to an earlier experience first.

Shortly after the experience that brought me back to Church I had very many experiences and some I have spoken of. There is one particular one I wish to mention.

I was driving from Utah to Idaho; I was going to Idaho to finally go back to Church. I knew the Church was true, I had been shown my fallacy, ignorance, arrogance and wholly wrong direction. I was grateful for the loving patience and guidance of my loving Father in Heaven.

During the drive I was amazed and deep in thought and thought of how much love God has for me. I could clearly see His greater hand in all aspects leading up to me finding the truth that is in the gospel and in His Son Jesus Christ.

I began to marvel and be amazed. I was going back to Church for the first time in so long and I was greatly thankful. I was so overwhelmed with gratitude and as I pondered and saw the vast workings of God I perceived that this was a graduation. The Lord had brought me back and I could finally see and see more clearly His vast beautiful symphony.

It was a great experience in the Spirit at that time, I was so grateful; He had brought me back. Though I had strayed so far He never left my side. His long suffering was apparent, His love was apparent. I realized this and it was as though I had graduated, to truly see clearly.

As my mind recognized the goodness of my Father in Heaven and how thankful I was that He stayed by me that I could, in a sense, graduate to truth, suddenly a large firework display began over the bay on the side of the freeway. This was a 'random' event scheduled and far after the 4th of July.

It was as though God was saying, "Yes, I wouldn't ever let you go, I love you dearly. Welcome back, I even prepared the way for you back home in celebration, with fireworks." My Dad sent fireworks. I had eyes to see and ears to hear.

This story continues but I will add some value to help understand here quickly.

In these types of instances, many may look at them in the physical understanding as coincidences. Coincidence is a word many use to explain something greater they yet do not understand.

Albert Einstein put it this way; "A coincidence is a small miracle when God chooses to remain anonymous."

Regardless of Einstein's opinions, coincidences truly are more than they appear. And when we are led in the Spirit of God in resonance with Him in truth they can be grand.

There are many, and most, who rely entirely on the physical, even those who know the gospel of our Father in Heaven. People will also often write off many spiritual amazing things as curiosities of our physical brain. Though many have the truth, they still look through physical eyes.

Some who look at things through physical eyes see a symphony of our Amygdala, Hippocampus, and Rhinal Cortex, parts of our physical brain, instead of a symphony of the Spirit of God.

This is similar to marveling at the inside of a radio for the messages given through it.

Even the 'wisdom' in the incorrect way of understanding that is in the world, that of missing the truth of God that we have talked so much about to help all see truth in our Savior, even in that the physical is confounded. And that 'great wisdom' that many in the world hold so dear, as we know, is confounded by He who created all things, our Father in Heaven, God Almighty. Faith and trust in Him becomes true wisdom as we can be taught humbly from on high, in truth, the greater things.

I say this to lift perspectives of all, to put your eyes on things of eternity and things of Spirit and of God. He is above all, in all, through all, nothing is too hard for Him, to say the least. All is of Him. He is truly the source of all good.

If you seek to learn more from our Father in Heaven and hope to be quickened in His Spirit you must lose your thoughts and perceptions that the physical reigns; God reigns forever.

All is His, and all is far deeper and more perfect and more amazing that you can imagine, and that's only a glimpse at His perfection. When we see above the physical and see in the Spirit we can then have the 'eyes to see and ears to hear.'

We must be faithful that He reigns, for if we do not accept this in faith the greater things will be withheld.

I tell you this story of fireworks, yet I keep personal far grander things that have come in similar fashion by exercising strong faith in Him. Grand things by simply recognizing He is always there, and infinite and perfect, my loving Father; things that most probably wouldn't believe because of the 'physical' stumbling block, things that are sacred and personal. I illustrate even this that you will keep focus beyond physical 'laws' (which aren't laws or rather the Spirit is above such significantly); we must keep our focus in His Spirit. All is His. We must be born again, of the Spirit.

Romans 8:5 "For they that are after the flesh do mind the things of the flesh; but they that are after the Spirit the things of the Spirit."

Romans 8 has much good on the subject.

I would liken this to a story in scripture. Jesus had just called to our Father in Heaven, and there came a voice from Heaven. People were around and some said they heard only thunder. What an interesting coincidence that it thundered just after Christ finished talking. There were other people that said an angel spake to Him.

John 12:28-30 "Father, glorify thy name. Then came there a voice from heaven, saying, I have both glorified it, and will glorify it again.

29 The people therefore, that stood by, and heard it, said that it thundered: others said, An angel spake to him.

30 Jesus answered and said, This voice came not because of me, but for your sakes."

We must leave the things of this world and walk not of the physical or of the understanding of the flesh, but graduate to the understanding of the Spirit and walk in the Spirit. This comes by recognizing the vastness and glory of God, who has easily created all things and nothing is hard for Him.

He is within all things, closer than we can imagine. Our thoughts are more understood by Him then ourselves. Will we hear thunder or the voice of our Father in Heaven?

Doctrine and Covenants 88:41 "He comprehendeth all things, and all things are before him, and all things are round about him; and he is above all things, and in all things, and is through all things, and is round about all things; and all things are by him, and of him, even God, forever and ever."

I have a, perhaps, silly thought, but will give an idea. That is, think of the talking inanimate objects in the story Beauty and the Beast. They don't want to talk and speak, though they are aware of those in the story. They watch and don't want to scare. Eventually they are realized that they are right there. Similarly, God is that close, He is our loving Father in Heaven and guides us in His perfect wisdom. The veil is thin.

When we recognize this, we too can hear the voice of the Spirit of our Father in Heaven. We can hear and perceive incredible things of our Father in Heaven, who is endless. We can hear His voice; His voice is Spirit, while others hear only the things perceived physically, the thunder.

The physical is nothing before the spiritual and all is God's.

This is yet another similitude of how Christ taught in parables. Those who heard physically about drinking His blood and eating His flesh were scared off. Christ sifted in a single moment those who would hear spiritually. Alas the greater things are protected by humble faith.

John 6:63 "It is the spirit that quickeneth; the flesh profiteth nothing: the words that I speak unto you, they are spirit, and they are life."

Continuing on.

At this moment, seeing the fireworks, I could see greater the blessings and love of my Father. When the fireworks happened at that moment, I knew how it would be in the physical, and I knew what it was in the Spirit. I was so thankful. The way was prepared back home, with fireworks and celebration.

The prodigal son had a fatted calf and a ring after his loving father ran out to him, they celebrated and made merry that though his son was dead, he was alive again. I had been blessed with a wealth of understanding in truth, healing, blessings and more grand blessings to come, He ran out to me, and He celebrated my return in many amazing ways.

Doctrine and Covenants 88:49-50 "The light shineth in darkness, and the darkness comprehendeth it not; nevertheless, the day shall come when you shall comprehend even God, being quickened in him and by him. Then shall ye know that ye have seen me, that I am, and that I am the true light that is in you, and that you are in me; otherwise ye could not abound."

63 "Draw near unto me and I will draw near unto you; seek me diligently and ye shall find me; ask, and ye shall receive; knock, and it shall be opened unto you."

All is His, He reigns. Oh that men would praise Him!

Now back to after X Games, to continue the story, trying to gain revelation about the injury. I am back at the hotel after leaving the hospital. I knew there was perfect purpose to all of this. I simply wanted to know what it was.

I was 100% healed from everything that mattered and grateful. My wife and I decided to go down to the hot tub in the hotel and see my parents. I didn't get in but I sat and pondered and continued praying and pondering, awaiting my answer.

I began to think of the whole amazing process that I had had over the past while. The Lord had blessed me as I had asked and brought me quickly into His fold, right back to where I was lost.

Nothing is too hard for Him. He placed the most incredible wife in my path and all these amazing blessings. He had healed me spiritually and physically. Memories could have been wiped out, but in trusting Him and His goodness, I was healthy, whole and new.

I had received a wealth and breadth of knowledge in truth, I had learned many things and above all else I had learned to rely wholly on Him. I began to see all of the many things of eternal value that I had been blessed with; as my thoughts changed I could see more clearly.

This was a great blessing, and perhaps a test to pass. All times that we are able to humble ourselves to God instead of any other reaction, we go in through the gate and are shown the greater things. It is, in a sense, a test passed.

This was a great blessing indeed. I had to personally look at myself and in my personal perspective and not in the 'normality' of the world, again to see the progress, as it always is.

The blessing was seemingly the final bit of teaching of everything for me. I had received revelation and understood yet more even the week leading up to the contest where I wrecked. This seemed the graduation point of everything I had been taught, incredible and great things, winding up into a simple, yet very glorious truth.

This blessing I was realizing more and grander as I pondered, that no matter what the issue was, the Lord was always there, as I was entirely humble and perfectly reliant on Him, He will always come through.

A few short days before the wreck, in the hotel room, I made a note, "POWER IS IN TRUSTING GOD!" I wrote it after seeing abundantly and round about that all power and strength is God's. All is His.

His goodness is significantly beyond what we can yet see. We must live in love and trust Him. Trust His will and have faith in His goodness. The thought was deeper than I can express and I had learned it first hand.

I am a child, I will always be His child, though He can give me all things I am His child and a baby compared to Him and His literally baby. I cannot of myself bring my memory back when hurt, I cannot heal myself, I can do nothing of myself; He alone is above all. But, when I trust fully in Him, and don't lose sight, and trust in faith, He will always be there for me. He will carry us up to be with Him and we can trust Him.

This blessing was a huge lesson in utter reliance on Him for all things. I could see the immense blessing of this in a way that the average person or viewpoint of today could not see as a blessing. After all I had went through and been taught I saw clearly and I could see the vastness and immensity of it.

I realized that power is childlike trust and reliance on God. That will not make entire sense to many, seek discernment given by the Spirit, but the glory and depth of such a statement is vast.

"Whosoever therefore shall humble himself as this little child, the same is greatest in the kingdom of heaven."

Oh how I was seeing the depth of truth of the vast wisdom of our Savior and seeing the vast grand perfect glorious symphony of our Father in Heaven!

The ends of certain deeper understanding were being finalized and I was thanking my Father in Heaven again for everything. The incredible deep and vast things I had been learning of Him were again being perfected, simplified and made most effective in pure humble childlike trust before Him, yet again.

His humble trusting child is the greatest in the kingdom of heaven. All good and all strength is of Him. What perfected faith in our loving Father!

It was as though I was being told by Him, "Few other than you could see what is really going on here. You gave yourself to me wholly. You have wanted all good things. You have stood up for me and longed to serve me above all. You needed to do well and make money here yet your eye was single to my glory and you sought to win for my glory alone and I know your heart. You knew I could and would provide and you put my words and purposes above the world. You have sought learning diligently. You have come to know my vastness and that I guide you in perfect purpose. You have been taught large things and have sought my glory with it all. You had faith in and knew that I could show you what all this meant. For your sake this test was given you, for that which you seek I will give. You are blessed for seeking the things of greater value, of Me. I love you."

Most times that grand revelation comes it comes with a grand understanding of how close we are, how much I am loved, and how much I truly am His son.

My eyes widened as I could start to truly see much of this. I was prepared for the greater things, the things of the world are not the ways of God, what is a BMX contest? The things He cares about are much higher; as He changes us and perfects us we can be made better servants and Sons of our Father in Heaven.

We made our way back up into the hotel room. I was continuing to think deep about all of these things in amazement. I was so very grateful. I had been truly taught and had utter trust. Trust like a child would to their parents. Deep and real trust; I could totally rely on Him. He completely has me in all things and I knew His power is to help and bless all.

I began to think of the many greater things I had learned of many things and of the Priesthood and was simply amazed at all the things I had learned that were continually built upon. How good our Father is! Oh that men would praise Him!

The things that are foolish in the eyes of the world truly come to ultimate wisdom in Him and confound the wise. Surely none can glory in His presence, all glory is His. Oh that men would praise Him! And I forever will!

I began to see that I was having yet another 'graduation.' A grand one. I had just lived through a serious situation made easy and clear and calm. And I was seeing the path of it all leading up to it. It was incredibly grand. My words cannot convey the depth of what the Spirit taught. I had been blessed greatly and was utterly amazed to see the good hand of my Father in Heaven every step of the way.

I could see the perfect faith, childlike faith. "Blessed are ye because of your faith. And now behold, my joy is full."

The fireworks started. Loud explosions and bright flashes of celebration, situated outside the large window of our hotel, 'randomly' began. Again after the 4th of July, having no tie to it.

The 'Minneapolis Aquatennial' firework show, one of the biggest in the nation, had begun outside the large window of the hotel room amidst downtown Minneapolis. It was a celebration of the famous lakes, streams and rivers. My room was perfectly situated to see it all. It was a beautiful show and the 'eyes to see and ears to hear' filled me with joy and praises to my Father in Heaven.

My wife and I watched the firework show at our window. The celebration was grand and culminated perfectly everything that I had been blessed to come to know. I was so grateful; our Father is so vast, so perfect, and so good.

I write notes all the time, often to remember some important spiritual things. At that time one of the notes I wrote was, "How much I've been given. Because I've been given much I too must give."

I also wrote my thoughts then that it was as though He was saying, "Trust me, and have faith and hope to do all good things; I have given you everything."

Humble trust and faith in Him, even like a child, to where we can trust Him, and have faith and hope to do all good things by Him and receive all good things by Him is immense. Especially when we can see He alone knows the utter perfect path and as we allow Him and seek it He will guide us so perfectly.

Ether 12:28 "Behold, I will show unto the Gentiles their weakness, and I will show unto them that faith, hope and charity bringeth unto me – the fountain of all righteousness."

333

Oh the subtle yet not so subtle things that are amazing. Oh the grand symphony and perfect goodness of our Father in Heaven.

I still learn new things through things He has given me previously.

Oh the long forgotten peaceful feeling of being a child who relied wholly on their parents. No worries, just full of wonder and love. No stresses, able to laugh at things others see as stressful. How grand it is to see it on the larger scale and fall into His perfect arms that have always been there for us to realize and see. How great and amazing and glorious His perfect love is!

Oh how we should leave our fears and stresses and trustingly fall into His arms. Humble as a child, for we are His. How I love the feeling that even I am His child. How peaceful, how comforting, how taken care of we are when we choose to see it and trust our loving Father.

Oh how He fills us with His incredible unconditional love! I pray all to come to see it. When you do you will strive for all to see it, His great love. How free we are in Him. Oh that men would praise Him!

'How Firm a Foundation,' The hymn lyrics are amazing.

The greatest in the Kingdom of Heaven are truly those humble as His children.

2 Corinthians 4:7 "But we have this treasure, in earthen vessels, that the excellency of the power may be of God, and not of us."

All is His and by Him and He is perfect!

I'd been saved and brought back to the gospel. My story and miraculous blessings inspired my step father to again try faith and to then see that it was all true. He also was brought back to the fold. I had prayed for him.

I am incredibly grateful for this as he was back in the fold of our Father in Heaven and is the one who gave me the Priesthood blessing in the hospital. This is a great lesson in needing each other and the importance of standing for and spreading the truth of our Father.

I am grateful to my Father in Heaven for every step of the way and continually guiding my path, going before me being on my right and left and His angels round about me.

My friend that I had helped get into X Games the year prior had his parents coming to watch. His dad was leaving his house when his mom stopped him as they left. She said she felt he needed to go grab some consecrated oil. They went back inside, got the blessed oil for healing, and headed out across the country.

It was this man and oil that anointed my head for healing in the Priesthood of our Savior, before the blessing was given that I would heal quickly; and so I did.

A friend of my wife had a relationship end after engagement and had been going to the temple and praying a lot to find the right person. She decided to come with us to watch me compete. After being injured we were at the hotel, she decided to go down to the hot tub alone and talked to some kind people there. She met a brother of one of my friends who is an X Games athlete as well; he also happened to be a member of The Church of Jesus Christ of Latter-day Saints and lived not far away in Utah. They fell in love and will probably be married soon.

I posted about how I was healed and how good God is on instagram; many people were worried and I wanted to let them know I was ok and that God lives and Jesus Christ is the Savior of us all.

Some months after this experience I receive this message from a missionary through a friend, he asked that it would be forwarded to me.

"Today we went to visit a friend that is getting baptized today and he had 4 seizures this morning and the ambulance was on the way cause he was also having extreme chest pain. We quickly taught him about the Priesthood power and blessings and shared the story of your crash at X Games and the brain bruising and how a blessing healed you. And he really believed that and said if it worked for you it will work for me and so we gave him a blessing; then immediately his pain went away and the ambulance arrived right after and did all the testing and could find no sign of anything wrong and he is good to go. So basically I wanted to thank him for sharing that story on instagram so that we could share that with others."

This same kid I had ridden with before he left on his mission and before I had the experience that brought me back to the gospel. We had a short conversation. I don't remember what was said, though we were kind, I believe I said something against his belief in the Church. It probably went something like, "You don't fully understand everything yet, but there is more to understand and that isn't it." I always genuinely wanted to help, but oh how silly I was. Oh how thankful I am for my living Savior. He has made my crooked paths strait and healed me.

It wasn't long after that experience that I hear from a friend he's coming to ride where we ride again and wants to buy some riding pants of my small company. I showed up and gave him the pants for free and told him that I was wrong and that the Church was indeed true. I was so blessed to have been saved and brought back to the fold. I am glad he went on his mission.

The very same day that I received the text from him while on his mission about the healing he was blessed with I was doing a fireside talk at a stake in Utah. I told the kids briefly and solemnly my story and taught them the importance of faith, that truly they were called to be here at this time, the Lord is counting on all of us to help bring truth to His children.

Some people came up to me to talk to me, some of which were this missionary's family. They knew we had ridden together a few times. They said he was doing well but briefly mentioned that he had had a hard time at times with the gospel. I was glad however he went on his mission and glad that I could, at least with him, do my best to rectify my incorrect words. I was happy to see him doing amazing good for the Lord. We all knew who was to thank, the Lord.

It has been hard at times to even think of myself in the past not knowing and following the gospel. I couldn't even imagine it now. It is hard to sometimes tell of experiences past that I want to forget; but my sorrow is swallowed up in my joy that is in the glory of my Father in Heaven.

The story is of His incredible and vast mercy, His amazing grace, His truly wondrously perfect and healing love, His perfect redeeming strength. I have been greatly blessed to say the least. Words will not do justice; I simply want all to know of Him, and His perfect love and glory.

The hand of the Lord is vast and infinite; His symphony of love is amazing. All good is truly of Him. He reaches out to save and bless. I cannot say the smallest part which I feel. All good is from Him. The good in you and I is of Him. Our strength is in Him alone. Trusting in Him is the greatest strength. Even as His child.

Alma 26:12 "Yea, I know that I am nothing; as to my strength I am weak; therefore I will not boast of myself, but I will boast of my God, for in his strength I can do all things; yea, behold, many mighty miracles we have wrought in this land, for which we will praise his name forever."

Doctrine and Covenants 98:3 "Therefore, he giveth this promise unto you, with an immutable covenant that they shall be fulfilled; and all things wherewith you have been afflicted shall work together for your good, and to my name's glory, saith the Lord.

336

Home After X Games

I came back from X Games, having gained far more than I lost, and far more than if I had simply won the event. Good things of eternal value.

I had seen many scriptures the two weeks leading up to X Games that said, "Seek my face." I had begun to pray that if it were in His wisdom that I would.

A few nights after getting home I had some deep thoughts suddenly come to me simply walking out of the kitchen. I suppose some may call it a vision.

It was a thought of a glorious and perfectly strong pillar of white marble. The pillar was clean and beautiful and it was a pillar of the authority of God. It was a beautiful thought. It was bright and shining and filled with love.

The next thought I had with it was, "This is you."

I sort of thought "Hmm, wouldn't that be nice." My thoughts continued. "Wow, imagine if that truly was me, I would just literally praise God all day long and serve Him forever."

I didn't think much of it at first, I just marveled at the thought of the pillar and continued to ponder it. "If that was me, wow, if He could make me into that, I would just use that in love in every way possible for His perfect glory!"

As I continued to think about it, and if it were really me, it felt as something I couldn't yet put on myself; but if it were, how I longed to truly do all things for His perfect glory and light which shined within me.

I started to realize something; my thoughts began to be enlightened to a place that I was marveling at the glory of God. I could see it far more clearly than I ever could previous.

Though I wanted to do all things for the glory of God I couldn't see perfectly how glorious that was and what it truly meant. With this new frame of thinking my heart swelled and I could see with an understanding I couldn't before. My eye was truly becoming single to His glory.

As I continued to think about it, I thought, "Wow; truly, all I want and all my joy is bringing you glory; I see eye to eye." As the scriptures state it, my eye truly was becoming single to my Father's glory.

Before my logical side was single and I did that which I knew was right because of the things I had been greatly blessed to learn, now my heart was wholly becoming involved and my heart was becoming enveloped in wanting to live always for His glory.

337

It was a new experience; I have been amazed how though we are committed to certain things the Lord will show us even more the importance and blessings of what we are truly doing; the vastness and purpose of His love.

As I marveled over this I had the thoughts come to me of how to discern the Spirit of God.

Moroni 7:13 "But behold, that which is of God inviteth and enticeth to do good continually; wherefore, every thing which inviteth and enticeth to do good, and to love God, and to serve him, is inspired of God."

I had known these grand keys and used them before to gain real revelation. Suddenly I saw it; "That was of God and that is how He sees you!"

I could hardly believe it. It was too grand too accept. My next thought jumped to a scripture.

Doctrine and Covenants 88:33 "For what doth is profit a man if a gift is bestowed upon him, and he receive not the gift? Behold, he rejoices not in that which is given unto him, neither rejoices in him who is the giver of the gift."

This also was a grand key that I had been blessed with in receiving grander and grander things. If I didn't step up one step I couldn't see the next one. This was a big step though. I do my best to forever be worthy of such sight of my Father in Heaven.

The point of the matter though was more centered on the fruit of the blessing. My mind and heart was totally single to the glory of God. My eye was single to His glory, truly and like never before.

Alma 32:28 does a great job at explaining this experience. The word was good for, "it beginneth to enlarge my soul; yea, it beginneth to enlighten my understanding, yea, it beginneth to be delicious to me."

Though I was and am incredibly imperfect, every ounce of me wants to do the will of my Father always.

I began to take notes on all of this, realizing that it was about to pass midnight. It was again the 24th of July, Pioneer Day. It had been a year since the Lord brought me back to His fold. The greatest year thus far. He saved me and I hungered and thirsted all year long to be close to my Father in Heaven and to be taught by Him and every step of the way He guided me in such incredible love. A year later I was incredibly blessed.

The Lord has given incredible promises for those with their eye single to His glory.

Doctrine and Covenants 88:67 "And if your eye be single to my glory, your whole bodies shall be filled with light, and there shall be no darkness in you; and that body which is filled with light comprehendeth all things."

This scripture was the last part of the note I wrote that night, I didn't realize until proof reading this book and the note that this was the case. And I followed it with, "Know as you are known."

The scripture right after that is this one, I didn't write that night but became significant quickly.

68 "Therefore, sanctify yourselves that your minds become single to God, and the days will come that you shall see him; for he will unveil his face unto you, and it shall be in his own time, and in his own way, and according to his own will."

A couple days later was Sunday. We went to Church, we came home, my wife napped and I turned on a constant play of the life of Christ, many short videos done by the Church of the stories of Christ. I was so thankful for the goodness of our Savior.

I relaxed next to my wife. I was caught up. I was blessed with the promise in Doctrine and Covenants 88:68. I will not elaborate on this as it is sacred and certain things are to be experienced in good time and all have their time and season. My brothers and sisters, HE LIVES!

If I made an attempt I could not convey the love and absolute immensity of perfection in every area. It has been the most life changing, and strengthening blessing I could have ever received.

There has not been any other single life-changing event for me. The experience that brought me back was obviously important but nothing can give such a zeal to serve Him from the heart. I am forever grateful and I will forever serve Him!

Remember back to the note I took just before leaving the hospital. I didn't recognize this for myself until after this book was written and during times in going back to add things that I feel must be added, I stumbled again upon the notes of that day before leaving the hospital.

Apparently I had been telling my mother, and I recorded in my notes, that Jesus was coming back within 10 days. I recorded that she misunderstood a little bit and that I meant that big signs would happen within the time; that he was coming back soon. I recorded that it was a deep thought because something on that side of the veil certainly had me thinking and feeling such a way.

I was injured the 20th of July. The next morning the 21st I took the note about the event of the injury. 9 days after the injury, on the 29th of July I was caught up and was with Him. And how very, very real and amazing.

Within 10 days indeed. Oh the perfection of our Father in Heaven. How blessed we are! I forever praise and serve Him for He is perfect and the source of all good and love!

2 Corinthians 4:6 "For God, who commanded the light to shine out of darkness, hath shined in our hearts, to give the light of the knowledge of the glory of God in the face of Jesus Christ."

We are children of God! When we truly realize what this means, just how big and how perfect and good He is, oh what a fullness of joy!!! How divine our heritage is, for He is as He is, so perfect. Incomprehensibly perfect. Glory and honor and praise forever to you Father in Heaven!

I will say this, as Christ said, the greatest in the Kingdom of Heaven is he who humbles himself as a little child. I will also say again, God is our Father. Jesus Christ is our very perfect Savior. I pray you will be striving to serve Him. After you behold Him you will truly and wholeheartedly wish you were and always had been serving Him.

We will gain a sense of the utter immensity He has done for us, and He of all didn't deserve to go through such for us, but He is perfect and His love for us all is such that He would do anything for us. Oh the love.

I so wholeheartedly want to be like Him and pray I will be able to. Our Father is so good! How we are children. Oh the memory forgotten that is brought again of being but a child. Oh the comfort. How I long to bring the truth of His love to all of His beloved children, my brothers and sisters. How He loves us! How good our perfect Father is! How close He is! Oh that men would praise Him!

We Are Children of the Kingdom

Brothers and sisters have faith in this truth, we are from the Kingdom of God; it is our home. We are His children. He has chosen us in these last days for very specific and important tasks. He wants His children home.

He sent His Son for us. He knew we would not be perfect. We must exercise faith in Him and move on from our past of sin, we are new in Christ. We must be new and remember our true home, our eternal home. We must be reborn and see Spiritually. The Kingdom of Heaven is with us. "Fear not; for they that be with us are more than they that be with them."

We are the children of God; we are the children of light. We are of the Kingdom of our Father in Heaven. We chose to come here to learn and to serve, that we may serve better that our joy will be full, and it will be.

I know nothing that will bring anyone a more fullness of joy than knowing that God Almighty, in His utter perfection, calls us His Son or Daughter. When you see this clearly, and truly who our Father is you will see and have a fullness of joy. I have seen this little by little; I am amazed in the grandest sense of the word.

We are here now, to walk the right way, and to gather His children. We live in the last days, the Prophet of the Lord has told us the gathering of Israel is now; it truly is. He has gathered me in and I will do my best to gather the more.

I have been blessed that I can see the grander picture and I pray you will too. We are eternal children of God, here for a short time. Though it took me longer to realize it, I am of great use and worth; as are all of us.

He wants us to see our worth and infinite potential. He can make all of us of infinite and glorious use in freedom for His perfect purposes of love. Oh how He loves us.

All things have been done in the wisdom of He who knows all things, even our Father in Heaven. Through Him we can truly know all things, for His perfect purposes, for His perfect glory.

Alma the Younger in the Book of Mormon fought against the Church of Christ though his father was over it. He was corrected and saved and healed and made new through Jesus Christ our Savior. He became one of the greatest prophets and missionaries ever and a great testimony of the redeeming power of Jesus Christ. His words are preserved in The Book of Mormon and are of great value. Many were brought to salvation and he was of incredible and great use to the Lord.

The Apostle Paul fought against the Church of Christ as well and was shown the right way that is our Savior. He was healed and made new through Jesus Christ our loving Savior as well and he did an incredible and a great work for the Lord. The words he wrote are preserved in the Bible and are of great value.

There is a quote I once heard, "Often God recruits from the pit and not the palace." I like this quote. Though there are incredible men that humble themselves and truly judge none and love all, yet many come to the same blessings through hardship. Many can learn much and see clearly and know of themselves by their own experience the need of our Savior. We all utterly need Him the same.

Though we all utterly need Him equally, many can see the vast power that is in His atonement and in Him. Many love and understand deeply without as much trial and misstep and many come to understand and love Him deeply in sheer amazement of His saving grace and love when all seems lost. I truly forever praise Him and am so thankful for His perfect love and saving grace. I think of the story given in at the end of Luke 7.

Luke 7:38 "And stood at his feet behind him weeping, and began to wash his feet with tears, and did wipe them with the hairs of her head, and kissed his feet, and anointed them with the ointment."

47 "Wherefore I say unto thee, Her sins, which are many, are forgiven; for she loved much: but to whom little is forgiven, the same loveth little.

48 And he said unto her, Thy sins are forgiven."

50 "And he said to the woman, Thy faith hath saved thee; go in peace."

I have seen fully the incredible need we have for Him and I am so incredibly thankful. I can judge none; I want to serve Him to the best of my ability forever. I am constantly amazed at His perfection and goodness. I am eternally thankful and forever am His so thankfully! He has done all to bring us back home!

As we see that we are children of God sent here from our heavenly home trusted to do a great work we can begin to see things in the eternal light that is of great value and truth.

We are here for a short time. In the hospital I had a thought come to me that I had had come to me a few times earlier in the year. "If you love me, feed my sheep."

Though I continually try to do this, the thought became bigger and I consistently had the context of the thought in the way Elder Jeffrey R. Holland says in a great talk titled, "The First Great Commandment." How I love Elder Holland.

After Christ was crucified for us His Apostles were obviously heartbroken and didn't know what to do. They decided to go fishing again, back to what they were doing before the Son of God came into their life; after all, they had to live.

Christ is resurrected and yells out to them, calling them children. He asks if they have caught anything. It turns out they had fished all night and caught nothing.

He yells out to cast the net to the right side and they will find. They do so and the net is so full of fish that they cannot pull it in. Quickly Peter and others recognized it was Christ. They jumped over and went to Him.

They sat and spoke with our Lord. Jesus asked Peter, 3 times, "Simon, son of Jonas, lovest thou me more than these?" Jesus asked him 3 times if he loves Him. Each time he replied, "Yea, Lord, thou knowest that I love thee." And each time Jesus replied, "Feed my sheep."

As Elder Holland puts it frankly, In a sense Christ is saying, "Do you love me more than you love all this? If I want fish I can clearly get fish. What I want is disciples and I need them forever. What I want is my children back. I need someone who loves me, truly, truly loves me." "Our is not a feeble message, it is the work of God and it is to change the world."

Do you love me more than fishing?

In my life it was, 'Ok, back to BMX again, that's great you can bring glory to me here in a way; but haven't I shown you far grander things? Don't you have a clear picture and understanding of those enslaved and with the stumbling block of false wisdom before them? Who else can see this? Ok it is great that you are putting forth effort, I appreciate it, but how much do you love me? I have shown you incredible things and even the greater things. Do you love me? Feed my sheep.'

When I came to in the hospital, I was asking all manner of questions. The same ones over and over again and they were answered over and over again. I was trying to understand what happened, pretty normal for the occasion. One of the questions I was asking was if I was writing a book?

I hadn't been actively writing a book but I knew I had always taken deep notes. Since then the push to write one and what the Lord would have me put in it has been strongly growing. It is unlike me, and it is quite difficult. Yet when I write I can continue and overflow with more and more.

At times when I would see the weakness of my writing I was reminded of the Lord's words in the same concern to Ether, the Lord's grace is sufficient for the meek.

It is not something I would do, though at times I felt it something I must do. "Lord, thou knowest that I love thee."

343

I humbly pray the love in this book will be evident. I truly judge none and neither could I. I truly wish to be of help.

I do not intend to make myself seem smart or lift myself up in any way; rather, show my folly, utter weakness and the true wisdom and goodness in our perfect Father in Heaven alone. My story is that of His glory. I have been blessed to have been taught much in a way that I hope I can help others to see His perfection and know His love as I do.

I have been blessed and want to share that blessing that it may bring glory to our Father in Heaven. I hope to bring His children back to Him and strengthen the faith of all; that we may have joy forever together. I should like to help everyone if possible. He dearly loves all of His children.

John 14:31 "But that the world may know that I love the Father; and as the Father gave me commandment, even so I do. Arise, let us go hence."

I am weak but in Him I am strong. I am imperfect yet in Him alone I am made perfect. We truly can do all things in Christ. Let us keep our eyes focused on the reason these blessings are given. We are here for a reason. It is true.

As these last days continue and we get closer to the return of our Lord and Savior Jesus Christ stay on the rock of Him our Savior. This book lightly details some of what is out today to deceive and a great stumbling block that I hope to be a help in the mighty hands of the Lord to free many. Be careful, be humble, stay on the rock that is our Savior and you will be fine.

"But to be learned is good if they hearken unto the counsels of God."

May we walk humbly and meekly before Him, utterly relying on and trusting in Him in great faith. May we walk through life as His child, never fearing but relying on Him and His perfect wisdom, smiling that we are so perfectly taken care of. May we be filled with His love and bring His love and light from our home, His Kingdom, into this world for all to see and come to!

Doctrine and Covenants 6:32-37 "Fear not to do good, my sons, for whatsoever ye sow, that shall ye also reap; therefore, if ye sow good ye shall also reap good for your reward.

34 Therefore, fear not, little flock; do good; let earth and hell combine against you, for if ye are built upon my rock, they cannot prevail.

35 Behold, I do not condemn you; go your ways and sin no more; perform with soberness the work which I have commanded you.

36 Look unto me in every thought; doubt not, fear not.

37 Behold the wounds which pierced my side, and also the prints of the nails in my hands and feet; be faithful, keep my commandments, and ye shall inherit the kingdom of heaven. Amen."

"To all within the sound of my voice, the voice of Christ comes ringing down through the halls of time, asking each one of us while there is time, "Do you love me?" And for every one of us, I answer with my honor and my soul, "Yea, Lord, we do love thee." And having set our "hand to the plough," we will never look back until this work is finished and love of God and neighbor rules the world. In the name of Jesus Christ, amen."

- Jeffrey R. Holland, The First Great Commandment Oct. 2012 General Conference

The day we are with Him again, our true joy will be in Him and in the things we did for Him. "Arise, let us go hence."

Isaiah 42:18 "Hear, ye deaf; and look , ye blind, that ye may see.

19 Who is blind, but my servant? Or deaf, as my messenger that I sent? Who is blind as he that is perfect, and blind as the Lord's servant?"

1 Nephi 14:1

"And it shall come to pass, that if the Gentiles shall hearken unto the Lamb of God in that day that he shall manifest himself unto them in word, and also in power, in very deed, unto the taking away of their stumbling blocks-"

2 Nephi 10:7-8

"But behold, thus saith the Lord God: When the day cometh that they shall believe in me, that I am Christ, then have I covenanted with their fathers that they shall be restored in the flesh, upon the earth unto the lands of their inheritance.

8 "And it shall come to pass that they shall be gathered in from their long dispersion, from the isles of the sea, and from the four parts of

the earth; and the nations of the Gentiles shall be great in the eyes of me, saith God, in carrying them forth to the lands of their inheritance."

Matthew 11:28-30
"Come unto me, all ye that labour and are heavy laden, and I will give you rest.

Take my yoke upon you, and learn of me; for I am meek and lowly in heart: and ye shall find rest unto your souls.

For my yoke is easy, and my burden is light."

Psalm 107:8
"Oh that men would praise the Lord for his goodness, and for his wonderful works to the children of men!"

Made in the USA
San Bernardino, CA
22 February 2020

64834448R00212